RED ELEGY

A Memoir of Existence in Communist China

By Chengmo Bao

Bouden House, New York

[Contemporary Chinese Thinkers Translation Series]
Academic Adviser: Andrew J. Nathan, Tom Kellogg
Chief Editor: David Rong
Deputy Editor: William Luo
Cover Designer: Flora Bao

Published by Bouden House, New York
ISBN: 979-8-90257-004-2 (Paperback)
       979-8-90257-005-9 (eBook)

RED ELEGY—*A Memoir of Existence in Communist China*
Author: Chengmo Bao

Publisher: Bouden House New York
Email: boudenhouse@gmail.com
Distributor: Google (Digital), Amazon (Paper)
Edition: First Edition, June 2025
Price: $40.00 USD

This book is dedicated to all those who suffer in the world,

especially to those who are desperate in both their countries and their homes.

I experienced it. I endured it. I documented it. I bore witness to it.

Where there is freedom, there is my homeland.
People possess the liberty to decide whether to cherish their country or not.
No force can quell the innate human longing for freedom!

The love for one's country may wane, especially when one endures relentless oppression from a formidable state apparatus.
Even familial love has its limits, fading when one faces repeated abandonment and victimization. However, my devotion to freedom knows no bounds.
The essence of being human lies in freedom of thought, expression, and self-realization. To love freedom is to love humanity. I cherish America because it embodies the spirit of freedom that I hold dear.

Table of Contents

FORWARD I I

FORWARD II VI

PREFACE 1

Chapter / Ancestors 11

    1. Tangyue / 11

    2. Wuxi / 44

Chapter 2 My Parents's Generation 85

    1. Bao family in Baoshan / 85

    2. Bao Family in Shanghai / 88

    3. Liu family in Shanghai / 112

Chapter 3 My Generation 138

    1. The Childhood Lost / 138

    2. The Old Three Cohorts / 152

    3. Go up the Mountain and Go Down to the Village / 170

    4. At Anhui Normal University / 274

    5. After College / 289

Appendix I The Specter of Communism 317

Appendix II In the Name of Revolution 323

    1. The British Glorious Revolution / 324

2. French Revolution   / 327

3. Soviet Union   / 335

4. Hungary   / 345

5. China   / 352

6. Summary   / 369

EPILOGUE 379

Treasured Documentary Footage 385

FORWARD I

A famous saying in journalism goes: "Today's news is tomorrow's history." But if today's news cannot be accurately reported, will tomorrow's history already be forgotten?

Sociologist C. Wright Mills (1916~1962) once said: "Behind the suffering of individuals lies inevitably the distortion of structures." We might add that behind an individual's ability to fully realize their subjectivity, there must also be supportive structures and institutional cultures.

This book is a testimony: it chronicles how the author endured profound suffering in Communist China and how, in a land of freedom, he was able to rise from the ashes like a phoenix.

It is also an indictment: through the author's personal experiences, it accuses the Communist Party of its systemic and fundamental evil born of a demonic ideology combined with the tyranny of authoritarian dictatorship. This system amplifies and catalyzes human greed and the pursuit of self-interest, rapidly eroding familial bonds, friendships, and all ethical human relationships in society. To whom is this indictment addressed? It is believed that the human conscience is the ultimate judge!

Looking back is looking forward: After retiring, the author courageously confronted a harrowing past—even the ugliness within his own family—and wrote this biography. This courage and perseverance clearly stem from his sense of justice and mission: to ensure that history does not fade into ashes, that tyranny is not forgotten, and that conscience can still be awakened!

I first met the author of this book, Mr. Chengmo Bao, in the early 1980s. At that time, I was pursuing a Ph.D. in mass communication at the University of Iowa in the United States. On campus, several students from mainland China began to appear—the earliest wave of students to study abroad after the Cultural Revolution (1966~1976). Most of them were exceptionally talented, yet they spoke of the horrors of the Cultural Revolution with lingering fear. For us students from Taiwan, such a hellish human experience was unimaginable. They often teasingly called us "kind but naive little white rabbits."

In the textbooks of my generation—those born in the fourth grade—we were taught about the belligerent nature of the Chinese Communist Party (CCP) and its various campaigns that harmed tens of millions of people over the years. But as young children back then, our understanding was limited.

By the time I studied abroad in the U.S., Deng Xiaoping had begun to gradually open up China after the Cultural Revolution, reforming its economy. Especially in the 20 years following China's successful entry into the World Trade Organization in 2001, its foreign trade grew more than eightfold, surpassing the U.S. to become the world's largest trading nation. Within less than a decade, it became the second-largest economy globally. "Made in China" products flooded our daily lives, and millions of people traveled between the two sides of the Taiwan Strait each year. Our perception and imagination of China seemed to drift far from that "evil" Communist regime marked by constant struggle and harm to its people.

Yet, has the Chinese Communist Party truly transformed itself and embraced a capitalist market system? Has the authoritarian regime that launched the Cultural Revolution and its oppressive structures gradually shifted toward democracy, freedom, and the rule of law? Has that dictatorial CCP regime, rooted in struggle, ceased to persecute its people and manipulate the world?

In fact, the CCP's history keeps repeating itself: After the Cultural Revolution, the peaceful 1989 Tiananmen Square student protests for political reform were once again met with armed suppression ordered by the so-called "reformer" Deng Xiaoping. To this day, the CCP spares no effort to conceal and suppress this history. Notably, Deng was also a key figure in the "Anti-Rightist Campaign" that targeted and persecuted intellectuals.

Similarly, Jiang Zemin, Deng's successor, who also supported the Tiananmen crackdown, launched a brutal persecution of millions of Falun Gong practitioners in 1999. This campaign involved the illegal use of dozens of torture methods and the horrifying practice of organ harvesting for profit. International investigations have revealed that this gruesome organ harvesting has long been an industry orchestrated by the Party-state, involving a seamless chain of military, police, judicial, and medical systems. Recent reports suggest it has expanded internationally and to other groups, including teenagers and children. This has continued under Xi Jinping's 12-year rule with no signs of improvement.

This demonstrates that the Chinese Communist Party, regardless of its leader, consistently upholds a demonic nature and conduct under its authoritarian regime: preserving the interests of the Party, eliminating dissent, pursuing wealth and power, and operating without any baseline of human ethics.

In fact, the CCP regime does not merely suppress dissent and allow the privileged elite to run rampant domestically; it also leverages the hegemonic momentum of its economic rise. In recent years, it has disregarded international legal norms in the South China Sea and Indo-Pacific region, arrogantly expanding its influence and causing unease among neighboring countries. Then, in 2019, under global scrutiny, it unhesitatingly and violently suppressed millions of Hong Kong citizens demanding democratic reforms, further unilaterally tearing apart the "one country, two systems" promise for Hong Kong. International investigations have successively exposed its atrocities, such as the concentration camp abuses against a million Uyghurs in Xinjiang and the eradication of their religious and cultural identity. Globally, the CCP's reckless disregard for human life—concealing and shifting blame for the Wuhan pneumonia outbreak (later called COVID-19)—unleashed a virus that has ravaged the world since 2019, resulting in a nightmare that has claimed millions of lives!

The free world, which has long coveted the vast market dividends of China, including prominent media outlets, has rarely condemned or imposed sanctions on human rights issues in recent years. It was not until the Trump administration came to power in the United States that various actions were launched to counter China's violations. Both parties also jointly awakened to the Chinese Communist Party's infringements on free nations in areas such as the economy, politics, human rights, and even drugs. This led to the so-called U.S.-China trade war, technology war, and financial war, as well as a series of chip blockades and punitive legislation directly targeting the CCP's disruption of the free world's international order.

To maintain and expand its authoritarian rule, Xi Jinping's communist regime has accelerated its leftward turn, abolishing term limits and employing various methods—especially digital control technologies—to centralize power, suppress freedom, and manipulate dissent on one hand, while using lies to manipulate information warfare, cognitive warfare, and hybrid unlimited warfare on the other. Amid the wave of free trade integration over the past three decades, the global landscape, fueled by the spreading conflicts of the Russia-Ukraine and Middle East wars, has been forced to transform into a confrontation between the camps of freedom and authoritarianism.

The international wave of resistance against communism formed by the free democratic world is actually based on an understanding of the CCP's authoritarian system. This wave of resistance is not only about economics, technology, politics, and national defense, but more importantly, it is rooted in the human rights values of upholding freedom, democracy, and the rule of law.

In this moment of global turmoil and pervasive crises, how should the free world, especially Taiwan, understand this phenomenon of confrontation? How can it uphold human values? In an era of online spaces flooded with disinformation and cognitive warfare, how can one truly recognize the essence of the CCP, remain unswayed by the temptations of lies and unthreatened by violence, and maintain clear rationality and judgment? This is the fundamental key to winning the battle between freedom and enslavement, democracy and authoritarianism, and the rule of law and tyranny.

Mr. Chengmo's thick biography is written with a mission to prevent history from turning to ashes. It is a profound and righteous work that looks back on the path taken and forward to the future, while also serving as foundational historical material in this movement of awakening against communism.

Of course, in examining the suffering under Communist China, the author also offers his personal insights, questioning whether the ethnic character of Chinese culture failed to prevent this Communist catastrophe. He earnestly encourages those of us of Chinese descent living in free regions to deeply reflect: How can we safeguard our existing freedom and democratic legal systems, ensuring that the Communist regime's manipulations through violence and lies do not prevail?

Winston Churchill once said, "The farther backward you can look, the farther forward you can see." I hope we can look deeper and farther, better recognizing the urgency and necessity of upholding human goodness and breaking free from the evil system of Chinese Communist authoritarianism. Opening this book is an important step!

-----*Chin-hwa Chang, Emeritus Professor*
National Taiwan University
August 2024, Taoyuan

FORWARD II

Communism is a tragedy for humanity, though ironically, it initially appeared as a savior. The same is true of Chinese communism. Since 1921, the Chinese Communist Party (CCP) has proclaimed its intention to establish a paradise on earth—a society without classes, exploitation, oppression, or injustice. In this new communist society, everyone would be equal, every family would live in peace and happiness, with ample food and clothing, and the nation would be prosperous and joyful! Imagine what a beautiful ideal that would be!

However, almost no one—certainly not the communists—could have foreseen that once the Communist Party took power in China, it would devastate Chinese society to an extent unprecedented in Chinese history—indeed, in all of human history.

Since 1949, the CCP has launched countless political campaigns on the Chinese mainland, cloaking them in grandiose terms such as "purging the class ranks," "eliminating counter-revolutionaries," "smashing the ox-demons and snake-spirits," and "rooting out traitors, spies, and capitalist roaders." The result was not only the destruction of hundreds of millions of innocent lives but also the downfall, one after another, of many ardent communists who had once vowed to "struggle for communism their entire lives"—including high-ranking officials like vice chairmen and even one president of the country.

The political campaigns launched by the CCP were as numerous as the hairs on an ox. Among the most significant were the Five Major Campaigns, the Three Transformations, the Three Antis and Five Antis, the Anti-Rightist Campaign, the Three Red Banners and Great Leap Forward, the Cultural Revolution, and the persecution of Falun Gong. Each of these plunged millions of Chinese people into a hellish existence where they could neither live nor die. Unfortunately, the author of this book, Mr. Bao Chengmo, was born at the wrong time and into the wrong family—one in which both his father and uncle were labeled counter-revolutionaries by the CCP. As a result, the first half of his life was entangled with nearly all these political movements, relegating him to the lowest rung of Chinese society and subjecting him to unimaginable suffering beyond the comprehension of the outside world.

Human societies have always had classes; in a normal society, however, class mobility is permitted and occurs "naturally." It is the result of a combination of one's family background, personal effort, and countless chance circumstances. Under CCP rule, however, social class is determined by political forces, leading to profound upheaval and injustice. In CCP-ruled China, politics reigns supreme—determining everything and distorting everything. It has warped the moral fabric of Chinese society and twisted the humanity of hundreds of millions of Chinese people.

As Mr. Bao himself states, simply because his father and uncle were "deliberately and erroneously" branded counter-revolutionaries by the CCP, he and his family became "relatives of counter-revolutionaries" in the eyes of the Party, condemned to live subhuman lives. Tragically, even the emotional balm of familial affection was denied him as solace for this misery. His mother, a "Party member who never joined the Party," became the Mao Zedong of their household. Her humanity was utterly crushed by the CCP's Party ideology, rendering Mr. Bao's early life even more unbearable.

Because of his status, opportunities for education, employment, love, marriage, and even choosing a future were stripped away from him almost entirely. Mr. Bao's life story is not an isolated case—there are likely millions like him on the Chinese mainland.

Yet, in a way, Mr. Bao is fortunate. After the age of 32, he miraculously secured an opportunity to study in the United States, an event that completely transformed his life. This allowed him to observe and experience firsthand how vastly different one's life can be and how starkly a democratic society contrasts with a communist one.

For decades, the CCP has propagated the slogan: "The evil old society turned people into ghosts; the new communist society turns ghosts into people." Mr. Bao Chengmo's life experience thoroughly refutes this propaganda.

Traditionally, the Chinese have said, "How can we let history turn to ashes?" As the author notes in his book, if those who survived the CCP's tyranny choose silence or forgetfulness, history could indeed be reduced to ashes. Mr. Bao is a survivor, but he has chosen to speak the truth—not out of an unwillingness to let go of hatred or to dwell on pain, but out of a conviction that if the living do not speak, the grievances of the dead will remain buried forever, never to see the light of day. Exposing evil serves to deter it, to warn the world, to learn lessons, and to prevent history from repeating itself!

I am of the same generation as Mr. Bao, fortunate to have been born and raised in Taiwan, spared from the great calamity of communism. Reading Mr. Bao's masterpiece stirred a torrent of emotions within me—waves of thought surging powerfully. With this preface, I solemnly recommend this book, hoping readers will take its lessons to heart and work to create a human society free of communism and injustice for future generations.

----- Chu-cheng Ming, Emeritus Professor
National Taiwan University
February 18, 2025

PREFACE

What truly matters in life is not what you have experienced, but what you remember and how you cherish those memories.

> ---*Gabriel García* Márquez, *A Hundred Years of Solitude*

Yu Youren (1879~1964) said, "I do not believe that youth can be recalled, nor that history will entirely turn to ashes." Peng Dehuai (Oct. 24, 1898 ~ Nov. 29, 1974) was a military leader, one of the greatest in Chinese communist history, and minister of national defense of China from 1954 until 1959. When he was removed for criticizing the military and economic policies of the party, he said, "I don't believe that history can be reduced to ashes. But I am deeply concerned that it may crumble into dust." Let's consider the famine of 1960. Officially, it claimed 35 million lives. Where is the record of those lost souls? Who were they? How did they live and die? Where were they born, and who were their loved ones? How many seasons did they see? How much joy and sorrow did they experience? Thirty-five million lives extinguished in silence, without a trace, without accountability, without remembrance. How do we honor the dead? How do we educate future generations? How do we hold those in power responsible? The study of the Cultural Revolution has largely been left to the generation of the Red Guards, among whom there are both perpetrators and moderates. But expecting perpetrators to confess their crimes or moderates to seek justice is futile. Even if some individuals in these groups were willing, they cannot truly understand the depth of humanity's sins unless they suffer them firsthand. The voices of the victims are drowned out, the previous generation has faded away, and the next generation is silenced, aging into twilight. The urgency of recording these victim narratives cannot be overstated, for once they are gone, the history of our world will vanish with them. And this is precisely what those in power are striving to achieve.

During Mao Zedong's 27-year rule in China, countless innocent intellectuals, officials, and ordinary citizens suffered brutalization. Concurrently, a significant number of so-called "activists" rose to prominence within the regime. Some were complicit in the atrocities, while others directly contributed to the bloodshed. However, due to the deliberate concealment of facts by the ruling regime, discussion of historical truths, rights, and responsibilities was forbidden. This stifled any chance of societal reflection and repentance. Consequently, those responsible for these actions have adamantly refused to acknowledge their wrongdoings or offer apologies or reparations to the victims. For seven decades, those in power have perpetuated a monumental falsehood, aiming to obliterate historical truth. In recent times, the authoritarian government has intensified its oppression, employing not only the full force of the state but also leveraging advanced surveillance technology to orchestrate informant networks. This has led to an unprecedented constriction of freedom of speech. Some outspoken intellectuals have faced severe repercussions, including expulsion from universities, loss of pensions, false accusations of immorality or corruption, and arbitrary detention leading to their demise.

George Orwell (1903~1950) said, "The past was erased; the erasure was forgotten; the lie became the truth." In a context where official historical accounts have faltered in their duty, individual documentation and civilian reassessment of history assume paramount importance. As Mo Yan aptly stated, "Spoken words may be carried away by the wind, but written words endure." Hence, I commit to record. Throughout China's modern history, the identities of countless individuals have been effaced, their visages lost to time, leaving behind only a government-crafted facade of history. Ultimately, it is personal recollections and reconstructed narratives that draw closest to the truth. Memory stands as our most invaluable intangible cultural heritage. Every individual's tribulation and firsthand encounter contribute to the collective national suffering, thereby serving as fragments in the mosaic of truth and historical restoration. It is through the narratives tied to each specific name that the essence of our shared journey through time is revealed, ensuring that future generations remember our names and the ordeals we endured.

In 1984, when I came to the United States, I had only $200 on me, which was less than many refugees had. After more than 30 years of study and work in the New World, today, I finally have the time to pick up a pen and record the vicissitudes of life. I am just a scholar, but I am living in a big era. This memoir may portray the story of an ordinary individual within an extraordinary era, yet it provides an irreplaceable footnote to the history of a nation spanning a century. My personal experience, intertwined with my family history, represents the true and unaltered history of the nation. I personally witnessed and experienced the suffering brought about by the revolution. I suffered what I should not have suffered, and I endured what I should not have endured. I have accumulated rich and unique experiences and insights during my torturous and difficult life journey. This spiritual wealth should be contributed to the community and left to future generations, not disposed of in the incinerator. The value of a person's life does not lie in money and power. When a person dies, he or she cannot take away money and power. The value of life lies in the contribution to society. Mo Yan said, "I have a prejudice that literary works should not whitewash reality, and that literature and art should expose darkness." In my opinion, exposing the darkness can play the role of enlightenment. Exposing the darkness is for the love of mankind. Exposing darkness requires not only a sense of justice but also courage and responsibility.

The title of this book is Red Elegy. The term "Elegy" carries two layers of meaning. One layer is a requiem for my own 32 hellish years in China. For many years after leaving China, I would often wake up from nightmares. Fortunately, those days are finally over. The second layer is a tolling of the death knell for the Chinese Communist regime. The suffering endured by three generations of the Bao and Liu families has its roots in the "Communist Revolution." This is why, after completing the firts three chapters of the book, I added two appendices. The first chapter, "The Ancestors," was written to fulfill the trust placed in me by the elders of the Bao family. After experiencing decades of political movements, my relatives in China have deep-seated fears that are difficult to dispel. They dare not speak openly for fear of repercussions. Since I am abroad, they hoped I could write down the family history. They provided me with extensive materials, including rare ancient texts documenting the Bao family and our genealogy. In the second chapter, "My Parents' Generation," I recount many stories about my father's generation in the Bao family and my mother's generation in the Liu family. The third chapter, "My Generation," documents my own 72 years of life in China and the United States, as well as the experiences of my peers during my time in China.

This memoir aims to unmask the four toxins that gave rise to the communist dictatorship in China: Marxist theory, class struggle, the despicable character of the people, and a lack of humanity and love. It is the combination of these four toxins that has caused the Chinese people to be stuck in a saucepan for more than 2,000 years. Unfortunately, I was born in the wrong place, at the wrong time, in the wrong family. In 1952, I was born in Shanghai and experienced important periods in Chinese history, including the Cultural Revolution and the transformative Reform and Opening Up era. I belong to a generation that was "born in the new society and grew up under the red flag." I lived for 32 years under the dark clouds of Red China. I have always suffered double discrimination in society, and my family, and I am a person who has been humiliated and damaged.

My autobiographical memoirs unfold along two overarching dimensions: "revolution" and "humanity." The dimension of the Red Revolution draws me back to the echoes of the French Revolution. In Hugo's works, such as Ninety-Three and Les Misérables, characters endure tragic destinies akin to gods and saints. What did the Revolution yield? It commenced with the guillotine's blade falling upon Louis XVI and concluded with Napoleon's reign. Blood was shed, and the nation's system traced a circular path from imperial rule back to its origins. Subsequently, a 19th-century German socialist political theory migrated from Russia to China, morphing into the envisioned ideal society for all humankind. Under the banner of "revolution," Mao transplanted infernal horrors into the mortal realm, resulting in the deaths of tens of millions. "Revolution" acted as Pandora's Box, unleashing jealousy, sorrow, grief, impoverishment, famine, massacres, and pandemics upon the world. A tree has roots, water has a source; a wrong has a cause, a debt has an owner. My personal tribulations, spanning three generations of my family, all trace their origins to the "revolution." Consequently, I allocate two comprehensive sections in the Appendix to delve into its core. Appendix I, "The Specter of Communism," endeavors to dissect the fallacies of Marxist theory. Appendix II, "In the Name of Revolution," seeks to denounce the egregious crimes against humanity perpetrated in communist-governed nations.

Another dimension is the suffering caused by the dark side of human nature. When we are trapped in a dark world, the absence of familial love manifests with particular cruelty. Moreover, it fosters an environment ripe for the seeds of the communist revolution to take root. Let us delve into Balzac's magnum opus, La Comédie Humaine (The Human Comedy). Taking nearly two decades to complete, this monumental work comprises 91 volumes, delving into the lives of over 2,400 characters, encapsulating every facet of French society. It stands as a collective portrait of an era and its people. Balzac titled his work The Comedy of Men in homage to Dante's "Divina Commedia" (The Divine Comedy). The Chinese rendition typically divides it into three parts: Inferno, Purgatorio, and Paradiso. While Dante's masterpiece navigates the realms of Hell and Paradise, Balzac grounds his narrative firmly in the earthly realm. "Old Goriot" pays homage to "King Lear" with a stark realism, while shades of Colonel Shaw echo the return of Odysseus in "The Odyssey." The unexpected twist in "Eugénie Grandet" satirizes the conventions of classical romance. Balzac's sweeping portrayal encompasses every conceivable character one might encounter in life. To read "La Comédie Humaine" is to traverse the annals of French social customs in the 19th century and explore the intricate depths of human nature. Family, humanity, love—these are ostensibly the most exquisite aspects of existence, yet Balzac dismantles them one by one, revealing their flaws. While labeled a comedy, it is, in essence, a tragedy. Within my memoirs, readers will discover the Chinese versions of "Old Goriot" and "Grandet," presenting these timeless tales to a new audience.

The darker aspects of human nature—miserliness, selfishness, greed, and indifference—are not confined to any particular nation but were and are ubiquitous in "Revolutionary" societies like those which have risen for various spans of time in France, Russia, and China. In environments where a flawed system prevails, these negative traits often proliferate unchecked. In societies characterized by absurdity, virtue is punished, evil is rewarded, and opportunism thrives unchecked. While a great deal of traditional Chinese culture has been swept away, remnants of its authoritarian past persist and have even strengthened. Authoritarianism isn't merely a feature of the political system, but a pervasive cultural trait deeply ingrained in the fabric of society. Almost every Chinese individual, consciously or unconsciously, carries traces of this authoritarian mindset. The specter of authoritarianism looms within the psyche of every Chinese, shaping not only the actions of dictators but also the behavior of those subjected to its influence. This book documents the endless and heartless events that occurred within a family, completely betraying traditional ethics and moral principles. The tragedy of my family is a subversive blow to traditional culture, a precipitous collapse. Moreover, such unfortunate families are not isolated cases, which is terrifying upon deeper reflection. At the root of it, the cruelty of the Chinese communist revolution and the evil inherent in human nature are two intertwined ropes that cannot escape blame.

My mother never concealed her interest in politics; at times, she reminisced about her highlights when she held a leadership position in Sanmin Youth Corps. However, with the advent of the Communists, she was branded a "counter-revolutionary key member." The official record characterized the clashes between the opposing factions as internal conflicts of the people. Politics is a perilous terrain where the right to choose freely and the burden of consequences are inseparable—much like the unpredictable fluctuations of the stock market, where one's losses cannot be blamed on others. While parents typically feel remorseful for any misfortune that befalls their children, my mother's perspective was starkly different. She harbored a deep resentment towards her sons, viewing them as constant reminders of her tainted status as a "counter-revolutionary spouse." The good thing for her was that her wishes were fulfilled when her sons departed Shanghai, and she remarried a member of the Chinese Communist Party (CCP), thereby shedding her "counter-revolutionary spouse" label. As I navigated the bureaucratic hurdles to leave the country, my mother observed with an indifferent gaze. Following my departure, my friend Shi Taihua visited her, only to be met with a cynical remark: "It's futile for Chengmo to venture to the U.S. empty-handed; for he will soon be driven back." Having endured a society where mutual victimization was rampant, she could hardly believe the existence of a government genuinely serving its people and a populace characterized by kindness. The irony deepened when, after I had settled in the United States, my mother brazenly requested that I purchase a property in Shanghai and facilitate her relocation to the U.S. to bask in a life of luxury. Her sense of entitlement perplexed me, defying all logical explanations. As Mark Twain astutely observed, "Truth is stranger than fiction, but it is because Fiction is obliged to stick to possibilities; Truth isn't." I could only marvel at Twain's insight, realizing that the absurdities within my own family surpassed anything conjured in fiction, while bearing a weight heavier than imagination could conceive.

In the Book of Genesis, it is written that God created the world in six days, fashioned man and woman, and ordained the equal value of every life. According to this narrative, each individual possesses the inherent right to free thought and the potential for nobility of the soul. However, throughout history, there have emerged dictators who arrogantly claim sole possession of lofty ideals and believe themselves uniquely qualified to construct a utopia on earth. They propagate the abhorrent notion that certain segments of society are unworthy of existence and advocate for their extermination in pursuit of their supposed higher goals. Prime examples include Hitler's genocidal campaign against the Jews and the Communist regimes' targeting of property owners and capitalists. The leaders of these oppressive regimes stand as embodiments of evil. Wherever their decrees are enforced, rivers of blood flow, and suffering abounds. By transgressing the boundaries of morality and conscience, they commit the gravest sin—the mass slaughter of innocent lives. Despite professing to represent the people, they demand nothing less than servitude, reducing individuals to mere tools or screws to be manipulated at will. Tragically, many among the oppressed masses, the very ones subjected to the scythes' blade, perceive themselves as comrades of the powerful rather than victims. They willingly align with those in authority, displaying hostility towards any who challenges or questions the established order.

I have a friend whom I first met in my teenage years, and we reconnected in my later life. She imparted this advice: "It's been decades; dwelling on the past will only hinder your happiness." I believe that only after justice is served, and sincere reflection and remorse have taken place, can forgiveness and pardon be possible. I believe that those who trivialize hatred will likely undervalue others' kindness; those who dismiss benevolence and righteousness will likely lack affection for others. I believe that true contentment stems from fulfilling one's responsibilities. Contrary to her perspective, I refuse to forget; I choose to document. By penning this memoir, I fulfill my duty. It is incumbent upon me to chronicle my own experiences and to unveil a corner of the grand deception. I am obligated to educate future generations about how malefactors and miscreants erected a dystopia in the guise of revolution. Amidst the clash of civilizations and ideologies—between democracy and autocracy—my act of defiance against autocratic authority in these memoirs holds greater significance than any personal grudge. The characters featured in this memoir are real individuals, some identified by their actual names. Their names should be nailed to the pillar of shame in history. My earnest hope is that readers will comprehend the depths to which human wickedness can thrive under tyranny. I pray that future generations will learn from past mistakes and never endure similar suffering. What purpose does our present existence serve if it condemns our progeny to live in perpetual fear as we did?

This memoir strips away the facade of the "revolution" during dark times, compelling readers to confront the evils that lurk within society.

My aim is to provoke contemplation, igniting a spark of introspection within the reader. I firmly believe that inherent within every individual's heart lies a core of goodness and purity. My writing endeavors to rouse and revive the morality of the human spirit, which has been deceived by tyranny. What constitutes this morality of the heart? It is the capacity for empathy and compassion—to derive joy from others' happiness and to feel their pain as if it were our own. Conversely, evil manifests as indifference to the suffering of others, accompanied by a lack of remorse for causing harm.

In 1911, Maurice Maeterlinck (1862~1949), acclaimed as the "Shakespeare of Belgium," was honored with the Nobel Prize for Literature. He frequently depicted characters from the town of Ghent in his works, yet his candid portrayal led to his expulsion from his hometown. The response of Ghent's inhabitants, directing their ire at Maeterlinck rather than addressing the evil that he exposed, serves as a sign of human depravity. During my visit to Ghent in 2022, I discovered that his former residence had been preserved as a poignant memorial, a testament to the enduring legacy of his truth-telling. Among the numerous vestiges of traditional Chinese culture, one of the most egregious is that instead of teaching people integrity, decency, and morality, it teaches them to be worldly-smooth and to protect themselves. What Chinese society, particularly its intellectual elite, lacks is not intellectual acumen but rather conscience and courage.

Embarking on the writing of this memoir felt akin to traversing through hell once more. Yet upon completion, I found a profound sense of fulfillment, as if my life's purpose had been fulfilled. I anticipate that the readers of this book will possess a baseline of emotional intelligence, devoid of the callousness and self-absorption characteristic of those who "sweep the snow from their own doorstep without regard for the frost on others' roofs." I impose certain expectations upon my readers—they must embody the fundamental qualities of humanity and adhere to the bedrock principles of civilization. What constitutes this existential bottom line? The answer is deceptively simple: "property rights." Contrary to the Communist Party's original doctrine of "Deprivation of private property," my readers must uphold the sanctity of "property rights," as they form the cornerstone of all legal and moral frameworks, as well as the primary foundation of human rights.

The evil of dictatorship and totalitarianism lies in its deprivation of people's legitimately acquired property, their right to freely dispose of that property, and all their freedoms. Contrary to the original intent of the Communist Party's "class struggle," my readers must possess humanity, compassion, and empathy for others. I believe human nature tends to fall into corruption, but it also has an instinct for elevation and refinement. In contemporary China, mired in oppression and corruption, individuals who embody these virtues are regrettably scarce. Thus, I pen this memoir with a blend of despair for the present generations and hope for the future, placing my faith in the generations yet to come.

Chapter 1

Ancestors

1. Tangyue

In ancient China, the people valued their genealogy, meticulously observing filial piety and ancestral reverence. They dreaded criticism for neglecting their ancestral roots, thus meticulously preserving the lineage of their ancestors spanning eighteen generations. They especially enjoyed recording the achievements of their forebears, and the Bao family was no exception. Historical records indicate that the surname "Bao" is of diverse ethnic origins and ranks 62nd in the "Hundred Family Surnames." "Bao" as a surname has a long and illustrious history, tracing back to the era of Confucius in the Spring and Autumn Period. According to the historical text "Xing Yuan" (Surname Collection), it originated with a descendant of the Xia dynasty, named Si, who served in the state of Qi during the Spring and Autumn Period. He was fond of gathering abalone, hence adopting the surname "Bao," which means abalone in Chinese. According to accounts in historical texts such as "Brief Review on Clan" and "Yuanhe Surname Review," Bao Shuya (BC? ~ 644 BC) befriended Guan Zhong in his youth and recognized Guan Zhong's virtue. Initially, Bao Shuya served the young master Xiao Bai, while Guan Zhong served the young master Jiu. However, in the twelfth year of King Ji Tuo's reign (685 BC) of the Zhouzhuang era, in their bid for the throne of Qi, Guan Zhong shot an arrow that grazed the young master Xiao Bai. Upon Xiao Bai's return and ascension to the throne as Duke Huan of Qi, Bao Shuya was appointed as the Prime Minister and advocated for Guan Zhong's release from imprisonment, facilitating his reinstatement and serving alongside him. The enduring friendship between Guan Zhong and Bao

Shuya, epitomized by phrases such as "Baozi's legacy" and "Guan Bao's friendship," contributed to Duke Huan of Qi's hegemony during the Spring and Autumn Period. Consequently, in later generations, close friendships were often likened to the bond between Guan Zhong and Bao Shuya, and their story was passed down as a tale of camaraderie. During Duke Huan of Qi's reign, the state of Qi reached unprecedented power, and Bao Shuya recognized Guan Zhong's extraordinary political talents, always treating him with courtesy, respect, and trust. Guan Zhong himself once expressed admiration, stating, "My parents gave birth to me, and Baozi knows me!" Many of Bao Shuya's descendants adopted their ancestor's name as their surname, perpetuating the lineage of the Bao family through generations.

Another origin story suggests that the Bao surname originated from the Mongolian ethnic group, specifically from descendants of the "Golden Family" of Mongolia, who adopted Han Chinese surnames through sinicization. The Borjigin clan of the Mongols, known as the "Golden Family," traces its lineage back to Temüjin, the fourth son of Yesügei Baatar, and the younger brother of Genghis Khan. The Borjigin clan, also known as the Borjigid, Borjiginjin, Borojiqin, Borochiqigit, Borochigin, Bo'erchijin, and Bo'erchijinjin, is one of the ancient tribes of the Mongolian Nüürwü (Nine Wells). The Borjigin clan originally belonged to the Kiyat tribe, one of the oldest tribes among the Mongols. The Borjigin clan later became known as the Borjiginjin after Yesügei Baatar established the clan. The name "Borjigin" is derived from the title "Börte Chono," as mentioned in "The Secret History of the Mongols": "Yesügei Baatar was a member of the Borjigin clan." During the reign of Genghis Khan's fourth-generation ancestor, Khabul Khan, Kiyat was placed before Borjigin, expressed as Kiyat-Borjigin. By the time of Genghis Khan, only the Borjigin name was used as the surname. During the tumultuous period of Genghis Khan's rise to power, many members of the Borjigin clan sought refuge with other branches of the Mongolian tribes, leaving only the descendants of Genghis Khan as the true Borjigin clan. Therefore, after Genghis Khan became the Great Khan of the Mongol Empire, he despised those who "chose otherwise" and strictly decreed that the Borjigin name could only be used by his five brothers and their descendants, earning them the title of the "Golden Family." From the time Genghis Khan assumed the title of Great Khan of the Mongol Empire until the surrender of Borjigin E'erkhonggor (the son of Lin Dan Khan) to the Jin Dynasty—a period of more than four hundred and thirty years—the leaders of the Mongol Empire, the emperors of the Yuan Dynasty, and the khans of the Northern Yuan Dynasty all descended from the Borjigin clan. During that time, Mongolians of the Borjigin clan had become widely distributed, with communities found inside and outside the Great Wall, along rivers, and across plateaus and lakeshores, as is still the case today.

Various scholars and bureaucrats wrote histories telling of the migration of northern ethnic groups to the south, such as the Hakka people and the Bao clan. During the pre-Qin period, the Bao surname primarily resided in the Shandong region. The origin of Tangyue Village in Shexian County can be traced back to Bao Hong, the prefect of Xin'an during the Xianhe period of the Eastern Jin dynasty (326~335). The Bao surname belongs to the descendants of Bao Hong. They originally resided in Jinkeitun, the Fengle River's south bank, known as Baotun. According to the Ming clan records, there were already 29 branches of the Bao clan scattered from Baotun. Bao Hong's tenth-generation descendant, Luo Jie, settled in Hexian County's Hesiwu, and Bao Rong, the twelfth-generation descendant, is considered the founder of the Tangyue faction. After the Southern Song Dynasty, more than 40 factions descended from the Tangyue faction can be verified.

The village of Tangyue derives its name from a rich historical tapestry. In this name, "tang" represents the stately tangli tree (sweet pear tree), while "yue" signifies the comforting shade cast by two such trees. "Tangyue" thus beautifully encapsulates the image of a place nestled beneath the protective canopy of the tangli tree. The origins of this name can be traced back to the enchanting story of Zhou Xian and Lu Taibo, first told in the Book of Songs poem titled Gantang ("Sweet Pear Tree"). In this narrative, Lu Taibo earnestly carried out King Wen's decree, demonstrating unwavering care for his people. His work was centered on

13

a gantang tree thoughtfully positioned close to the community. Over time, Taibo undertook the special task of preserving the venerable gantang tree, ensuring its branches and leaves flourished, thus offering abundant shade. Consequently, Tangyue symbolizes the embodiment of "virtuous governance." Yet the village is also named "Tangyue" for another reason. Here, "Tang" pays homage to the illustrious Tang Dynasty, while "Yue" venerates "The Duke of the State Yue." These characters can be found etched on ancient farm tools and tombstones of that era. This name commemorates the heroic endeavors of Bao Anguo, who, alongside his wife's brother Wang Hua, played a pivotal role in the late Sui Dynasty uprising to safeguard six states from impending disaster. In recognition of their remarkable valor, Emperor Taizong of the Tang Dynasty conferred upon Wang Hua the titles of Duke of Yue and King of Loyalty. The people, deeply moved by Wang Hua's sacrifice and dedication, elevated him to the status of a deity, leading to the construction of King Wang temples in every village. The enduring spirit of reverence and the continuation of these sacred traditions thus inspired the village's name "Tangyue".

From a geographical perspective, Shexian County is situated at the southern foothills of Huangshan (Yellow) Mountain, within the undulating terrain of southern Anhui. The Xinan River Valley stretches in an east-west direction through this region, with Shexian County and the Xiuning Basin forming significant, expansive valleys. As far as the eye can see, the landscape is adorned with chickens, dogs, mulberry trees, and hemp fields, while villages bustle with life. Tangyue, nestled in the heart of Huizhou, lies upstream along the Xinan River. To the north, Huangshan Mountain often veils itself in mist, while to the south, Tianmu Mountain flaunts its jagged peaks. Surrounded by mountains, streams, emerald-green peaks, and villages that stretch into the horizon, it's aptly described as a place where "Yellow and White Mountains face each other, offering scenery as enchanting as that found in the southern reaches of the Yangtze River." Tangyue is located 7.5 kilometers west of Shexian County town, nestled to the north by Longshan and shielded to the south by Futingshan. Three streams, constructed by ancient people, encircle the village, creating an exceptional environment characterized by being"embraced by mountains, encircled by water, and sheltered by a protective screen." It is within this favorable environment that the brilliant cultural heritage of the Bao clan, embodying the essence of Huizhou culture, has flourished. Tangyue is an ancient village, and the prominent Bao clan, one of its major surnames, has thrived for over 800 years since the Song and Yuan dynasties.

From a historical perspective, Shexian County, formerly known as Xin'an, was established during the Qin Dynasty. In the third year of Emperor Huizong of the Northern Song Dynasty (1121), it was renamed Huizhou. Since the end of the Sui Dynasty, Shexian County has been the location of prefectures, states, and government offices, serving as the political, economic, and cultural center of Huizhou. During the Song, Yuan, Ming, and Qing dynasties, Huizhou governed six counties (Shexian, Yixian, Xiuning, Wuyuan, Jixi, and Qimen). In terms of family lineage, clans were quite high-achieving in Huizhou. Since the Tang and Song dynasties, there have been numerous families with clear and extensive vertical lineages. Simultaneously, due to migrations and interactions among various lineages, favorable conditions for the vertical transmission of family legacies were established. The people of Huizhou predominantly lived among those of their own surname, preserving the purity of their customs. Each surname was overseen by its respective ancestral hall, and members of the same clan showed great respect for one another. As the "Jiyuanji Note" recounts: "The tombs of thousands of years have not been disturbed; the clans of thousands of people have not dispersed; the genealogy of thousands of years remains unaltered; the strict hierarchy between masters and servants has endured for decades." During the Ming and Qing dynasties, Huizhou culture flourished, exemplified by Huizhou woodblock printing, Huizhou architecture, Huizhou Confucianism, Shexian seal carving, Xin'an Neo-Confucianism, Xin'an painting, Xin'an medicine, etc. Shexian County was renowned for its rich cultural heritage, with tales of "father and son both being imperial scholars," "siblings being both members of the Hanlin Academy," "four generations holding high imperial ranks," and "four siblings all being members of the Hanlin Academy" passed down through generations. In modern times, Shexian has been home to numerous politicians, thinkers, scientists, educators, and writers, further enriching its cultural heritage.

During the Jianyan period of the Southern Song Dynasty (1127~1130), Bao Rong, who held the position of "literature official" in Huizhou Prefecture, saw that Tangyue was a beautiful place with clear mountains and rivers. He built a house in the Pingtou area of Tangyue Village and named it "Zhangshu Garden." He also buried his deceased wife and concubine in the garden during his lifetime. This is the ancestral cemetery of the Bao clan in Tangyue Village today. It was Bao Jumei, the great-grandson of Bao Rong, who moved the entire family from Ximen River in the west of Huizhou Prefecture to Tangyue, where they settled permanently. Bao Jumei once praised Tangyue as a place "with prosperous mountains and rivers with expansive fields capable of supporting countless generations of descendants." It was from his generation that the Bao clan flourished in Tangyue Village, gradually becoming a prominent family. The descendants of the Bao clan in Tangyue Village honor Bao Rong as the "ancestor of the Tangyue Bao clan." The ancestral cemetery is located in the center of Tangyue, adorned with green grass and colorful flowers, surrounded by pine and cypress trees, solemn and majestic, serving as a place for descendants to pay their respects. Starting from Bao Jumei, Tangyue Village underwent extensive construction projects, with large-scale village industries being established. During the Yuan Dynasty, in the period of Yuzheng (1341~1368), Tangyue Village had well-established production and living facilities. During the transition from the Yuan to the Ming Dynasty, Tangyue Village underwent large-scale water system renovations. The water source for Tangyue came from Lingshan Mountain, divided into two streams: one came from Dongshan and Hui Pond, passing through the northern part of the village into Molu Pond; the other went to the west of the village along the Lingshan Mountain range to Xisha Creek, serving as the main water source for the village. During the Yuzheng period, Bao Baiyuan advocated for the construction of the "Thumb Dam," which irrigated more than 600 mu of fields (approx. 99 square acres), ensuring the harvest of Tangyue's farmland in times of drought and flood. At the same time, water was brought into the village, encircling the southern part of the village like a belt, with water channels in the front and back streets. The front channels were hidden underground, while the back channels were visible and accessible. The water from Molu Pond Creek flowed around the east of the village, where two streams converged at Congbu Pavilion, flowing gently to the mouth of Qixingdun Yishanting. During the 18th to 19th years of the Yongle period of the Ming Dynasty, the Thumb Dam was rebuilt, and a series of mountain reservoirs were excavated below it. As a regulatory measure, Degong Pond, located on the mountain northwest of the village, was a large reservoir constructed with stone walls, ensuring agricultural water supply in times of severe drought in the village.

The Tangyue Bao family branch has maintained its lineage for 34 generations since its founding ancestor, Rong Gong. Bao Yuankang, a scholar from the Yuan Dynasty, constructed the Kindness and Filial Piety Hall in Longshan, to the north of the village, as a place of reverence for Bao Zongyan and Shousun. These two individuals were father and son, who lived during the late Song Dynasty and early Yuan Dynasty. They valiantly fought to the death when they encountered thieves. The Kindness and Filial Piety Hall encompasses several courtyards and serves as an equivalent to a family temple. It stands as the original ancestral hall of the Bao family in Tangyue. During the Yuan Dynasty, the village's structures were predominantly centered on the ancestors' cemeteries. Notable features that remain identifiable today include the "Mother of Kindness and Filial Piety" located west of the tomb, Bao Tongren's Mongolian Zhuangyuan Square to the north of the tomb, the Dahe Society, and Xichou Academy situated to the east of the tomb. The Tangyue Bao Family Branch Temple was initially constructed during the Jiajing period of the Ming Dynasty. Duke Xiangxian, the 16th-generation ancestor, oversaw its construction during his approximately ten-year stay (circa 1550) at the site of the former Xichou Academy. This temple is often referred to as the "Xichou Temple" and was erected to venerate the "Ancestral Duke Qingyun." As Duke Qingyun held the title of Wansi, it's also known as the "Duke Wansi Branch Temple." This site, known as "Dunben Hall," is the ancestral temple of the Bao clan in Tangyue, commonly called the "Male Temple." By the Jiaqing period of the Qing Dynasty, the Wansi Temple, initially constructed during the Jiajing period of the Ming Dynasty, had experienced 250 years of various challenges and had fallen into a state of disrepair. It was during this time that the Bao Zhitong family, prominent merchants in Tangyue's Huai River Region Salt Industry, decided to honor their ancestors by performing virtuous deeds. Bao Zhitong and his son Shufang generously donated a significant sum to reconstruct the Male Temple. Additionally, they established the "Wenhui" on the left and created the "Forever Filial Piety Temple" to honor the filial sons of the Bao family since the Southern Song Dynasty. Simultaneously, they undertook the preservation and maintenance of cultural relics and historic sites such as the Dahe Society, Shuikou Archway Garden, and Sanyuan Temple. Bao Qiyun, the younger brother of Bao Zhitong, built a Female Temple, Qingyi Hall, located south and facing north, opposite the Dahe Society, to commemorate the heroines of the family. Furthermore, he donated over 1,200 acres of land for charitable purposes, establishing the "Four Poor Warehouses" to provide support to widows and single individuals. The Bao family's commitment to charity extended to include the provision of assistance to less fortunate clan members each year.

In the summer of 1998, I embarked on a journey with my daughter, Bao Fuluo, to Shexian in search of our ancestral roots. Our exploration began with a visit to the majestic Yellow Mountain, and from there, we made our way to Tunxi, which is known today as Huangshan City (Yellow Mountain City). The renaming of Tunxi, a place rich in both geographical and cultural heritage, has always left me puzzled. The name "Tunxi" itself holds a deep significance. "Tun" symbolizes gathering, while "xi" represents a brook. This name, "Gathering Brook," perfectly encapsulates the essence of the place. In the heart of Tunxi, the Hengjiang River and Lushui River converge, creating a tranquil haven where the Tunxi River nourishes a picturesque valley. As the evening sets in, misty waves dance in the fading light, a few beach gulls soar above, fishermen sing their timeless songs, and the curling smoke from chimneys adds to the enchanting atmosphere. But what truly sets Tunxi apart is its famous old street. This historical thoroughfare has roots dating back to the end of the Yuan Dynasty and the beginning of the Ming Dynasty. Merchants hailing from Wuyuan and Shexian counties recognized the strategic location where the Lushui, Hengjiang, and Zhejiang Rivers converged near the mouth of the Three Rivers. Here, they established warehouses to stock goods, facilitating the transit of local products and salt. During the Yongle period of the Ming Dynasty, Xiuning businessman Cheng Weizong built new shops on this foundation and even erected pavilions between them, providing pedestrians a place to rest. This marked the start of Tunxi's flourishing commercial district, known today as "Old Street." As the Ming and Qing Dynasties unfolded, Huizhou merchants took center stage, further boosting the district's prominence. Tunxi's market district evolved into a bustling hub for both water and land transportation in Huizhou. Its rapid development was possible thanks to its favorable positioning at the crossroads of Anhui, Zhejiang, and Jiangxi provinces. The confluence of the Hengjiang and the Lushui River, whose combined waters flow directly into the Qiantang River, only added to its prosperity. During the Ming Dynasty, Tunxi's commercial district earned its reputation as an influential central county market, and by the Qing Dynasty, it had become a renowned metropolitan tea city.

Today's Tunxi Old Street, in the heart of Tunxi District in Huangshan City, Anhui Province, is a remarkably preserved ancient pedestrian thoroughfare, brimming with historical charm. Nestled between Huashan Mountain to the north and Xin'an River to the south, it is a testament to the region's rich heritage. Stretching for a total length of 1,272 meters, Old Street's core segment spans 832 meters, commencing at Qingchun Lane (Youth Lane) in the east and culminating at Zhenhai Bridge (Towered Over Sea Bridge) in the west. This charming street boasts a width of 5 to 8 meters and encompasses one straight path, three cross streets, and 18 charming alleys. Distinguished by its architecture, Tunxi Old Street comprises over 300 Huizhou buildings, constructed in various eras, giving it a distinctive character. These buildings are artfully arranged, forming a fishbone-like pattern that narrows toward the west and broadens to the east. Sitting adjacent to the confluence of the Hengjiang, Lushui, and Xin'an rivers, Tunxi Old Street is aptly known as "The Riverside Scene during Spring Festival." It offers a picturesque setting and stands out as one of China's most comprehensive ancient street markets, showcasing architectural styles from the Southern Song, Ming, and Qing Dynasties. The structures along Tunxi Old Street faithfully display the unique architectural style of Huizhou. The town's planning layout and architectural design exhibit distinct Huizhou characteristics. Nestled amid the natural contours of mountains and rivers, the street follows a gentle curve, and its road is paved with brown-red granite slabs. Adorning both sides of the street are elegant and unassuming buildings with whitewashed walls and black-tiled roofs, their structures harmoniously dispersed and neatly stacked. These buildings, together with the iconic high horse-head walls that separate many of them, collectively embody the exquisite beauty of Huizhou architecture.

The five-tiered horse-head wall, with its distinctive stepped profiles, was originally constructed to protect homes from the threat of fire damage. As a safeguard, a series of volcanic sealing walls was erected. However, over time, this practical structure evolved into a distinctive decorative element. With its undulating profile and embellishments such as depictions of creatures like beasts, turtles, and sparrows, it now embodies the distinctive rhythm of southern Anhui folk architecture. Among locals in Huizhou, this architectural wonder is affectionately known as "Five Peaks Facing the Sky."

In contrast to the "Five Peaks Facing the Sky," another hallmark of Huizhou architecture is the "Four Waters Back to the Hall." Most of the ancient homes in Huizhou are designed as enclosed compounds with a central courtyard as the focal point. They are encircled by towering walls on all four sides, featuring only a limited number of exterior windows. The inner courtyard is elongated and narrow, serving multiple purposes such as providing natural light, ventilation, and drainage. On the roofs, strategically placed water troughs direct rainwater into the courtyard, preventing any leakage and symbolizing the conservation of resources, mirroring the pragmatic values of the merchant culture that thrived in the region.

Water, considered the primary lifeline in human existence, holds deeper significance for the people of Huizhou. They view water as wealth, as well as the pathway to the external world, embodying the saying, "a propitious location must have water," and "gathering water is like gathering wealth." "Four Waters Back to the Hall" also symbolizes prosperity in descendants and the enduring lineage of a family, akin to the unending flow of rivers. Huizhou residents often say, "With a courtyard in the home, each generation will thrive."

Shops that line the old streets of Tunxi typically stand as two-story structures of brick and wood, with sturdy beams and columns forming their framework. Despite their often compact single-room layouts, their design principles are ingenious. The door lintels and window lattice come in various shapes, square or round, ridged or flat, adorned with intricate patterns. These elements boast brick and wood carvings, showcasing impeccable craftsmanship. Within the Hui-style wood carvings on the lintels, opera characters come to life, folk tales exude subtlety and emotion, and Xin'an landscapes paint vivid and beautiful scenes. Jutting out from the shops, you'll find the "flying chair" or "beauty chair," not only expanding the usable space within the store, making it convenient for both store owners and customers to enjoy the street view, while enhancing the exterior grandeur of the store itself. The majority of shops on Old Street are characterized by their narrow and deep structures, often featuring patios brightening the interiors. Upon scrutinizing the internal layout, one can identify two main types: open-front shops facing the street and inner-patio designs. They may also be categorized into those with a "front shop and back workshop," "front shop and back residence," or "front shop and back warehouse," some with two compartments and others with three. These shops generally exhibit a deep layout, with the front area designated for business operations and the inner compartments reserved for processing or storing goods. You'll find the shop in front with living quarters at the rear, or a retail space on the ground floor and living quarters above. In front of the shops, large vermilion wooden doors stand prominently, designed to be flexibly opened and closed during the morning and evening hours. The interior of these establishments is often adorned with couplets and shelves displaying calligraphy and paintings, reflecting the refined sensibilities of Huizhou merchants, who skillfully navigate between the worlds of Confucian wisdom and commerce.

Strolling on the large red sandstone-paved roads, one can see vermilion pavilions with double eaves, tea houses, wine shops, and antique stores lined up in an orderly fashion, with banners, flags, and calligraphy studios still retaining the charm of the Ming and Qing dynasties. Despite the strong commercial atmosphere, the area remains steeped in historical ambiance, overwhelming the senses with its nostalgic charm. Numerous shops are selling the "four treasures of the study," as Hui ink, She ink stones, and Xuan paper are all local products. The extraction and production of She ink stones began in the Tang Dynasty, over 1,300 years ago. Since the Southern Song Dynasty, the stone supply dwindled, with mining gradually decreasing until intermittent periods of excavation continued until 1963, when the She County Arts and Crafts Factory (Anhui She Ink stone Factory) resumed extraction based on historical records. She ink stones are characterized by their hard and smooth texture that doesn't absorb water, releasing ink like oil without damaging brushes. They are described as "not clinging to the brush or rejecting ink," and with age, they become even more radiant with each wash. They possess the eight virtues of "hardness, smoothness, flexibility, strength, fineness, delicateness, cleanliness, and beauty."

Bao Fuluo and I walked into a tea house. Perhaps because it was lunchtime, there were few customers in the spacious hall. Despite the sparse clientele, the two girls performing the tea ceremony on stage were quite dedicated. They wore two small braids, dressed in short-sleeved shirts with large collars that were popular among rural girls in the Republic of China era, along with plain trousers and a simple half-moon apron. One girl's shirt had blue flowers on a white background, while the other had white flowers on a blue background. Standing on stage, the two girls resembled two clean and simple blue-and-white porcelain vases. Before the tea ceremony began, they played traditional Chinese stringed instruments and softly sang a prelude reminiscent of ancient poetry. The props on stage were also common in the households of the water towns of Jiangnan (Southern Yantze Region) during the Republic of China era: a lengthy altar desk, an Eight Immortals table, and two armchairs. We savored the spectacle for two hours, indulging in fragrant tea and delectable tea-time snacks.

From Huangshan City to She County, it's about 26 kilometers. Yu Liqing, Director of the Huangshan City Education Committee, graciously offered us a ride. Along the way, villages appear every two or three kilometers, displaying views of pink walls standing tall, tiled roofs overlapping, and towering gates beckoning. Despite being of small size, these striking elements give each a presence more akin to a city. Amidst the verdant trees and lush foliage, the distinctively tiled pink walls stand out. Upon arriving at the county seat of She County, Yu Liqing led us to Xu Guo Archway. Yu Liqing brought us to see Xu Guo Archway for another reason: Xu Guo and Tangyue's Bao Xiangxian were in-laws. Xu Guo's eldest son, Lide, married Bao Xiangxian's granddaughter. In the Ming Dynasty, Bao Xiangxian (1496~1568) started as an imperial scholar before being appointed as an assistant censor in Hu Guang Provinces. Later, he led troops to Yunnan, governed Shaanxi, became a censor-in-chief, and then served as an assistant minister of war. Upon retiring, he returned to his hometown and was appointed as the assistant minister of war in Shandong, overseeing military affairs in Guangdong and Guangxi. He was both a civil servant and a renowned military commander, with illustrious achievements in battle, posthumously awarded the title of Minister of Construction, and honored with an archway and a memorial. Bao Xiangxian served in various official positions in seven provinces. Due to his unwavering integrity, he faced ostracism and slander from the jealous and corrupt officials at court, so he did not receive the emperor's favor or promotion. Xu Guo, his in-law, who served as prime minister for three reigns and was the teacher of Emperor Wanli, was deeply dissatisfied with this situation, calling out, "Significant contributions, yet scant rewards." However, Bao Xiangxian remained calm. He famously said, "I do not choose the place of service, nor do I seek the position of office," demonstrating the demeanor of an ancient virtuous official.

The Xu Guo Stone Archway, also recognized as Grand Scholar's Square, is popularly referred to as the "Eight-Legged Archway." This distinctive monument is situated on the eastern side of Yanghe Gate (Sunshine Gate) in Shexian. It stands across the street as a prominent landmark. Xu Guo, the proprietor of this remarkable archway, hailed from Shexian and gained acclaim as a prominent statesman during the Ming Dynasty. In 1565, he achieved the esteemed title of Jinshi in the Jiajing Yichou examination. His illustrious career spanned the Jiajing, Longqing, and Wanli reigns, marking him as a veteran of these significant periods. In the 11th year of Emperor Wanli's reign, Xu Guo assumed a role in the imperial cabinet, serving as the Minister of Rites and earning the distinguished title of Grand Scholar at Dongge Institute. Subsequently, he was honored with the title of Guardian of the Crown Prince and bestowed the position of Grand Scholar at Wenyuange Institute. Notably, in the 12th year of Emperor Wanli's reign, his exceptional service in quelling a rebellion on the Yunnan border led to a promotion to the position of Prince Guardian. He was further granted the prestigious title of The Grand Scholar of Wuyingdian, housed within the Hall of Martial Heroes. Emperor Wanli, delighted by the successful pacification of the Yunnan border turmoil, rewarded his loyal ministers generously. Xu Guo, as an integral aide to the emperor, was commended for his unwavering dedication and significant accomplishments, which resulted in the receipt of various honors and rewards. Emperor Wanli of the Ming Dynasty, also known as Ming Shenzong, personally approved the establishment of the Xu Guo stone archway in October of the 12th year of Wanli (1584). The archway was commissioned to record Xu Guo's remarkable achievements and contributions to the dynasty. What sets the Xu Guo Stone Archway apart is its unconventional design. Unlike the typical four-pillar archways, this archway boasts eight pillars, forming an enclosure on all sides. The octagonal structure is magnificent and unparalleled in China. This innovative design defies conventional norms regarding the interaction between monarchs and ministers, making it the sole exemplar of its kind in the nation. Today, the Xu Guo Stone Archway is the only existing octagonal archway in China and has become an iconic symbol of the ancient city of Huizhou, serving as a testament to the enduring legacy of Xu Guo and his extraordinary contributions to Chinese history.

The Xu Guo Arch epitomizes the apex of Huizhou stone arch technology. Comprising two stone archways with three rooms, four columns, and three front-facing floors, as well as one single room on the left and right sides, it spans an area of nearly 80 square meters. Crafted from resilient and substantial green tea garden stone, it stands as a prominent architectural landmark in the ancient city of Shexian. It features two types of cupolas, characterized by their robust structure and plump form, serving as the local archetype for four-column, three-story cupola-style stone houses renowned during the Ming and Qing Dynasties. Xu Guo's stone abode exudes majesty and grandeur, adorned with extraordinarily intricate carvings. The eight pillars are interconnected by beams and squares, with the upper cupola being slightly smaller in size, supported by 12 imposing lions, which ensure structural stability. The pillars and horizontal squares are meticulously etched with brocade motifs, depicting flowers, auspicious clouds, and cranes, accentuating the primary design on the moonbeam. These motifs symbolize Xu Guo's accomplishments and prominence within his contemporary society. Among these motifs, the dragon in the south symbolizes reverence for royal authority, the flying carp in the west signifies Xu Guo's substantial academic background, and the "three leopards and magpies" allude to Xu Guo's consecutive promotions through three levels. The most prominent plaque above the archway bears the inscriptions, "Student first, minister later," and "Venerable elder stateman who came to power," inscribed in large, regular script characters. These inscriptions were composed by Dong Qichang, an illustrious calligrapher and painter during the Ming Dynasty and one of the four great talents of the southern Yangtze River region. "Venerable elder statesman who came to power" underscores Xu

Guo's service as an official during the Jiajing, Longqing, and Wanli reigns. Adorned with solemn Hui-style sculpture art, the Xu Guo Archway's stone pillars, beams, plaques, brackets, and spandrels are graced with lifelike carvings, including flying, colorful phoenixes, galloping animals, powerful lions, and numerous cloud patterns. The overall effect transforms the Xu Guo Archway into a captivating constellation of art, akin to a small-scale art exhibition hall.

The center of Shexian's Huizhou Town houses the millennia-old Huizhou government. The historic city of Huizhou is segmented into an inner and outer city, each fortified with gates at the cardinal points of east, west, south, and north. This ancient town boasts a remarkably well-preserved heritage, encompassing the urn city, city gates, ancient streets, and venerable alleyways. The city abounds with notable landmarks, including: the Huizhou Government Office, the South Bell and Drum Tower (Nanqiao), the East Bell and Drum Tower (Dongqiao), the Yanghe Gate, Hui Garden, the Kindness Tower (Renhe), the Close to the Moon Tower (Deyue), the Tea House, the Street Crossing Tower, the Ancient Theater Tower, the Poet Li Bai Tower (Taibai), the Uphill Street (Doushan), the Ancient Shexian Bridge, the Favorable Wind Archway (Huifeng), the Xin'an Monument Garden, the Fishing Dam, the Tao Xingzhi Memorial Hall, and the former residence of Huang Binhong. Moreover, the city is a repository of Huizhou culture, encompassing Xin'an Neo-Confucianism, Hui School Pu Xue, Xin'an Medicine, Xin'an Painting School, Hui School Printmaking, Hui School Seal Engraving, Hui Opera, Hui Merchants, Hui School Architecture, and Huizhou's "Four Carvings" (brick carving, wood carving, stone carving, and bamboo carving). The rich tapestry of Huizhou culture also includes its renowned cuisine, tea ceremonies, dialect, and more. Shexian is not only famous for its cultural heritage but is also the primary production hub for Huizhou ink and Shexian ink stones, which are integral to Huizhou culture and Peking Opera. Tang Xianzu, a distinguished playwright from the late Ming Dynasty, once wrote: "If you want to know gold and silver, you often travel from Yellow Mountain to White Mountain; but I have never had a dream of going to Huizhou." Tang Xianzu's reluctance to visit Huizhou likely reflects the scholarly elite's longstanding disdain for the merchant class, unease with travel outside major cultural centers like Beijing, Nanjing, and Suzhou, and concern over the rising power of Huizhou's commercial magnates amid the instability of the late Ming era. However, neither I nor my daughter, Bao Fuluo, shared these concerns. Today, Huizhou is celebrated as one of China's four exceptionally well-preserved ancient cities. These include: Huizhou Ancient City in Huangshan, Anhui; Langzhong Ancient City in Langzhong, Sichuan; Pingyao Ancient City in Pingyao, Shanxi; and Lijiang Ancient City in Lijiang, Yunnan.

From the county seat of Shexian County to Tangyue is only 5 kilometers. When we arrived at the village entrance, we got out of the car to buy tickets. It turns out that Tangyue Village has become a tourist attraction, and tickets must be purchased to enter the village. Surrounding the ancient archways are ancient ancestral halls, old residences, and ancient pavilions, all set amid the picturesque rural scenery. More than 30 films and TV shows have been shot in Tangyue Village, such as "Dream of the Red Chamber," "Smoke in the Locked Room," "Tea Sage Lu Yu," and "Ye Ting." Tangyue Village is primarily centered on two intersecting main streets, surrounded by ancient ancestral halls and archways, forming a large square with a strong classical taste. To the west of the archway, there are three ancestral halls: Dunben Hall, Qingyi Hall, and Shixiao Hall. Moving eastward, there is the Congbu Pavilion and seven tall stone archways extending into the distance in succession. The ancestral halls are magnificent and solemn, with tall gatehouses and imposing drum-bearing stone sculptures at the entrance, exuding an aura of power and authority that commands respect. Green stone archways reach across the paths, towering high above, forcing pedestrians to look up at them in awe. Passing underneath, one can't help but feel an overwhelming presence that enhances the supreme authority of the rulers, wherever they may be.

Dunben Hall, originally known as "Duke Wansi Temple" and colloquially referred to as "The Male Temple," is a remarkable architectural gem that graced the late Jiajing period of the Ming Dynasty (1522~1567). In the Xinyou year of Jiaqing during the Qing Dynasty

(1801), a philanthropic effort led by Bao Zhidao and his son Shufang funded the reconstruction of this venerable edifice. Dunben Hall is celebrated as an exemplar of Huizhou ancestral hall architecture during the Qing Dynasty, characterized by the distinctive "fat beams and thin columns with an inner patio" design. This architectural marvel boasts slender, towering pillars and robust, imposing beams, aptly earning it the moniker "Winter Melon Beam." The structure, with its southern orientation, comprises three courtyards deep and five rooms wide, stretching 15.98 meters in width and 47.11 meters in depth, encompassing a sprawling area of more than 750 square meters. Outside the entrance, a meticulously crafted brick-carved eight-character wall captivates the eye. The addition of door hairpins and drum-holding stones to the entrance gate enhances its grandeur. The welcoming entry hall is graced by the Five Phoenix Tower, its wings soaring to the heavens. The subsequent Joy Hall (Xiangtang) spans five rooms in width, featuring four pillars in the central and side rooms, and five pillars in the wing rooms, with square stone pillars in both the front and rear sections. The timber and beam frame is left exposed on the exterior. The entire hall structure is a masterpiece of architectural ingenuity, combining platform beams and bucket-type frames with the front eaves carefully designed as a canopy pavilion. Notably, in the open and side halls, you will find 16 gray lacquered screen doors, bearing the entire text of "Bao's Five Ethics" meticulously engraved in official script by Deng Shiru. Atop the rear eave room pillars, a stele bearing three edicts from Emperor Jiaqing proudly stands. The rear courtyard assumes a deep pool shape, and two verandas on the walls display a stele titled "Reconstruction of Duke Wansi Temple." Venturing deeper into the ancestral hall, one encounters the dormitory, flanked by inscriptions of "Charity Fields Forbidden Monuments" in the Ti Yuan and Dun Ben versions, embedded on both sides of the front eaves. The corridor along the stone steps reveals "Bao Family Journal," a literary work by Liang Tongshu, Liu Yong, Huang Cheng, and others. The structural materials of this ancestral hall are a testament to its understated elegance, with ginkgo wood pillars and camphor wood beams complemented by simple yet intricate brick, wood, and stone carvings. These elements embody the essence of Confucian philosophy and cultural depth, epitomizing the virtue of neutrality. The overall structure of the ancestral hall exudes simplicity and grace, evoking a sense of serenity and grandeur, a fitting tribute to the illustrious Tangyue Bao family. Notably, the ancestral hall proudly displays a couplet composed by Emperor Qianlong, declaring: "There are no peers in the world for mercy and filial piety, and the beautiful township is the number one in the south of the Yangtze River."

Qingyi Hall, more commonly referred to as the Female Temple, was constructed during the early Jiaqing period of the Qing Dynasty and stands in direct opposition to Dunben Hall. This temple is oriented with its front facade facing north and its rear to the south. Its design is deeply rooted in the philosophical concepts of the male (qian) and female (kun) principles as outlined in the Book of Changes (Yi Jing), reflecting the dichotomy between the earth (yin) and the sky (yang). Ancient tradition held that to reach the Mother's (Xuan) Temple, one should journey to the back of the village, with "back" indicating the northern hall, where the mother lives. The establishment of a temple dedicated to women, especially one that venerates a heroine, was a revolutionary departure from the prevailing custom of "women not entering the temple." This made Qingyi Hall a truly exceptional and rare structure in the region. The unique layout of Qingyi Hall spans five rooms in width and extends three houses deep, incorporating two courtyards in between. Its dimensions are characterized by a width of 16.9 meters and a depth of 48.4 meters. The temple exhibits an imposing, mountain-like appearance (known as Ying Shan), and the external eight-character wall in front of the foyer is adorned with exquisite, translucent, and colorful brick carvings, heralded as some of the finest examples of such craftsmanship among Huizhou's temples. Originally, a large decorative openwork window graced the front wall of the courtyard, with a rooftop attic behind it. The entrance hall of Qingyi Hall is five rooms wide and extends four steps deep, featuring three sturdy columns. Eaves and pillars are crafted from bluestone, with a drum-shaped stone serving as the central pillar's door, adorned with painted door gods. The beams in the foyer are fashioned in the bucket style, featuring a front canopy. A prominent plaque inscribed with the three characters "Qing Yi Tang" hangs prominently in the middle of the Joy Hall's (Xiang Tang) screen wall, bearing the hand of calligrapher Bao Zhen. Another horizontal plaque reading "Zhen Lie Liang Quan" (Both Chastity and Loyalty) was composed by Zeng Guofan. The name "Qing Yi" translates to "innocent, chaste, virtuous, and beautiful," serving as an ode to women. The patio of the Joy Hall is paved with bluestone slabs and is encircled by drainage ditches, with a central aisle and side corridors. A screen wall originally stood between the golden pillars at the rear of the well-lit room. The dormitory area resembles a deep pool, featuring verandas on both sides and stone steps providing access. At the rear of the hall, there stands a 1.2-meter-high Sumuru platform with auspicious "As One Wishes" (Ruyi) patterns engraved on its waist. The entire ancestral hall boasts a well-conceived layout, clear functional divisions, a compact beam structure, streamlined and elegant contours, intricate carvings, meticulous craftsmanship, and a refined yet straightforward interior and exterior. In essence, Qingyi Hall exemplifies the quintessential Qing Dynasty ancestral hall in Huizhou.

During the reign of Jiaqing in the Qing Dynasty, specifically in the year 1801, the Shixiao Temple, dedicated to Forever Filial Piety, was established. This revered edifice was built by Bao Zhidao, the 24th son of the esteemed Bao family, who also penned the temple's inscription. Serving as an ancestral hall devoted to honoring filial sons, the Shixiao Temple aimed to perpetuate the virtues of their forebears and instill a profound sense of filial piety in future generations. It stood as a testament to the enduring tradition of ethical values upheld by the Bao family, emphasizing human virtues and transmitting the noble essence of filial devotion through generations. Since the Song and Yuan Dynasties, the Shixiao Temple has been a sacred site where the names and deeds of illustrious members of the Tangyue Bao family are enshrined. Adorning its walls are inscriptions detailing the remarkable acts of filial piety performed by these individuals. The entrance to the Shixiao Temple features an elegant archway-style door cover, meticulously crafted from water-milled bricks, supported by four pillars spanning three rooms in width. Exquisite carvings embellished the beams, rafters, and ornamental elements, showcasing the artisans' skill and dedication. At the heart of the temple is a tablet inscribed with "Shixiao Temple" (The Forever Filial Piety Temple) and six steles of "The Facts of Forever Filial Piety," penned in an official script by Deng Shiru, a distinguished calligraphy master from the Qing Dynasty. The dormitory comprises five rooms, adopting an open bay style with four pillars and a top bay style with five pillars. Towards the rear of the dormitory stands a Sumuru pedestal, reflecting the simplicity typical of the Qing Dynasty era. On the east and west corridor walls, there are writings by the painter Wang Gong, dated to the 42nd year of the Qianlong reign, "Recording the Reconstruction of the Halls of Kindness and Filial Piety." In addition to the names and filial deeds of generations of the Bao family, the walls of the ancestral hall also feature a stele titled "Record of Filial Piety Hall" authored by Tiebao, a renowned Qing Dynasty scholar. In the 41st year of the Qianlong reign, Bao Zhidao returned to his hometown, Tangyue, from Yangzhou. Collaborating with his brother Bao Qiyun and his son Bao Shufang, they embarked on a series of initiatives aimed at promoting filial piety within their community. These endeavors included the construction of bridges and roads, the donation of a substantial 1,200 acres of charitable land, and the establishment of four destitution relief centers dedicated to aiding the disadvantaged categories within the clan: widows, widowers, orphans, unmarried, the disabled, and the indigent.

Situated along the eastern avenue of the village, the Tangyue Archway Group stands as a testament to ancient craftsmanship and moral values. Comprising seven stone archways, three from the Ming Dynasty and four from the Qing Dynasty, these structures serve as the entrance to several ancient hall buildings. The theme of these archways is the concept of "righteousness," reflecting a moral hierarchy that includes loyalty, filial piety, integrity, and righteousness itself. Positioned in a specific order, they gradually progress towards the central arch, emphasizing the paramount value of "righteousness." Arranged in a semi-circular formation stretching from west to east, the archways create a unified composition. The archways include: the Bao Can Filial Piety Arch, the Mercy and Filial Piety Arch, Bao Wenling's Wife Royal Arch, the Being Good and Giving Arch, Bao Wenyuan's Wife Royal Arch, Bao Fengchang's Filial Son Arch, and the Bao Xiangxian Shangshu Arch. Each arch exudes a solemn and majestic presence, embodying centuries of tradition and virtue. Designated as national key cultural relics under protection, they stand as enduring symbols of China's rich cultural heritage.

The village's surrounding landscape encompasses farmland, trees, ponds, rivers, and man-made structures, including ancient bridges. This environment reflects the fundamental principles of adapting to local conditions and maintaining a harmonious coexistence between humanity and nature. In ancient times, these principles guided the selection of the village site and the construction of its structures. A group of archways spans the road, constructed using substantial flat bluestone slabs, with permanent farmland preserved on either side. As a young peasant girl emerges from the paddy fields, she diligently washes her hands and feet before venturing barefoot onto the immaculate bluestone corridor. It is a rarity in rural China for the daily habits of ordinary farmers to be so hygienic. This observance of cleanliness is a testament to the honest customs, exquisite houses, and picturesque scenery in two villages, Tangmo and Tangyue, as expressed in a local folk song, "Tangmo and Tangyue, no regret to starve to death." Even in times of scarcity, the villagers could still find contentment in their surroundings. As one gazes around, cement structures are absent. The distant archway group, comprising seven majestic arches, appears to emerge from the very farmland itself, creating a striking visual presence. The structural layout of the Tangyue Archway Group adheres to strict central axis symmetry, evoking a profound sense of stability. The design emphasizes a visual focal point and meticulous craftsmanship. The Tangyue Archway Group is a remarkable example of architectural art from the Ming and Qing Dynasties. Despite spanning several centuries, the architectural style of each archway maintains a seamless and cohesive aesthetic. The transition from wood to stone in the Tangyue Archway Group signifies a significant change from earlier iterations. Almost all archways are constructed from the exceptional "Shexian qing" blue stone, known for its outstanding texture. These bluestone archways stand solid, tall, and straight, exuding a sense of grandeur and magnificence. Their construction is a marvel, as they require no nails or rivets, and the ingenious arrangement of stones ensures their longevity for thousands of years without failure.

The westernmost arch is the Bao Can Filial Piety Arch, originally erected during the early 13th year of the Jiajing reign in the Ming Dynasty (1564). Later, it underwent reconstruction in the 11th year of the Qianlong reign in the Qing Dynasty (1746). This archway features a distinctive design with a three-room width, a gracefully curved grass-shaped roof ridge. Standing at an impressive height of 8.4 meters and spanning 8.27 meters in width, it is supported by four stone pillars. The central column dates to the Ming Dynasty, while the lower beams in the two chambers and brackets are crafted from pristine white granite from the same era. Other components of the arch were refurbished during maintenance in the Qing Dynasty, using tea garden bluestone. An intriguing detail of the Bao Can Arch is the "dragon and phoenix board" embellishing the eaves, adorned with the words "imperial edict." Enhancing its allure, a pair of relief lions adorn both the front and back beams, exuding an aura of valor. Although Bao Can never held an official position during his lifetime, the exceptional upbringing of his descendants earned him a commendation from the emperor. His grandson's remarkable contributions in defending the Ming Dynasty in battles led to a special honor known as "honored for three generations," bestowed by the emperor. In honor of this remarkable individual, a memorial was constructed for his ancestor.

The second arch from the west, known as the Cixiao Li Arch (the Mercy and Filial Piety Arch), was built in the 18th year of the Yongle reign in the Ming Dynasty (1420). It underwent multiple renovations during the Ming Hongzhi, Qing Qianlong, Tongzhi, and Guangxu eras. This archway consists of four pillars and three chambers, with a distinctive design featuring a rolled grass-type pattern on the roof ridge. It spans 8.57 meters in width, 2.53 meters in depth, and stands at a height of 9.6 meters. The pillars are made of white marble, while the rest of the structure is built from solidified stone from the Qinghui Tea Garden. The marble components date back to the Ming Dynasty, while the construction using bluestone is from the Qing Dynasty. Inscribed on the arch's lintel is the phrase "Cixiao Li," while the dragon and phoenix board bears the inscription "Imperial Edict," signifying the emperor's personal approval. The Cixiao Li Arch was erected to commemorate the sacrifice of Bao Yuyan and Bao Shouxun, two Confucian scholars from the end of the Song Dynasty, who chose to die to save each other's lives. According to historical records, during a rebellion led by the Yuan Dynasty's county governor Li Da, the Bao father and son were captured by the rebel forces. The rebels demanded that one of them be killed, leaving the decision to the pair themselves. Unexpectedly, the father and son competed to sacrifice themselves to save the other, and even the rebel forces couldn't bring themselves to carry out the execution. To honor their actions, the imperial court ordered the construction of this archway. Inscribed on the archway is also Emperor Mingle of the Ming Dynasty's poem "Cixiao," which reads: "When a father faces danger, life and death hang in the balance. The Bao family parents' filial piety shines through the ages." Later, when Emperor Qianlong of the Qing Dynasty visited Tangyue and learned of the "Cixiao" story, he inscribed a couplet, "There are no peers in the world for mercy and filial piety, and the beautiful township is the number one in the south of the Yangtze River." and allocated funds to renovate the "Cixiao Li" archway, adding his own inscriptions to the couplet. It's extremely rare for an archway to receive such recognition from multiple emperors over several dynasties.

The third arch from the west, known as the Jiang Clan's Virtuous and Filial Arch dedicated to Bao Wenling's wife, was constructed in September of the forty-first year of the Qing Qianlong era (1776). This archway is constructed from the Qinghui Tea Garden bluestone, 8.75 meters in width and 11.1 meters high. Inscribed on the lintel are the phrases "Maintaining Integrity, Exemplifying Filial Piety" and "Upholding Virtue, Protecting the Orphan." The fourth arch, named the Benevolent and Charitable Arch, was built in January of the twenty-fifth year of the Qing Jiaqing era (1820). It too was constructed using bluestone from the Qinghui Tea Garden. This archway features a "piercing heaven pillar" design with four pillars and three chambers, spanning 9.19 meters in width, 2.85 meters in depth, and standing at a height of 11.70 meters. The pillars contain no decorative patterns, but the arch board under the eaves is intricately carved with floral patterns, and the rings and sparrows on the moonbeams are also finely carved with delicate patterns. The large beams and pillars are roughly polished without adornment. According to tradition, the Bao family in Tangyue once had archways symbolizing "Loyalty," "Filial Piety," and "Integrity," but lacked one for "Righteousness." When Bao Shufang, a prominent figure in the family, rose to the position of Salt Commissioner of Lianghuai, controlling the salt trade in Jiangnan, he sought imperial approval to erect an archway featuring the missing virtue to honor his ancestors and bring glory to his lineage. He donated 100,000 bushels of grain and 30,000 taels of silver, financed the construction of river embankments spanning 400 kilometers, and provided military provisions for three provinces. His efforts earned him approval from the imperial court.

As you wander away from the "Being Good and Giving" archway, you'll soon stumble upon the unassuming yet charming "Congbu Pavilion" (the term "cong" refers to a dappled bluish-white horse, and "bu" refers to a step). Nestled amidst picturesque surroundings, this square pavilion with a single eave and pointed peaks exudes simplicity and allure. Delicate wind bells sway gently from its corners, and its distinct square top has earned it the nickname "official hat top." Flanked by gates to the east and west, connecting it with the surrounding archways and corridors, the pavilion bears the elegant three characters "Congbu Pavilion" in official script, attributed to the renowned calligrapher Deng Shiru. Its eight pillars, four of which are partially concealed within the walls, provide discreet support, creating an uncluttered ambiance. Once adorned with flying chairs on its southern and northern sides, stone benches now invite visitors to rest and soak in the tranquil scenery. An arched water channel beneath the pavilion diverts water into the stream, filling the air with the soothing melody of flowing water. Amidst the pastoral beauty of its surroundings, the pavilion stands as a serene oasis, seemingly untouched by the commotion beyond its boundaries, offering solace to those seeking refuge. The origins of this pavilion date back to the Longqing period of the Ming Dynasty, with a history spanning over four centuries. It is believed to have been erected in honor of Bao Xuan, an esteemed ancestor of the Bao family who served as an imperial envoy for three successive generations during the Western Han Dynasty. Bestowed with a status akin to that of a prime minister, Bao Xuan was renowned for his candor and courage in offering advice, embodying principles of integrity and righteousness. Often seen patrolling the realm on his fine piebald steed, he was known for his prompt action and diligent reporting. A popular folk song from the Han Dynasty's capital attests to his influence: "Walk slowly and make stops, avoid the envoy on the Cong horse." The Congbu Pavilion stands as a timeless tribute to Bao Xuan's enduring legacy.

Upon leaving the Congbu Pavilion, you'll encounter three more archways to the east. The fifth arch, known as the Wu Clan's Virtuous and Filial Arch dedicated to Bao Wenyuan's wife, was built in the winter of the thirty-second year of the Qing Qianlong era (1768). Constructed from bluestone from the Qinghui Tea Garden, it stands at a height of 11.9 meters, featuring a "piercing heaven" style with four pillars. Inscribed on the lintel are the phrases "Virtue Endures Three Winters" and "Pulse Preserved with a Single Thread." The sixth arch, named the Bao Fengchang Arch, was built in November of the second year of the Qing Jiaqing era (1797). This archway, the second from the east, also utilizes bluestone from the Qinghui Tea Garden. It features a "piercing heaven" style with four pillars and spans 9.28 meters in width, standing at a height of 11.79 meters. The forehead of this archway is graced with inscriptions such as "Heaven's Sincerity," "Human's true filial piety," and "Bless Filial son Bao Fengchang." The seventh arch, dedicated to Bao Xiangxian, a Shangshu official, was originally built in August of the second year of the Ming Tianqi era (1622) and rebuilt in the autumn of the sixtieth year of the Qing Qianlong era (1795). This is the first archway from the east. Featuring a "piercing heaven" style with four pillars and three chambers, it is constructed primarily from bluestone from the Qinghui Tea Garden, except for the four pillars made of white marble. Spanning 9.35 meters in width and standing at a height of 11.9 meters, the archway boasts minimal adornment, with only slight decorations on the honor and glory boards. Inscribed on the lintel are phrases such as "Destined with Edicts" and "Linked to the Ministers," commemorating Bao Xiangxian's meritorious service in Yunnan and Shandong. According to county records, Bao Xiangxian, a Jinshi scholar in the eighth year of the Ming Jiajing era (1529), initially served as an Imperial Censor before being appointed as the Right Assistant Minister of War. He played a crucial role in stabilizing the Yunnan border, earning gratitude from the local populace who erected a shrine in his honor after his death. He was posthumously promoted to the position of Minister of Construction.

Within Tangyue Village, a thousand-meter-long main street runs east-west, its flat and clean stone surface stretching out seamlessly. Numerous smaller streets crisscross the village from north to south. Ancient ancestral halls, pavilions, archways, and traditional homes are scattered throughout, creating a serene and magnificent atmosphere that reflects the village's past grandeur. The intersection of Main Street and winding alleys, centered on the antique pavilions and the ancestral tomb of the Bao family, forms a classic architectural district in the Huizhou style. On the front street stands the "Cun'ai Hall," originally the ancestral home of Bao Can, now refurbished during the Qing Dynasty and adorned with a plaque from the Jiaqing Emperor bestowing the title of "Five Generations Living Together." A stone tablet engraved with the "Double Dragon Imperial Decree" from the Jiaqing era is prominently displayed. The house features three spacious rooms, adorned with intricately carved Ming Dynasty wooden decorations, displaying elegant lines and vivid patterns, exuding a sense of antiquity and grandeur. In the rear garden, peach blossoms bloom in early spring, brimming with vitality. The spacious main hall proudly displays the inscription "Cun'ai Hall" on its plaque. Adjacent to the antique hall is the "Bao'ai Hall," with delicate brick carvings adorning its gatehouse. The original structure boasted 36 courtyards and 108 rooms, a testament to the prosperity of the Huizhou merchants. The "Bao'ai Hall" now retains 8 courtyards and 40 rooms, with one room adorned with a plaque reading "Ansu Pavilion," inscribed by the contemporary calligrapher Wang Shiqing. Through the neatly designed flower walls, one can catch a glimpse of the "Cunyang Mountain Residence," showcasing calligraphy and paintings from ancient and modern literati, along with various antiques, embodying the refined taste of the Tangyue Huizhou merchants and reflecting the Bao family's aspiration for glory and success through generations. Under the gentle glow of the moon and the shimmering stars, the village showcases a variety of Tangyue ancient houses. These structures are characterized by towering buildings and spacious courtyards adorned with pristine white walls and classic black-tiled roofs. Each building is enveloped by ornate flower walls, creating an enchanting atmosphere. Beyond these walls, one can glimpse intricate wood and stone carvings in the deep courtyards, inviting visitors to explore the world of "a swing out of the wall" and "a branch of rainbow apricot coming out of the wall." It's as if the Ming and Qing Dynasty Huizhou merchants deliberately left a veil of mystery, inviting all to engage in boundless contemplation.

The beauty of Hui-style architecture lies in its simplicity, a stark contrast to the grandeur of contemporaneous Beijing palaces. Using only bricks, wood, and stones as building materials, Hui-style residences, whether ordinary homes, opulent merchant estates, government mansions, or even temples, pavilions, shrines, and archways, all feature small blue-gray tiles instead of glazed ones. Stone archways, bridges, and shrine railings are crafted from pure stone materials such as bluestone and white marble, without any painted embellishments. Even the brick carvings on gatehouses, no matter how finely detailed, are left uncolored. Wood carvings on screens and beams are left unpainted, preserving the natural texture and color of the wood. Thus, Hui-style homes exhibit a monochromatic effect, with a simple and unified color scheme of black, white, and gray. In terms of architectural form, Hui-style homes are characterized by straight lines. The high walls and roofs create a dignified horizontal profile, conveying a sense of spaciousness and tranquility. The vertical lines of the walls appear sturdy and upright. The curved roofs, covered in blue-gray tiles, gracefully arch upwards at the eaves, forming elegant curves to channel rainwater away. Internally, Hui-style homes embody a sense of softness, reflecting the Ming-era philosophy of "che ming dao" or "thorough enlightenment." Massive exposed beams crisscross the interior, resembling a labyrinth of pathways. The profile of the large wooden beams spanning across the pillars resembles a lute, with a curved shape known as the "moonbeam." Its rounded form, akin to a winter melon, earned it the nickname "winter melon beam." The massive wooden pillars, circular in cross-section, taper slightly at both ends, resembling a weaving shuttle, hence called "shuttle pillars." Their resemblance to the Doric and Ionic columns of ancient Greek temples is striking, despite the cultural and temporal differences.

Throughout the ages, the Bao family has produced respectful children, virtuous husbands, chaste wives, and loyal officials. Even those branches of the family tree with humble beginnings produced many descendants who pursued knowledge, engaged in commerce, and succeeded in ascending to positions of wealth and influence. During the Ming and Qing dynasties, the rise of the Hui merchants in Tangyue gave birth to a thriving cultural scene, featuring successive generations of self-made scholars who "rose with ink-stained hands" and self-made civil servants who became "climbers of the nine ranks of the bureaucracy." Notable figures include Bao Xiangxian, a Ming Dynasty Vice Minister of War, and the distinguished descendants of Bao Shidao, Bao Shufang, and Bao Jun, renowned salt merchants in the Qing Dynasty. These individuals amassed great wealth. Then they enhanced their hometown by constructing grand pavilions to host visitors, expanding temples to honor their lineage, and erecting archways to perpetuate their glory through the ages. Bao Zhidao, courtesy name Chengyi, was a direct descendant of Bao Xiangxian, a Ming Dynasty Minister was born in the eighth year of the Qianlong reign (1743) during the Qing Dynasty. He was a direct descendant of Bao Xiangxian, who served as Assistant Minister of War twice during the Ming Dynasty.

Bao Zhidao and his eldest son, Shufang, received favor from both the Qianlong and Jiaqing emperors, monopolizing the salt trade in the

Huai salt region and becoming the wealthiest merchants in Jiangnan. The Qing court conferred Bao Chengyi six official titles, including Cabinet Secretariat Member, Provincial Governor, Cabinet Reader, Deputy Director of the Ministry of Justice, and Salt Inspector. Alongside Bao Chengyi and Bao Shufang, Bao Zhidao also served as a leading salt merchant in the Huai salt region. The bustling city of Yangzhou, a vital southeastern stronghold of the Qing Empire, hosted the headquarters of the Huai salt trade. During six imperial visits to Jiangnan, three of which were to Yangzhou, the Qianlong Emperor was financially supported by the Huai salt merchants. Bao Zhidao respectfully accompanied the imperial procession as a representative of the salt merchants. These merchants engaged in fierce competition, spending millions of silver taels and constructing extravagant projects seemingly overnight. Among these, the creation of the White Pagoda, a marvel erected in a single night, astonished Emperor Qianlong. Bao Tingbo, courtesy name Yiwen, was born in the nineteenth year of the Jiaqing reign (1728) and passed away in 1814 at the age of 86. Renowned for his vast library of over 600 volumes, he was esteemed for his erudition and authored "The Collected Poems of Huayong Xuan." Almost a century and a half later, his descendant, Bao Zhaoda, was a student of the pioneering scholar-statesman and master, Yu Youren. In 1952, Bao Zhaoda and Bai Suihan co-founded the Youren Middle School in Tangyue.

During the War of Resistance against Japan, the entire Chinese nation faced dire challenges. In 1938, the 19th Group Army of the Kuomintang, commanded by General Luo Zhuoying, was stationed in Tangyue Village. Later, the 23rd Group Army, led by General Tang Shizun, and the 32nd Group Army, commanded by General Shang Guanyun, were also stationed there. General Luo was deeply impressed by the artful and harmonious architecture of the village. He first paid respects to the elders of the Bao clan and local dignitaries, perused the genealogy of the Bao clan, and gained insight into the history and present state of Tangyue Village. Under General Luo's leadership, strict military discipline was enforced, fostering harmonious relations between the military and civilian residents. The improvement of the village's appearance was particularly notable. At that time, not a single weed grew on the paved stone streets of Tangyue Village, and the drainage channels remained clear, even during heavy rains, drawing praise from the villagers. The garrison attentively protected the ancient plum, pine, crepe myrtle, locust, and other flowering trees beside the archways and waterways, and planted large numbers of new trees around the village. They strictly prohibited the unauthorized cutting down or damaging of any of the grand mature trees on the old streets. The garrison was noted for making equally strenuous efforts to preserve the town's architectural treasures. They refrained from damaging ancestral halls, temples, and residential houses, and even conducted repairs on some dilapidated buildings. Amidst the towering ancient trees and the dense shade cast by the archways, General Luo Zhuoying composed two poems, preface as follows: "In the west of She, Mr. Bao and others presented the genealogical image of his ancestors, where he was called Cixiao, and his hall name was Proclaiming loyalty. Bao Sian, a Minister of the Ming Dynasty, excelled in both military and political affairs, leaving behind a reputation for honesty and upright conduct. At the beginning of his official career, he was known for his saying, 'Choose not the office, nor the place,' embodying the spirit of a noble statesman." These two poems, composed by General Luo, reflect the respect and admiration he held for the village and its noble heritage.

As I arrived in Tangyue,
the rustling trees stirred deep reflection.
Serving the nation, upholding loyalty,
passing down filial piety, and nurturing benevolence within the family.
In the heavens, the hues of antiquity remain,
striving to innovate in steadfastness.
Who can truly grasp this profound meaning?
I humbly bow and express my thoughts.
Look up to the Master,

and race to fulfill the duty of serving the country.
His candid voice, a testament to his righteousness,
and his strategic wisdom make him a capable leader.
Ashamed to seek official positions,
I pursue achievements without seeking fame.
In today's resistance against Japan,
I, too, stand as a scholar.

In modern China, wars have been ongoing, and after 1949, political movements have been relentless, with many people suffering the calamity of imprisonment. Many outside the prisons also felt fearful, and to varying degrees, everyone was endangered. Interactions between the descendants of the Bao family in Baoshan and Shanghai and their relatives in their ancestral home of Tangyue virtually ceased. I belong to the 12th generation with the character "Cheng." Between 1949 and the 1980s, few of the older generations and cousins born in Shanghai had visited Tangyue in Shexian. This situation didn't change until the 1990s. In 1998, when I took Bao Fulo to Tangyue to trace our roots, we received warm hospitality from the local government of Huangshan. Ms. Yu Liqing, Director of the Huangshan City Education Committee, took the time to accompany us to Shexian and Tangyue. She also arranged for a local writer specializing in the history of the Bao family to accompany us and gave me several books about Shexian and Tangyue. Before leaving Tangyue, Ms. Yu Liqing specifically bought an inkstone from the gift shop at the village entrance and gave it to Bao Fulo. It was a rectangular stone measuring 5 inches by 8 inches, two and a half inches thick, with rounded corners. The stone was predominantly bluish-gray, featuring a shiny gold inkwell and relief carvings of auspicious clouds and ruyi (as one wishes) motif above and around the inkwell. It felt smooth and solid, resembling jade, and was priced at 500 yuan. Ms. Yu Liqing was very courteous, saying it was a souvenir. She also warned me not to buy it myself, as I would surely be overcharged. Later, I saw the news: In September 2019, Tangyue was named one of the first batch of beautiful rural demonstration villages in Anhui Province; on December 31, 2019, Tangyue Village was selected for the second batch of national forest village lists.

As the sun dipped below the horizon and the gentle new moon cast its glow, Yu Liqing suggested taking us to a farmhouse restaurant. After a short drive, we arrived at a rural household. Though it was an old house, it was neatly kept, with the floors swept clean. A middle-aged couple welcomed us at the door. Yu Liqing introduced them, saying this was a designated restaurant by the Huangshan City government. The farmhouse was secluded, not on the main streets of the town. Without guidance, one would hardly expect to find a restaurant here. Government officials often speak in bureaucratic jargon and anecdotes. Yu Liqing quipped, "County leaders focus on eating enough, provincial leaders on eating well, and central leaders on eating greens." The specialty of this restaurant was wild vegetables and game. In the courtyard, originally designed to reflect the "Four Waters Back to the Hall," were seven or eight basins filled with various wild vegetables and game soaking in water. I quickly explained to the owner that I had a delicate stomach and was not accustomed to exotic delicacies. The owner was understanding and did not insist. Knowing my preference for vegetables and tofu, the hostess immediately went to the vegetable garden to pick a few bunches of greens. The water in Huizhou was good, and the quality of soy products was particularly high. The owner sliced some ready-made braised dishes, and we enjoyed a very hearty and homey dinner. The owner seemed to be a jovial person, and since we were the only guests that day, he came over to chat with us. It turned out they were a pair of Shanghai Educated Youths. After the Cultural Revolution, most Educated Youths returned to Shanghai, and they had also gone to Shanghai for a while. However, they faced difficulties without jobs or housing. Their parents were also struggling and couldn't help much. Considering survival as their priority, they returned to Shexian County. They were familiar with the area and, after settling in this house, decided to open a restaurant to ensure their livelihood. In Shanghai, until the 1990s, there were still many families facing housing shortages for three generations. The spaciousness of this house, with its own courtyard, made them very content. As we bid our hosts farewell, we extended our heartfelt thanks once more, deeply appreciative of the warmth and hospitality they had shown us.

2. Wuxi

My maternal grandmother's house is located outside the west gate of Wuxi City. My warm and dreamlike childhood was spent by my grandmother's side. Afterward, until she passed away, I would visit Wuxi once or twice a year. I went to visit my grandmother, relive the old dreams in the cradle, admire the beautiful and delicate Wu Mountain and Yue Water, and enjoy the prosperity of the land of fish and rice. Wuxi is such an enchanting place! Wuxi, also known as Xi, was formerly known as Liangxi and Jin Gui, and is known as the "Pearl of Taihu Lake." The Wuxi Taihu Scenic Area and Xihui Scenic Area have been renowned throughout China since ancient times. My grandmother's maternal home is located in Sunxiang, which is between the Taihu Lake Scenic Area and the Xihui Scenic Area, about 5 kilometers west of Wuxi City. Today, it has long been incorporated into the urban area of Wuxi and belongs to the Binhu District. Coming east from Rongxiang Station on Metro Line 2, there is a lane called Rongxiang, less than 400 meters long. At the eastern end of Rongxiang is Sunxiang, which is only a short 100 meters. Rongxiang and Sunxiang are actually the same alley in the same village, just with different names at each end.

Rongxiang was famous in modern times because of the Rong conglomerate, which was one of the most influential business empires in Republican-era China and later played a key role in post-Mao economic reform, through the founding of CITIC—China's first state-owned enterprise created to attract foreign capital and engage with international markets. The first-generation founders of the Rong family include Rong Zongjing and Rong Desheng, the second generation includes Rong Yiren, and the third generation includes Rong Zhijian. Near Rongxiang Subway Station, located on the former site of Rong's ancestral home at 165-166

Liangxi Road, Rongxiang Street, the Rong Yiren Memorial Hall was established. The memorial hall consists of an exhibition hall, the Rong ancestral home, the Dagong Library, and the relocated former residence of Rong Yiren in Beijing. When I visited Sunxiang in the summer of 2000, there was no Rong Yiren Memorial Hall yet. I observed that Rongxiang still retained its old-world charm, featuring over 150 historic houses with blue brick walls and black-tiled roofs. In Sunxiang, the ancestral house of my grandmother's maternal family is still inhabited by her nephew's descendants.

In 1892, my grandmother was born in Sunxiang. There were three sisters in the family, and she was the middle one, often referred to as the "second maiden." She was the outstanding figure in the village at that time. Although my grandmother was illiterate, she had a broad mind, was rational and insightful, and her words and deeds were always sensible. Whenever relatives or friends had requests, she would readily accommodate them without hesitation, handling everything effortlessly. When there were disputes or conflicts in the village, people often sought her mediation, and her words were respected by all. Therefore, she often played the role of resolving difficulties and disputes among relatives and friends. At the age of sixteen, my grandmother coincided with the beginning of Rong Desheng's entrepreneurship in her hometown. The flour mill and cotton mill were the two main pillars of the Rong family. The cotton mill needed female workers. So, in the villages of Rongxiang and Sunxiang, many girls from local families went to work in the cotton mill, becoming the first generation of the working class in China. One of them was my grandmother. Because of her work in the factory, she gained a formal name, "Sun Miaoying." The factory environment gave rise to gossip and discord among the female workers, affecting productivity and causing considerable concern for Rong Desheng. As they were all fellow villagers, living in close proximity, the question of how to address these issues weighed heavily on him. It was then that Rong Desheng approached my grandmother and entrusted her with the role of foreman. Recognizing the nuances of human nature and the complexities of right and wrong, he left it to the "Second Maid" to make decisions regarding rewards and punishments. Delegating this responsibility greatly eased Rong Desheng's burden. The female workers would turn to the "Second Maid" whenever they had grievances, and her intervention helped maintain harmonious relations between laborers and management. Throughout the ten years my grandmother worked at the cotton mill, major conflicts between the two groups were virtually non-existent. Rong Desheng was 41 years old when his son, Rong Yiren, was born in 1916. My grandmother was 24 when Rong Yiren was born, and he referred to her as "Second Uncle," because people in Wuxi traditionally referred to aunts as "uncles." My grandmother had a ten-year acquaintance with Rong Desheng, but little interaction with the younger generation represented by Rong Yiren.

After ten years as a foreman at the mill, it was time for my grandmother to marry. Though members of the working class, my grandfather's family was on the rise, paying for him to receive some private home schooling, which later enabled him to get a job as a bookkeeper in a local seed-oil mill. Grandma's dowry was quite impressive. Rong Desheng gave the "Second Maid" a big house with two courtyards and a lovely backyard garden. This house had more than a dozen rooms and was at No. 35 Cotton Lane, just outside the west gate of Wuxi City. It was not only a large house but also well-situated. In contemporary real-estate terms, it occupied a prime location. Wuxi was a small city with a layout typical of old Chinese cities. It was surrounded by a brick and rammed-earth wall and a moat filled with water, connecting to the Liangxi River and the ancient canal. Four city gates in the North, South, East, and West led in different directions. It was just 1.5 kilometers from Wuxi Railway Station to No. 35 Cotton Lane, only a 20-minute walk. To reach my grandmother's place, you would exit the west gate, cross a narrow wooden bridge, walk down an alley for half a kilometer, and arrive at her house. The part of the alley in front was called Xizhi (West Straight) Street, and the back was called Cotton Lane. My grandfather's sister and her kids lived on Xizhi Street, and I fondly called her "Good Grandma." Cotton Lane's pavement was made with a mix of brick and stone and sometimes got wider or narrower as it wound westward for about a kilometer until it reached the banks of the ancient canal. The river was filled with boats covered by awnings going back and forth. On the other side of the river was the Xihui Mountains Scenic Area. Until the late 1950s, Cotton Lane was the only route linking Wuxi city to the Xihui Mountains.

My Grandmother's house faced north and had white walls with black tiles. Two big, round iron rings were attached to the naturally finished wooden doors. When you pushed open these thick double doors and stepped inside, you'd see a large empty foyer with blue brick flooring. People used to park sedan chairs in this area. On the right side, there was a room called the wing room. Its door opened on the opposite wall from the main entrance, and its window faced the hall. Because the doors and windows were all on the inside wall, this room didn't get much light. As you continued inside, there was another wing room on the right. This room was quite long and had two parts: one on the inside and one on the outside. The inner part of the wing was connected to the main hall and was quite dark. The outer part had walls that faced the courtyard, so the doors and windows opened into the courtyard, providing plenty of natural light. This courtyard was shaped like an inverted L, with its longer sides facing the outer walls. There were two raised flower beds, facing each other under the east and west walls. Many family photos were taken in this courtyard.

The second entrance led to the main building at the front of the courtyard. At its center stood a grand main hall, flanked by wings on either side. The main hall had a lofty structure without an inner ceiling. Looking up, one could see the red-painted beams and rafters, with rows of small blue bricks neatly arranged between them, topped by roof tiles. The main hall itself was further divided into a central chamber and a rear chamber. A series of floor-to-ceiling partition doors adorned both the central and rear halls, serving as passages to and from the adjoining courtyards. These partition doors were slender and tall, sheltered by eaves above and resting upon wooden thresholds below. The upper half of each door featured a lattice window, adorned with milky white, translucent mica sheets that allowed light to filter through while keeping dust and wind at bay. The lower halves of the doors were solid wood panels, blocking the slanting winds and fine rain falling from above the courtyard. The central hall was reserved for significant events, such as ceremonies, celebrations, formal family meetings, receptions, and banquets. Adorning the Taishi Wall were plaques, paintings, and wooden couplets. This was the ceremonial or display wall, named for the post of Taishi—"Grand Preceptor"—one of the three highest ranks in Imperial China's civil government. Below this wall, an elongated altar table and a square Eight Immortals table were set. At the center of the altar table, a white jade Guanyin Bodhisattva was enshrined, standing gracefully upon a lotus, holding a flower, and smiling with a tranquility that could dispel worldly troubles. A vase graced the eastern end of the table, while a delicately carved glass mirror adorned the western end, symbolizing "peace in the east and tranquility in the west," a wish for harmony worldwide. Beneath the altar table, a square table was slightly shorter than the long table. This design allowed it to be pushed underneath to save space when not in use and easily pulled out when required. On either side of the Eight Immortals table were Taishi chairs. Originating in the Song Dynasty, these now-iconic high-backed, formal-looking chairs give distinct impressions of dignity, prestige, and authority.

Flanking the central hall, on its left and right sides, were the east and west wing rooms. Both the Taishi Wall and the walls of the wing rooms were constructed from wood. In the central hall, aligned against the wooden walls of the east and west wing rooms, four Taishi chairs were neatly arranged on each side, their footrests concealed by bamboo bars. These pieces of furniture were known for their sturdiness and deep, luxurious tones. My grandmother often recounted that these were all selections made by my grandfather, a man with a penchant for items that could endure for generations. Beyond the wainscot in the central hall lay the back hall, an area scattered with several small tables and chairs, where the female family members diligently attended to their household chores. Doors led from the back hall to the east and west rear wing rooms, completing the layout of this stately abode.

On both sides of the central hall were side rooms. The side rooms were slightly narrower than the main hall, but had the combined length of the central and rear halls. My grandmother's bedroom was in the left-side eastern side room, known as the master bedroom. The western side room served as another main bedroom. Hanging above the door of my grandmother's bedroom was a yellow plaque with Tibetan script. The floors of the side rooms were elevated and covered with red-painted wooden planks, raised one step higher than the main hall, making the side rooms relatively dry. Above the middle section of the bedroom was a red-painted loft for storing miscellaneous items. Along the window was a redwood writing desk and dressing table. A large four-poster bed was placed horizontally against the back wall, dividing the side room into two sections. This bed resembled a small house when viewed from the outside. Overall, it could be divided into two parts: a canopy bed and a surrounding corridor in front of the canopy bed. The canopy bed was designed for hanging curtains, and to allow for spaciousness and brightness, the sides and back of the bed were lowered. The canopy bed was like a smaller room within the room. In the space in front of the bed, a toilet could be placed on one side, allowing one to use the toilet without leaving the bed in the morning. The carved eaves and lintels depicted ancient stories, while the railings and surrounding panels were engraved with patterns of kylin [Chinese unicorn], phoenix, peony, and rolling leaves. Each marble screen on either side of the front door had landscape patterns, depicting mountain peaks, vegetation, and faintly visible scenery, adding a lot of interest to the canopy bed.

My grandmother once shared with me a remarkable story from her fifties when she discovered a tumor in her breast. Despite seeking assistance from prominent doctors in Shanghai, the situation appeared hopeless. My grandmother and her peers were devout believers in Buddhism. That year, she and several female relatives from Liu's family went to the Lingyin (Hidden Gods) Temple in Hangzhou to listen to the teachings of the Panchen Lama. After absorbing the wisdom of the lectures, they continued their journey, taking in the breathtaking sights of A Thread of Sky. It was there that my grandmother experienced a profound moment. Gazing through a rift in the sky, she saw the

Bodhisattva seated serenely upon a white lotus cloud. The Bodhisattva smiled warmly and extended her hand, pointing at my grandmother's chest. Upon returning home, the tumor that had once plagued my grandmother miraculously vanished, astonishing both her family and the medical professionals. My grandmother adopted a vegetarian lifestyle as a testament to her gratitude and newfound commitment to her faith. She transformed the back room of her master bedroom into a dedicated Buddhist hall, adorning it with an Eight Immortals table serving as an altar. A magnificent brocade Tibetan painting adorned the center of the wall, radiating grandeur and solemnity. The altar was decorated with butter lamps, prayer wheels, holy water cups, and seasonal fruits. Among the sacred water cups, she placed peacock feathers whose slender and iridescent beauty resembled golden-green velvet, adorned with large eye-shaped spots comprising purple, blue, yellow, red, and other colors. These feathers reflected a vibrant and dazzling light, akin to colorful satin. A long, red-painted board lay diagonally on the floor beneath the altar, roughly three feet wide and spanning the length of a door panel. The outside was flush with the ground, while the inside was slightly elevated, featuring two concave marks at the ends for kneeling. This board was specially designed for prostration. Following Tibetan Buddhist traditions, prostration involved the "five-point prostration." It entailed first raising the hands skyward, followed by kneeling and touching the ground with the five points of the body: two hands, two feet, and the forehead. My grandmother's devout dedication to Buddhism was evident in her daily routine. She rose before dawn to recite sutras and perform her devotional practices, a ritual she referred to as "Reciting the Buddha's Scriptures." Seated beside the altar table, she methodically counted the prayer beads while keeping the prayer wheel in perpetual motion. Upon completing her recitations, the first rays of dawn illuminated the room. During the years I lived with her as a boy, she would then wake me and invite me to prostrate myself on the kowtow board. She dipped a peacock feather into a few drops of holy water, placed it in the palm of her hand, and let me sip a little bit of the holy water from her palm. Then she wiped the remaining holy water onto my hair. She gently sprinkled the peacock feather over my hair, all while invoking blessings with the words, "great virtue and great sage, good luck, and good blessing." Following this sacred ceremony, she would change her attire and set out to the market for her daily errands.

Pushing open the French windows of the rear hall led to the back courtyard. The back courtyard was shaped like an inverted T, with outer walls at both ends and a central corridor leading to the back garden. On both sides of the corridor, the rooms were flanked by side chambers. In the long room on the east side was the bedroom of my great aunt. When she was young, my grand aunt married far away in Wuhan because her husband worked under Zhu Wenxue, the director of the Hankou Telegraph Office at the time. Later, my grand aunt became a young widow without children of her own, so she returned to Wuxi to live with my grandmother. At that time, my grand aunt was specifically designated by my grandmother to take care of me, so I slept in her room on the east side. Although my grand aunt was my grandmother's older sister, she respected my grandmother's authority as the head of the household. My grand aunt did not adhere to a vegetarian diet and enjoyed indulging in culinary pleasures, which my grandmother always tried to accommodate. However, sometimes my grandmother had to remind her to "mind her manners" when there were guests present. My grand aunt's entertainment consisted of going to the theater to see local operas, and as a child, I was reportedly very well-behaved and often taken along by her to the theater.

Due to the early deaths of my grandfather and uncle, my grandmother found herself lacking the financial means to maintain the house, and the eaves and drainpipes were often damaged. As a boy, whenever it rained, I enjoyed hiding indoors to listen to the rain. Raindrops danced upon the pointed iron cap that covered the sauce vat, creating a crisp and resonant tinkling melody. Rainwater slid down from the eaves into the water accumulated in the tile basin, creating a rhythmic pattern. Small waterfalls gushed out from the holes in the broken pipes with a rush. The combination of persistent rain and intermittent wind created a constantly changing but continuous rhythm—like music. The rustling sound of the rain drowned out human voices, submerging the sounds of the city and bestowing peace and tranquility on everything in the world. Since I left my grandmother, I have never heard such an intimately familiar and comforting sound again, nor have I been able to find that same inner peace and tranquility.

On the western side of the patio stood a spacious kitchen, complete with a tall stove and a chimney extending through the roof. This kitchen boasted a large pot atop the stove, along with midsize pots and a pot of simmering water. Whenever the water in this simmering pot reached its boiling point, it was used to fill a thermos. At other times, the residual heat from the stove was sufficient to maintain the temperature in the simmering water pot. This convenience provided us with the luxury of having warm water available throughout the day. The kitchen saw its busiest moments during the Chinese New Year celebration. On regular days, our meals consisted of rice. However, when the Chinese New Year arrived, it was a tradition for Grandma to steam special buns as an offering to our ancestors. These buns came in two varieties: pleated buns filled with vegetables, and smooth buns adorned with a red dot on top, which were sweet buns. Upon leaving the kitchen, a path led down the patio to a door that opened into the back garden.

In the garden, there was a firewood shed and a deep well. The well had a small opening but held plenty of clear water. My grandmother told me that when my grandfather dug the well, he used tiles to line the walls. After using up all the spare tiles without finding water, my grandfather became very anxious. He persisted, and eventually, he dug through to the aquifer. Because the water source was deep, the well water was exceptionally clear and abundant, and neighbors from far and near liked to fetch water from my grandmother's well. The back gate of my grandmother's yard was always open to neighbors. For several years, a dyeing workshop rented my grandmother's backyard, and even they couldn't use up all the water. My grandmother enjoyed planting flowers and herbs. A peach tree and a fig tree she planted grew particularly well, yielding sweet fruit every year. In flowerpots, my grandmother grew peonies and mint, using fresh leaves to brew tea. Besides storing firewood, the firewood shed also housed a large pot doubling as a bathroom. After heating the water in the pot, a wide plank was placed across it, allowing people to sit on it and scoop water for bathing. This three-section courtyard was protected by a courtyard wall, and all the exterior walls of the side rooms had no doors or windows, giving a sense of strict security.

The liveliest time at 35 Cotton Lane was the decade after my grandmother married into the Liu family. Suddenly, the Liu's had a brand-new estate, and the whole extended family could finally live together happily under one roof. When my grandmother married, my grandfather's father had already passed away. In the Liu family, there were six siblings, the youngest being a sister. The eldest brother was sickly since childhood and remained unmarried. My grandfather was the second eldest, with three younger brothers and a sister nicknamed "Good Grandma." My grandmother transitioned from being the "second maid" in the Sun family to being the "second aunt" in the Liu family. The matriarch of the Liu family was delighted to have gained such a capable daughter-in-law and, from that point on, enjoyed a peaceful life. My grandmother took on many responsibilities, especially after the matriarch passed away, assuming the role of the family head. While my grandfather worked as an accountant at a seed oil mill, his three brothers were in the rice business. All three brothers were married at No. 35 Cotton Lane. The third brother married a neighbor girl from down the street at No. 6 Cotton Lane. My grandpa's sister also married a neighbor, residing a stone's throw away on Xizhi Street. With the Liu family being quite large, it was inevitable that disputes and conflicts arose between uncles, aunts, sisters-in-law, nephews, and nieces. In such situations, they often turned to my grandmother for guidance, seeking her counsel to mediate and ensure fairness. Grandma possessed a sharp intellect, a discerning eye, an eloquent tongue, and a reputation for arbitrating disputes to the mutual satisfaction of those involved. Even more than two decades after her passing, her nephew couldn't help but remember her authority when recalling those times. He remarked, "When Second Aunt spoke, not a soul in the whole family dared not listen."

My mother both revered and feared my grandmother. She used to say, "If your grandmother were educated, she would be formidable."

There's a Chinese saying: "No enmity, no father-son relationship; no grievance, no husband-wife relationship." The relationship between my mother and grandmother was never harmonious. My mother said she couldn't stay with my grandmother in Wuxi for more than three days, and it was true. During those first three days, my grandmother treated my mother like a guest, but after that, she would start criticizing her, and my mother couldn't bear it, so she would leave. I think the root cause lies in their differing belief systems. My grandmother believed in Buddhism, with compassion for all beings, and she did many charitable deeds throughout her life. My mother, on the other hand, was a selfishly pragmatic opportunist, believing that if one didn't look out for oneself, no one else would. She would cozy up to those who were fortunate and step on those who were not. My grandmother saw through her and was deeply disappointed. However, dealing with a stubborn and disobedient daughter like my mother also left her feeling helpless. Human psychology can be strange. At a certain point, I realized that my mother actually cared a lot about winning my grandmother's approval and tried hard to earn her praise. However, her principles clashed with my grandmother's, so her efforts were often in vain. My mother's pragmatic pursuit of worldly success couldn't impress my grandmother, so even when my mother seemed to be doing well, she couldn't hide her inner sense of defeat.

The strange pattern of "No enmity, no father-son relationship" repeated itself in the relationship between my mother and me. This pattern initially emerged when my mother rebelled against her own mother. In China, the tradition of favoring boys over girls has a long history, dating back thousands of years. This is primarily because in an agrarian society, physical labor was the most highly valued. Regrettably, my grandmother was not exempt from this bias. To make the matters worse, my mother was naturally sensitive, and this sensitivity may well have left emotional scars from her childhood. Consequently, my mother took a different approach when raising her own children. As my brother and I recall our childhood, our mother rarely embraced us or displayed love. This behavior seemed to be deeply ingrained in her. Another significant factor in this complex dynamic was my relationship with my

54

grandmother. Among all her grandchildren, I spent the most time with her. She believed that I had a special bond with the Buddha and often took me to the temple. The Grand Master at the temple also had a special fondness for me. My grandmother's beliefs and actions greatly influenced my perspective on life, creating an unspoken bond between us, a spiritual connection. My mother, recognizing the strength of this connection, found herself unable to penetrate the world shared between my grandmother and me, fostering an unspoken resentment towards me.

In the era when my grandmother was young, working-class girls didn't have the opportunity to receive an education, so they lacked formal schooling. However, her intellectual depth was far beyond that of an ordinary citizen. When faced with sudden adversity, my grandmother could grasp profound principles, her perspective transcending personal gains and losses, regarding wealth lightly. On August 13, 1937, the Battle of Songhu erupted, putting Suzhou and Wuxi in peril. In response, Grandma led her extended family on a journey to escape Wuxi. They initially followed the Shanghai-Nanjing and Jinpu railway lines northward to Xuzhou. From there, they transferred to the Longhai Line, which took them to Wuhan, where they reunited with Grandma's sister in Hankou. After resting in Wuhan for several days, they took a southbound train along the Beijing-Guangzhou Line to Hong Kong. Once the war had subsided, they traveled by sea from Hong Kong to Shanghai and circled back to Wuxi.

Before leaving the Cotton Lane, Grandma's nephew, who lived on Xizhi Street with his parents, volunteered to look after the Liu family's estate house. Before their departure, Grandma hid some of the Liu family's treasures, including gold, silver, jewelry, and silver dollars, in iron cans from State Express 555 cigarettes, burying them under a fig tree. After everyone had left, the nephew dug three feet into the ground and unearthed the cans. He took them and disappeared. The theft of the Liu family's treasures became a major scandal in the neighborhood, causing many members of the Liu family to be furious. They believed that the Good Grandma and her husband had a history of taking advantage of others and that it was their fault to have such a thieving son. They confronted her, saying, "A monk can escape, but the temple cannot. Your son is a thief, and you're definitely involved." Amidst the accusations and anger, everyone awaited Grandma's response. She stated, "What a disgrace to the family! Isn't this enough? Open the lid! In the chaos of war, who would dare carry gold and silver with them on the road? He's young and ignorant. It wasn't a wise move!" "Open lid!" was a derogatory term in the Wuxi dialect, referring to people with foul mouths, much like an open lid toilet. Although everyone was upset about Grandma's lost treasures, her main concern was the safety of the thief. The collective outrage suddenly subsided. Yes, you considered it, on a journey filled with refugees, even in bright daylight, people got shot and robbed. Clearly, Grandma's concerns weren't unreasonable. No one ever saw the nephew again. The Good Grandma often visited Grandma, shedding tears. Grandma would say, "It's a pity, it's a pity!" and then she would take the Good Grandma to her Buddhist altar to kowtow and pay respects to the Bodhisattva. After the victory over the Japanese, the civil war erupted once again. In later years, many unfortunate individuals sought solace in Grandma. She would tell them, "Human wisdom has its limits. Things the human heart can't bear must be entrusted to the Bodhisattva, Amitabh!" I've known since I was a child that people with faith have big hearts.

I was born in Shanghai in 1952. That year was Grandma's sixtieth birthday, and since both Grandma and I were born in the Year of the Dragon, she believed that we had a special bond. Perhaps due to some inherent weakness, I grew slowly after birth, still resembling a newborn even after three months. Grandma was deeply concerned when she saw my weak breath and heard my cries, which resembled those of a kitten. She said to my mother, "Will this child survive with such weak health?" My mother's indifferent attitude angered Grandma greatly, prompting her to take me away immediately. When I arrived in Wuxi, my uncle Liu Hongying had recently passed away. After completing high school in Shanghai, my uncle worked as an assistant alongside his fifth uncle. Unfortunately, he contracted tuberculosis, and his condition worsened in 1951. He returned to his hometown in Wuxi to recuperate in the Meiyuan of the Rong family. His wife brought her mother and son from Shanghai to live in Cotton Lane together to care for my uncle. After my uncle's passing, my aunt returned to Shanghai to work. Grandma kept her grandson Yuanyuan and his maternal grandmother in Wuxi for a while. Yuanyuan's grandmother took care of him full-time, while my grandmother's sister Da Yipo focused on caring for me. My brother Chengquan was born in Shanghai in 1953. Since my mother didn't like boys and was reluctant to care for him herself, Grandma brought Chengquan to Wuxi as well. She treated her three grandchildren as treasures. Grandma hired a distant relative from her maternal family in the countryside to be Chengquan's nanny and also hired a wet nurse for him. Thus, 35 Cotton Lane once again bustled with activity. Three old ladies took care of three babies, with help from two wet nurses, and Grandma overseeing them all, making a total of six adults eating together, keeping the kitchen very busy. Although the three caretakers were of grandmotherly age, they were not old, and the wet nurse had a big appetite. Grandma took charge of buying groceries and cooking, keeping herself busy all day. Grandma was always generous to others but strict with herself. Despite serving lavish meals to the wet nurse and caretakers every day, she ate nothing but leftovers. On one occasion, my wet nurse took me to Shanghai to visit my mother, but hastily returned to Wuxi after just three days. Grandma asked her, "How have you lost weight in only three days?" The wet nurse tearfully explained that she didn't have enough to eat and was hungry the whole time. Grandma was furious and called my mother to Wuxi to deliver a stern rebuke: "I've never seen anyone not feed a wet nurse properly!"

The second bustling period at 35 Cotton Lane didn't last long. Yuanyuan was the first to leave Wuxi and go to Shanghai to attend kindergarten. Then, Chengquan's nanny took him to Shanghai as well, continuing to work as his nanny at my mother's house. After I left Wuxi at age four, only Grandma and Da Yipo remained in the house. In 1962, with some economic recovery in the country, Wuxi began to establish nursing homes. Since Da Yipo was a lonely elderly person, it was arranged for her to live in a nursing home near Liyuan. The conditions of that nursing home were decent, not far from Cotton Lane, Sun Lane, and Yuantouzhu. I visited her there several times. Later, we were shocked to receive news of Da Yipo's passing. Grandma said, "Your Da Yipo had a big mouth." It emerged that during her time at the nursing home, Da Yipo had inadvertently shared her past experiences of a prosperous life, which was misconstrued as evidence of her belonging to the privileged class of the old society. Consequently, Da Yipo was swiftly expelled from the nursing home and relocated to a place with far less decent conditions. Soon after, she passed away. My grandmother wasn't informed of her sister's death for a year or two. The circumstances surrounding her demise remained shrouded in mystery. Perhaps worst of all, no one knew where she was laid to rest after her passing.

What I am personally familiar with is Cotton Lane in the fifties and early sixties. The alley was primarily lined with residential houses, featuring high walls and deep courtyards, punctuated by a few small convenience stores like soy sauce shops, salt shops, cigarette paper stores, and a large funeral wreath paper shop. During that era, lifespans were relatively short, and deaths were not uncommon. The bamboo-bound horse-drawn hearses and the black coffins tucked away in the dimly lit back rooms were truly eerie sights. Diagonally opposite the coffin shop, there was a quaint little Xi opera theater where Da Yipo enjoyed taking me to pass the time. The backyard of No. 35 Cotton Lane faced south. Just a stone's throw to the south lay a medium-sized pond where nearby residents would gather to wash clothes and clean wooden toilets. Back then, wells were not as plentiful, and well water was too valuable for cleaning purposes. Perhaps due to the smaller population and less pollution at that time, the water in that pond remained remarkably clear. In the 1950s, the West Gate Bridge underwent expansion and was renamed the "People's Bridge." People's Road was also straightened to accommodate cars en route to Xihui Mountains. This new road happened to pass by the pond, leading to its eventual filling. This road marked a significant development as the first asphalt road in Wuxi. Consequently, "Asphalt Road" became the colloquial name for it, while its official name of "People's Road," fell into relative obscurity.

Grandma experienced numerous hardships throughout her life. Apart from fleeing from the Japanese during the war, she lost her husband in middle age, her only son in old age, and her son-in-law faced imprisonment. With no financial support from her children, Grandma relied on renting out houses for her livelihood. After 1949, due to the housing shortage in urban areas, the government temporarily tolerated the existence of privately-owned houses and their rental activities. However, according to the logic of the Communist Party, all private property was considered obtained through exploitation and could be nationalized at any time. The Communist Party aimed to overthrow the exploiting class entirely. However, for reasons unknown, Wuxi's largest capitalist, Rong Yiren, was designated by Mao Zedong as a "Red Capitalist" and even ascended to the high position of "National Leader." The Sun family, Grandma's maternal relatives, had intermarried with the Rong family for generations, a fact that mattered in the past and the present. Local authorities were aware of my grandmother's employment at the Rong family factory, and despite this knowledge, they dispatched investigators to engage with the Rong family. Rong Desheng had passed away in 1952, so the officials went to Beijing to find Rong Yiren. Fortunately, Rong Yiren remembered Grandma and issued her a "worker-class" certificate. This certificate safeguarded the house originally bestowed upon her by the Rong family. The government affixed a "self-retention" sign to each rental room in the house, allowing my grandmother to continue collecting rent, a crucial source of income that remained undisturbed even during the tumultuous period of the Cultural Revolution.

The winter of 1960 was very tragic. Many beggars arrived in the streets and alleys of Wuxi, most of them speaking with northern accents, mainly from Henan and northern Anhui. Every day, there were carts on the streets carrying corpses. Grandma, upon seeing people who couldn't walk, even if she had only one bowl of rice, would still share half of it with them. The households along Cotton Lane, who were well-off families in the past, all extended their helping hands. That year, there were no starving corpses in Cotton Lane, and the local government received commendation from the higher-ups because of this. One day, a family from northern Jiangsu went from door to door in Cotton Lane begging for food. The couple had three young children, with runny noses and tears staining their clothes. Seeing how cold it was, Grandma took them in and let them spend the night in the firewood shed in the backyard. The next day, the children couldn't get up after lying down. And so, this family stayed for a long time, eventually changing their Household Registration from northern Jiangsu to Wuxi.

Grandma had another tenant named Axiang, who lived at her property for over twenty years. Axiang's family consisted of five members: her, her husband, their two boys and one grandmother. Grandma and Axiang's family got along harmoniously, as if they were family. Grandma liked Axiang's sons; they were very sensible and took care of her when they grew up. So Grandma and Axiang signed an agreement that after Grandma passed away, the property at No. 35 would be sold to Axiang at a low price, so she and her husband could stay and—once they married—their sons could both raise their own families there. The family from northern Jiangsu in the backyard also grew up, found jobs, and were allocated houses by their workplaces. Grandma asked them to move out, but they refused and even demanded a hefty sum from Grandma as relocation expenses, blatantly bullying the lonely old woman who decades earlier had likely saved their lives. Since Grandma didn't have the money to give them, they refused to leave. They dug out all the soil under the fruit trees Grandma planted in the backyard. After the trees died, they used the vacant land to build makeshift houses, hoping to get more money from Grandma when the demolition came. Grandma said, "You stand up to offer help, but you have to kneel down to collect debts. Sometimes, when you lend a hand, people are grateful, but they might turn against you when they want more. It's hard to believe but true." After Grandma passed away in 1981, they still occupied the backyard. In the 1990s, my younger brother, Chengquan, was transferred to work in Wuxi. Chengquan had graduated from Jiangxi Institute of Political Science and Law and was quite familiar with the law. He took them to court and finally got them evicted. This story shows that being poor doesn't necessarily make someone good, and some poor people are rogues.

Grandma had two sisters, and one sister was younger than her. She passed away early; I never met her. Before she passed away, she called her two young sons, Lu Puhong and Lu Puyun, to her bedside, "kowtow to Grandma," and asked Grandma to take care of them. Grandma brought them up alongside her own children and sent them to Shanghai for schooling. The Rong family had many yarn factories in Shanghai. Grandma introduced them to work in a yarn factory in the Yangshupu district, Shanghai. As Lu Puhong and Lu Puyun were both educated, they worked as technicians in the factory and earned a good income. Lu Puhong participated in student activities at school and was recruited into the Communist Party. In 1949, when the Communist Party took over private enterprises, Lu Puhong naturally became the workshop director and the party branch secretary, with a salary of 120 yuan, which was a high income at the time.

During the "Free Airing of Views" movement, Lu Puyun couldn't withstand the repeated mobilizations and spoke up at a meeting. He said that in the past, the capitalist managers respected his technical expertise, allowing him to work freely, which made him happy. However, the current state managers often gave blind commands without understanding the business, resulting in unnecessary losses and causing him a lot of trouble. Following the "Free Airing of Views" movement was the "Anti-Rightist Campaign." With just these few words, Lu Puyun was accused of "opposing the leadership of the Party" and was labeled as a rightist and dismissed from his official position. Because his wife resided in a village near Wuxi, he was sent back to the village, unlike other rightists who were sent to Qinghai. Lu Puyun was fortunate to have an old house in Sun Lane to live in. However, he was completely unfamiliar with farming and physically not strong enough to meet the challenges of working in the fields, unable to support himself, let alone his three children. The family was in rags, barely able to make ends meet.

In the meantime, ever since Lu Puhong had grown up, he had treated my grandma (his aunt) like his own mother, giving her a monthly subsidy of 15 Yuan. When Lu Puyun became destitute, Grandma handed this money to him every month. On the 15th of each month, Lu Puyun's wife would eagerly come to Grandma's house, anxiously waiting for the money to buy rice.

Grandma had only one son, Liu Hongying. He had passed away early. Liu Hongying's wife worked in Shanghai with a moderate income. She had to support her son and elderly mother, so she simply didn't have the ability to financially support her mother-in-law. Despite my mother's relatively high salary of 80 Yuan a month—at a time when university graduates earned only 53 Yuan and factory apprentices earned 18 Yuan per month, increasing to 36 Yuan after three years—she never provided any financial support to her mother. My mother also inherited sixty thousand Yuan from my father's savings, a substantial amount for that era, yet she never offered any financial assistance to Grandma. My mother held onto that money tightly all her life, and when she passed away in 1999, she left behind forty thousand Yuan. But its purchasing power was only equivalent to four hundred Yuan in the 1950s.

In 1978, Lu Puyun was finally rehabilitated, receiving some compensation economically. One day, Lu Puyun, along with his wife and children, dressed neatly, came to my grandmother's house to express their gratitude. Grandma patted Lu Puyun's new blue jacket and the black synthetic leather briefcase on his back, happily saying, "Indeed, when one's fortune changes, appearances change too." I saw Lu Puhong a few times in Shanghai, but this was the first time I met Lu Puyun. Previously, it was always his wife who came to visit Grandma, and he hadn't dared to contact Lu Puhong for decades, fearing he might cause trouble for his brother. Despite relying on his brother's compassionate generosity for decades, he hadn't dared to write him one letter of thanks.

From the 1950s to the 1970s, life was very difficult due to the shortage of goods and inadequate food supply. No one could eat their fill. My grandmother lived a very frugal life, getting by on the meager rent she collected from a few tenants. The stove in Grandma's kitchen had long gone cold. Grandma lived a rather frugal life, relying on the modest rent from a few tenants. Her daily life was extremely simple. She would light a small coal stove, but to save coal, she wouldn't cook breakfast. At night, she would pour boiling water into a thermos, add some rice and mung beans, and by the next morning, there would be porridge to drink. Grandma herself followed a vegetarian diet. But whenever I visited Wuxi, Grandma would always buy a live chicken and cook me a clay pot dish. She believed that soup made from an old hen was especially nourishing. As Grandma entered her twilight years, she rarely went out, usually sending someone to buy her groceries. But when I visited, she would be delighted and insisted on going to the market herself. Grandma walked with her tiny bound feet and leaned on a cane. Walking next to her, we left two and a half pairs of footprints in the alley.

In Rongxiang Lane and Sunxiang Lane, when it came to hosting major events like weddings and funerals, Grandma was often asked to take charge. Despite lacking formal education, Grandma managed to organize the banquets, handle the etiquette, and ensure all guests were happy. Another reason people liked to ask Grandma for help was her exceptional cooking skills. Grandma's culinary prowess was renowned far and wide since she was young. The poultry and fish she picked out always resulted in exceptionally delicious dishes. One of Grandma's talents was her skill in selecting ingredients. She had a knack for choosing pork, often picking out the best pieces from the market. Pork vendors would hang slices of meat on large hooks, and she would point to the stall and say, "This is a 'fragrant pig', and that one is a 'stinky pig'." The pork that she chose always turned out tender and fragrant, unlike some meats that retained an unpleasant odor no matter how they were cooked. So, at the market, you would often find a few "fans" trailing behind her, buying more of whatever she picked. Grandma never claimed to have any secrets; it was perhaps just intuition, something not everyone possessed. The fish vendors used large wooden basins filled with lively freshwater fish. Grandma usually bought crucian carp and freshwater herring. She made crucian carp egg soup and braised or smoked herring. However, Grandma's specialty was meat dishes, each one prepared to perfection: marinated pork, pork ribs, pork-stuffed gluten, sausage, and old hen soup. Her marinated pork, made with red wine marinate and pork belly, had translucent skin and melted in the mouth. Pork ribs, cooked in

Grandma's homemade bean paste, were flavorful to the bone. Anyone with sharp teeth would chew the bones to pieces. The pork-stuffed gluten had a perfect balance of texture, both firm and juicy. Grandma's sausage casings were impeccably cleaned, fatty but not greasy. Grandma liked to keep it simple when cooking, using minimal tools besides her knife skills. Neighbors believed in Grandma's "magic touch," thinking she had "fragrant hands" that could turn any dish delicious with just a touch.

One of Grandma's banquets unexpectedly ended in tears. Good Grandma had a son named Ruizhen. He worked as a traditional Chinese medicine doctor in Nanjing. From 1964 to 1965, the government promoted "acupuncture anesthesia." Ruizhen specialized in ear acupuncture therapy for myopia. He became a notable figure after impressing some superiors. When he came to Shanghai for a demonstration, he visited my mother. Both my older sister and younger brother suffered from nearsightedness, and he personally administered ear acupuncture to them, but it had no effect. However, in China, during the so-called "Great Leap Forward" era, everyone followed the government's directives blindly. Whether or not his acupuncture could cure poor eyesight, Ruizhen had attracted the government's positive attention. Liu Yihou (the eldest son of my third grandmother) also lived in Nanjing and became enthusiastic about his cousin's newfound fame. He was determined to find Ruizhen a girlfriend. However, before all this, Ruizhen had met a girl in Wuxi, and they were already considered engaged, with their wedding date set for the second day of the Chinese New Year in 1965. Good Grandma asked Grandma to take charge, and she prepared several banquet tables at home. On the wedding day, the groom was absent, and the bride was in tears. Good Grandma was utterly bewildered and distressed, struggling to even stand on her own feet. In those days, it was not easy for ordinary people to host banquets. The preparations for the banquet had started days earlier, and the guests who came to the wedding had all brought gifts. The atmosphere was extremely awkward. Grandma took it upon herself to address the situation, offering a humorous perspective. She greeted the relatives and friends and said, "Whether they choose to get married or not is their business; our business is to enjoy the meal." In response, some guests settled down to partake in the food and drink, while others decided to take their share of the provisions home. As a child, it was the first time I witnessed the tragicomedy of life.

After I left Wuxi, Grandma often asked people to bring two types of medicine to Shanghai. Grandma's maternal ancestors' favorite prescriptions: Placenta Powder and Wound Healing Medicine. The main ingredient of Placenta Powder is, unsurprisingly, placenta. After washing the placenta, it is sliced, dried in the sun, fried, ground into powder, and mixed with other medicinal herbs according to the prescription, along with sesame powder and white sugar in proportion. This prescription is said to be a useful supplement for young boys. Since I was weak since childhood, Grandma prescribed Placenta Powder for me. Since it contains sesame and sugar, making it very tasty, she turned it into a treat. This was the only special treat I enjoyed at home in Shanghai. The main component of Wound Healing Medicine is lime. Raw lime is packed in reed bags and buried under fruit trees for at least 20 years. Then mixed with various medicinal herbs in proportion. After applying Wound Healing Medicine, its effect is to stop bleeding, relieve pain, and leave no scars. Wound Healing Medicine has always been a staple in our family's first aid kit.

The city of Wuxi is rich in cultural relics and has long been a place where many scholars and literati linger. Among this illustrious list are Lu Yu (Tang Dynasty author of *The Classic of Tea*) and Su Shi (Song Dynasty poet and statesman) by the No. 2 Erquan Spring; Pi Rixiu and Lu Guimeng (Tang poets) at the foot of the Xihui Mountains; Wen Zhengming (Ming Dynasty painter and calligrapher) by Taihu Lake; and Wen Tianxiang (Song loyalist and poet) at Huangbudun—the famous islet in the Grand Canal. Grandma grew up in the picturesque Jiangnan (Southern Yangtze Region) and had a broad outlook from a young age. She visited some famous mountains and ancient temples, believing that personal cultivation and character development are inseparable from the influence of the environment and culture. Because of her bound feet, as she grew older, Grandma rarely went out. But every time I visited Wuxi, she always suggested that I go to Xihui Mountains or Taihu Lake to relax. Standing at the door of Grandma's house and looking west, you would see Huishan (Mount Hui), a mountain formerly known as both Xishenshan and Huashan, which is part of the Tianmu Mountains. At the top of Huishan, there are three peaks called First, Second, and Third Maofeng, with the highest peak reaching 329 meters. Walking the three peaks, you can see several Taoist nunneries, Buddhist temples, and historic sites like the stone gate known as Wanggong Dock, the White Cloud Cave, and the Immortal Residence of Lü Dongbin. Besides Huishan, there is Xishan (Mount Xi), where you can find attractions like Longguang Pagoda and the Xishan Neolithic Site. Longguang Pagoda, standing at the foot of Xishan for more than four hundred years, has been a landmark architectural symbol of Wuxi city for centuries.

Huishan Ancient Town is not a traditional "town" in the conventional sense, but a historical relic composed of many ancestral temples. It can be traced back to the Tang Dynasty, when it was established to commemorate Chunshen Jun (Lord Chunshen). It developed into 118 ancient ancestral temples dedicated to ancestors of various surnames during the Republic of China period. Among the surviving temples, there are temple halls such as the Taibo Zhide (Taibo Ultimost Integrity) Hall, the Dongyue (East Mountain) Great Emperor Temple, and the six major god temples of Tea, Dreams, Earth, Water, Warfare, and Insects. There are also temples dedicated to historical figures, such as the Qian Wusu King Temple dedicated to Qian Liu, the Lord Lu Zhongxuan Temple dedicated to Lu Zhi, the Lord Fan Wenzheng Temple dedicated to Fan Zhongyan, the Guangji Temple, also known as the Mr. Zhou Lianxi Temple dedicated to Zhou Dunyi, the Lord Sima Wen Temple dedicated to Sima Guang, the Lord Yu Zhongsu Temple dedicated to Yu Qian, and so on. Additionally, there are temples dedicated to local scholars, including the Li Shen Temple honoring Li Shen, the author of the poem "Min Nong" (Compassion for the Farmers), the Lord Li Zhongding Temple honoring Li Gang (a prime minister of the Southern Song Dynasty), the Youmao Temple honoring You Mao (a poet of the Southern Song Dynasty), the Ni Yunlin Temple honoring Ni Yunlin (one of the "Four Families of the Yuan and Ming Dynasties"), Mr. Gu Dongyang Temple honoring Gu Dongyang (teacher of Hai Rui), and various other temples dedicated to local sages of Wuxi.

It takes about twenty minutes to walk from No. 35 Cotton Lane to the Huishan Town ancestral hall. The hall is located in the northeast foothills of Liangxi District, also known as "Huishan Ancient Town" or "Huishan Old Street." The ancestral hall complex occupies two main thoroughfares—one running north-south and the other east-west— that intersect in an "L" shape, with halls lining both legs of the corner. The east-west street, originally named Xiuzhang Street (Pretty Mountain Street), has a plaque at its entrance called "Wuli Xiangcheng Archway." This name originated from the fact that in the past, people passed through this road to Huishan Temple to offer incense, and this road used to be Wuli (five li = 2.5 kilometers) long, hence the common name "Wuli Street." The inscription "Huilu Zhongling" (Smart Bell at the foot of Huishan) on the archways at the entrance of Huishan north-south or Vertical Street (Xiuzhang Street) and Huishan east-west or Horizontal Street was inscribed by Ma Yinchu in 1930. During the Qianlong Emperor's southern tour, while staying at Jichang Garden (Pleasure Keeping Garden) at the foot of Huishan, local officials renovated this road with expensive Jinshan stones for the emperor's procession. This led to a local saying, "You can wear new shoes right after the rain in Wuli Street." Apart from Zhi Street and Heng Street, there are also two rivers: GuanDao (Broad Sword) and Longtou (Dragon Head). The latter is a tributary of the ancient canal and was initially called Huishan Bang. However, after the Emperors Kangxi and Qianlong visited Huishan, it was renamed Longtou River. This area was accessible by both water and land, making it a natural commercial port during the canal transportation era. It is worth mentioning that due to its proximity to canal transportation, many Huizhou merchants chose to settle here, and they also followed the local customs, establishing ancestral halls. Examples include the Zhu Xi Temple, which serves as a Huizhou guild hall, and the Lord Li Temple, dedicated to Li Hezhang, the younger brother of Li Hongzhang of the late Qing Dynasty, forming a unique blend of Jiangnan and Huizhou architectural styles at the foot of Huishan. In addition, influenced by the integration of Eastern and Western cultures in modern times, many ancestral halls in the ancestral hall complex now feature a combination of Chinese and Western-style temples. The Yang Family's Yang Zonghan Temple is a typical example. Many of these ancestral halls also have garden pavilions, such as the Yang family's Grass Hut, the Shiyou Garden inside the Gu Kejiu Temple, and the lake stones in Zhusu Garden, where one can relax while admiring the scenery, adding to the serene elegance of Huishan. The prosperity of the ancestral halls also brought prosperity to handicrafts. The temple attendants made mud figurines known as "playthings" from Huishan clay to supplement their income. Because there were many practitioners, not only did they establish a guild called the "Plaything Guild," but they also formed the distinct and charming scene of the "Huishan Mud Figure Street" that still exists today. From then on, the reputation of Huishan mud figures spread far and wide.

Huishan Temple can be found nestled at the base of Huishan in Beitang District, Wuxi. This temple is renowned and holds a special place in the Xihui Scenic Area. Its history dates back to the time of the Northern and Southern Dynasties. Originally, it was called the "Lishan Thatched Cottage," built by Situ Youchang Zhanting during the Liu and Song Dynasties in the Southern Dynasties period (420~479). In the first year of the Jingping era of the Liu Song Dynasty, this humble cottage was transformed into a dwelling for monks and came to be known as "Huashan Monastic Chamber." Then, in the third year of the Liang Datong era (537), Huashan Monastic Chamber was officially renamed as the Huishan Temple. Over more than a millennium, this temple has seen its share of ups and downs. Many respected monks have lived here, and it has hosted numerous well-known figures who visited or stayed for some time. During the Tang and Song Dynasties, the Huishan Temple was a hub of spiritual activity. It encompassed Yugong Valley and Jichang Garden and boasted 1,098 rooms for monks. Within the temple grounds, you'll discover a treasure trove of historic relics, including a stone scripture building from the Tang and Song Dynasties, the King Kong

Hall, the Fragrant Flower Bridge, Sun and Moon Pond, the Golden Lotus Bridge, the Golden Lotus Pond, the Royal Stele Pavilion, the Listening to Pine Stone Bed, an Ancient Ginkgo Tree, Datong Hall, Bamboo Furnace Mountain House, and Cloud Rising Mansion, among others. Even emperors couldn't resist the allure of the Huishan Temple. Emperors Kangxi and Qianlong, who reigned during the Qing Dynasty, visited the temple multiple times during their southern journeys. They paid their respects by burning incense and offering prayers to Buddha. Emperor Kangxi, during one of his visits, even had the pleasure of tasting the spring water in Yilan Hall. Emperor Qianlong, on his southern tour, found rest in Qinyuan (also known as Jichang Garden) and Zhufoulu Mountain House. He was so moved by the temple that he composed poems and inscribed a special dedication to the Huishan Temple.

Jichang Garden was built by the descendants of Qin Guan, a famous poet from the Northern Song Dynasty and a grand academician of the Dragon Pavilion. Since then, the descendants of the Qin family have continuously expanded the garden. During the Wanli period (1573~1620), based on the line "Take joy in benevolence and wisdom, find solace in mountain scenery" from Wang Xizhi, it was renamed "Jichang Garden." In the late Shunzhi period and early Kangxi period, Qin Yao's great-grandson Qin Dezao inherited the garden and carried out repairs and expansions. He invited the renowned garden expert Zhang Lian and his nephew Zhang Shi to meticulously renovate Jichang Garden, arranging springs and rocks, shaping mountains and managing water, making the scenery even more enchanting. Jichang Garden became a model of classical Chinese gardens with its superb garden artistry. The garden is lush and expansive, with ancient and serene mountains, murmuring streams, and echoing springs, resembling a fairyland. It was not only favored by literati and scholars but also became a beloved destination for Emperor Kangxi and Emperor Qianlong during their tours of Wuxi. Emperor Kangxi visited Huishan seven times and personally inscribed plaques with phrases like "Stream light, mountain scenery" and "Pine breeze, moonlight Reflection." During Emperor Qianlong's southern tour, he followed in the footsteps of Emperor

Kangxi's seven visits to Huishan and Jichang Garden, expressing even greater affection for the mountain and the garden. He remarked, "Only Huishan is elegant and tranquil. Among the famous mountains of Jiangnan, Huishan is unparalleled," and "Among the famous attractions of Jiangnan, Qin Garden in Huishan is the oldest." He also inscribed numerous plaques and poems alongside Kangxi's inscriptions. The green peaks, ancient pagodas, and elegant pavilions are reflected in the garden's pond, hence its grand name "Yingshan Lake" (Reflection Mountain Lake). Half an acre of square pond, reflecting the sky's light and clouds drifting together. The clear water surface, like a mirror, merges with the scenery of the Xi and Hui mountains. To ensure that Qin Garden could always be by his side, Qianlong even replicated Huishan Garden based on drawings in the Wanshou Mountain area of Qingyi Garden in Beijing (later renamed the Summer Palace Yiheyuan), setting a precedent for cloning Chinese gardens. Although he recreated eight picturesque scenes, he couldn't replicate the authentic charm of Jichang Garden, which was nestled between the Xi and Hui mountains and connected to the Hui Spring. Qianlong left behind a regretful line: "My imitation of this place already ranks among the Eight Wonders, yet still cannot compare to the Great Wu Palace."

Jichang Garden is long from north to south and short from east to west. Upon entering the garden near the Day and Night Pool of Huishan Temple, the first structure you see is Fenggu Xingwo. On both sides, the embracing pillars are adorned with couplets: "Shaded by miscellaneous trees, with light clouds and faint mist" and "Clear and smooth breeze, refreshing and harmonious atmosphere," both lines from poems by Weng Tonghe. In the eastern part, there is a long and narrow water pool named "Jinhui Yi" (Gathering Splendors Pond), which is splendid and colorful, earning its name. The pool stretches from north to south, and in the middle of its long bank, there is a protruding platform called He Bu Tan, where two large trees are planted. Across from Hebu (Crane Step) Beach is the Zhiyu (Knowing Fish) Pavilion, which divides the water surface into two parts. It seems to stop, but keeps going. The hexagonal pavilion called Yupan, located in Jinhui Yi, is also remarkable. According to folklore, Emperor Qianlong once played chess here with a monk from Huishan Temple. The monk trapped Qianlong, leaving him unsure of his next move. Although the monk eventually let Qianlong win, knowing that his chess skills were inferior left Qianlong displeased. Hence, he named the pavilion "Yupan" (brooding frustration). Nearby, there is a stone called "Beauty Stone," leaning against the wall like a beautiful woman, hence its name. The western part of the garden is dominated by artificial mountains, with undulating contours of varying heights. The central part is higher, mainly made of soil, while the flanks are lower, mainly composed of rocks. Vines and trees are planted between the soil and rocks, blending with nature. Although the hills are not high, the tall trees on them enhance the man-made mountain scenery. Streams run through the artificial mountains, bringing water from Huishan Mountain into the garden. The water flows gently, creating a soothing sound that resonates throughout the valley. This melodious stream is known as the "Eight-note Stream," as it mimics the sound of music played in harmony.

Huishan is surrounded by the "Nine Dragons and Thirteen Springs," with Hui Spring being the most renowned. According to Dudu, the provincial governor of Changzhou during the Tang Dynasty, as mentioned in the "Record of the New Springs of Huishan Temple," this spring was opened by Jing Cheng, the magistrate of Wuxi County, during the Dali era (766). Originally named Huiquan (Hui Spring), it was formed by the natural mountain water of Huishan, with two wells and one pool divided into upper, middle, and lower sections. The spring water, stored and filtered through countless pine roots and sandstone, is pure and sweet. Once opened, the spring attracted guests of great renown from all directions, asking where the clear water came from, as it had such a pristine source. During the Tang Dynasty, Lu Yu, a native of Tianmen in Hubei Province, lived in Huzhou, Zhejiang, to escape the turmoil of the Anshi Rebellion. During his stay, he visited famous mountains and explored mountain springs while studying tea, resulting in the creation of the world's first specialized tea book, "The Classic of Tea." He evaluated twenty famous springs in the world, ranking Lu Mountain's Kangwang Gulianquan as the best and Huishan's Shiquan (Stone Spring, Huiquan,

71

Hui Spring) as second-best, thus making the two springs famous. Another tea expert of the Tang Dynasty, Liu Bochu, believed that "the Cold Spring in the Yangtze River is the best, and Hui Spring is the second best." Therefore, while the ranking of the top spring may have shifted over time, the second-ranked in Huishan remained consistent. Eventually, the water of Erquan (meaning "Second Spring"—the name by which the consistently runner-up second-ranked spring water of Huiquan became widely known) became the preferred choice of tea connoisseurs worldwide, especially when paired with Yangxian tea from Yixing, highlighting its high quality. Su Shi once said, "Snow buds ask me for Yangxian, and milk water should be offered from Huishan." By the Song Dynasty, the water of Erquan had become a tribute. Emperor Huizong of Song ordered the construction of a pavilion to protect the spring, with the imperial inscription "Source of Living Water," praising it as a tribute, with hundreds of barrels delivered monthly. The great literary figure of the Song Dynasty, Su Dongpo, admired it and visited many times, writing the verse "Alone bringing the small round moon from heaven, coming to taste Erquan of the world." When Emperor Gaozong Zhao Gou crossed south, he disregarded the chaos and specially came to drink water by the spring, and built a pavilion on the spring, which still exists today. Later, the calligraphy master Zhao Mengfu inscribed a stele "Erquan of the World" inside the pavilion. Although Huishan's spring ranks second, there have always been those who dispute this. Wang Shizhen of the Ming Dynasty once wrote a poem: "In vain does Lu Yu lightly rank and title, who in the world should be the first spring?" When Emperor Qianlong of the Qing Dynasty toured the south and reached Huishan, he also said, "The Huiquan is famous throughout the world, and the cold spring of the Yangtze River should indeed yield."

On the 15th night of the lunar months, with the moon casting its glow halfway up the wall, the bamboo shadows swaying gently, and the spring water murmuring softly, how many people throughout history have been moved to feelings of wistfulness and melancholy by this beautiful scene? It was on such a serene evening on Mount Huishan that Ah-Bing's inspiration was sparked, leading to the resounding fame of his composition "Erquan Yingyue" (Moon Reflected on the Second Spring). The melodious and tender tune brings me back to my hometown time and time again, where I see the full moon hanging over the peaks of Mount Huishan. Setting aside the enchanting evenings, even the daytime at Jichang Garden is enough to intoxicate one. Adorable children chase and play on the grass, retired elders enjoy coming here to sit in the teahouse, sipping tea and socializing, while lovers cherish the tranquility under the flowers. With a scroll in hand, I often find myself lingering all day without the heart to leave. The ancient temples and monasteries add a touch of solemnity and spirituality to Mount Huishan's beauty. During my childhood, the temples on Mount Huishan were thriving with incense, and pilgrims coming from the city to worship Buddhas filled Cotton Lane all day long. I often went to the temples with my grandmother back then, becoming accustomed to the drumbeats and bell-tolls of Buddhist rituals. I always held a sense of reverence for the smiling Bodhisattvas and fierce-looking Vajras. Stepping out of the temple gate, listening to the evening prayers carried by the incense breeze, and watching the sunset gradually disappear into the dusk, even those heavily burdened with worldly desires could sense the transcendental meaning of emptiness beyond the six Buddhist desires.

Walking out of the backyard of No. 35 Cotton Lane, it takes less than five minutes to reach Wuai Square. It used to be a spacious square, but today it is surrounded by tall buildings. From the West Gate Bridge to Wuai Square is just one stop away, making it both a commercial center and a transportation hub. In the past, there were buses to Taihu, but today there is Metro Line 2, making transportation very convenient. Every time I went to Wuxi, Grandma always insisted on my going to a wonton shop in Wuai Square for a bowl of wontons before heading to Yuantouzhu (Turtle Head Island).

During the Spring Festival of 1975, I entered my sixth year of being sent down to Anhui, which was the darkest moment of my life. My friend Liu Gengnian and I went to Wuxi together. Liu Gengnian was my middle school schoolmate and also a fellow struggler. By that time, he had been recruited to work as a coal miner in Huaibei No. 8 Mine. Coal miners had high wages, but it was a high-risk occupation, with work-related injuries being common and deaths occurring frequently. Many local farmers were afraid and refused to become miners. We, the Educated Youths sent down to the countryside, had no other choice. Another schoolmate of mine, Shi Taihua, and I, due to family issues, had desperately tried to find a way into the coal mines but failed. Before the Spring Festival that year, I went to the No. 8 Mine to find Liu Gengnian, and then we traveled together to Shanghai, stopping in Wuxi on the way to visit my grandmother.

Grandma not only loved me, but she loved other people's children, too. Wuxi's winter nights were quite cold, and when Liu Gengnian and I stayed at my grandmother's house, she cared for Liu Gengnian just as she did for me. Wuxi people love to eat xiaolongbao (soup dumplings), with the saying "If you're not eating xiaolongbao, you're on your way to eat xiaolongbao." One of the most famous xiaolongbao restaurants in Wuxi is Wang Xing Ji, a time-honored brand. There is a branch of Wang Xing Ji on Wuai Square. The next day, Liu Gengnian and I went to Wuai Square for breakfast before heading to Taihu. Before we left, my grandmother handed me ten yuan and said, "Go to Wang Xing Ji and have a good meal." She reminded me, "Although Liu Gengnian has a high salary and you are particularly poor, when spending money outside, you must not take advantage of your friends." At that time, my financial situation only allowed me to deal with dimes, and even one Yuan was a big deal. My grandmother's financial situation was not at all affluent, and she lived very frugally, spending only 15 Yuan a month. Looking at the ten Yuan bill in my grandmother's hand, I couldn't bring myself to take it.

Liu Gengnian and I took a public bus, and after a few stops, we arrived at Li Lake. Li Lake, also known as Wuli (Five li) Lake, Qi Lake, or Xiao Wuhu (Little Five Lake), is shaped like a gourd and is an inland lake extending into Wuxi from Taihu. It covers an area of 8.6 square kilometers, and the Southeast connects to Taihu through the 10-Li-long Guangxi River. The Baojie Bridge, over 300 meters long, lies across the lake, dividing it into East Li Lake and West Li Lake. Baojie Bridge was donated and built by the renowned local industrialists Rong Zongjing and Rong Desheng. Li Lake is named after Fan Li, a great minister of the Yue State during the Spring and Autumn Period. Legend has it that during the Spring and Autumn Period (500 BC), after Fan Li, a great minister of the Yue State, helped King Yue conquer the Wu State, he took his beloved Xi Shi boating on this lake. In the early years of the Republic of China, Yu Xunzhen from Qingqi Village built the Eight Scenic Spots of Qingqi, including Plum Pier Fragrant Snow, Singing Orioles in the Willow Waves, South Bank Spring Dawn, Qu Pond Fish Watching, Japanese Beauty, Guilin Belle, Maple Stage Music, and Moonlight Lookout. This marked the beginning of Li Garden's history. From 1927 to 1936, Wang Yuqing and his son Wang Kangyuan from the same village used the original foundation to build Li Garden. In 1930, Chen Meifang, a relative of the Wang family who became wealthy in Shanghai, built a "Fisherman's Village" on its west side, also known as "Saili Garden"(even better than Li Garden). In 1952, the new government merged the two gardens and expanded the Li Garden corridor by about 200 meters to connect it with the Fisherman's Village. Most of Li Garden and Fisherman's Village were closed off and were only available for senior Communist officials to enjoy. Li Garden mainly includes the central rockery area, the lakeside long embankment in the west, Four Seasons Pavilions, and the Thousand-step Long Corridor by the water in the east, along with the Lakeheart Pavilion and the newly developed Layered Ripple area built in 1982. The Four Season Pavilions, built in 1954 with yellow roofs and red pillars, are the main scenic area of Li Garden. Plum blossoms are planted near the Spring Pavilion, oleander near the Summer Pavilion, osmanthus near the Autumn Pavilion, and wintersweets near the Winter Pavilion. Adjacent to the waterside are the Water Pavilion and the delicate and exquisite Spring Tower, which symbolize Li Garden. Because it was winter, and during the Cultural Revolution, there were very few tourists in Li Garden. Even in this bleak season, the beauty of Li Garden's scenery could not be erased. As the sun rose, its warmth could be felt on the body.

Yuantouzhu is an island protruding into Taihu, named for its resemblance to a turtle's head. It is acclaimed as the number one scenic spot of Taihu and the finest place of Taihu. At the Snowing Pavilion on Yuantouzhu, there is a pool of water with the Changchun (Spring Forever) Bridge, modeled after the Yudai (Jade Belt) Bridge in the Summer Palace. There are lake embankments before and after the bridge, separating it from Taihu. Changchun Bridge was built in 1936, and at the same time, Japanese wild cherry blossoms "Somei Yoshino" were planted on the bridge, blooming in April each year with pale red and white flowers, called the Cherry Blossom Embankment, or the Changchun Flower Ripple, a famous landscape of Yuantouzhu, hailed as the "Ueno Park of China." Yuantouzhu boasts magnificent mountains and rivers, grandeur, classical structure, and a northern style. Standing at the head of the island, one can enjoy the scenery of Taihu, with waves crashing against the shore and distant cliff carvings of "Horizontal Clouds" and "Embracing Wu and Yue," displaying extraordinary magnificence. The archway of "Finest Place of Taihu" was built in 1931, with a brick arch wall on the right side inscribed with the characters "Lishe" (Landing) and "Wenjin" (Inquiring) on both sides. Before 1934, there was only waterway access to Yuantouzhu, where boats docked, hence the "Lishe." Travelers arriving here by boat would inquire about the direction, hence the "Wenjin." Beyond the archway stands a screen wall, blocking the view of the garden. Behind the wall, overlooking the water, is the "Hanwanxuan" waterside pavilion, named for its ability to encompass the waves of thousands of acres. Inside the pavilion hangs a plaque reading "Hanwanxuan," written by Zhu Ruzhen in a fan shape. Another plaque, "Hu Shan Yan Hua" (Lake and Mountain Painting), inscribed by Emperor Qianlong, was originally from the Jingming Garden in Beijing, acquired by the garden owner in 1934, and relocated here. Passing through the archway into the "Deep Lotus Area," one arrives at Yuantouzhu and sees the lighthouse for the first time. This tower, built in 1924, was constructed with funds raised by local residents to celebrate the opening of navigation by the Wuxi Lake Steamship Company. After several renovations, it reached a height of 13.1 meters. Behind the lighthouse is an inscribed stone, with "Yuantouzhu" on one side, written by Qin Dunshi, and "Spring Waves of Yuantouzhu" on the other, originally inscribed by Liu Chunlin, a Qing

Dynasty scholar, but destroyed during the Cultural Revolution…

After exiting the bus, Liu Gengnian and I turned around from behind the archway and were suddenly struck by the vast expanse of the lake, which was very impressive. It was Liu Gengnian's first time at Yuantouzhu, and he said the scene left a very deep impression on him.

In the afternoon, we spent twenty cents to hire a farmer's boat from Yuantouzhu and rowed towards the Plum Garden. In the lazy winter sunset, the lake seemed a bit intimate. The Plum Garden was built in 1912 by the brothers Rong Zongjing and Rong Desheng, originally the site of the "Xiao Taoyuan" owned by the Qing Dynasty Jinshi scholar Xu Dianyi. In 1912, it was purchased by the Wuxi entrepreneur Rong Desheng, with the aim of "spreading fragrance for the world", and 3,000 plum trees were planted, comparable to the Little Xiangxuehai (Fragrant Snow Sea in Guangfu Town, Suzhou), and named "Plum Garden." The garden is centered on the Rong family's private residence, backed by Longshan (Mount Dragon), with the garden built against the mountain, using plum blossoms to adorn the mountain and the mountain to embellish the plum blossoms, giving it a unique style. The plum blossoms in the Rong family's Plum Garden are diverse, including varieties such as Jade Butterfly Plum, Green Calyx Plum, Palace Pink Plum, Cinnabar Plum, Ink Plum, and Rambling Dragon Plum. There are also attractions such as Tianxin Terrace, Xixin Spring, Qingfen (pure and pleasant) Pavilion, Nianqu Pagoda, Zhaohe Pavilion, Xiaoluofu (Little Luofu Mountain— referencing a mountain in Guangzhou renowned for its plum blossoms), Songbin Hall (Nanmu Hall), Huoran Cave (Suddenly See the Light), and Kaiyuan Temple. Xixin Spring was excavated in 1916, with its name chosen by Rong Desheng, meaning "washing the material makes it clean, washing the heart makes it clear." Tianxin Terrace was built in 1914, meaning "every plum blossom is like a piece of heaven," and the three peaks of Taihu Stone in front of Tianxin Terrace resemble the characters "Fu, Lu, Shou" symbolizing fortune, wealth, and longevity, hence it is called the "Three Stars Stone." Nianqu Pagoda is a hexagonal three-story brick pagoda, 18 meters high, and is a great place to admire the plum blossoms from a high vantage point. In 1930, the brothers Rong

Zongjing and Rong Desheng built it to commemorate their mother's 80th birthday. The name "Nianqu" is derived from phrases in ancient poetry, expressing deep respect and love for their mother. In 1951, my uncle stayed in the Plum Garden to recover from pulmonary tuberculosis. He took a photo at the Nianqu Pagoda, still elegant and full of vigor. Unfortunately, this photo now serves as a posthumous memory.

Grandma often said, "To be tough in life, you need to have a big heart. With a big heart comes great blessings." The Communist Party's most skilled method of rule is to divide people into different categories and break them down one by one. They even categorized the "black five categories" into different levels, with direct relatives who have been killed or imprisoned ranked at the bottom of the 18 levels of hell. Because both my father and uncle were locked up in prison, one sentenced to life and the other to twenty years, I became a descendant of a dual-category counter-revolutionary. It was as if I had crossed the "Bridge of Sighs" in Venice, abandoning all hope from then on! I left Shanghai on January 16, 1969. Before that, some Educated Youths went to farms in Dafeng, Jiangsu, and to military farms in Heilongjiang. The people on the state farms are considered agricultural workers. They receive wages with benefits and eat at the cafeteria. Due to my family background, I didn't have the opportunity to go to a farm. I was among the first to settle in as part of the "up to the mountains and down to the villages" movement. My younger brother, Chengquan, and elder sister, Shenjie, were sent to Jiangxi to "resettle in rural production squads" in March 1969. Chengquan met someone influential who helped him, and by 1972, he had already found a job and moved to Nanchang. Shenjie returned to Shanghai in 1974, where she quickly married and had children. Her return was made possible by the "No Child Around" policy the government had begun to use to address one of the many unintended consequences of their Educated Youth "resettlement" policies, instituted early in the Cultural Revolution. This particular consequence was the creation of a growing cohort of elderly with no children around to look after them, a phenomenon that threatened to become a severe drain on the already limited resources of major cities. As for me, after nine years spent being "resettled", I felt doubly desperate for the country and for my family.

Regarding my family, Grandma understood the unfairness I was born into the best. She advised me, saying, "From the day you were born, various hardships have been waiting for you. You must be tough and endure. Everyone has their own fate; you can't do anything about it." She said a truly successful person must be able to endure hardships that others cannot bear when they are unlucky and grit their teeth through it. There's no other way now, just waiting for an opportunity. She said, "I don't believe that a child from a good family will be unlucky for a lifetime." Then she raised her thumb and shook it behind her, saying, "Even the big shots will die. You're so young, what are you afraid of? One word - wait! I've seen many regime changes." I was shocked to hear this and quickly scanned Grandma's bedroom, then walked briskly out of the room, checking the central and back halls, fearing the walls had ears. Thank goodness, there was no one around.

Looking at it today, Mao has been dead for 50 years, and the Soviet Union has been dissolved for 35 years. Grandma's words can be said to be a big truth. But before Mao died, in the era when millions of people shouted, "Long live Chairman Mao!" anyone who dared to say what she did had committed a "deadly" capital crime! In the age of everyone crazily praising the emperor's new clothes, Grandma dared to say that the emperor was running naked. Where did her confidence come from? I think it can only be understood as coming from her steadfast faith. People will die one day, and the red regime will eventually disappear. Grandma believed this was a simple truth that couldn't be changed by human will. I've heard that when Mao fell seriously ill, Ye Jianying said that no action should be taken as long as Mao was still breathing. He believed any action would be futile, and they could only wait for him to pass away. In this regard, Grandma's insight and foresight are no less than Ye Jianying's. In the past, I was brainwashed by materialism and didn't believe in the existence of God. Now, although I haven't been baptized, I have a firm faith. Because I've begun to understand that the existence of humanity and the universe is evidence of God's existence. God will not tolerate the moral decay of humanity for long. In the past, God punished humanity with a great flood. Today, just as the banishment of educated urban youth did in the past, China's more than three decades of implementing the one-child policy have led it to face many unintended negative consequences, such as the dilemma of having no available manpower. Additionally, the new coronavirus pandemic makes me wonder if it's a warning from God to humanity.

Grandma's words were like a flash of lightning, illuminating a lamp in my heart. After returning to Huaibei, I mustered the courage to face reality and gave up the fantasy of performing so well at my job that my cadre would reward me with an opportunity to return to the city. Instead, I seized the opportunity to work as a private teacher, obtained textbooks from before the Cultural Revolution, and self-studied the curriculum from the third year of junior high school to the senior year of high school in mathematics, physics, chemistry, and English. Teaching during the day and studying at night. By the end of 1977, the first college entrance exam after the Cultural Revolution had resumed, and I initially applied to be tested for a science major with a foreign language option. However, the county education office informed me that I needed to apply for a liberal arts major before taking the additional foreign language test. I switched my track to study history and geography instead of physics and chemistry. The county education office found that it was a mix-up. However, it was too late to correct the mistake. Nevertheless, my total score in the liberal arts exceeded the cutoff for national key universities, and I scored 103 on the English test, the highest score among all eight counties in the entire Suxian Region. During the Spring Festival of 1978, after receiving the university admission notice, I went to Wuxi to share the good news with Grandma. Sitting on the train, I imagined how excited and overjoyed Grandma would be to hear the good news I brought. But I guessed wrong. Grandma didn't seem surprised at all. She just laughed a few times, and then with a smile, she leaned closer to me and said, "I knew you would definitely pass the exam. I've been praying to Bodhisattva for you every day. I told Guanyin Bodhisattva, this child has been kowtowing to you on this wooden board since he was a child; you must bless him. I don't believe that a child from such a good family will be unlucky for a lifetime."

How her confidence and pride resonated in my heart! The radiant smile on Grandma's face remains vivid and brilliant in my memory forever. Every wrinkle unfolded, laughing with profound satisfaction and joy. Every time I recall it, tears well up uncontrollably.

In early 1981, as usual, I visited Grandma before the Spring Festival. I took the train from Wuhu to Shanghai, stopping in Wuxi for a few days. It was already night when I got off the train. I hastened my steps, passing by the China Hotel, skirting around Chong'an Temple, crossing Ximen Bridge, walking along Xizhi Street, and entering Cotton Alley. When I arrived at Grandma's house, her tenant Axiang warmly greeted me. She had already set up a single bed for me in Grandma's bedroom. I knew Grandma had been weak and bedridden for a long time. After greeting Grandma and seeing her peaceful expression, I lay down and fell asleep. Like most elderly people, Grandma enjoyed telling old stories. She talked to me about everything and didn't treat me like a junior. What I admired most about Grandma was her ability to judge people. She was very observant, casually picking up a few small things from the daily lives of my relatives that others missed, and with just a few words, she could analyze a person's character and appearance thoroughly. Sometimes she spoke so vividly that it made me laugh, while other stories made me feel the inevitability of karma. Finally, Grandma always ended the topic with "just laugh it off." Grandma had a natural emotional intelligence. Her friends and relatives liked to talk to her when they encountered problems, as if they had met a psychologist.

Since 1949, political campaigns have been endless. From the confiscation of landlords' and capitalists' property to the house raids during the Cultural Revolution, countless families were broken, and lives were lost. Chen Yi was the first mayor of Shanghai. It is said that during the "public-private partnership" movement, Chen Yi used to ask his staff every morning, "How many paratroopers are there today?" referring to how many capitalists had jumped off buildings to commit suicide that day. Later, the government adopted the method of paying "fixed interest" to capitalists for their assets. Some relatives came to Grandma in tears, saying that public-private partnerships were worse than being kidnapped, wasting half a lifetime of hard work, and cutting off their source of wealth for the rest of their lives. Grandma guided them with her own experience, saying, "You know, I've been through tough times too. When the Japanese troops came, I had to leave my home. The Japanese didn't ransack our house, but it was robbed by a thief. Now you're being offered a fixed interest rate. Think of it as catching salt in water. Just be open-minded, it's all external." Grandma may not have known "understanding is the best sympathy," but that's just how she was. On this day, Grandma opened up her heart again. However, it was clear that she was starting to run out of breath as she spoke. After a while, her eyes dimmed, and she needed a few minutes to recover.

On the third day of my visit, Grandma said she wanted to have a sip of thin porridge. I served her half a small bowl, mixed with a little sesame oil and half a preserved duck egg. She said it was so nice to have a sip of hot porridge. She asked me to change the clean sheets for her and assist her in using the toilet. She put on a thin silk jacket and silk cotton pants and lay back down. I tucked her in, and she happily said, "All clean inside and out." Then she urged me to leave, saying, "You and Yuanyuan have grown up together. He's getting married tomorrow, and you must attend his wedding. Don't worry, I'll not die on the day of my grandson's wedding." She added, "The furniture in the house was left by your grandpa. It needs to go to his grandson, Yuanyuan. I buried an iron box under the floor tiles against the wall in the main room, and it holds some jewelry from my family. Take the jewelry for yourself. There's 30 yuan under my pillow, you take it too, I don't need it anymore." I replied, "You're fine, why are you talking nonsense?" When Grandma saw that I didn't move, she said, "It's alright if you don't want to take it. It can save you some trouble. Everyone has their own destiny. You're blessed, and I know that. I won't be mistaken." Finally, she reminded me to leave the lights on in the bedroom and the Buddha hall, as she liked having the rooms brightly lit.

Three days after Yuanyuan's wedding, Axiang called to inform us that Grandma had passed away. My mother, brother, and I hurried to catch the overnight train to Wuxi immediately. Without delay, my mother took the initiative to collect Grandma's jewelry to bring along. The next morning, Yuanyuan and his mother, Wu Mingqi, arrived, but Yuanyuan's wife couldn't make it; as a bride, she had to tend to her new home according to tradition. As expected, my mother had a disagreement with Wu Mingqi, her sister-in-law, and Yuanyuan, her nephew, over Grandma's jewelry. This turned close relatives into enemies. Wu Mingqi argued that her son was the only rightful heir to the Liu family and its legacy. My mother, on the other hand, insisted that these jewels were part of Grandma's dowry from her own family and had nothing to do with the Liu family. I'm not sure how the dispute ended, and honestly, I don't need to know. I'm just relieved I stayed out of that mess. I knew my mother very well; she was extremely protective of her interests. With those jewels under her control, it would be hard for Wu Mingqi and Yuanyuan to make her give them up.

When Grandma passed away, she looked peaceful, and her face was turned slightly toward her beloved Buddha hall. She had reached the age of eighty-eight. We placed her ashes in a serene spot on a sunny hillside in Huishan. The Sun family had their private cemetery, which had been cared for by privately hired graveyard keepers for generations. Behind the cemetery were towering mountains and clouds, and in front of us, there stretched a vast, flat plain. Looking into the distance, I could see the winding rivers and canals, providing a breathtaking view of the beautiful Jiangnan. During that time, I was in my third year of college, just one year away from graduation. College graduates received a monthly salary of 53 yuan back then, which was considered quite decent, higher than what factory workers earned. A worker's apprenticeship paid 18 Yuan per month for three years, rising to a salary of 36 Yuan after completing the apprenticeship. I could have easily afforded to support grandma with ¥10 a month, and a bit more during holidays. But, sadly, Grandma didn't wait for that day to come. It's a lifelong regret of mine.

After my grandmother passed away, the kowtow board and some furniture were sent to my mother's house in Shanghai. In May 1983, my daughter Luoluo was born in Shanghai. It was a scorching hot summer, and she needed to take showers multiple times a day. The kowtow board had a slanted surface, making it easy for water to drain away. We found it very convenient to bathe Luoluo on the kowtow board. The red lacquered kowtow board felt smooth, providing a cooler surface for Luoluo to rest on. Perhaps the countless kowtows performed by my grandmother on this board had blessed Luoluo. Since childhood, Luoluo has been healthy, free from illness and misfortune, and has excelled in her studies and career.

In 1984, I left China to study in the United States. For the first ten years, I juggled a full-time job with being a full-time student, until I returned to China for the first time in 1994. During that visit, my mother asked me to purchase burial plots at Qinglongshan (Mount Blue Dragon) Cemetery in Wuxi for her, my father, and her second husband. My father passed away in 1998, and my mother followed in 1999. In 2000, my siblings and I escorted our parents' ashes to Qinglongshan in Wuxi for burial. Accompanied by my brother, I revisited Sunxiang to see my grandmother's old house. Sunxiang and Rongxiang remained intact. Grandma's old house was now occupied by her nephew and his son's family. Many new buildings had sprung up in the village, and there were no longer any fields beyond its borders. Wuxi's urban area had expanded significantly, transforming the once quiet Sunxiang and Rongxiang into bustling cities. In 2010 and 2017, I made additional trips to Wuxi with my good friends Shen Jianwen and his wife Liu Ying to visit my grandmother's cemetery and former residence. An extension of Cotton Lane had changed the landscape, and No. 35 had been demolished, resulting in the disappearance of Grandma's old house. The spiritual connection I once felt to my grandmother's Xihui Mountains was now devoid of its old scenery, leaving me feeling mournful. It has been over forty years since I left China. As I write this, I am reminded of the words of Yu Yingshi: "I have no nostalgia. Wherever I go, there is China." My heart resonates with these sentiments. I, too, do not feel homesick. Wherever I go, there is China. Wherever I go, there is my grandmother's Xihui Mountains.

Chapter 2

My Parents's Generation

1. Bao family in Baoshan

The "Brief Chronicle of Huizhou" records, "The descendants of the kinfolk that migrated to Huizhou continued to live in the areas which their predecessors had first occupied and named after their ancestral clans. These migrations had begun when conflicts arose due to limited land and dense populations in their original places of residence, driving previous generations to settle in other regions. The development of a clan is like a tree growing branches, and the branches giving rise to leaves, resulting in the clan's members being spread all over the world." In the mid-17th century, because of famine, a branch of the Bao family, descendants of Lord Liangyu, moved from Shexian to Jiangsu Province. They settled in Chengxiang Town, Jiading County. After four generations, led by Lord Guochang, they moved from Jiading to Chengxiang Town, Baoshan. Lord Guochang had three brothers. Lord Guoxin and Lord Guoxiang relocated to Liuhe Town, Taicang County, but their branch became sparsely populated and eventually lost contact. Only one branch of the Bao family that moved from Shexian to Chengxiang Town, Baoshan, thrived and multiplied for generations. Three generations of Lord Liangyu's family had graveyards in Jiading. From 1930 to 1949, these grave fields were rented to a man named Zhang Xinquan for farming, who was entrusted with maintaining the graves in lieu of paying rent. Zhang Xinquan lived outside the south gate of Jiading and ran a construction material shop near the city wall. Before 1949, descendants of the Bao family in Baoshan would visit Jiading to pay their respects at the cemetery, where Zhang Xinquan would serve as their guide. However, after the 1949 Communist "Liberation", turmoil and uncertainty ensued, leading to the disappearance of the cemetery and the loss of contact between the Baoshan family and Zhang Xinquan.

According to the clan genealogy, from the first-generation ancestor Liangyu, who moved to Jiading, to my father of the eleventh generation with the "Xian" name, most members of the Bao clan have resided in the northwest corner of Chengxiang in Baoshan, particularly concentrated in "North Third Street." Because many Bao families lived on both sides of the street, it was also called "Bao Family Lane." The postal address at that time was: Bao Family Lane, within the west gate of Baoshan. The Bao clan's long history and cultural heritage have thus been passed down in Baoshan. There is a local saying, "First there was Bao Family Lane, then there was Chengxiang Town; first there was Chengxiang Town, then there was Baoshan County." Clan members working and living elsewhere often returned to Baoshan on holidays, and it was rare for entire families to move away permanently.

The genealogy of the Bao family branch in Baoshan has always been consistent with the Tangyue clan genealogy. This can be referenced in the 200-volume "Recompiled Genealogy of the Three Bao Clans of Tangyue in Shexian, Anhui," edited by Bao Guangchun in the 25th year of the Qianlong reign (1760), printed with wooden movable type by Yiben Hall in twenty copies. A copy is currently preserved at the National Library of China, with only 199 of the 200 volumes remaining, and another at the Huizhou Museum in Anhui Province, completely intact. The Tangyue genealogy uses 20 characters to represent 20 generations, repeating in a cycle. They are: Liang, Hou, Ru, Guo, Ci, Zong, and Zu (the seventh generation uses both "Zu" and "Yi"), Wei (the eighth generation uses both "Wei" and "Sheng"), Si, Er, Xian 賢 (women use "Xian"嫺), and Cheng (women use "Shen"), Fu 福 (women use "Fu"馥), Yi, Jia, Yong, Da, Chang. In China, such generational names define and strengthen the family bond of the clan. The names of the Bao family descendants follow the ancestral system, consisting of three characters. The surname comes first, followed by one character indicating the generation, and one for the given name. My grandfather Bao Ershao belonged to the "Er" generation.

The generation following "Er" is "Xian," so my father's name is Bao Zuxian. The generation after "Xian" is "Cheng," so my name is Bao Chengmo, and my brother's name is Bao Chengquan. For females in the "Cheng" generation, the character used is "Shen," so my sister's name is Bao Shenjie. My daughter is the "Fu" generation. Her name is Bao Fuluo.

Our old house in Baoshan was a two-story, square-shaped building. The house layout resembled the traditional "Four Waters Back to the Hall" style from Huizhou's hometown. In the middle, there was a large courtyard, and all the rooms on the ground floor had doors and windows facing the courtyard. The first floor had a living room, dining room, study room, family room, kitchen, and a woodshed. Once the main door on the ground floor is closed, the whole family can rest peacefully. On the second floor, a gallery encircles the courtyard, connecting the bedrooms. The toilets are attached to the bedrooms, a design that enhances the living standards. When I was in elementary school, I stayed in this house several times, where there was a room assigned to my father. My memories of the old family home in Baoshan also include the seawall. Since Baojia Lane in Chengxiang is located at the eastern edge of Baoshan, near the Yangtze River, relatives visiting the old family home could climb the seawall for a distant view. This is the estuary of the Yangtze River and one of China's most important gateways to the sea and a vital hub of trade. The vast water surface and the merging of the river and sea offer a broad and open view. Growing up in such an environment, one's mind should also be broad and open. The seawall serves as Baoshan's barrier along the river. In the 12th year of the Yongzheng reign (1734), Baoshan magistrate Hu Renji oversaw the construction of a new earthen city wall for several years. In the 15th year of the Daoguang reign (1835), during Lin Zexu's tenure as Jiangsu governor, the seawall was renovated. The cross-section of the seawall measures 80 ft. wide at the base, 20 ft. wide at the top, and 12 ft. high, with large stones placed outside the wall to withstand the tides.

Far from the Baoshan seawall, a memorable event occurred during the difficult period of 1961. Uncle Kuanxian lived in Baoshan and worked in Shanghai. One day, he came to visit us on Xinchang Road in

87

Shanghai. At that time, the transportation from Baoshan to Shanghai was very primitive, taking at least two hours one way. Therefore, relatives in Baoshan and Shanghai only visited each other during holidays. Uncle Kuanxian was my father's first cousin, and they shared the same grandfather. On that day, he brought a live rabbit with him and wanted to prepare it for us to eat. Uncle Kuanxian worked in an office, and it was clear that handling rabbits wasn't his expertise. Nevertheless, in front of two kids under the age of ten, he had no choice but to complete this difficult task. My brother and I still vividly remember how he struggled with that rabbit. We couldn't help but watch with a mix of excitement and fear. During those years, when people were going hungry and times were tough, the people of China felt like the impoverished and abused Little Match Girl who froze to death in Hans Christian Andersen's story. That rabbit was like a miracle, bringing us immense joy and hope. In the 1990s, I lived in Forest Hills, Queens, New York. Uncle Kuanxian and his wife paid a visit, bringing their nephew Bao Feng (the son of my Uncle Changxian), who was studying in the United States. This unexpected visit was another delightful surprise.

2. Bao Family in Shanghai

The area where Yuyuan Road is situated was originally farmland in the western suburbs of Shanghai, crisscrossed by several small rivers. In the tenth year of Xianfeng (1860), when Li Xiucheng led the Taiping Heavenly Kingdom army's attack on Shanghai, the Shanghai Magistrate constructed a short military road on the north side of Jing'an Temple, which formed the easternmost segment of what would become Yuyuan Road. By the fourth year of Tongzhi (1865), this military road came under the management of the Shanghai Public Concession Industry Bureau. In 1899, Shanghai's public concession underwent significant expansion, pushing its western boundary to the west of Jing'an Temple. Consequently, the original section of Yuyuan Road fell within the public concession, and the renowned Yuyuan Garden at the intersection on the east end of Changde Road lent its name to this road. In 1911, the

Shanghai Public Concession Industry Bureau commenced the process of filling in a small river located outside the concession and extended Yuyuan Road westward to Edinburgh Road, which is known today as Jiangsu Road. This construction was a transboundary or "overstep the border" road project, furthering foreign encroachment into Chinese sovereignty. Jiangsu Road is a north-south avenue intersecting with Yuyuan Road, representing a trans-boundary road in the western part of Shanghai. In 1913, the road's extension continued westward, ultimately extending to reach Baili South Road, now recognized as Changning Road.

In the decade following the conclusion of World War I (1919~1928), a remarkable transformation took place along Yuyuan Road, stretching from Changde Road to Jiangsu Road. This area saw the construction of garden residences and modern-style lanes, and soon established itself as one of the most exclusive residential districts in Shanghai. Notably, numerous prominent figures in history called this neighborhood home. Yuyuan Road became a hub for celebrities, from the worlds of politics, science, literature, music, academia, and the military, including Kang Youwei, Cai Yuanpei, Chen Duxiu, Qu Qiubai, Li Jishen, Huang Yanpei, Shen Junru, Wang Boqun, Zhang Bojun, Dong Zhujun, Lin Yutang, Fu Lei, Shi Zhecun, Zhang Ailing (aka: Eileen Chang), Mao Dun, Du Yuming, Jiang Guangnai, Chen Heqin, Gu Shengying, Qian Xuesen, and Wang Jingwei. Among the well-known modern-style lanes in the area were Andingfang, Lane 284 on Jiangsu Road, Lane 285 on Jiangsu Road, Yongle Village, Lane 389 on Jiangsu Road, and Qishan Village, Lane 1032 on Yuyuan Road, to name a few. Alongside Andingfang Lane, you can find the residence of the renowned translator Fu Lei, while on the other side stands the Huimu Church, a Christian landmark.

In August 1937, the Japanese army launched an attack on Baoshan County and Wusongkou. In response, the Chinese army began the August 13 Battle of Songhu during the same month. This turned Baoshan into a battleground. To escape the horrors of war, many members of the Bao family abandoned their old homes in Chengxiang Town, Baoshan, and relocated to the comparatively safer Shanghai Concession. Bao Erliang, Erjing, and Erjia, representing the tenth generation of the Bao family, took their children from the Xian generation and moved to urban Shanghai. They settled in Yongle Village, situated at the southeast corner of the intersection of Jiangsu Road and Yuyuan Road. Upon entering the lane, a row of three-story British-style townhouses, facing south, came into view. There were about ten households in total. The townhouses were made of yellow refractory brick on the outside, and inside, they were designed as two-family homes. There was a small garden behind the front door, and from the entrance, you would find a living room, dining room, storage room, bathroom, and kitchen. The kitchen was equipped with a gas stove and flush toilets on every house floor. The bathrooms on the second and third floors even had large bathtubs. From as far back as I can remember until the 1980s, a few Bao families resided in Yongle Village. On the first floor of No. 17 Yongle Village, there lived Bao Erliang, his wife Jin Lan, and their youngest son Qingxian. The second floor of the same building was home to Bao Erliang's eldest son, Bao Zhixian, his wife Ma Keyu, and their kids Shenjue and Chengzuo. Meanwhile, the third floor housed Bao Erliang's younger brother, Bao Erjing's family. In a nearby house, No. 11, Bao Erliang's youngest brother, Bao Erjia, and his wife Yan Enzhen resided on the second floor. I used to call these three elders from the Er generation "Gonggong." These Gonggongs' father, Sihan, and my grandfather Ershao's father, Sirun, were brothers. That made them and my grandfather Ershao first cousins. Ershao, born in 1898, was the eldest son of Sirun, while Erliang, born in 1899, was Sihan's eldest son, just one year younger than Ershao. Therefore, in the "Er" generation, my grandfather should have become the future head of the Bao family. However, Ershao was irresponsible from a young age. After getting married, he and his wife, Chen Lanying, became opium addicts and passed away at a young age. My mother never had the chance to meet these in-laws.

Bao Erliang subsequently became the head of the two branches of the Bao family. My father referred to Erliang as Grand Uncle. I called him Grand Gonggong. In his younger years, Bao Erliang worked at the Baoshan County yamen (government office). By the time I was old enough to remember, he had long since retired. He was a member of the

Revolutionary Committee of the Chinese Kuomintang, but he usually kept a low profile and rarely went out to participate in activities. Despite the numerous political movements after 1949, Bao Erliang was not significantly impacted and managed to navigate them smoothly, which was likely related to his reclusive philosophy. Whenever I visited Jiangsu Road, I mostly saw him reading or writing at his desk, sitting very straight and in excellent health. Bao Erliang did not talk much, but when he did, his voice was loud and clear, speaking in a distinct Baoshan accent. He often smiled when he saw us grandchildren. Because he was the clan head, we would visit Jiangsu Road to pay our respects to him and other elders every New Year's Day. One of the joys of these visits was setting off firecrackers. Bao Erliang's youngest son, Qingxian, whom we called "Maomao" uncle, would lead us in setting off firecrackers in the small garden. He had many colorful firecrackers, and we children would follow him, shouting and excited, amazed by the spectacle. However, there were also unpleasant moments, like being marginalized by other children. Many uncles and aunts from the "Xian" generation would visit Jiangsu Road during the New Year, bringing their children of the "Cheng/Shen" generation, who were my age. The differences in each family's circumstances were stark. Some of them had parents who were proud Communist Party members. They formed exclusive circles, flaunting their material and spiritual superiority, along with a few sycophants. Unfortunately, with my father and uncle both imprisoned, I had no choice but to occupy the lowest rung of the social ladder. Some children would point at me, whispering intentionally, warning each other not to talk to me. Children's words and actions can be very cruel. Grand Gonggong Erliang noticed my plight and tried to comfort me in his way. He said, "Your father is a political prisoner, not a deceitful person. There's no need to feel ashamed." Although I didn't fully grasp the meaning of Grand Gonggong Erliang's words at the time, his kind intentions were unmistakable. As I grew older, I gradually came to understand his philosophy of "not judging a person based on their success or failure."

Grand Gonggong Erliang had eight children of his own and even more grandchildren. My father was not his direct nephew, and I was not his direct grandnephew. However, during holidays, he would send Da A-po (his wife) to our house, for instance, to deliver rice dumplings during the Dragon Boat Festival. Da A-po's maiden family, the Jin family, was also prominent in Baoshan. I met two women of her generation, though I'm not sure if they were her sisters or her brothers' wives. We called them Plump Auntie and Slim Auntie. They both lived on Wuyuan Road, and their home seemed frozen in time, with furnishings reminiscent of the 1930s. Most of their food and clothing were imported goods, which were not seen in ordinary households. They belonged to the minority who relied on foreign exchange. Due to a shortage of foreign exchange, for many years, including the Cultural Revolution period, the Shanghai government was lenient towards those who had foreign cash. Not only were they allowed to bring in foreign currency, but a special currency called "RMB Exchange Vouchers" was also invented. People with foreign currency could enter special supply stores like the "Friendship Store" and the "Overseas Chinese Store" to buy food and daily necessities unavailable on the open market. These stores sold everything from chocolate to bicycles. Some of these people were beaten to death by the Red Guards during the "Red August" of 1966, while others committed suicide. Those who survived the disasters of 1966 and 1967 were mostly taken abroad by their relatives in the 1980s. Da A-po passed away in 1976 at the age of 78. Grand Gonggong Erliang passed away in the summer of 1984 at the age of 86. I left China for the United States to study in August 1984. Just before I left, I managed to attend Grand Gonggong Erliang's memorial service.

Grand Gonggong Erliang's oldest son was Zhixian, who worked as an accountant at Shanghai No. 4 Radio Factory. Uncle Zhixian's wife, Ma Keyu, was once the object of my mother's envy. This was because Ma Keyu and her husband had good jobs, a spacious house, parents, and children. However, life is unpredictable. In 1966, Ma Keyu died of cancer at the age of 42. Grand Gonggong Erliang's second son, Bao Haoxian, was born in 1928. Uncle Haoxian was relatively well-known, and I have a strong memory of him. In 1949, after Bao Haoxian graduated from

Wusong Business College at the age of 21, he became a liaison officer and joined the People's Liberation Army representatives to take over the Kuomintang Investment Promotion Bureau and organize the China Shipping Fleet. In 1954, he was assigned to work at the China-Polish Company. Three years later, he climbed from being a third mate to becoming a first mate, which was the highest rank among the Chinese crew members in the company at that time. When China started building its ocean-going fleet, he was one of the very few selected for promotion to independent captain. In 1962, he led his crew to establish routes to East and West Africa. In October 1982, he commanded the new container ship "Fenhe" on its first voyage to New York. Later, Bao Haoxian served as the leading captain of the Shanghai Ocean Shipping Company. Unfortunately, in 1989, he passed away from overwork at the relatively young age of 61. Uncle Haoxian received many honors during his lifetime, such as being named a Shanghai Model Worker, a National Outstanding Captain, a Member of the Sixth Shanghai CPPCC (Chinese People's Political Consultative Conference—a powerless "advisory" body, created by the CCP in 1949 to conceal its total political control of the country behind a veil of pluralism), and a Representative of the Seventh National People's Congress. His wife, Tang Jingyi, was a close colleague of Uncle Zhixian's wife, Ma Keyu. It was Ma Keyu who introduced Tang Jingyi to her brother-in-law, Bao Haoxian. My brother and I still vividly remember the scene of attending Uncle Haoxian's wedding banquet. At that time, we were children under ten years old, with blurred memories of many things. However, in an era of extreme material scarcity, especially food shortages, nothing was more important to perpetually hungry children than having a lavish meal. The restaurant, possibly located on Jiangsu Road, was not luxurious. Yet, it managed to serve four cold dishes, four hot stir-fries, desserts, a whole chicken, a whole duck, and a pork knuckle—a true feast. My brother recalls that he was so full that day he almost couldn't make it home, lying in bed with a stomach ache all night, unable to sleep, and didn't dare tell the adults. The bride, Tang Jingyi, was very beautiful, resembling the female leader Jin Hua in China's number one blockbuster movie of that era, "Five Golden Flowers," even surpassing her. Consequently, we called Tang Jingyi "Pretty Aunt."

Great Uncle Erjing lived on the third floor of No. 17 Yongle Village. My father fondly called him 4th Uncle. Grear Uncle Erjing graduated from Tongji University Medical School. He and my father had a strong friendship, and he often visited our home for a drink. Sadly, he passed away at a relatively young age. I never had the chance to meet him because I wasn't in Shanghai when I was young. Great Uncle Erjia was the second of four siblings and resided at No. 11 Yongle Village. He and his wife, Yan Enzhen, were a very stylish couple. Both were graduates of Fudan University. They were known for their open-mindedness and wit, and for being excellent dancers. Together, they had two sons and four daughters, all of whom were both attractive and talented. In the 1960s, I had the pleasure of meeting their third daughter, Lin Xian, who was a college student and a volleyball player, full of youthful vigor. In the 1980s, I met their second son, Jiming. Jiming graduated from the Beijing Institute of Aeronautics and Astronautics and began working as an engineer at Shanghai No. 2 Radio Factory after his graduation. Being a dedicated professional, not aligned with communist beliefs, and coming from a family with a questionable background, he encountered significant challenges during the different political movements of the Chinese Communist Party, enduring substantial hardships. My departure from China had a significant impact on him, as he longed to leave China. Unfortunately, by that time, he was already older and later fell ill, making it impossible for him to fulfill his dream of leaving the country.

My father, Bao Zuxian, had a tough life along with his two brothers. He was born in Baoshan in 1920. His younger brother, Bao Zongxian, was born in 1924, and the youngest, Bao Hongxian, arrived in 1926. Life took a hard turn when he lost his dad at just 9 years old and his mom at 17. This meant he had to step up and take care of his two younger brothers. At the age of 16, he began working. In 1938, a schoolmate of his named Zhuang Pengcheng brought him from Shanghai to Taicang County to do anti-Japanese underground work. The following year, in 1939, Zheng Fengshi introduced him to join the Kuomintang, aka: Nationalist Party. At that time, the Kuomintang and the Communist

Party were working together to fight against Japan. Bao Zuxian was on the side of the Kuomintang. During the two years he spent in Taicang from 1938 to 1940, he held various important roles, like being the County Government Secretary and Lieutenant Secretary of the local Self-Defense Regiment. He even became the Director of the Taicang County Party, Government, and Military Joint Office. In 1940, he withdrew from Taicang and went to Shanghai to make a living. In 1941, his uncle Jiang Lansheng, who was a grain merchant, helped him get a job as an accountant at the Xiechangde/Yichangde Rice Shop on 208 Beijing West Road in Shanghai. At the same time, he started his own trading business in Wusong, which he managed until 1950.

In 1944, Bao Zuxian's schoolmate Zhuang Pengcheng introduced him to become a member of the Sanmin Youth Corps. During this time, he established a connection with Chiang Ching-kuo. The Sanmin Youth Corps was founded in the early days of the Anti-Japanese War. Even though it was officially linked to the Kuomintang, it operated independently with support from Chiang Kai-shek. The Kuomintang had a long history with various factions and senior figures still actively involved. Party affairs were largely overseen by the Chen brothers, Chen Lifu and Chen Guofu, which led to the saying: "Chiang's country and Chen's party." Although Chiang Kai-shek had largely consolidated leadership of the KMT by the late 1930s, he still faced internal factionalism and ideological dissent. So with the aim of solidifying his power, on July 9, 1938, he created the Sanmin Youth Corps to imbue the next generation of KMT membership with a sense of personal loyalty to him as their unchallengeable leader. After the defeat of the Japanese in August 1945, Chiang Ching-kuo replaced Kang Ze as the head of the Central Organization Department of the Sanmin Youth Corps, further tightening his control over the organization. In September 1947, during the sixth plenary session of the Kuomintang Central Committee and the Central Party-Corps Joint Conference, it was decided to merge the Sanmin Youth Corps into the Kuomintang. This merger allowed Chiang Ching-kuo, who had limited seniority and position within the Kuomintang, to smoothly become a senior official on its central committee. Simultaneously, all central officials of the Sanmin Youth Corps were converted to central executive committee members of the Kuomintang. Bao Zuxian and those in Chiang Ching-kuo's inner circle, who previously held the title of "central official of the Sanmin Youth Corps," became members of the Kuomintang Central Executive Committee after the merger. (The position of a Kuomintang Central Executive Committee member was equivalent to a member of the CCP's Politburo.)

After Japan's surrender, Chiang Kai-shek's prestige reached its zenith. Kuomintang officials seized enemy assets and amassed significant wealth. Though not a high-ranking official, my father, Bao Zuxian, had made notable contributions to the fight against Japan. In 1945, his specific role in the Sanmin Youth Corps was as an instructor for the third division of the Shanghai branch. After the party and the youth corps merged, from 1946 to 1948, he served as a member of the Kuomintang's Shanghai Municipal Executive Committee and a committee member of the Party Department in Dachang District. In 1947, he established a trading firm in Wusong. Serendipitously, a former junior high school classmate, Wang Shouchang, occupied a key role in Wusong as the Station chief of the Central Bureau of Investigation and Statistics (CBIS). The CBIS was the intelligence and secret police agency of the Nationalist government. Wang Shouchang recruited Bao Zuxian to join the CBIS. He filled out an application and received the credentials of a "CBIS special agent" (a name card, identical to a Western business card), but he was not listed on the CBIS official roster, never took on any tasks, and did not receive a salary. This part of history was repeatedly verified by the Communist courts and the special investigation team and is considered credible. In the business world, the credentials of a "CBIS special agent" brought Bao Zuxian many conveniences. At that time, dealing in rice was highly profitable, and it was impossible to do so without special privileges. Politically well-connected and economically prosperous, Bao Zuxian rented the ground floor at 122 Lane 340, Xinchang Road in the British Concession. The residence had entrances at both the front and back. The back entrance led to a private kitchen. He converted the courtyard at the front entrance by adding a glass roof and flooring, thus creating an additional large room. He built a loft above the rear living room to use as a storage room. Looking down from the loft, the full set of rosewood furniture, crystal chandeliers, and ceiling fans were quite eye-catching. In the front room, besides a complete set of rosewood furniture, there was an additional large wardrobe and a washstand with a marble countertop. The wardrobe was filled with British wool suits. He owned a British Raleigh bicycle, a German Leica camera, and a Watson electric fan. During his underground anti-Japanese activities, he held a military rank and had a fondness for guns. Living on Xinchang Road, he would go in and out in a suit, carrying a German pistol across his chest, which drew the attention of his neighbors. At the time, Bao Zuxian could be described as a quintessential diamond bachelor.

In 1945, Shanghai held the prestigious title of the most cosmopolitan city in the Far East, often referred to as the "Paris of the Orient." The aftermath of World War II marked a unique era for Sino-American relations. Hollywood films graced the screens of the Shanghai Grand Theater almost simultaneously with their release in American cinemas. Meanwhile, the Baxianqiao Young Men's Christian Association—YMCA—of Shanghai served throughout the Japanese War as a vital hub of patriotic resistance in the city. Ambitious individuals like my mother, Liu Hairong, knew where to seek opportunities. She had a long-standing interest in politics and was captivated by its aura of power. When the aforementioned Sanmin Youth Corps first established a branch in Shanghai, she eagerly applied for membership and actively recruited new members. Her unwavering dedication and competence swiftly earned the admiration of her immediate superior, Tang Mingkang. Recognizing her potential, Tang Mingkang appointed her as the captain of a Sanmin Youth Corps branch.

At that time, Tang Mingkang's superior, Bao Zuxian, came into her view. Politically, Bao Zuxian held positions in both the Kuomintang and the Sanmin Youth Corps. In terms of personal wealth, he owned his own rice shop and business. In the family, his parents had passed away early. In Liu Hairong's own words, the absence of her future in-laws was actually a welcome thing. She immediately sought Tang Mingkang's assistance in getting introduced to him.

Liu Hairong, who later became my mother, chose to keep this chapter of her life story concealed from her children. In a twist of fate, in 1965, I enrolled in Shanghai No. 62 Middle School. Tang Mingkang was one of the teachers there, and his daughter, Tang Lili, was one of my schoolmates. Although my time at the middle school was brief, I perpetually sensed Mr. Tang's watchful eye. In 1998, during a visit to China, my schoolmate Shi Taihua and I visited Tang Mingkang at his home, where we were joined by his daughter, Tang Lili. It was during this visit that Mr. Tang revealed to me the untold history between him and my parents. He recounted how, following the Era of Reevaluation, he had been labeled as a historical counter-revolutionary, a classification that had deterred him from reestablishing contact with my parents. The burden of their shared past was a secret they all carried, keeping their experiences hidden away. It was only with the advent of reform and openness in China that the silence could be broken. Mr. Tang had earned a well-deserved reputation as a prominent and accomplished figure within Shanghai No. 62 Middle School. In the past, when academic excellence held paramount importance, he had served as the head teacher of a key class. Though he had retired since the period of reform and opening up, the year-round bonuses and benefits for all the school's faculty and staff were intricately tied to the school-run factory established and managed by Mr. Tang. When asked about the impression left on him by my parents, Mr. Tang smiled and highlighted the stark contrast in their personalities. My father leaned towards conservatism, while my mother embodied a radical spirit; they appeared as two opposite ends of the spectrum. Mr. Tang often mused on what might have brought these two extremes together. Perhaps it was a match made in heaven.

As I write this, I think of Yuan Tengfei. In his book "Analysis of Women from Various Regions across the Country," Yuan offers vivid portrayals of Chinese women. He says that based on similarities in personality traits, Chinese women can be divided into nine major regions: the Jiang-Zhe-Hu region (Jiangsu, Zhejiang, and Shanghai), the

Shanhaiguan region (Shandong, Hebei, and Northeast China), the Chaoshan region, the Greater Wuhan region, the Xiangjiang region, the Bashan region, the Sichuan region, the Capital region, and the Central Plains region. In the "Jiangsu/Zhejiang/Shanghai Bloc" section, Yuan Tengfei states that, as someone born in the Jiangsu/Zhejiang/Shanghai region, he begins his analysis with the women from his home territory. The women from Jiangsu, Zhejiang, and Shanghai have similar personality traits and can be categorized into the first bloc. More precisely, this bloc includes the triangular areas of Shanghai, Nanjing, and Hangzhou. The first characteristic of Jiangsu/Zhejiang/Shanghai women is their adeptness at managing the household. This does not mean simply saving money, but rather spending where necessary and not spending where unnecessary. In terms of household management, Jiangsu/Zhejiang/Shanghai women rank first. The second characteristic is that they are the most practical and realistic. For instance, if a woman's husband suffers from kidney disease and the family is in poor financial condition, her first thought would not be to donate her own kidney to him, but rather to find another man who is strong and healthy. The third characteristic is that they have high intelligence and good fashion sense, and they are very adept at sweet-talking and deceiving men, making them willing to work hard for them. The hidden secret of Jiangsu/ Zhejiang/Shanghai women is that, although they are said to be gentle as water, they can actually be as fierce as tigresses, turning hostile without warning and leaving no room for reconciliation, showing no mercy or kindness. If one does not truly understand the dynamics, it is easy to be misled by the gentle facade of Jiangsu/Zhejiang/Shanghai women. You'd better remember this well. As for my mother's utilitarian nature, I am well aware. When the Kuomintang was in power, she married into the Kuomintang; when the Communist Party took over, she remarried into the Communist Party. But to be fair, she was not the only Chinese person who adhered to the principle of "I would rather betray the world than let the world betray me."

Grand Gonggong Erliang's eldest daughter was named Bao Qinxian and was one year older than my father. I affectionately referred to her as

Niangbo. My father and Niangbo were cousins, and they grew up together in the old Baoshan house. They were not only classmates in primary school but also attended Wusong Middle School together. Wu Chenghao, who later became Niangbo's husband, was also an alumnus of Wusong Middle School. Niangbo initially worked as a private teacher before her marriage, but she transitioned to being a housewife and raised three children after getting married. In those days, it was not common for women to pursue careers after marriage. Her husband worked as a civil servant in the Salt Bureau of the National Government, which required him to follow government postings. During the Anti-Japanese War, Niangbo and Wu Chenghao resided in Chongqing, and they later moved to Nanjing after the war. Their son was born in Nanjing. Wu Chenghao also worked in Building 18 on the Bund in Shanghai. However, before the Communist Party came into power, the Salt Bureau retreated to Taiwan, and they assisted Wu Chenghao's family in relocating there. His youngest daughter was born in Taiwan. Wu Chenghao was proficient in English and found employment with the American Aid Association, leaving his position at the Salt Bureau. Later, when the American Aid Association was dissolved, he began working at the U.S. Embassy in Taiwan. As a result of these opportunities, all three of Niangbo's children had the chance to pursue graduate studies in the United States and eventually establish families there. Her son and daughter resided in Los Angeles. Upon Wu Chenghao's retirement, he and Niangbo also relocated to Los Angeles to settle down.

In 1984, my first stop in the United States was Los Angeles, where I stayed with Niangbo for a few days. Niangbo shared stories of their generation with me. She said, "Your father just made one wrong move. When we went to Taiwan, he refused to go. But we didn't have a choice. We had three children, and our family of five relied solely on your uncle's salary. We had to follow his job". She went on, "Look at the people Little President (referring to Chaing Kai-shek's son and successor, Chiang Ching-kuo) is using now; they are all from your father's small circle back then. If your father had gone to Taiwan, you wouldn't need to work so hard to survive." Since the 1980s, Niangbo had visited mainland China for family reunions and sightseeing more than a dozen times. She and my father had met many times. The choice to leave or stay had always been a recurring topic. This decision determined their fate for the rest of their lives and the fate of the next generation. My father told Niangbo that within his circle of friends in the Kuomintang and Sanmin Youth Corps, including Chiang Ching-kuo, many decided to leave. The reason he didn't leave was straightforward. He said, "At that time, the Kuomintang was collapsing. Even Chiang Ching-kuo's future seemed bleak. I thought it was better to stay put. When the Kuomintang was in power, everyone knew my two brothers were in the Communist military, and no one troubled me. When the Communists came, having two brothers in the Party, I shouldn't face significant problems." At that time, Hong Kong was several tiers below Shanghai, and Taiwan was seen by many as a provincial backwater. Shanghai was my father's beloved home, and he couldn't bear to leave either the atmosphere or physical comfort of the place. Not to mention, he couldn't take the house and land in his nearby ancestral hometown of Baoshan with him. Later, I also asked my father the same question, and he gave the same answer. He said, "Back then in the Kuomintang, many had family members in the Communist Party. For example, Chiang Kai-shek's speechwriter, Chen Bulei's daughter was a Communist, and everyone knew it, and it was fine. I never expected the Communists to be so ruthless."

Starting in 1940, during the period of cooperation between the Kuomintang (KMT) and the CCP, my father Bao Zuxian, acting as an underground KMT member, was involved in the anti-Japanese resistance in Taicang. He introduced his two younger brothers to the Jiangnan Anti-Japanese Guerrilla Force, which was affiliated with the Communist Party's New Fourth Army. At that time, Bao Zongxian was 16 years old, and Bao Hongxian was only 14. The three brothers had very different personalities. Bao Zuxian was of medium height, conservative in nature, and adhered strictly to rules. At five-feet, eleven-inches, Bao Zongxian, the older of his two younger brothers, was tall and rebellious, and displayed bravery and cunning on the battlefield, making him a natural soldier. Admiring General Ye Ting, he replaced his given name of

Zongxian with Ting. Bao Ting joined the Anti-Japanese Guerrilla Force in the suburbs of Shanghai in 1939, the New Fourth Army in 1940, and the Communist Party in 1941. He then rose through the ranks from squad leader to platoon leader, company commander, battalion commander, commissar and chief of staff. After the national liberation, he was made an instructor at the Central Military Commission's Advanced Infantry School in Nanjing. In 1956, he was promoted to the rank of Lieutenant Colonel.

On the night of April 20th, 1949, the People's Liberation Army (PLA) crossed the Yangtze River on their way to the KMT capital of Nanjing. The next day the General Headquarters of the PLA issued a proclamation titled: "Statement of the Chinese People's Liberation Army on Crossing the Yangtze River." Thanks to the efforts of underground organizations embedded in various regions, this proclamation was widely disseminated even before the PLA arrived. The proclamation stated: "Except for incorrigible war criminals and extremely lawless reactionary elements, all officials of the Kuomintang central, provincial, municipal, and county governments, as well as representatives of the National Assembly, legislative and supervisory commissioners, senators, police personnel, and local administrators, who neither resisted with arms nor engaged in sabotage, would not be captured, arrested, or humiliated". These individuals were instructed to remain at their posts, obey the orders of the PLA and the People's Government, protect government property and archives, and await further instructions. Those among them who had skills and no serious reactionary behavior or records of misconduct were allowed to be employed by the People's Government. (Selected Works of Mao Zedong, Vol. 4, p. 1458.) Before the collapse of the Nationalist Government, many officials who saw this proclamation but accurately predicted they would not be tolerated under the new regime fled to Taiwan or Hong Kong. Those who trusted the proclamation and stayed behind did not meet a good end. In the spring of 1949, when his former classmate and KMT mentor Wang Shouchang of the Central Bureau of Intelligence and Statistics, retreated to Taiwan, my father lent him some gold for his journey. In April 1950, Zhang Yahua, a former secretary of the Baoshan County Kuomintang Party Committee and Bao Zuxian's cousin, retreated to Hong Kong, and my father provided him with financial assistance. These actions later became irrefutable evidence of my father's "counter-revolutionary crimes" and were recorded in his file.

When PLA units entered Shanghai, my father, Bao Zuxian, was standing at his rice shop on the corner of Huanghe Road and Beijing West Road. He immediately recognized his younger brother, Bao Zongxian, with the troops. The brothers had been separated for nearly ten years. Bao Zuxian said, "Let's go home." Bao Ting (Bao Zongxian) replied, "I'm leading the troops now. I'll see you tonight." When my uncles, Bao Ting and Bao Hongxian, were stationed with their units in Shanghai, they didn't have their own home. The family property in Baoshan hadn't been divided yet, so their elder brother's home was also theirs. Bao Ting always had guards and orderlies with him. The Xinchang Road community CCP made a red plaque reading "Glorious Family" to hang outside the door. Bao Zuxian also had military experience, albeit with the Kuomintang (KMT). During the anti-Japanese war efforts with the KMT underground party in Taicang, he held the rank of lieutenant. Although he never saw combat, he practiced his shooting skills and became an excellent shot. After the war, he held civilian positions in the KMT and the Youth Corps, but his fondness for guns remained. He liked to carry a finely crafted Browning pistol in a leather holster, which was quite stylish. However, under Communist law, possessing a firearm privately was a serious crime, and this gun became a source of anxiety for him. One day, he expressed his concern to Bao Ting. Bao Ting casually said, "I've confiscated thousands of guns. One more won't matter. Just give it to me." Bao Ting took the gun and gave his older brother a receipt. After 1950, grain trade and sales were nationalized. My father's business and rice shop closed, leaving him unemployed. His cousin Liu Yihou's wife, Zhu Shuizhao, had established the Yunhua Yue Opera Troupe in Shanghai and invited him to be the troupe's accountant. In 1954, Zhu Shuizhao moved the Yunhua Yue Opera Troupe to Nanjing, and my father went with them.

After the Chinese Communist Party (CCP) seized power, the

movement to suppress counter-revolutionaries, the land reform movement, and the Korean War effort were all carried out simultaneously and in coordination with each other. This created an atmosphere of fear and intimidation where virtually everyone was terrified of the Communist Party, allowing the CCP to strengthen its totalitarian rule. Among those executed during the "counter-revolutionary" campaign were many who had fought in the Anti-Japanese War to defend China, helping to save the country. These individuals were firsthand witnesses to the CCP's treasonous actions during the Anti-Japanese War—collaborating with Japanese forces while attacking the Nationalist army. They stand as living proof of this betrayal. The CCP knew that keeping these national elites alive meant preserving the truth about the Anti-Japanese War and the Chinese Civil War.

While the CCP did not take the more extreme approach of predecessors like the Jacobins or the Red Terror, or successors like the Khmer Rouge, in trying to execute all enemies and erase all traces of "counter-revolutionary" history in one blow, they never hesitated to kill a dozen or a hundred or a thousand such "enemies" when political campaigns presented the opportunity. The sentencing and execution of people during the suppression campaign were not based on the actual crimes of the individuals but on population ratios, with specific numbers of executions mandated for certain regions and cities. Which, from any perspective other than that of a CCP zealot, was a vile and absurd approach to government prosecutions. Initially, Mao Zedong demanded an execution ratio of 0.5 per thousand of the local population, and in more severe cases, up to 1 per thousand. Later, he allowed for exceptions but not exceeding 1.5 per thousand, with a maximum of 2 per thousand. On February 12, 1951, Mao Zedong directly telegraphed the leaders of the Shanghai and Nanjing municipal committees, saying: "Shanghai is a large city with a population of 6 million. Considering that over 20,000 people have been arrested and more than 200 executed, I believe that in 1951, at least 3,000 major criminals, habitual bandits, tyrants, spies, and gang leaders should be executed within the year. In the first half of the year, at least about 1,500 should be executed. Please consider whether this number is appropriate. In Nanjing, according to a February 3 telegram from Comrade Ke Qingshi to Comrade Rao Shushi, 72 people have been executed, and it is proposed to execute another 1,500. This number is too small. Nanjing is a large city with a population of 500,000 and was the capital of the Kuomintang, so it seems that more than 2,000 reactionaries should be executed. More executions are needed in Nanjing!"

According to the CCP's own statistics, the "Suppression of Counter-Revolutionaries" campaign resulted in the killing, imprisonment (labor reform), and surveillance (mass control) of approximately 3 million "counter-revolutionary" elements. In a report from January 1954, Deputy Minister of Public Security Xu Zirong stated that a total of 2.62 million people were arrested during the campaign, of which 712,000 were executed, representing 1.31 per thousand of the national population. Additionally, 1.29 million people were sentenced to labor reform, 1.2 million were placed under mass control, and 380,000 were released after ideological education. Further, according to a report compiled in 1996 by the Central Party History Research Office and three other departments, titled "Facts about Historical Political Movements since the Founding of the People's Republic of China," from early 1949 to February 1952, over 1,576,100 "counter-revolutionaries" were suppressed during the campaign, with more than 873,600 sentenced to death.

During the "Suppression of Counter-Revolutionaries" campaign, my father, Bao Zuxian, was arrested on September 16, 1955, in Nanjing due to his status as a "historical counter-revolutionary." He was held at the Nanjing Public Security Bureau Detention Center. In April 1957, he was sentenced to two years of public surveillance and supervision and returned to the theater troupe to serve his sentence. Typically, those labeled as "historical counter-revolutionaries" were treated as "internal contradictions among the people" and were not usually arrested or sentenced. However, less than three months later, in October 1957, he was imprisoned again. This time, he was charged with the crime of being a "current counter-revolutionary." Those convicted of "current counter-revolutionary crimes" were not only arrested but often sentenced to death.

An incident occurred in the summer of 1960 when Bao Zuxian was assigned to work in the drawing room at the Nanjing Detention Center. Someone discovered a piece of tracing paper used as a bookmark in a book, which had reactionary slogans written on it. The detention center's management concluded that Bao Zuxian was responsible. In December 1960, the Nanjing Intermediate People's Court issued a criminal judgment, charging Bao Zuxian with "writing reactionary slogans", and he was sentenced to life imprisonment. However, the "reactionary slogans" used as evidence of the crime were never shown or archived anywhere. Bao Zuxian repeatedly appealed, stating that he did not know what the "reactionary slogans" were and requesting verification. His appeals were all rejected, and the truth remained a mystery. One indisputable fact is that Bao Zuxian was arrested in October 1957 for "current counter-revolutionary crimes," but the incident of "writing reactionary slogans" occurred in the summer of 1960. It was evident that the verdict was decided first, and the evidence was sought afterward.

What is even more puzzling is that shortly after my father's second arrest in October 1957, his People's Liberation Army officer brother, Bao Ting, was also arrested in 1958. The brothers were convicted in the same case. My father was sentenced to life imprisonment, and Bao Ting was sentenced to twenty years in prison. The charges against Bao Ting were: "After entering Shanghai, he followed the instructions of his brother Bao Zuxian to provide information on the codenames of the 60th Division of the 20th Army, the unit's organization, deployment situation, and significant military intelligence about the Zhoushan Islands and the Korean War to his brother, who then passed it overseas." To substantiate my uncle's guilt, additional crimes were charged against my father: "He arranged for his younger brother Bao Ting to infiltrate the Jiangnan Anti-Japanese Guerrilla Forces to gather information on our troops' deployments and activities. After the liberation, Bao Ting followed our army into Shanghai and reconnected with the defendant. The defendant then instructed Bao Ting to continue collecting military intelligence for him." Due to my Uncle Bao Ting's unyielding attitude and refusal to admit his guilt and accept the verdict, he served the full twenty-year sentence without any reduction. In 1981, he was finally rehabilitated, with his party membership and military rank restored, and he was given a retirement status equivalent to that of a General Officer rank.

Upon his release from prison, Bao Ting discovered that his old comrades from the New Fourth Army, who had been promoted to various military command positions during Ye Ting's tenure as commander, had all experienced a transformation from revolutionaries to counter-revolutionaries. This process happened without exception, differing in timing and charges but always ending with the same result. Bao Ting and his fellow survivors may not have known that Gaozu Liu Bang, the rebellious peasant-turned-first-Han-Emperor, once said: "When the birds are gone, the good bow is hidden; when the cunning rabbits are dead, the hunting dogs are cooked." However, they knew it was their efforts and sacrifices that won victory over first the Japanese and then the Nationalists, through bloody battles, and then, when it was time for them to enjoy the fruits of their labor, they all ended up as prisoners.

In later years, when these surviving old comrades gathered, a regular topic of discussion was the "Southern Anhui Incident." This was a key event of the Chinese Civil War, also known as the "New Fourth Army Incident," when virtually the entire headquarters element of that army was annihilated in an ambush by the 36th Division of the Nationalist Army. This occurred in January 1941, during the Second United Front (1937~1945) truce between the KMT and CCP. At that time, the military forces of the Chinese Communist Party consisted primarily of two armies—the New Fourth Army and Eighth Route Army—so one would expect it to have been a severe blow to the overall military capacity of the CCP at the time. However, in the aftermath of the incident, the New Fourth Army managed to swiftly rebound from its severe leadership losses, almost all of which were suffered by individuals and factions seen by Mao as potential rivals, and all of which were quickly replaced by devoted loyalists. This enabled Mao to consolidate his personal control over both the New Fourth Army and the broader Communist Party apparatus. Before their arrest and imprisonment, noting these facts would have been punishable by imprisonment or worse, but after their release, my uncle Bao Ting and his comrades did not hesitate to theorise that the tragic Southern Anhui Incident, in which many had lost friends and brothers-in-arms, was a result of Mao employing the strategy of "killing with a borrowed knife". It was well-known that Mao was adept at eliminating political rivals, and Ye Ting— commander of the New Fourth Army—was not aligned with Mao, whereas Chen Yi was Mao's trusted ally. After Ye Ting's death, Mao appointed Chen Yi to take over the New Fourth Army. During the war, Chen Yi needed the surviving veteran officers from Ye Ting's system to competently lead the fight on the battlefield. Once the fighting ended in 1945, they were sidelined. After the professional combat leaders from Ye Ting's system had been purged, Chen Yi's people were promoted to their positions.

After gaining his freedom, Bao Ting visited his old superior, Su Yu, and his former subordinate, Chi Haotian. The old cadres of the New Fourth Army and the Third Field Army held Su Yu in high regard. When Su Yu saw my uncle, he expressed sympathy for his plight but explained that he couldn't help, fearing that any attempt to assist might backfire and do more harm than good. Several of the highest-ranking members of the Chinese Communist Party had always disliked Su Yu, making his life difficult. Despite considerable military achievements that should have earned him the rank of Marshal, his success made him a target of jealousy. When Mao Zedong needed Su Yu's service, he praised him lavishly. However, once Mao secured his own power, he disparaged Su Yu as a "bad person," causing Su to suffer for decades. In 1958, criticism against Su Yu was disseminated down to the regimental level, affecting the entire party and army. On October 9, 1979, Su Yu wrote a letter of appeal to then-Party leader Hua Guofeng, mentioning that the heavy criticism from over twenty years ago had been a painful burden on him. After the Third Plenary Session of the 11th Central Committee, many cases of wrongful persecution were redressed, and Su Yu earnestly requested that the central authorities review and redress his case. However, until Su Yu's death on February 5, 1984, his case was not rectified. Su Yu's wife summarised his life, saying that Su Yu suffered in war, suffered from persecution during peace, and suffered from illness in his later years. He followed the Communist "revolution" for sixty years, spending thirty of them in adversity.

The ultimate vindication of Su Yu was delayed until the end of 1994, after Deng Xiaoping had become too ill to manage affairs. At that time, Jiang Zemin had become both General Secretary of the Communist Party and President of the People's Republic of China, but still lacked a strong base of support in the military. Jiang was looking for opportunities to diminish Deng Xiaoping's unparalleled influence in the military and establish his own authority. Reassessing Su Yu's case was a good opportunity to do so. Su Yu's old subordinate, Vice Chairman of the Central Military Commission Zhang Zhen, proposed revisiting Su Yu's case. Another significant figure was Wang Daohan, who had been Su Yu's subordinate during the Japanese war and deeply admired him. Wang Daohan had consistently supported Jiang Zemin for decades. After Jiang became President in 1993, Wang Daohan believed the time was right and advised redressing Su Yu's case. Jiang Zemin readily agreed. By then, Su Yu had been dead for almost ten years, so it is questionable what this posthumous rehabilitation meant to him.

Chi Haotian enlisted in the military in 1945 and joined the Communist Party in 1946. From 1948 to 1950, he served as a company-level Political Officer in the Third Field Army, with Bao Ting serving as a battalion Commissar in the same unit. The military is a place with a strict hierarchy and respect for seniority. Bao Ting joined the military in 1940 and the Party in 1941, making him senior to Chi Haotian. Chi Haotian never faced any purges throughout his career and rose smoothly through the ranks, eventually becoming the Chief of the General Staff in 1987 and the Minister of National Defence in 1998. Despite his high position, Chi Haotian politely received his old superior, my uncle, when he came to visit. Bao Ting, however, was filled with anger and mocked the party's post-Cultural Revolution compensation policies meant to make up for past wrongs. He complained to Chi Haotian, "My former bugler is now a military region commander, yet I still am treated like a division-level commanding officer?" Chi Haotian tried to calm him down, saying, "You have a valid point. Your previous subordinates have risen to the rank of military region commanders, but they have reached retirement age. Is it appropriate for you to assume their positions?" When comparing their military qualifications and the fact that Bao Ting received his first military rank in 1955, it was clear that he held a higher standing than Chi Haotian. However, the two individuals were fundamentally different. Bao Ting had little choice but to accept his circumstances. The verdict of the Military Commission regarding his 20-year imprisonment was that "things happen for a reason, but no substantial evidence is found." The Kafkaesque nature of his case summary added insult to the injury of his two decades in prison and inflicted a severe blow to his spirit. The Party was right when they arrested him, and it was right when they released him. The Party is always great, glorious, and correct. Bao Ting's life experience made him realise this bandit logic, and after becoming its victim, he finally saw the true nature of the "revolution" as a demon. The summary of the investigation into his wrongful imprisonment case was both the last straw that broke the camel's back and the final incineration that enabled the phoenix's rebirth. The "lofty ideals" he had pursued since his student days, for which he was willing to sacrifice his life, completely collapsed. Bao Ting, who was over 5 ft. 11 in. tall, suddenly seemed to shrink. As a veteran of the War of Resistance against Japan in 1940, Bao Ting retired with the status of a General Officer rank, which provided him with a very generous compensation package. However, he refused to pay Party dues. The structure of the Communist Party is akin to joining a gang. The Party oath includes the phrase, "Keep the Party's secrets, and never betray the Party." Once you join the Party, you can never quit. Resignation is seen as betrayal, an impossible action. Bao Ting cursed the Communist Party at home every day, shouting out loud: "If you have the guts, drag me out and shoot me!" The managers at his retirement home had no way to silence his reckless declarations, so they restricted his activities and treated him like a madman.

In the summer of 1998, my father, Bao Zuxian, passed away in Shanghai. At the memorial service at Longhua Funeral Home, I met my two uncles for the first time. In the summer of 2000, my brother and I went to Nantong to visit our elder uncle. He was living in a retirement home specially built for former senior cadres of the New Fourth Army. This was the second time I met him, and the first time we ever had a heart-to-heart talk. I said, "My father was undeniably a member of the Kuomintang, so he could not complain about being imprisoned by the Communist Party. However, it was unfair for you and Uncle Hongxian to be implicated. After all, you both risked your lives for the Communist Party." Bao Ting replied, "It's debatable who implicated whom. It's quite possible that to solidify the counter-revolutionary case against me, your father had to be labeled as a current counter-revolutionary." Bao Ting had discovered that while he was still fighting on the Korean battlefield, his unit had already designated him as a target for the "Suppression of Counter-Revolutionaries" target to meet the quotas set by higher authorities. Since his brother Bao Zuxian was a historical counter-revolutionary, it was convenient to label Bao Ting as a "class alien element infiltrating the revolutionary ranks." He sighed and told me, "Chengmo, our Bao family served the emperors, your father served the Kuomintang, and I served the Communist Party. Serving the Communist Party was not as good as serving the Kuomintang, and serving the Kuomintang was not as good as serving the emperors." Hearing these words from a 74-year-old veteran who joined the revolution at 18 and risked his life in battle for the Communist Party was truly shocking for me! Uncle Bao Ting's words summed up the essential truth of the Chinese Communist revolution. It's not new; it's just a repetition of history, another regime change with a different group of people sitting on the throne. If there's any difference, it's that this group is worse than the previous ones.

Unlike his older brother, Bao Ting, Uncle Hongxian didn't hold a high position in the military and had been severely injured in the Korean War, so the Communist Party spared him and didn't give him a hard time. However, the experiences of his two brothers terrified him, and for decades, he severed all ties with the Bao family. After transitioning out of the military, he began working as the Communist Party Secretary at Suzhou Medical College. Over time, his position gradually declined until he was the least significant among the deputy secretaries. Unlike Uncle Bao Ting, who was fiery and strong-willed, Uncle Hongxian had a gentle personality. He endured hardships without complaints and did not seek power. Therefore, despite facing numerous challenges during the various political movements, he ultimately avoided imprisonment.

3. Liu family in Shanghai

In 1919, at the age of 25, my third maternal great-uncle followed his fellow townsman from Wuxi, Uncle Lu, to Shanghai. By then, Uncle Lu had already become prosperous by running a rice shop in Shanghai. He facilitated Third Great Uncle's entry into the industry by securing a position at a rice store and arranging accommodations for him. In the vicinity of Quyuan Lane's entrance, a small subdivided room was occupied by Mr. Fu and his family, who also hailed from Wuxi. Fu Lanfen, Mr. Fu's eldest daughter, developed an affection for the handsome Third Great Uncle. But he was already married and had a little daughter back in Wuxi, where he returned to once a month. When he told his family about Fu Lanfen, they were all opposed. However, Fu Lanfen was willing to be a concubine without first-wife status and still very much wanted to marry him. Eventually, two years later, my Third Great Uncle married Fu Lanfen. One year later, in 1922, his business flourished. He rented No. 7 in Quyuan at the intersection of Jianguo West Road and South Shaanxi Road, and brought his wife Wang Peizhen and their eldest son, Yihou, who was born in Wuxi in 1921, to Shanghai. My Third Great Uncle and Third Great Aunt Wang Peizhen had four sons: the second son Chenghou, the third son Dinghou, and the fourth and youngest son Shaohou. My Third Great Uncle passed away in Quyuan in 1932. Back in 1922, he had also brought his two younger brothers to Shanghai to learn the business. The Fourth Great Uncle lacked ambition and was addicted to opium, and he passed away relatively young. Subsequently, the Fifth Great Uncle also moved to Quyuan, renting No. 8 next door.

Good flowers don't bloom all the time, and good times don't last forever. With the passing of my grandmother's mother-in-law and my grandfather, and with my grandfather's three younger brothers moving to Shanghai, the bustling atmosphere of No. 35 Cotton Lane faded away. The old house in Wuxi seemed to have completed its historical mission. My Third Great Uncle and Fifth Great Uncle worked as brokers at foreign firms, dealing in trade and stocks. Their households suddenly became prosperous, attracting many relatives who formed a close-knit circle around them. At that time, my grandmother's financial situation was not as good, with one son and one daughter still minors. The Liu family reached an agreement: my uncle Liu Hongying would live with my Fifth Great Uncle, who would act as his guardian, while my mother, Liu Hairong, would live with the Third Great Aunt, who would serve as her guardian. My grandma remained in her ancestral home, becoming a revered figure in the Liu family. The Third and Fifth Great Aunts repeatedly invited my grandmother to Shanghai to enjoy a comfortable life. My grandmother accepted their kindness with gratitude and stayed in Shanghai for a few days. They treated her with the utmost respect, as if she were their own mother, providing private cars, delicacies, and fine clothing to please her. Seeing her husband's brothers and their wives enjoying good lives made my grandmother genuinely happy, and she blessed them. She said, "You deserve your success, but I can't accept such treatment. A gold home or a silver home is not as good as one's own straw home." She had little interest in the endless, frivolous "icing on the cake" activities, and her heart was tied to her Buddhist hall. Soon, she bid farewell to her sisters-in-law and returned to her old home in Wuxi, never to visit Shanghai again. My grandmother always undervalued material pleasures, adhering firmly to principles of self-respect and self-discipline. She would say, "Wealth and glory are fleeting; virtues and morals are timeless."

My mother's feelings toward her mother were quite complex; she respected and admired her, while also fearing, and later rebelling, against her. During the years in Cotton Lane, Wuxi, the Liu family was able to live together under the same roof. My grandmother had her mother-in-law above her, and below her were brothers-in-law, sisters-in-law, and nieces. She was the backbone of the large family. Her mettle was somewhat legendary. She worked for the Rong family for ten years, earning the trust of both Rongs and the female workers, serving as de facto foreman, and eventually bringing a house to the Liu family. My mother once said, "If your grandmother were educated, she would certainly have been remarkable." On the other hand, my grandmother's favoritism toward my uncle (her son) and disregard for my mother (her daughter) were a perpetual source of pain for my mother. My grandmother had strong beliefs: she believed in Buddhism and that boys were the hope of the family, so it was natural for her to favor sons over daughters. This attitude infuriated my mother from a young age. After moving to Shanghai to live with her third aunt, my mother grew close to her and treated her like her own mother, even making us call her "Grandmother." Deep down, my mother desperately wanted her own mother's approval, but their values were fundamentally at odds. Grandma revered moral principles, while my mother worshiped power; Grandma stood for conscience, while my mother sided with the winners; Grandma valued self-reliance, dignity, and self-discipline, while my mother saw opportunism and outshining others as the markers of success.

My mother spent her teenage years in the illusory prosperity of Shanghai, and the success of her third and fifth uncles' families broadened her horizons. The profit-driven mentality of businessmen began to take root in her. She had a relentless spirit and her own ambitions, and was determined not to live at the mercy of others. Grandma once introduced a suitor to my mother, a Wuxi native who ran a modest shop in Shanghai, and told her, "Peace is a blessing." This notion was utterly unacceptable to my mother. She was determined to show her mother and everyone else what she was capable of. When she succeeded in marrying my well-off father, she felt triumphant, but Grandma did not share her excitement, which left my mother with a sense of loss. My mother's unscrupulous methods to achieve her goals disgusted my grandmother, who accepted her failure in raising her daughter and placed her hopes on the next generation. Under Grandma's guidance, I grew up with a reverence for the divine and embraced her values of helping others in times of need rather than opportunistically exploiting them. I understood Grandma's deep disappointment in my mother. My mother, realizing she could not connect with my grandmother or me, often felt frustrated. She found herself powerless against my grandmother and even feared that I, her son, would grow up to be just as difficult to deal with. From an early age, my mother saw me as an adversary, constantly setting up barriers and obstructions. An acquaintance familiar with our family dynamics once remarked, "Your mother guards against fire, theft, and her own son."

My mother and grandmother never had a close relationship. After my uncle passed away, my mother was my grandmother's sole remaining child. Logically, they should have lived together to take care of each other, especially since Wuxi and Shanghai are geographically close. However, from what I can remember, Grandma never came to Shanghai. Upon Grandma's request, my mother took me to Wuxi to visit her twice a year, during the winter and summer vacation times. My grandmother was illiterate and couldn't read or write, so there was no way for my mother to communicate with her through letters, and they had little daily interaction. This arrangement may have been wise on both their parts, as they understood that maintaining a distance allowed them to remain polite to each other.

My Uncle, Liu Yihou, the eldest son of my Third Great Aunt, made a name for himself in Shanghai through great success with stock market speculation. First, he flaunted his wealth by renting long-term rooms at the prestigious Park Hotel. Later in 1948, he used ten gold bars to secure the property at 11 Taira New Village, Taiyuan Road. After he and his mother's joyful relocation, Taira New Village experienced a few years of lively and glamorous days. Following the end of the Japanese war, as people began to enjoy peace, the soft and melodious Yue opera became very popular in Shanghai. My Third and Fifth Great Aunts became Yue opera fans. Famous Yue opera stars like Yuan Xuefen, Qi Yaxian, Yin Guifang, Fan Ruijuan, and Fu Quanxiang recognized my Third Great Aunt as their godmother and frequently visited 11 Taira New Village. Among the most popular celebrities of that post-Japanese-War era were the critically acclaimed stars known as the "Ten Sisters of Yue Opera".

Yihou became romantically involved with Yin Guifang, one of the famed Ten Sisters. They spent private time together on the third floor of my Fifth Great Uncle's house, where Yihou resided. In those days, an unmarried couple cohabitating was considered a serious transgression. But my Fifth Great Uncle, a devout Buddhist, found himself unable to do anything to change the behavior of his nephew, Yihou, other than pleading with the Bodhisattva during his daily sutras to forgive his nephew Liu Yihou's misconduct. Before long, however, Liu Yihou became captivated by another of the "Ten Sisters"—Yin Guifang's stage partner, Zhu Shuizhao, whose real name was Zhu Yunhua. Zhu Shuizhao was widely celebrated in the Yue Opera world not only as a peerless beauty but also for her remarkable talent and radiant stage presence. Among devoted fans, she was affectionately known as the "Xi Shi of Yue Opera" (China's Helen of Troy). Xi Shi was one of the Four Great Beauties of ancient China, a legendary figure from the State of Yue during the Spring and Autumn Period, around 500 BC. She played the key role in the famous "beauty trap" strategy used by the statesman Fan Li in the service of King Goujian of Yue to usher in the defeat and ultimate destruction of his rival, King Fuchai, and the state of Wu. Because of this, Xi Shi is often referred to as the Chinese Helen of Troy. According to legend, she was so breathtakingly beautiful that when she washed silk by the river, her reflection on the water so mesmerized the fish that they would forget how to swim and sink to the bottom.

In September 1947, Zhu Shuizhao founded the Yunhua Yue Opera Troupe at the Shanghai Cathay Theatre. In February 1948, the troupe moved to the Longmen (Dragon Gate) Theatre. My uncle Liu Yihou succeeded in winning Zhu Shuizhao's favor, and in 1949, they fled to Hong Kong and got married there. It is estimated that one million Chinese fled Mainland China for Hong Kong in the year 1949, driven by the looming Communist takeover, which came to fruition with the official establishment of the People's Republic of China on October 1st, 1949. However, unlike the vast majority of Chinese, Liu Yihou and Zhu Shuizhao were not fleeing from the Communists but from the society pages, scandal-sheet reporters, and paparazzi in Shanghai.

In fact, Yin Guifang and Zhu Shuizhao had shared a deep and complex friendship long before my uncle came into both of their lives. The two became close during their teenage years, forged through hardship. In a memoir published in Nanking Daily in 1988, Yin wrote: "Shuizhao was like a sister to me—sisters not by blood, but by suffering...In 1937, I was nineteen, and she was seventeen when we began performing together. From the very beginning, we weathered a storm of adversity side by side." That year, the two were unjustly detained in Huangyan, Zhejiang Province, and held for fifty-one days. After their release, they took a vow of sisterhood at the Chenghuang Temple and became inseparable, supporting each other like family.

In the autumn of 1940, Yin Guifang and Zhu Shuizhao performed together at the Tongle Grand Theater in Shanghai, staging traditional Yue opera classics such as Liang Shanbo and Zhu Yingtai (China's Romeo and Juliet) and the Legend of the White Snake. Yin Guifang played the male lead (Xiaosheng), while Zhu Shuizhao took on the female role (Huadan). Their onstage chemistry was said to be "seamless" and "brilliant." Offstage, they shared nearly every aspect of daily life—living, eating, and working together. Audiences adored them, calling them the "Golden Couple" and "Stage Lovers." However, as their careers took different paths and romantic entanglements complicated their relationship, the two eventually went their separate ways.

Liu Yihuo and Zhu Shuizhao returned together from Hong Kong to Shanghai in 1951, and Zhu Shuizhao gave birth to the first of their three daughters, named Liu Kemei. While they'd been gone, the new Communist Party government had shut down the Shanghai stock market, along with virtually all other forms of market-based and speculative investment. This left my uncle Liu Yihou, the financial speculator, without prospects, while his opera star wife continued her success. She reorganized her Yunhua Yue Opera Troupe with the noted singers Shang Fangchen, Xiao Shuizhao, Jiang Hong'ao, and others. In 1954, Liu Yihou accompanied Zhu Shuizhao and her troupe to perform in Jiangsu province, and then settled in its capital city of Nanjing, where it went on to become an experimental private-public partnership. In March 1956, it was nationalized and renamed the Nanjing Yue Opera Troupe, with Zhu Shuizhao as leader.

Throughout the 1950s, most of the "Ten Sisters of Yue Opera" left Shanghai and took their opera companies with them. A perfect example of this was Yin Guifang moving her Fanghua Yue Opera—which she had reorganized in 1948—to Fuzhou, Fujian Province, in 1959, opening a new chapter in her career. Yin would go on to survive physical persecution during the Cultural Revolution, but it left her partially paralyzed. In the 1980s, she visited my Third Great Aunt in Shanghai, arriving in a wheelchair, visibly frail and aged. It was a sad reunion. In the year 2000, Yin Guifang passed away in Shanghai at the age of 81.

The relocation of virtually all the leading opera companies from Shanghai in the 1950s was spun by the government as a patriotic movement to "spread revolutionary culture to the people," but in reality, these artists wanted to escape the heightened sensitivity and extreme visibility of Shanghai for the less highly-charged atmospheres of secondary cities. Before 1949, Shanghai had been a KMT stronghold and the commercial and cultural capital of China, so the new Communist government's scrutiny there was extremely intense.

Zhu Shuizhao had a fierce and unyielding personality. Zhu Shuizhao's tragic death in 1968 has remained the most sensitive and unspoken subject within the Liu family. Between 1967 and 1968, as the campaign against "those in power taking the capitalist road" intensified in Nanjing, and as the head of her Yue Opera troupe, Zhu Shuizhao became a prime target. She was repeatedly paraded on stage to be publicly criticized and humiliated. The troupe had an affiliated performing arts school, where her eldest daughter, Liu Kemei, was a student, along with several children of her husband, Liu Yihou's, old friends. This group of young performers, whom Zhu had personally raised and mentored since childhood, later became the most zealous Red Guards and showed her no mercy during the struggle sessions. At this time, Kemei was romantically involved with a man surnamed Wu, a member of the troupe's "investigation group," which was responsible for humiliating Zhu. Later, with the support of her father, Liu Yihou, she would marry this man. As for how Liu Yihou himself treated his wife Zhu Shuizhao while she was the ongoing public target of politically-driven personal attacks—despite years of trying, I have never been able to learn that part of the story from anyone with firsthand knowledge. But what cannot be ignored, denied, or swept under the rug is that combined weight of political persecution and family betrayal tragically led to the end of Zhu Shuizhao's life.

After one public denunciation meeting led by her troupe's Red Guards, Zhu ran into Kemei outside the opera troupe's communal water room and asked for a drink from her thermos flask. Her daughter refused, saying, "The water's not boiled." Zhu opened her daughter's flask anyway—only to have the scalding heat from the cap burn her fingers. Soon after this incident, Zhu Shuizhao committed suicide in a disturbingly painful way, repeatedly stabbing herself in the abdomen with a small fruit knife.

Since learning the truth behind Zhu Shuizhao's death years after it occurred, I have been unable to separate her spectacular success performing and directing love stories on stage from the profoundly dismal way those she loved the most in real life treated her offstage. I have also wondered whether her choice of how to die was driven by guilt or anger. Anger at the husband who failed to support her and contributed to her suffering, and at the daughter who, with chilling indifference, turned her back on her, or guilt for choosing to marry and stay with one, and giving life to and raising the other. Whether the reason was one or both of those, or something completely different, neither I nor the rest of the world will ever know. But I do know it would not have happened if not for the 1949 communist "Liberation" and resulting creation of the People's Republic of China, and its 1966-1976 Great Proletarian Cultural Revolution. Her death stemmed from a profound despair brought on by both political persecution and the absence of familial love; it also served as a powerful indictment of authoritarianism and the cruelty of human indifference.

Ironically, years later, after the end of the Cultural Revolution, Liu Kemei adopted the stage name Zhu Xiaozhao—meaning "Junior Zhao"—identifying herself as her mother's legitimate heir and the torchbearer of her artistic legacy. To this day, she relies on her mother's name to make a living. In the late 1980s, Liu Yihou's second daughter, Liu Xunmei, married a mid-level Communist Party cadre's son in Nanjing. This was the subject he liked to discuss with visitors: boasting about Xunmei's successful marriage. When I visited China in the year 2000, I invited several Liu family cousins to a dinner party at a restaurant in Shanghai owned by Liu Yihou's nephew, Liu Zhengyang. Liu Xunmei showed up along with her teenage daughter. It turned out her husband couldn't make it because he was serving a prison sentence for corruption. Later, I learned that after her husband was arrested, Liu Xunmei went to the courthouse and knelt on the ground outside the entrance, asking for mercy. When I first heard the story, I felt as if we were still living in the Middle Ages. Even now, looking back, I still feel shocked.

I feel that the tragedy of Zhu Shuizhao and many others is like a story out of Kafka. They lived in a world that was like a nightmare— strange, confusing, and unfair. They were trapped by a powerful system that didn't make sense and didn't care about people. As individuals, they were small and powerless. Their dignity was taken away, and they were left at the mercy of a cruel fate. They tried to fight back, hoping for a better life, but instead were completely crushed. Their pain and loneliness weren't just their own—it was the shared fate of countless silent families.

My Third Great Aunt had four sons and no daughters. She treated my mother, Hairong, as if she were her own daughter. However, the condescending attitude of "big brother" Liu Yihou towards Hairong left an indelible shadow in her heart. She described herself as "the poor relative of a rich family" and lamented that her "warm face couldn't melt a cold heart." Yet, Liu Hairong was not one to admit defeat easily; she was determined to make others look at her with new respect. As Bao Zuxian's wife, she could finally hold her head high. She bid farewell to her impoverished past, transforming perfectly from an ugly duckling into a beautiful swan. Her wedding photo was in the style of British and American. She wore a pristine white wedding dress, had her hair styled in large Hollywood waves, held a bouquet of lilies, wore a Swiss Enicar gold watch on her wrist, and had high heels on her feet. This photo hung on the wall of their room on Xinchang Road for over a decade. She wore a satisfied smile in the photo, and she had every reason to feel proud of herself. She enjoyed working as a teacher and had no interest in being a housewife. After getting married, she continued teaching at a small school. All her salary went into a private savings account, while all household expenses were covered by her husband. My mother had a firm grasp on my father's easygoing nature, and it wasn't long before his savings and bank accounts were all placed under her name.

She considered her Third Aunt's prosperous family as her own. Her relationship with her Third Aunt and her cousins was amicable and harmonious. They didn't live together and so were spared the daily frictions of life. After giving birth to her first child, she returned home from the hospital in a rickshaw with her new daughter, Shenjie. Two of her cousins, Chenghou and Dinghou, rode bicycles in front and behind her, like bodyguards. However, relationships between people can be strange. Whether it is between spouses or relatives, once a pattern is established, it is hard to change. After her "big brother" cousin Yihou made a fortune on the stock exchange, he assumed a prominent leadership role in the extended family and looked down on everyone. Though born at 35 Cotton Lane in Wuxi, he never revisited the old home. He disdained to look back, convinced that his wealth made him a big boss. Though he lived in Shanghai, he never visited Xinchang Road, even when passing nearby, even though his mother visited often, and later even when his own daughters were guests there. My mother spent her whole life trying to integrate into her Third Aunt's family, but "big brother" Yihou's attitude constantly reminded her: no matter how close, you are still an "outsider." This remained a lifelong pain in her heart.

My Third Great Aunt's house was at Taira New Village, Lane 188, Taiyuan Road. However, the large Iron Gate at the entrance of Lane 188 was always locked, so residents had to enter through Fulu (Prosperity) Village, Lane 384, Jianguo West Road. On the north side of Lane 188 was a wall. Inside the wall at No. 160 Taiyuan Road stood Taiyuan Villa. The wall wasn't very high, so from the second or third floor of my Third Great Aunt's house, the entire Taiyuan Villa was visible. When I was young, my friends and I would play soccer in the alley, and sometimes the ball would accidentally fly over the wall into Taiyuan Villa's lawn. Taiyuan Villa's main gate was on Taiyuan Road. We would run to the gate on Taiyuan Road and knock, and the soldier on duty would throw the ball back over the wall. This building is an exemplar of French Second Empire architecture, featuring a Mansard roof, French windows, intricate fleurde-lis motifs, and castle-like conical towers that exude a subtle grandeur. Originally constructed at the end of World War I for Comte Maurice Frederic Armand du Pac de Marsoulies, a retired French civil servant, it was later owned by the Dieckmann Trading Company. This villa witnessed subsequent historical moments. In December 1945, American General George Marshall stayed here, making the residence famous in Shanghai as the "Marshall Mansion." At that time, he was attempting to negotiate peace between the Chinese Communist Party and the Kuomintang. In November 1946, the negotiations broke down, and two months later, Marshall left Shanghai with sorrow. In 1947, Marshall proposed the European Recovery Program (ERP), also known as the Marshall Plan. The plan was officially implemented in 1948, playing a significant role in helping Western European countries recover their postwar economies and achieving great success.

The first floor, once Marshall's dining and drawing room, now serves as a Shanghai-style restaurant. Nearly eighty years have passed since Marshall's regretful departure, but the structure of the rooms remains the same, and even the wooden floor has no cracks. Marshall's second-floor bedroom was a two-room suite furnished with exquisite rosewood furniture, including antique wardrobes flanking a Chinese-style rosewood bed. The spacious bathroom was richly adorned with white marble. The expansive garden, an 8,780-square-meter fairyland, resonates with the melody of birds and features green camphor, red maple, and golden Chinese parasol trees. For the first 30 years after 1949, Taiyuan Villa served as a government guesthouse, hosting notable figures such as Liu Shaoqi, Zhu De, Dong Biwu, Zhou Enlai, and Jiang Qing at various times. During the 1980s and 1990s, Taiyuan Villa was an important location in Shanghai for receiving dignitaries and distinguished guests from various countries. Over the years, Taiyuan Villa stood silent witness to countless stories and events. I remember a particular day in 1960 when the Communist Party's neighborhood committee issued strict instructions to all residents: a state leader was going to stay at Taiyuan Villa, and everyone with rooms facing it had to keep their curtains drawn all day and leave the lights on throughout the night. Soldiers patrolled the villa's lawn, closely monitoring any movement in the houses opposite and promptly issuing warnings to residents for any suspicious activities.

Taira New Village, where my Third Great Aunt and her family lived, was a Western-style lane built in 1943, featuring a row of three-story British-style terraced villas. The houses have three floors above ground. The kitchen is equipped with a gas stove. There is a boiler room in the basement, used for heating water during the winter. The house is equipped with a telephone. From Fulucun, Lane 384, Jianguo West Road, you enter Taira New Village. At the entrance of the lane, there is a row of garages for parking private cars. In the middle of the lane, there is a small garden with some shrubs and flowers. At the end of the lane on the right is Taira New Village. The exterior walls of the houses are light yellow cement with a textured finish. The outer walls and the balconies on the second floor feature curved corners. Each house has a black lacquered iron gate as the front door, and behind the gate is a small garden. When you open the front door, there is an open hall, the front half of which can be used as a living room and the back half as a dining room. Behind the dining room wall is a corner staircase. Going down a few steps behind the staircase, you reach the semi-basement kitchen. The kitchen has a gas stove, and going down a few more steps from the kitchen, you reach the boiler room, used for heating the house with a steam heating system in the winter. "水汀" (si tīng) is a Shanghainese Chinglish word for "steam," both a transliteration and a translation.

Such creative translations of English terms were popular in Shanghai at the time. For instance, "fry pan" was translated as "发来盘" (fā lái pán), and "starter" as "斯达特" (sī dá tè). In the late 1950s, some old workers from the gas company came to install a gas stove in our home. They were illiterate but spoke fluent English, which surprised me greatly. They explained that when they were apprentices, the supervisors at the gas company were all British or American, and the tools and parts were not available in China. Therefore, everyone in the company spoke English and had to speak English. The principle of the steam heating system is simple: water is boiled in the boiler, and the steam is sent through pipes to each room, providing powerful heating that keeps the entire house warm without being dry. Having a private telephone in the house was rare at that time. The south-facing, large room on the second floor was my Third Great Aunt's bedroom. Outside the large bedroom was a big balcony, with a small garden below. My mother lived in the small north-facing room on the second floor. Outside the window of the small room was the neatly trimmed lawn of Taiyuan Villa.

Between the large and small rooms was the bathroom. The bathroom was tiled in black and white, with a flush toilet and a large bathtub. The third floor originally was the bedroom of Liu Yihou, my Third Great Aunt's eldest son, and his wife, the famed Yue opera star, Zhu Shuizhao. The walls were decorated with large photos of Zhu Shuizhao in opera costumes. After 1954, Zhu Shuizhao and her husband Yihou had moved to Nanjing, so the third floor was empty for a long time. At that point, only two people lived in this three-story house: my Third Great Aunt and her granddaughter, Liu Jiemei. Jiemei later recalled her childhood in Taira New Village and the unsettling memories of the near-empty house, which made her scared at night. Later, the third floor was rented out to a relative, Shi Fengyi, and her husband. Shi Fengyi's sister, Shi Fengshu, was the eldest daughter-in-law of my Fifth Great Uncle. Their father, Shi Xiaoshan, was a famous Chinese traditional medicine doctor. In 1968, during the Cultural Revolution, the Red Guards of Zhu Shuizhao's troupe came to Shanghai and kicked my Third Great Aunt out of the house and she was forced to relocate to Yiyuan (Noble Garden), next to Jianye Lane on Jianguo West Road and Yueyang Road. In Taira New Village, she and her granddaughter lived in a three-story house, but in Yiyuan, she was allocated a living room on the first floor of someone else's house, and the two of them lived in that one room. Fortunately, the room faced south and received some sunlight. Outside was a small patch of open-air patio without any plants.

My Third Great Uncle and his concubine, Fu Lanfen, had six children: daughter Liu Yufang (1922~1996), son Liu Zhonghou (1924~2015), daughter Liu Guofang, daughter Liu Hanfang, son Liu Kunhou, and daughter Liu Yuefang. They have many stories. The eldest daughter, Liu Yufang, whom I called Big Aunt, was married to Shen Shenhua (1915~1976), who was proficient in five languages and had a thriving business in machinery import and export.

In the later stages of the civil war, the Nationalist government's economy collapsed, and its Gold Yuan notes became worthless. From that point on, Shen Shenhua conducted business with foreigners using gold as the medium of exchange. Six safes were filled with foreign currency, gold bars, and diamonds purchased to preserve value. Naturally, the Communist Party saw him as a big fish to devour. Their method was to accuse him of being a "German spy," send him to the Bai Maoling labor camp in Anhui for "reformation through labor," and confiscate all of his property.

For various stretches of time after Mao's reign began in 1949, the court system throughout China was purged and supplanted by political and administrative bodies. Of course, the most extreme and long-lasting of these periods was during the Cultural Revolution, when the entire Ministry of Justice was literally abolished in 1966 and not restored until 1979. Shen Shenhua was never formally tried or sentenced. By 1975, his health had seriously deteriorated. Since the authorities had no real evidence of espionage, they allowed him to return home to Shanghai. Neither he nor his family ever received a formal written notice of acquittal—they simply assumed he was cleared. After all, if he had been found guilty, he would have been sent directly to prison and would not have been allowed to return home. Even so, he was warned: "Behave yourself. We can take you back in at any time." After being sent back to Shanghai, he received a token amount of economic compensation. But two decades of physical and mental torment in the labor camp had completely broken Shen Shenhua. He didn't even dare to think about reclaiming his confiscated property and died less than one year later, of grief and despair.

When capitalists exploit people, it is fundamentally a transaction—you still have a choice. However, when the Communist Party exploits people through power, it is outright robbery. The essence of the Communist "revolution" was to legitimize robbery and murder. Shen Shenhua's story reflects the common practice of the CCP: they never admit to their mistakes. Have they ever apologized for the Great Famine of 1960, which claimed an estimated 37 million lives? Of course not. In the eyes of the CCP, Shen Shenhua was guilty regardless of any lack of evidence. His mere identity as a capitalist was considered a crime. Under the Party's ideology, capitalists are enemies by definition—facts or innocence are irrelevant. Shen Shenhua's story reminds me of Aesop's fable *The Wolf and the Lamb*: no matter how the lamb defends itself, the wolf insists it is guilty. The reasoning doesn't matter—the verdict is predetermined: "You're guilty, no matter what."

Big Aunt's home was at Lane 20, North Shaanxi Road, located at the northeast corner of the intersection of North Shaanxi Road and Yan'an Road. Lanes 10, 20, and 30 of North Shaanxi Road are typical examples of high-end residential areas in Shanghai's western district. Built in the 1930s, these three-story Western-style lane houses were designed by architect Fan Wenzhao, who also designed other notable buildings in Shanghai, such as the Nanjing Grand Theater (now the Shanghai Concert Hall), the Majestic Theatre, and the YMCA building at Baxianqiao. The house layout was neat, attractive, and elegant. The first floor contained the living room and dining room. The kitchen was a few steps lower than the main floor. The gas stove in the kitchen had four burners on top, with a square oven below. This style of gas stove was still popular in the United States as of 2020, showing how advanced it was 90 years ago. The second and third floors each had two large bedrooms with built-in closets and bathrooms with large bathtubs. The south-facing bedrooms had large steel windows, providing ample sunlight, and spacious balconies outside the French windows. There was also a north-facing attic room between the floors. Yue Opera actresses Qi Yaxian and Bi Chunfang also lived on this lane, and Big Aunt was friendly with them. When they went on tour to perform in other places, they left their house keys with Big Aunt, entrusting her to look after their homes.

From my home on Xinchang Road, Shaanxi North Road was within walking distance, so I often visited Big Aunt's house. I never saw her husband, Uncle Shen Shenhua, because, like my father, he was imprisoned for many years. Big Aunt's mother, Fu Lanfen, lived on Shaanxi North Road for a long time, so I saw her often. I called her

"Granny Lan." Granny Lan was skillful and humorous, with a pleasant personality that made her very approachable to the younger generation. Using ordinary white yarn and a crochet needle, she crafted pillowcases, coffee table covers, and other items, each a delicate work of art. Her crocheted items looked best against a dark background, with patterns that were always uniquely vibrant and distinct. Big Aunt was a skillful and eloquent person. We nicknamed her "Big Fat Aunt" because her elders and peers called her that. During Mao's era, China was a time of hunger, and it was rare to see a fat person. However, when Big Aunt sat in a rickshaw, she filled the seat completely. She knew people called her "Big and Fat" and didn't mind. She said, "Don't look at me being fat now. When I got married, my waist was only 18 inches." Her weight was entirely due to her love of food, and she was an excellent cook. The Liu family women were all skilled in cooking, each surpassing the other, but they all cooked Wuxi cuisine. Big Aunt was different; she could also cook Western dishes. Her specialty was Western pastries. The Western oven in her kitchen was her most powerful tool. Mao's era was a time of material scarcity. Everything, from food to daily necessities, was in short supply. Buying rice had limits; fish and meat required coupons, as did cloth. Even cigarettes, alcohol, soap, matches, and toilet paper required coupons. Big Aunt's skill was evident in that even with the most limited ingredients, she could create delicious dishes. With just a small bowl of flour, she could bake six shiny, fragrant round bread rolls, like a magician.

Liu Zhonghou, the eldest son of Granny Lan, also known as Liu Peizeng (1924~2015), was involved with study groups led by the CCP when he was a 16-year-old student in 1940. By the age of 18, in May 1942, he joined the CCP at Huxin High School in Shanghai. During various political campaigns after the establishment of the People's Republic of China, he was suspected of being a "class alien element infiltrating the revolutionary ranks." His benefactor was Jiang Weiqing, who had worked with Mao Zedong since the Jinggangshan period of 1927-1929 (when the CCP transformed from a faltering urban revolutionary movement to a powerful rural-based insurgency) and was trusted by Mao. Jiang Weiqing was also known as a leader who disliked persecuting others. For example, during the Anti-Rightist Campaign in 1957, when Mao personally asked Jiang to target rightists, Jiang responded, "Chairman, you said it yourself, everyone makes mistakes when speaking! If nine out of ten statements are correct, that's a score of ninety; if eight out of ten are correct, that's a score of eighty." Mao angrily slammed the table and demanded, "Are you going to target the rightists or not?!" Jiang stood up and replied, "Chairman, you can remove me from my position first and then appoint someone else to carry out the campaign, because I am the first to be a rightist!" As a result, Mao not only did not remove Jiang from his post, but throughout Jiangsu Province, not a single rightist was targeted among the three levels of cadres at the provincial, prefectural, and county levels. In the end, only a few intellectuals were targeted, for which Jiang felt deeply guilty. Jiang Weiqing served as the Party Secretary of Jiangsu Province for a long time, and Liu Zhonghou was one of his favorite subordinates. In January 1957, Liu Zhonghou was appointed as the Party Secretary of Qidong County, and in October 1965, he became the Deputy Party Secretary of Yancheng Region. In 1975, he was appointed as the Party Secretary of Yancheng Region. During the difficult period of the 1960s, he achieved outstanding results in grain and cotton production in rural areas, which caught the attention and praise of Zhou Enlai. During the Cultural Revolution, like most officials in power, he was subjected to both verbal and physical struggles. After the Cultural Revolution, his views remained at the level of Maoist thought. He said he did not understand the Cultural Revolution at its inception, but gradually came to understand it. He believed that the Cultural Revolution was necessary, that Mao's initiation of it was correct, and that there were indeed officials taking the capitalist road. After the Cultural Revolution, in 1977, he was transferred to the Ministry of Education, where he served as a member of the Ministry's Party Group and Vice Minister from May to October. During his tenure at the Ministry of Education, he opposed Deng Xiaoping's proposal to immediately restore the college entrance examination system in 1977 and eliminate the "leadership approval" requirement. This stance drew criticism from the reformists.

From 1974 to 1982, Jiang Weiqing served as the First Secretary of the Jiangxi Provincial Party Committee. In 1978, he requested Liu Zhonghou to join him as his deputy. From December 1978 to February 1982, Liu Zhonghou served as Deputy Secretary of the Jiangxi Provincial Party Committee, overseeing agriculture and political and legal affairs. At that time, rural reforms were marked by the dissolution of the people's communes and the implementation of the household responsibility system. Liu firmly opposed the new policies of reform and opening up, insisting on returning to Mao's old path. These actions were intolerable to the central authorities. He was quickly relieved of his real power and sent to establish an advisory committee. In August 1983, he was appointed Deputy Leader of the Preparatory Group for the Jiangxi Provincial Advisory Committee. From June 1985 to November 1992, he served as Deputy Director of the Jiangxi Provincial Advisory Committee and Deputy Leader of the Jiangxi Provincial Advisory Group. He retired on January 31, 1997. Liu Zhonghou passed away in Nanchang at 4:08 AM on October 15, 2015, at the age of 92.

The story of Liu Zhonghou openly defying the central leadership is very rare within the CCP system. This is because the organizational structure of the CCP is similar to the rules of a gang, where superiors have life-and-death power over subordinates. When Deng Xiaoping took power and began to govern, he encountered significant resistance within the party. The pro-Mao faction refused to acknowledge Mao's failures. The economic reforms of the thirty years following Mao's era began in the countryside, marked by the household responsibility system. Deng Xiaoping sent Wan Li and Gu Zhuoxin to Anhui to dissolve the people's communes and distribute land to households. Liu Zhonghou wrote a letter to Premier Zhu Rongji, firmly opposing the household responsibility system and insisting on following the path of agricultural collectivization. Liu Zhonghou had spent decades involved with and overseeing agriculture. From his time as a county party secretary to a regional party secretary and then a provincial party secretary, he spent most of each year administering in rural areas. He could not have been unaware of the backwardness of agriculture and the poverty of the farmers. So why was he unwilling to acknowledge the failure of Mao's policies? I think an important reason is that admitting Mao's failure would mean acknowledging the collapse of the utopia he had struggled for all his life, which would be equivalent to self-criticism. In his world, self-criticism was extremely dangerous. It would cause him to lose prestige and status. Therefore, as the key force behind his unyielding devotion to Mao, it is hard to exclude the primal motive of mercenary self-interest.

In the Liu family, Liu Zhonghou was known for his extreme leftist ideology, strong principles, strong party loyalty, selflessness, and refusal to show favoritism to relatives. During the Cultural Revolution, joining the military was considered an extremely honorable thing as well as a way to avoid being sent to the countryside. Becoming a female soldier was an especially enviable position. Liu Zhonghou's daughter was noticed by an officer, her uniform was issued, and she was just waiting for the notification to report. To demonstrate his adherence to principles and refusal to use connections, Liu Zhonghou forced his daughter to return the uniform. His daughter nearly succeeded in committing suicide as a result. I have a deep respect for those who sacrifice their lives for their beliefs, even though the utopia they believe in does not exist, because the price they pay is their own life. However, I am skeptical of those who sacrifice their kin for a cause because it is at the cost of others' lives to maintain their own integrity. For those with strong party loyalty, keeping their official hat and satisfying their desire for power is more important than anything else. The fate of others, even close relatives, is insignificant. Many people mistakenly believe that Communist Party members with strong party loyalty are impartial and selfless, but this is a huge misunderstanding. Such people are actually extremely selfish. Their sternness and cold-heartedness are directed towards others, and even close relatives can be easily abandoned. Thus, the family members of CCP officials can boast of the privileges of being the children of high-ranking officials in public but also suffer untold hardships in private. Li Nanyang, a visiting scholar at the Hoover Institution (whose father, Li Rui, was once Mao Zedong's secretary and a critic of the CCP), analyzed Communist Party members in her book "I Have Such a Mother" as follows: "The essence of the Communist Party is to abandon everything for personal gain. I want people to know the reasons why these peasants joined the revolution. They were originally peasants. They joined the revolution for their own personal gain. For personal gain, they have no morality, no feelings, and no marital affection—nothing. This is the essence of the Communist Party."

The relatives in the Liu family understood that reaching out to Liu Zhonghou was a futile endeavor, and it was better to keep their respectful distance. When I was in China, I never had any desire to meet this uncle. In the summer of 1996, I returned to China from New York to visit my relatives. At the invitation of a publisher in Jiangxi, I went to Nanchang and took the opportunity to visit Uncle Zhonghou. That was the only time I met him. By then, he had long since retired and held no position or power. He told me he had just returned from Canada after visiting his son. As a former senior CCP official, he was naturally very sensitive about issues of power, and the conversation turned to the Canadian elections. He believed that China's political system was also a democracy and even better than the Western system. He thought that the one-party rule of the Communist Party made the country more stable. He was very puzzled by the existence of opposition parties in Canada. I explained that competition between two parties and alternating administrations is common in Western countries. When a party loses the support of the people and the votes, it must step down. A one-party dictatorship and a system where one person holds power cannot be a democratic system; it can only be a totalitarian dictatorship. His facial expression changed dramatically, and he waved his hand repeatedly, saying, "Chengmo, let's not talk about that, let's not talk about that!" He joined the Communist Party at a very young age, reportedly because he was pursuing progress. Back then, the revolutionary slogans of the Communist Party were: "Oppose dictatorship, demand democracy, and strive for freedom." Unfortunately, he did not even have the most basic understanding of democracy and freedom in his mind.

Granny Lan's daughter Liu Hanfang also joined the Communist Party. I called her Auntie Hanfang. In her youth, she was also very progressive and was influenced by her older brother, Liu Zhonghou, to join the New Fourth Army in Northern Jiangsu. However, because she wasn't born into a poor family and had complicated social connections, she couldn't gain the Party's true trust. The Communist Party used "class struggle" as a tool to seize power and placed great importance on family background. Additionally, the Communist Party also emphasized "social relations" and would investigate who your relatives and friends were. This was essentially a distorted form of implicating one's entire family. Auntie Hanfang, based on her credentials, was a senior revolutionary, but her family background and social connections were questionable. As a result, she suffered a lot in various political movements and became an experienced "participant" in these movements. Fortunately, she managed to retain her Party membership and wasn't labeled as a "counter-revolutionary." Auntie Hanfang's husband, He Yifeng, also came from the New Fourth Army and served as the director of the Commerce Bureau in Nantong for a long time, wielding some power locally. Therefore, her children had relatively better lives and did not become "bastards" like Uncle Bao Ting's children. Her eldest daughter was even recruited and became a female soldier. She worked at the Shanghai Yan'an Hotel, which was part of the military system. Such a prestigious position was unimaginable for most people at the time, and this was undoubtedly due to Aunt Hanfang's careful maneuvering. I only met Auntie Hanfang once. In 2000, when I visited my uncle Bao Ting in Nantong, Auntie Hanfang was also living there. She knew Bao Ting, and they interacted with each other. Upon meeting Auntie Hanfang for the first time, I immediately felt her warmth and familial affection. Perhaps she inherited genes from Granny Lan, as she was very articulate and had a witty way of speaking. My younger brother Chengquan was more familiar with her, and when he was far away in Jiangxi, Auntie Hanfang and her husband put a lot of effort into helping him with job opportunities, introducing girlfriends, and so on. Such a good elder is indeed rare. Although Auntie Hanfang and Uncle Zhonghou both chose the path of joining the Communist Party, their personalities were completely different.

Granny Lan's second daughter, Liu Guofang, and her second son,

Liu Kunhou, died in the largest maritime disaster in Chinese history: the "Taiping" shipwreck. Taiping was a passenger ship owned by the China United Enterprises Company, with a displacement of 2,489 gross tons. The incident occurred on January 27, 1949, during the Lunar New Year period. This was the last voyage from Shanghai to Keelung before the Spring Festival. The Taiping had only 508 valid tickets available, and ticket prices had skyrocketed. Tickets were priced in gold at that time, but this did not stop the flood of ticket buyers. Although tickets were long sold out and exceeded capacity, many ticketless passengers managed to board the ship through connections and payments in gold. According to testimony from China United Enterprises Company in the Shanghai Local Court afterward, including the 124 crew members of the Taiping, ticketless "stowaways," and passengers with their children and families, the total number of people on board exceeded a thousand. The Taiping was originally scheduled to depart at 10 a.m. but was delayed until 4:18 p.m. to wait for a shipment of silver dollars from the Central Bank of the Republic of China. To leave Wusongkou before the curfew, the Taiping accelerated rapidly in the Huangpu River. In the winter, it gets dark early, and a ship as large as the Taiping should have lit its lamps when leaving port. However, due to the tense situation of the Civil War at the time, none of the ships navigating Wusongkou, large or small, used their horns or lights. The sea conditions that night were excellent—no wind, no rain, no fog.

At 11:45 p.m., the Taiping, near Baijieshan in the Zhoushan Archipelago, had just passed the curfew zone when it collided in the dark with the "Jianyuan," a ship carrying 2,700 tons of coal and timber from Keelung. The Jianyuan belonged to the Yixiang Shipping Company and had 120 crew members on board. The Jianyuan was struck amidships and sank immediately, drowning 72 people, with 3 rescued by the Taiping. At that moment, no one on the Taiping—including its captain—would have anticipated that the ship would sink. The Shengjing, another passing ship, received a distress signal from the Jianyuan minutes after the collision. When the Shengjing asked the Taiping if it needed assistance, the Taiping's captain responded that everything was fine. Consequently, the

Shengjing sailed away. Only a few minutes later, the captain received an urgent report from the passengers that water was entering the lower decks. He suddenly realized the Taiping was in danger of sinking and quickly issued orders to accelerate towards the nearby shore, hoping to beach the ship. However, the Taiping was sinking too quickly, and the shore was still far away. Just 45 minutes later, around 12:30 a.m., the Taiping sank completely. The screams and cries for help echoed over the sea near Baijieshan. Drifting in near-freezing water, there was only despair and endless waiting. By dawn, the sea was almost silent. When a nearby Australian warship received the distress signal and rushed to the rescue, only 38 of the over 1,000 passengers on the Taiping survived, while more than 900 perished. This was the largest maritime disaster in Chinese history and was referred to as the "Chinese Titanic."

In 2014, the "Taiping" shipwreck was brought to the silver screen as the Titanic had been almost twenty years before. However, in terms of amenities, the two ships were worlds apart: one was a luxurious cruise liner built to accommodate wealthy merchants and aristocrats on holiday, while the other was a hastily assembled refugee ship amidst the chaos of wartime. Fear of the civil war overshadowed people's concern for the sinking of the Taiping, and the authorities never investigated the true cause of the collision. Various legends and speculations floated around in that turbulent era. The theory that the Taiping sank due to "overloading" seems to lack historical evidence. Another theory suggests that there was a navigation error. All is speculation. The Taiping's "black box" was never found. The captain and most of the crew perished in the disaster, and these questions were forever buried in the deep sea of the Zhoushan Archipelago. Perhaps even the captain himself, at the end, was not aware of exactly what had caused the collision. To this day, the ship still lies with her countless secrets at the bottom of the sea, near Baijieshan. Liu Guofang's husband, Shen Dejun, was the first officer of the Taiping, and Liu Kunhou was the third officer. All three of them were on board at the time. It is said that Shen Dejun was an excellent swimmer. Survivors reported seeing Shen Dejun throw a table into the water. But in the freezing cold sea, how long can even the strongest person survive? It was

New Year's Eve, and Granny Lan suddenly lost her daughter, son-in-law, and son. It's unimaginable how she managed to get through it.

The Fifth Great Uncle was the only male elder from the Liu family's grandparent generation whom I ever met. Before 1949, he not only owned cars and Western-style houses but also employed two chefs—one for Chinese cuisine and one for Western cuisine. At the end of World War II, Sino-American relations were at their best. Shanghai was the most fashionable international metropolis in the Far East, known as the "Paris of the East." I enjoyed looking at the old photos left by my Liu family uncles and aunts. The men were all dressed in suits, and the women had their hair styled in voluminous waves and sported stiletto heels. My mom's brother, Uncle Liu Hongying, was a handsome man. With his shiny short hair, gold-rimmed glasses, and two generous dimples, he looked even more attractive in photos than the renowned Zhao Dan, China's preeminent movie star of the nineteen-thirties, forties, and fifties. My Fifth Great Uncle was very westernized, gentle in temperament, and the most popular among the younger generation. He liked to speak English and greeted his nieces with a kiss, then emptied his pockets to give them all his loose change. After 1949, Fifth Great Uncle lost his business and moved to Guangming Village, a Western-style alley near Ruijin Road on Nanchang Road. At that time, he still employed a Western chef. This chef had no family and lived with my Fifth Great Uncle until he passed away. When I was a boy, my mother would take us to visit my Fifth Great Uncle and Fifth Great Aunt during New Year's and other festivals to pay our respects. As soon as we arrived, Fifth Great Aunt would pull me into her arms and kiss me, calling me "Little Dragon." It turned out that Fifth Great Aunt was also born in the Year of the Dragon, forty-eight years before me.

My Fifth Great Uncle was a devout Buddhist and naturally timid. After 1949, he retired early but still couldn't escape misfortune during the Cultural Revolution. In 1966, the Red Guards came to ransack his home and confiscated his bank savings. Unable to bear the humiliation, my Fifth Great Uncle jumped out of a window attempting to commit suicide. His bedroom was on the second floor, and he only broke his leg in the fall. He lived another three years and passed away in 1969. Fifth Great Aunt had suffered from severe tuberculosis when she was young, and her old illness recurred during this time. Despite the excellent care provided by her children, who were medical doctors, she did not live to see the end of the Cultural Revolution, passing away in September 1976. I left Shanghai in January 1969, so I wasn't there when Fifth Great Uncle and Fifth Great Aunt died, and I don't know how their funerals were handled. During that time, so many people were dying that the Shanghai funeral homes couldn't keep up with the cremations.

Fifth Great Uncle had six children: two sons and four daughters. The eldest son resided in Changchun, the second son in Baotou, the eldest daughter in Hangzhou, and the third daughter, Liu Puqin, joined the military in Beijing early on, so I never met any of them. I am familiar with Second Aunt (Fifth Great Uncle's second daughter) Liu Deqin and Little Aunt (Fifth Great Uncle's youngest daughter) Liu Aiqin. They and their husbands were all college classmates and graduated from the First and Second Medical Colleges of Shanghai. Second Aunt Liu Deqin worked as the head of the obstetrics and gynecology department at Renji Hospital in Shanghai and later became the director of Nanxiang Hospital after the Cultural Revolution. When my wife was in labor at Renji Hospital, my Second Aunt rushed from Nanxiang to assist. Little Aunt Liu Aiqin worked in the pediatrics department at Zhongshan Hospital in Shanghai. When I was a child, she took care of all my medical check-ups. Little Aunt had a lively personality and a striking appearance, making her very popular. She loved it when I visited her at the hospital. Whenever I went, she would take me around and introduce me to every colleague, saying, "Look, this is my nephew. Isn't he handsome?" Little Aunt's husband, Wu Yongli, was the deputy director of Xinhua Hospital in Shanghai. After the reform and opening up in the 1980s, they moved to Macau. Due to their compassionate hearts and medical skills, they became well-respected in the local community. In 1994, my family and I travelled from our home in New York to visit Little Aunt and Little Uncle in Macau, where they received us with memorably warm hospitality.

I have only one First Uncle on my mother's side. He was Yuanyuan's father, Liu Hongying. He was the eldest among all the cousins in the Liu family and was known as Big Brother Hongying. Before I was born, he had passed away from tuberculosis. After finishing middle school in Shanghai, Uncle Hongying worked as an assistant alongside Fifth Great Uncle. It was said that he had exceptionally high emotional intelligence; he was beloved by everyone, whether dealing with small family matters or larger family issues. Old Granny (Yuanyuan's maternal grandmother) loved to talk about Liu Hongying. She would tear up every time, saying there could never be a better son-in-law. Yuanyuan's mother, Wu Mingqi, was very beautiful. She was from Tianjin and spoke Mandarin eloquently. Uncle Hongying and my mother attended a Mandarin class once, and Wu Mingqi was their Chinese language teacher; that's how they met. The three of them always had a very good relationship. Aunt Wu Mingqi lived two bus stops down from Xujiahui, in Shangtang Third Village. Before the Cultural Revolution, my mom took us to my Third Great Aunt's house for lunch every Sunday. Then I would take the No. 42 bus by myself from Jianguo West Road to Yude Road, getting off at the entrance of the Tianma Film Studio to visit Aunt Wu Mingqi and Yuanyuan. During summer vacations, I would stay at Aunt Wu Mingqi's house for a few days. At that time, Yuanyuan had just been accepted by Nanyang Model High School. He was an outstanding student. He inherited his father's excellent genes, standing five feet, eleven inches tall and looking like a movie star. Our favorite activities together were building ore radios—which use lead sulfide crystals to detect radio signals, so they don't require electrical power—and taking photographs.

Chapter 3

My Generation

1. The Childhood Lost

If reincarnation were a business, my big sister Shenjie's arrival in 1949 couldn't have been more profitable. It was when her parents, Liu Hairong and Bao Zuxian, were at the pinnacle of their lives. Within a mere two years, Liu Hairong had not only secured a prosperous marriage but also welcomed a daughter into the world. Thanks to Bao Zuxian's gentle demeanor, she seamlessly assumed control of the family's financial matters, solidifying her position in the marriage. She left the cramped room at the back of her Third Aunt's house, stepping out from under the cloud of being the "poor relative in a wealthy family." The joyous occasion of returning home from the hospital after giving birth to her daughter was accompanied by a bicycle procession led by her Third Aunt's sons, Chenghou and Dinghou, who rode next to her like protective escorts. When reminiscing about these events, her eyes gleamed with delight. The moments when she proudly brought her husband and daughter to her Third Aunt's home for display were the happiest for her. In those instances, mother and daughter were the natural focal point, basking in the enjoyable warmth of the spotlight.

Though my younger brother and I were born just a few years later, the situation had profoundly changed, and it was a much more challenging period in our family's history. A series of misfortunes unfolded as our father and uncle were successively imprisoned, narrowly escaping execution. With the absence of male figures in the family, our mother, Liu Hairong, focused more of her attention on her daughter, deeming her to be of utmost importance. In her eyes, a daughter was essential for future care in old age, while sons seemed unnecessary. From a young age, our mother made it clear that she never desired boys, and our birth only added to her dismay. Initially harboring a dislike for boys, her sentiments intensified over time, viewing her sons as burdens. Some individuals are considered "superfluous" after birth, while others face rejection even before entering the world. My brother and I fell into the latter category, experiencing pre-birth rejection. Recognizing our mother's inherent rejection of her sons, Grandma, concerned for our survival in Shanghai, took us to Wuxi and hired a nanny for us there. Consequently, we spent a few years in Wuxi with Grandma, out of Mother's sight. But as we approached school age, our mother had no choice but to bring us back to Shanghai.

While living at my Grandma's house in Wuxi, my younger brother, Chengquan, was fortunate enough to be looked after by a caregiver we called "Grandaunt," who was a distant relative of our Grandma. While still a young boy, Chengquan went to live with our mother at her house in Shanghai. Grandaunt accompanied him and, after arriving there, temporarily worked as a housekeeper for my mother. Grandaunt had a granddaughter named Ruyi, who was a few years younger than Chengquan, and harbored a desire to betroth this granddaughter to him. Later, in the 1960s, I visited her once at her home in Wuxi, near the Northgate, which was later renamed Triumph Gate. She proudly showcased a storage room containing an entire set of dowry items prepared by her and Ruyi's mother for Ruyi's eventual marriage to Chengquan. As we were all underage at the time, witnessing the array of items, including red-painted cabinets and a wooden portable bathtub, proved eye-opening. Despite the scarcity of supplies in that era, Grandaunt treated me as an honored guest, preparing a generous bowl of beef vermicelli soup with two boiled eggs nestled beneath the surface. Her sincerity left an indelible impression on me. Following my father's life imprisonment sentence and my mother's subsequent divorce approval, this Grandaunt—who had a son working in Luoyang—asked my mother to consider marrying him. The Grandaunt, a simple and honest person, would never have followed my mother's train of thought and decision-making process, which had little to do with the Grandaunt's son and everything to do with the Hukou—or Household Registration system. Though various Chinese governments dating back to the Qin and Han dynasties had maintained similar "Family Book" structures, in January 1958, the State Council issued the *Regulations on Household Registration of the People's Republic of China*. These turned Chinese household registration into a mandatory internal passport which determined access to housing, food rations, education, and employment—achieving maximum control over the people and depriving them of their right to move freely. At the same time, urban residency limits were artificially created. It was easy for the residents of big cities to move to small and medium-sized cities, but not vice versa. Hence, Shanghai household registrations became more valuable than gold. My mother, firmly rooted in Shanghai, viewed the proposal to relocate to Luoyang as nothing short of "madness."

When I arrived in Shanghai at the tender age of four, I was the latest addition to the family. By that time, my father had already departed for Nanjing, where he faced arrest. I possessed no memories of him, nor did I have a familiarity with my mother and sister, who regarded me as an unwelcome intruder. Our residence, occupying the entire ground floor of No. 122 Chengxing Lane, Xinchang Road, was adorned with mahogany furniture, a washbasin stand boasting marble countertops, and a wardrobe filled with my father's British wool suits. My mother's closet showcased various styles and colors of stiletto heels, while my sister's drawers held lace dresses and other fashionable clothes, white children's leather shoes, ivory-framed sunglasses, and blonde dolls. My brother and I shared a modest bed; otherwise, nothing else. Wuxi, a mere 140 kilometers from Shanghai, remained a rustic town in the 1950s, 1960s, and well into the 1970s. Hailing from Wuxi, clad in a homespun gown and speaking the local dialect, I recognized my status as an outsider. I understood my disconnection from this new world of my mother and sister.

My mother disliked having me around. The disdain in her eyes was unmistakable. At that time, when I was four years old, she began vehemently emphasizing to everyone in the house that her daughter mattered most, because she could expect her daughter to look after her in her old age. As for my brother and me, we were considered worthless, serving as constant reminders of her politically incorrect spouse and, like him, a perpetual source of her unhappiness. Cold stares and scolding were routine, often accompanied by derogatory names like "baldy" and "debt collecting devil." Our mother favored and highlighted the distinction by mistreating us. Her daughter, the recipient of her kindness, was repeatedly urged to repay her favors and become her caring "little cotton-padded jacket." My childhood effectively ended when I stepped onto Xinchang Road. The only solace I found was in a small family temple at the entrance to the alley. Exiting Chengxing Lane onto Xinchang Road, the first doorway on the left was a cigarette and paper store called Qinyu Li. The second doorway housed the lane's hot-water station, jokingly called the "tiger stove." Its front opening—where the fire was fed—was wide, dark, and arched, like the gaping mouth of a tiger. The third doorway was the small family temple. When the row of door panels was removed during the daytime, the clay statue of Buddha and the offering table were right in front of me. As I looked at the swirling incense smoke and the Bodhisattva with his eyes folded in front of him, I felt as if I had returned to my grandmother's Buddhist hall.

The greatness of motherhood and the sublimity of maternal love are themes often celebrated in literature. Yet, assuming that all mothers universally love their children is entirely mistaken. Li Nanyang Li Nanyang (born August 1950) is a biographer and mechanical engineer. She is the daughter of Li Rui, a former part-time industrial secretary to Mao Zedong. She left China in 1990 and worked at several research institutions in the United States. After retiring in 2014, she became a visiting scholar at the Hoover Institution of Stanford University. She expressed in her memoir, *I Have Such a Mother:* "I can empathize with her situation as a mother. Balancing the responsibilities of raising three children while dealing with challenges involving her husband undoubtedly brings stress and sadness into her life. However, I believe that exercising restraint is essential for any mother—or simply as a normal human being, for that matter. This means refraining from directing anger towards her children, especially avoiding violent disciplinary measures like severe beatings or depriving them of sleep. Resorting to offensive language to insult them is equally harmful. In my view, she falls short of embodying a typical mother because she neglects essential aspects of maternal care. She shows no interest in her children's well-being, never inquiring about their experiences at the factory or their ability to handle demanding work. Instead, her focus remains on daily news and political updates. It wasn't until I entered a relationship and later married someone from a working-class family that I realized mothers could be different. My husband's parents consistently demonstrated care and concern in their letters, asking about what we might be lacking and what we might need. It was a revealing contrast to my own mother's approach. Suddenly, I realized, oh, a mother can be like this. She will inquire about what you're lacking and what you need. When my husband reads my mother's letters, he says, oh, why is your mom like this?"

Right across from the entrance of my mother's house on Xinchang Road, there's an elementary school. In the era before the Communist Party took control, it was known as "Kun Fan" (a moral exemplar) and operated as a private elementary school. However, with the advent of the Communists, all private schools were abolished, and this school underwent a series of name changes: first, it became "Xincheng District Central Elementary School," later, after the dissolution of the Xincheng district, it was renamed "Xinchang Road No. 1 Elementary School". My mother had been a teacher at this school since its "Kun Fan" days. In the Republic of China period, elementary schools were categorized into junior elementary schools (grades one to four) and senior elementary schools (grades five to six). If a school covered all six grades, it was referred to as a complete elementary school. Xinchang Road No. 1 Elementary School was one such complete elementary school, complemented by a formal kindergarten. The kindergarten was organized into three grades based on age. The kindergarten's principal, Li Bifang, stood out for having graduated from a Normal University, a relatively rare academic qualification at that time. My sister Shenjie, my brother Chengquan, and I sequentially enrolled in the kindergarten.

In the early 1950s, the CCP adopted Stalin's post-World War II approach to incentivize childbearing and initiated the "Glorious Mother" campaign. By 1958, Shanghai was experiencing a "baby boom," resulting in a significant surge in the number of school-age children. The Communist Party responded by launching a campaign to convert available spaces into schools. This led to the simultaneous opening of four private elementary schools in my Changsha Road neighborhood. Due to the urgency, these makeshift school venues lacked adequate infrastructure in terms of facilities, teachers, and teaching materials. Classrooms were set up in vacant rooms within residential houses, often poorly lit and without desks. Students were required to bring their own stools, which varied in height. Any housewife with basic literacy skills could be recruited as a teacher. My first-grade teacher seemed to have limited education and little or no teaching experience. She was particularly impatient with her young students, frequently using the word "annoying" to describe us. Private elementary schools were perceived to have lower academic standards compared to public schools, making them less competitive. To attract students, private schools adjusted their admission policies, allowing enrollment one year earlier than public schools for interested students. In 1957, my sister Shenjie was already attending first grade at Xinchang Road No. 1 Elementary School. When I turned 6 in 1958, and Chengquan turned 6 in 1959, my mother sent us both to private elementary schools. One of my mother's colleagues, Chen Yuebo, who had a close relationship with her and was a graduate of Shanghai St. John's University, strongly disapproved of this decision. Ms. Chen, known for her insight and assertiveness, voiced her concern, stating, "Liu Hairong, you must be out of your mind. How could you send both your sons to private elementary schools?" My mother's response was pragmatic: "What's so special about skinheads? The sooner they start school, the sooner they can start working." Subsequently, when Chengquan completed elementary school, my mother enrolled him in a vocational school instead of junior high. Vocational schools, being directly linked to factories, offered immediate job opportunities upon completion. My mother's advice to my brother and me was to "leave home as soon as possible." In 1982, when my father returned to Shanghai, my mother discussed financial plans with him, expressing her readiness to support both her sons through college. Chengquan was exasperated by this sudden paradigm shift on our mother's part and exclaimed, "This is a lie. I didn't even get the chance to go to junior high or high school, so how can I go to college?"

After 1949, the urban area of Shanghai was divided into several districts. Beneath these districts were several sub-district communities, and under these were several neighborhood residents' committees. In rural areas, the corresponding administrative agencies, from top to bottom, were provinces, counties, townships, and villages. When the CCP came to power in Shanghai, district-level leaders established party committees, and sub-districts established general branches. The local neighborhood residents' committees did not yet have formal government agencies. In 1960, China experienced three years of famine, leading to widespread starvation in many provinces. In Shanghai, residents received a monthly food ration, but the government struggled to ensure a consistent supply. To address this issue, they sought to reduce the population. In our neighborhood, certain "activists" collaborated with authorities to identify target families to relocate their registered residence from Shanghai to Qinghai Province. Unfortunately, my family became a victim of these individuals. Those relocated to Qinghai faced harsh conditions, with some even succumbing to starvation. Upon returning to Shanghai—with what became known as the "reverse flow"—many found their homes occupied by opportunists, leaving them homeless. Some were also jobless and penniless, and resorted to menial tasks such as laundry and sanitation, while others begged for food.

Living next door was an "activist" who harbored jealousy toward our family. In 1949, due to two uncles being Communist army officers, a red plaque declaring us a "Glorious Family" adorned our door. This neighbor remarked, "This family was popular during the Kuomintang era, and it remains popular under the Communist Party." Sensing an opportunity, she began visiting our house daily, harassing us with questions like, "Why haven't you left yet?" Faced with this constant pressure, my mother felt desperate and turned to the principal of her school, Zhang Yaohua, the initial head of "Xincheng District Central Elementary School." Mr. Zhang, who hailed from Northern China and spoke the Northern dialect, once welcomed us to his house to extend New Year greetings. He proved to be a generous and warm-hearted person. Assuring my mother, he said, "Do not worry. I will take care of it." Mr. Zhang promptly called the Chengxing Lane residents' block Committee, stating, "Liu Hairong is on my staff. Please leave her alone." As it turned out, Principal Zhang held authority not only as the school principal but also as the immediate superior of the residents' block committee. Following his intervention, the troublesome "activist" ceased bothering our family, and we successfully weathered the "pushing-out" attack. Recognizing my mother's exemplary performance as a teacher, Mr. Zhang rewarded her with an opportunity to present a model lesson in a large lecture hall. Other teachers were invited to observe and learn. My mother taught the geography class and was appointed as the department leader for subject teachers in geography, history, general science, art, music, and physical education. Furthermore, she received an additional half-step promotion during the salary evaluation, increasing her monthly income from ¥60 to ¥80. Shortly thereafter, Mr. Zhang earned a promotion to the district government, and Wang Huarui, the school dean, succeeded him as the principal of Xinchang Road No.1 Elementary School.

In 1962, when I was in fourth grade, Changsha Road Sub-district No. 2 Elementary School finally moved into its own building. The school was located on Xinzha Road, a two-story wooden house facing north between Wenzhou Road and Changsha Road. This house used to have several small shops downstairs and a warehouse upstairs. Although the house did not look like a school, it could finally gather the scattered classrooms together. There were uniform desks and chairs in the classroom, and the teacher had an office. Public elementary schools had playgrounds. In the morning, the staff would assemble the students on the playground and turn on a radio program which would lead them in their daily gymnastics. Our private elementary school did not have a playground, and each class stayed in its own classroom for morning assembly. The content of the morning assembly was to listen to the dean's lecture on the radio, while teachers corrected homework in the classrooms. The dean's closing remarks every day were: "Boys and girls, how fortunate you are to live in the era of Mao Zedong! May you grow swiftly under the nurturing care of the Party!"

One day, the dean suddenly disappeared. She and her husband were both taken away by the police, accused of being Soviet revisionist agents. No one would have thought that a woman who praised the virtues of the Party and Mao every day could be charged with being a Soviet revisionist spy. Soon, internal news surfaced. It emerged that during the early and mid-1950s, when China and the Soviet Union were on friendly terms, her husband participated in the construction of the Wuhan Yangtze River Bridge, working under the guidance of Soviet civil engineer and railway/bridge-building expert, Konstantin Sergeyevich Silin. The bridge had opened in 1957, but then in 1958, the Soviet Union opposed both the People's Communes and the Great Leap Forward campaigns of the Chinese Communist Party, and Mao became furious. By 1960, Sino-Soviet relations had deteriorated to the point where the Soviet Union withdrew its experts from China. Further deterioration occurred in 1962, and in 1963, Mao personally presided over the publication of the "Nine Commentaries on the Open Letter of the Central Committee of the Communist Party of the Soviet Union." At this juncture, activists at the dean's husband's workplace reported that he was in communication with Soviet experts and was suspected of having ties with foreign countries. Whether or not he was ever formally convicted or punished is unknown. However, it was evident that his aspirations for a promotion and a new residence came to naught, and his wife, the dean of our elementary school, was also implicated in and tarnished by the ordeal.

Our class was fortunate to have two recent graduates from a teacher's college, one teaching Chinese reading and the other handling arithmetic. With their arrival, the atmosphere in our class immediately

146

became more formal. Being among the top students, I gained the affection of my teachers. The principal, Xu Yiying, lived right across from the school at Hongfuli, Lane 66, Xinzha Road. She frequently took me to her house, and several other nearby teachers also took a liking to having me over. When the school established the Young Pioneers battalion, a teacher nominated me for the role of Battalion Leader. However, the dean reminded her that my family background needed consideration. Consequently, it was deemed inappropriate for me to become Battalion Leader. Eventually, I was appointed as Company leader, while a classmate with a brother who taught at our school became the Battalion Leader. He often shared insider information with us. The Young Pioneers issued armbands to their leaders, specifying that they must be worn to school. The Battalion Leader had three horizontal red bars, the Company Leader had two, and the Squad Leader had one. The back of all the armbands was white. Upon receiving the armband, I chose to wear it inside out. A curious classmate asked me, "Wearing your armband in reverse could be seen as a commendable gesture of modesty if you were a Battalion Leader. What does it mean to wear it in reverse with just two stripes?" I replied, "It means I have zero stripes." While most of my elementary school classmates were friendly, thanks to us all being neighbors, some could also be cruel. Since all my classmates knew I didn't have a father at home, arguments could take a hurtful turn. Once, during a dispute, a classmate shouted at me, "Your father is a counter-revolutionary!" As a child, he might not have fully understood the term, but everyone knew prisons were for "bad" people. While I could defend myself in a typical argument, defending my father's honor was beyond my capacity. It was not on the same wavelength. Regardless of who was right or wrong, I could only choose to walk away.

At school, I felt like an outcast in society, and life at home wasn't much better. Whenever my mom was around, her eyes, sharp like broken glass, often scrutinized the back of my head. When trouble brewed, her voice grew excited, like a wolf marking its territory. She took pleasure in challenging children, especially those who stood their ground. The feeling of superiority and the enjoyment of oppressing others fueled her actions.

She boasted to her colleagues that her look could kill, claiming that any misbehaving child in her classroom would quickly succumb to her gaze. She often declared, "No matter how naughty they are, they won't dare to misbehave in my hands." I believed it to be true; she wouldn't relent until she had absolute control. At home, encountering my small figure and determined eyes, her sharp-as-broken-glass gaze transformed into icicles that seemed to freeze in my eyes. I distinctly remember the second half of the semester in fourth grade, just after winter vacation. Each night before bedtime, my mom summoned me to the kitchen for a one-on-one session, pressing me to confess any misdeeds from the day. Despite my best efforts, I couldn't come up with anything. Our neighborhood was relatively peaceful, with children seldom engaging in theft or fights. What could I have done wrong? I was clueless. The north-facing kitchen had a cold cement floor, making each minute standing there feel longer than a day. "Did you misbehave at school? Cheat on a quiz?" she probed. My arithmetic scores consistently hit a perfect 100, and the Chinese language tests were essays—how could I have cheated? My brother, Chengquan, and I consistently scored above 4 points in academics; in our home, falling below 4 meant physical punishment. We had to place our hands against a marble countertop while Mom struck them with a stick. Our sister, Shenjie, with mainly 3-point scores, was exempt from such punishment. Mom claimed Shenjie's brain development might be affected due to being asleep during her appendicitis surgery. Mom was well aware that I couldn't have committed any major transgressions. She aimed to humiliate me and relished the sense of control. One day, having nothing to confess, I started fabricating stories. The face of Comrade Mao, a young household registration policeman with the same surname as Chairman Mao, flashed in my mind. He often harassed our family. I confessed, "Teacher Gu invited me to her house today, and I told her that there was a gun hidden in our house." Mom's face turned pale, like a sheet of paper. Her eyes seemed to freeze in the air, losing focus. From that day on, my routine of confessing never returned. I did not know that my father actually had a gun and that it played a role in sending both him and his brother to prison. Mom, however, did know. That day, by chance, the tale of this gun became the unexpected savior of my life.

My years in third, fourth, and fifth grade, spanning from 1960 to 1962 in elementary school, proved to be challenging. In urban Shanghai, residents received a grain purchase certificate per household. The quantity of rice varied based on factors such as age, occupation, and whether one was a white-collar or blue-collar worker, ranging from 10 to 15 kilograms per person monthly. Beyond rice, essential items and supplementary foods were distributed using tickets: food stamps, oil stamps, fish stamps, meat stamps, soy product stamps, cloth stamps, soap stamps, toilet paper stamps, and even furniture, sewing machine, and bicycle stamps—everything had its designated stamp. This intricate system was a vivid representation of a planned economy. Among these tickets, food stamps were categorized into local and national types, with the latter being more valuable as they could be used nationwide. Shanghai residents enjoyed a slightly better supply than those in other provinces, receiving additional tickets for breakfast and snacks. Breakfast tickets could be utilized for freshly prepared hot foods like fried dumplings, steamed buns, sweet rice balls, and noodles. Snack tickets, on the other hand, were used for bakeries and dry snacks such as biscuits and cakes. Since arriving in Shanghai, Chengquan and I had never seen these items at home, and over time, we had almost forgotten they existed. In 1969, Shenjie and Chengquan went to a village in Jiangxi together. Mom sent them a monthly parcel containing snacks and other goodies. It was then that Shenjie revealed to Chengquan that she never ran out of snacks during the three years of famine; Mom had secretly provided for her. During festivals, we all receive special treats from relatives, which Mom divided into four shares—one for each of us. Seizing the opportunity, Mom often told us the tale of "Kong Rong giving way pears," a classic Chinese fable teaching the virtues of selflessness and generosity, and always designated Chengquan and me to pick a share first. Emulating Kong Rong's example, we would invariably choose the smallest and seemingly worst share. Mom nodded in approval, but fairness in sharing was a chance we seldom had.

During our time in Wuxi, Mom paid little attention to what

Chengquan and I ate or wore. Our clothes and shoes were handcrafted by my Grandma and grandaunt. Upon arriving in Shanghai, the rustic lifestyle persisted, and Mom, seemingly indifferent, didn't bother to update our wardrobes. When I entered the fourth grade, our housekeeper taught me how to make shoes. The local store offered small pieces of black cloth for the upper shoe and white plastic soles at an affordable price. I learned to cut the upper shoe material precisely according to the sole's size, reinforcing it with sturdy old cloth as lining. I then sewed piping around the shoe's mouth. Accuracy in cutting the upper was crucial, ensuring it fit the sole perfectly and didn't waste material. The stitches were essential when sewing the piping to achieve the desired result. After completing the uppers, I took them, along with the soles, to the cobbler at the alley entrance. Using extra heavy thread, he sewed the upper to the sole. The housekeeper's training paid off, and the shoes looked impressive. I crafted pairs for both myself and Chengquan, earning admiration from neighbors who marveled at a boy making his own shoes at such a young age. They credited my mother's job as a teacher for enabling her to raise such exceptional children. Shenjie, exempt from making her own shoes, preferred stylish ones that were purchased at the store; handmade shoes appeared not fashionable enough for her. With the shoes complete, it was time to tackle knitting a sweater. My brother's and my sweaters appeared dirty and ill-fitting, requiring disassembly, washing, and re-knitting. Unable to get Mom's attention to the matter, I sought the guidance of a kind neighbor. Knitting didn't seem too challenging, and I didn't aim for complexity; practicality was my focus.

The Grandaunt who took care of Chengquan in Wuxi and served as our caregiver in Mom's house returned to Wuxi before long. The subsequent housekeeper was an elderly lady who lived next door. I called her Arh-Po. She was nicknamed "foreign grandma." Born into a devout Catholic family in Xujiahui, she married a Brazilian seaman and bore ten beautiful mixed-race children, all talented in linguistics, proficient in multiple languages. Arh-Po lived a simple life. Lacking extra furniture, her home didn't appear too small. She washed the cement floor to a gleaming shine. A portrait of the Pope hung on the wall, and an altar shelf held several holy vessels. The most striking item was a relic housed in a gorgeous and exquisite chalice. When she started working in Mom's house, Arh-Po was already seventy years old, yet she enjoyed robust health. Serving as both our caregiver and bodyguard, she provided care when Chengquan had measles, isolating him at her place. If children bullied us outside, she would confront them with a poker, labeling them "barbaric brats" and driving them away. Mom was rarely home. Xinchang Road No.1 Elementary School was just across the street from the entrance to the alley where our house stood. She could hear the school bell and go to work on time. But mom didn't come home until late evening after dark, and she did not get up early on Sundays. Arh-Po took Chengquan and me to attend mass at a Catholic Church on Datong Road every Sunday, where we watched the adults receiving Holy Communion and singing hymns. I especially liked the angel sculptures on the wall. Their calm and joyful expressions calmed the melancholy in my heart. Chengquan and I wore necklaces and crosses given by Arh-Po, and we were able to recite the Latin Bible in sections. My brother Chengquan went on to be a sincere and conscientious man. He left the village after two years of hard work in the fields in Jiangxi. After securing a job in a factory, despite not being in Shanghai, he supported Arh-Po financially whenever he could.

Arh-Po, despite lacking formal education like my grandma, possessed considerable wisdom and a straightforward demeanor. She believed that my mother's arrogance, selfishness, lack of common sense, and extreme materialism stemmed from a lack of faith. According to Arh-Po, "Your mother doesn't believe in anything. She only believes in the two bowls of rice in front of her." She expressed her concern, stating, "People consider sons precious, but your mother treats her sons like debt collectors. What she's doing is selling her own sons to buy a son-in-law in return." Much like my Grandma, Arh-Po cautioned Mom that mistreating her sons would bring retribution. Mom's mental maturity appeared stunted, remaining in the rebellious phase of adolescence throughout her life without ever developing a truly adult mindset. Her stubbornness and aversion to heeding the advice of others were defining traits—it was always her way or the highway. While others anticipated relying on sons in old age, Mom preferred counting on her daughter. She argued that it was her right to decide and her freedom to choose, seemingly unaware that her choices bore consequences. Years later, it became evident that the results differed significantly from her initial wishes and expectations, but by then, all she could do was have regrets.

Arh-Po's candid words may have left Mom feeling unsettled. They certainly left her bitter. Once Chengquan and I became capable of taking care of ourselves, she promptly dismissed Arh-Po. With no caregiver or housekeeper and lacking a man in the house, the responsibility of household chores had to fall on someone's shoulders. Physical tasks, such as mopping the floor, washing large items like bed sheets, and conducting deep cleaning and painting each year before the Chinese New Year, became my responsibility. Despite being only 14 or 15 years old, I was assigned these demanding tasks. Some duties, like cleaning glass windows and skylights, posed physical dangers. I improvised by using tables, chairs, and stools to construct makeshift scaffolding to reach the tall windows and skylights. But who cared? This was the duty of the eldest son! Upon completing these physically demanding, labor-intensive tasks, Mom would reward me with two pieces of braised pork for dinner.

2. The Old Three Cohorts

The term "old three cohorts" specifically refers to those who came of age during the Cultural Revolution. They were junior high and high school students set to graduate in 1966, 1967, and 1968. This generation was profoundly influenced by extreme leftist ideology, leading them to engage in destructive actions such as looting homes, demolishing cultural artifacts, and even physically harming their teachers. They were also the generation that fervently promoted and implemented the theory of bloodline. Many of them later became part of the "Educated Youths," ultimately falling victim to the Cultural Revolution and political purges. When the Cultural Revolution erupted, my siblings and I were all in junior high school. Shenjie belonged to the 1966 class, I was in the 1967 class, and Chengquan was part of the 1968 class. In the summer of 1964, having completed my elementary school education, I applied for junior high school. Our classroom teacher recommended a more conservative approach, suggesting that a group of classmates choose No. 62 Middle School as our first preference. No. 62 Middle School, offering a 7-12 high school program, held a prominent status as one of the key schools in the Huangpu District. The teacher expressed unwavering confidence in our ability to secure admission and assured us of a smooth progression to the high school class in the future. However, she cautioned against prioritizing city key schools as our first choice, fearing that coming from private elementary schools might pose challenges to admission. When the test results were later announced, it became evident that our scores surpassed the admission threshold for city key schools.

After entering school, according to the year of graduation, we were referred to as the '67 class. Our '67 class had a particularly large number of students, with 16 parallel classes, each with over 50 students, giving our cohort over 800 students. Not long after entering school, the Air Force visited to recruit soldiers and requested all male students to undergo a physical examination. The whole school got excited. There's an old saying in China: "Good iron isn't used for nails, good men aren't made into soldiers." But in the Red Era, being a soldier became the highest honor, especially joining the Air Force and entering the Air Force Academy, where graduating meant becoming an officer. This was undoubtedly an unattainable dream for millions of youths. That year, I was only 12 years old, a perfect age for dreaming. The Air Force physical examination was quite detailed. After the examination, only two boys in the whole school passed, and I happened to be one of them. I excitedly went home to tell my mother. She cast me a familiar look—her cold gaze like shattered glass—as if I had committed a grave mistake, and coldly advised: "Don't even think about it." At the young age of 12, I somehow knew dual forces were driving her to mercilessly crush my boyhood dream. The first was her general dislike for me and related annoyance at seeing me dare to imagine I could succeed in living such an exceptionally successful life in the future. The second was her hard-earned insider knowledge of the new class system in the People's Republic of China. From then on, I began to understand it myself. Setting aside those who'd been executed or imprisoned by the state and dealing only with those who retained the ability to walk the streets or dirt roads of the country, it was those whose close family members had been executed or imprisoned that now occupied the lowest class of all. In my own family, my father, a Kuomintang member, was sentenced to life imprisonment, and my uncle, a CCP member, was sentenced to twenty years. My mother, associated with the Sanmin Youth Corps of the Kuomintang, avoided imprisonment but remained under strict surveillance by the local party agency. Consequently, I found myself bearing an original sin since birth, destined to be part of the lowest caste in the new society, and therefore—once I thought about it in this new, harsh but revealing light—unquestionably barred from even the slightest chance at recruitment and enlistment. If I were the scapegoat, my mother was desperately trying to elude her share of blame. She could divorce, remarry, and change her fate. She believed she still had that ability, and time would prove her right, to a degree. But children were a constant reminder of her status as a counterrevolutionary family member, forever obstructing her path.

On May 16, 1966, the Cultural Revolution officially commenced with the publication of the May 16 Notice in the People's Daily. During those days, my class was engaged in a two-week fieldwork session in the suburbs of Shanghai, where we slept on mud floors with damp straw underneath. Despite the uncomfortable conditions, the students were excited, reveling in the newfound freedom away from parental supervision. In the middle of this, our class teacher disappeared, and no one took notice. After a few days, the school informed us that we were free to return home. Upon our return to the city, the streets of Shanghai had transformed into a sea of red. Buildings were adorned with red paper and revolutionary slogans, while large trucks moved slowly along the streets, displaying red flags and blaring revolutionary messages from loudspeakers. A fervent crowd marched with red flags, contributing to the surreal atmosphere. When I arrived back at school on the first day, the campus had undergone a radical transformation. Every available space on the walls was covered with big-character posters. On the playground, high school students singled out and criticized several teachers, some of whom had past affiliations with the Kuomintang military and government. During the civil war, they had disobeyed their leaders,–surrendered, and in many cases helped the Communist Party successfully take power. Following the "Liberation", they were given jobs in the CPPCC (The Chinese People's Political Consultative Conference) and later assigned to be teachers in middle schools. Among the people targeted were individuals classified as rightists in 1957, both "those who removed their hats" and "those who continued wearing them"—this was the metaphoric terminology used to differentiate between rightists who had confessed to their crimes and those who had not. In response to the revolutionary fervor of the Central Cultural Revolution Team, the Shanghai Municipal Party Committee attacked those deemed enemies of the people throughout the city, and No. 62 Middle School was no exception. The school's party branch followed the directives from above, exposing personnel files detailing historical issues to target these "dead tigers." Already apprehensive due to their histories, these individuals had no recourse when confronted by revolutionary youth. They were made to wear tall hats made of white paper with a board around their necks bearing the inscription "Counter-revolutionary XXX" in black letters, marked with a red cross across the name. Circling the playground, they banged broken washbasins and chanted self-incriminating phrases like "I am a monster, an enemy of the people. I am guilty. I deserve to die, bang bang bang." The high school Red Guards urged them to sing loudly, while we, the young junior high school students, avoided the playground. Instead, we ran to the balcony outside our classrooms to observe from above. It was a surreal scene, as those teachers seemed to transform into ghosts and monsters, reminiscent of the paper craft bullheads and horse faces I had seen as a younger boy in a Wuxi funeral shop. The reality unfolding before my eyes seemed almost unbelievable.

No. 62 Middle School was situated at No. 270, Chongqing North Road, just a short distance from the horse racing track. Positioned in the city center, where land is highly valued, the school's main structures consist of three south-facing three-story buildings. Each floor's rooms were encircled by tile-paved verandas on the south, east, and west sides, featuring railings made of intricately twisted cast iron. Between the three buildings, there were two turrets with curved facades, connected by two wooden overpasses in front. Adjacent to these overpasses stands a massive magnolia tree, gracing the area with its vibrant white blossoms every spring. The translucent petals resemble porcelain rice bowls turned upside down, infusing the campus with a delightful fragrance. The buildings showcased a symmetrical and distinctive architectural style, crafted with high-quality materials and exquisite workmanship. Notably, these structures were historically significant as they belonged to the descendants of Li Hongzhang, a renowned statesman from the Qing Dynasty who visited America in 1896.

I belonged to Class No. 15, and our classroom was situated on the second floor of a turret. Upon arriving, I found senior students and teachers, identified by red armbands, guarding the classroom door. Upon entering, I observed that most students were already seated in a classroom enveloped in silence, where the air seemed frozen. The plum rain season in Shanghai had extended that year, lingering into late June. The atmosphere was humid and sticky, making the classroom feel even hotter. The collective breathing of my classmates resonated in the room. A thick line divided the blackboard into two sections. Those from red families sat on the left, while those belonging to the Five Black Categories occupied the right. Each of the Five Black Categories included individuals targeted by the Communist Party's dictatorship: landlords, rich peasants, counter-revolutionaries, bad people, and rightists. In urban areas like Shanghai, capitalists took the place of landlords and rich peasants. Originally covering lawbreakers like thieves, fraudsters, murderers, arsonists, hooligans, and other traditional criminals, the term "bad people" had now expanded to include religious individuals and those refusing to serve as party informers. Red Guards distributed a paper to those on the right side of the room, instructing each of us to stand and read it aloud. The note declared: "I am XXX, I come from a capitalist/counter-revolutionary/bad people/rightist family. I decide to draw a clear line with my family. I will report and expose the counter-revolutionary crimes of my parents. I will resolutely follow the path of revolution and be infinitely loyal to Chairman Mao." As students on the right side, we looked at the paper with despair. Sitting beside me was Sun Jinlian, a straightforward individual uninterested in compliance. She declared, "I will not read this." I urged her to consider the senior Red Guards wielding belts with brass buckles, which had been used to beat teachers black and blue. I conveyed, "We have no way out. I'll read it." After reading the notes one by one, the Red Guards proclaimed, "The Five Black Categories stay, and the others are dismissed." We were instructed to verbalize and then write our commitment to sever ties with our families on chart paper with prominent characters. The Red Guards emphasized: "The party's policy has always been that you cannot choose your family, but you can choose the path. We will see today which path you choose. You can go home when your statement is approved." When it was my turn, I expressed my distress. "When I was little, my Grandmother took me to her house in Wuxi. My father was absent, and I had never met him. I harbored no feelings for him. My mother, a teacher, was someone I perceived positively. At the onset of the Cultural Revolution, my siblings and I changed our surname from Bao to Liu to disassociate from our counter-revolutionary father. However, I now discover that my mother is deemed an enemy of the revolution as well. I am deeply upset and don't want to return home. Where can I go? Please tell me." The unexpected nature of my question left the Red Guards perplexed, and they dismissed me.

In May 1933, Joseph Goebbels, the head of propaganda in Nazi Germany, initiated a large-scale "Book Burning Movement." On the evening of May 10, 1933, thousands of students brandishing torches marched through Berlin's streets, converging on the square opposite the University of Berlin. In this square, numerous books chronicling human civilization's achievements were piled high. Subsequently, the students hurled torches at the books, sparking flames that illuminated the night sky. The objective behind this "Book Burning Movement" was to eradicate established freedoms and civilization, paving the way for the new Nazi era. Poet Heinrich Heine once prophetically asserted that there is only one step from burning books to burning people. From the early hours of November 9 to 10, 1938, under Nazi instigation and control, Hitler Youth, Gestapo, and SS forces unleashed a frenzy of beatings, destruction, looting, and arson against Jewish homes, shops, and churches throughout Germany. It was a catastrophic disaster for the Jewish population, resulting in approximately 267 synagogues, over 7,000 Jewish shops, and 29 department stores being set on fire and otherwise damaged. In Austria, 94 synagogues also suffered damage. The broken windows, illuminated like crystal in the moonlight, led to the night of destruction being termed "Kristallnacht."

The initial phase of the Cultural Revolution echoed the Nazis' actions by targeting the "Five Black Categories," engaging in the destruction of the "Four Olds" (old ideas, old culture, old customs, and old habits), and ransacking homes. This agenda drew parallels to both the "book burning movement" and "Kristallnacht" orchestrated by the Nazis, and the Red Guards shared striking similarities with the Nazi SS. The offspring of senior cadres in Beijing initiated the Red Guards. The "bloodline theory" was propagated by the "Zilaihong" (Born Red) children of Beijing's high-ranking cadres, asserting that their heroic lineage also made them heroes. When the "May 16 Notice" was issued, the cadres' children were oblivious to the impending disaster. Initially, they perceived the "Cultural Revolution" as a mere continuation of the various purges meant to eliminate remnants of the overthrown old regime of 1949. They saw themselves as the natural revolutionary forces and the driving power behind this new chapter in the book of Communist revolution. Consequently, a peculiar and unspoken phenomenon emerged in nearly every university and high school in Beijing. Those who chose to publicly display big-character posters critiquing the school party committee and leaders were predominantly the children of cadres. For instance, the offspring of Liu Shaoqi and He Long were responsible for posting big-character posters at Tsinghua University, characterizing Jiang Nanxiang, the then Minister of Higher Education and President of

Tsinghua University, as a counter-revolutionary gangster. At the No. 1 Middle School Affiliated with Beijing Normal University, one of Liu Shaoqi's daughters was the first to post a big-character poster targeting school leaders. These cadre offspring collaborated closely with party work teams dispatched by their fathers, intending to shape the Cultural Revolution to conform to their own vision. Their goal was to replicate the anti-rightist campaign of 1957, overthrowing a faction of capitalist roaders and the Five Black Categories, and positioning themselves as the "successors of the proletarian revolutionary cause." However, their plan came to naught. Mao accused the party work teams of "white terror," leading the Central Cultural Revolution Team to assume control of the movement. The elementary focus of this movement shifted from class enemies of the past to those in power at all levels, reaching up to and including Liu Shaoqi, who at the time was the President of China.

The initial cohort of Red Guards, primarily comprised of the offspring of high-ranking government officials, quickly became acutely aware of the imminent danger facing both themselves and their parents. Witnessing their parents' fearful expressions, these youths, accustomed to the privileges afforded by their powerful families, felt a profound sense of abandonment. Coming together, they reminisced about their fathers' past accomplishments, drawing strength from their legacy and seeking solace and solidarity from their peers. They harbored deep resentment towards the unjust treatment their parents endured and were incensed by their own worsening circumstances. Fueled by anger, they channeled their intensified hatred towards the Five Black Categories and their descendants, giving rise to the infamous saying, "Father is a hero, and son is a good man; father is a reactionary, and son is a bastard." Tan Lifu, an advocate of the "bloodline theory," was the son of Tan Zhengwen, Deputy Procuratorate-General of the Supreme People's Procuratorate, who passed away in 1961. Born in a cave dwelling in Yan'an in 1942, Tan Lifu was a third-year student at Beijing University of Technology when these events unfolded.

In October 1966, Tan Lifu and his fellow Red Princelings formed a collective action committee known as the "Capital Middle School Red

Guards Joint Action Committee," referred to as "Linkage," to resist the Central Cultural Revolution Team and safeguard their parents from the expected efforts to overthrow them. They also adopted the nickname "Linkage". This was done to closely align themselves with the "Great Exchange of Revolutionary Experience"—a nationwide campaign initiated in September 1966, four months after the start of the Cultural Revolution., which encouraged Red Guard groups from all across China to travel to Beijing and other cities to share revolutionary experiences, demonstrate loyalty to Mao Zedong, and participate in mass rallies and other political activities. The basic idea was to "link" revolutionary fervor across the nation, so the nickname for the campaign itself became "Linkage". From its start, this campaign was seen as being directly endorsed by Mao Zedong, so by adopting "Linkage" as their nickname, the Capital Middle School Red Guards Joint Action Committee aimed to gain favor with Mao and the central leadership, and enhance their political standing and influence.

Seeking to assert their multi-generational revolutionary bona fides, they dressed in their fathers' and brothers' old military uniforms, adorned with Red Guard armbands. The oversized military attire was cinched tightly with wide belts, with some even wearing heavy black leather boots to emulate the grandeur of the Red Guards. Adopting an arrogant demeanor, they employed coarse language referring to themselves as "big boss," and "top dog," and to others as "bastard," and "sonofabitch." This group initiated the "Red Terror," employing various forms of torture, including kneeling on glass, painting faces, hanging tests, head knocking, jet plane, burning hair, buttock shaving with knives, boiling water baths, beatings, live target shooting, and the sweep leg technique.

The "Linkage" Red Guards in Beijing spread the Red Terror across the country by targeting various locations. The Cultural Revolution's outset witnessed the Red Guards engaging in the destruction of the Four Olds. They forcefully entered the homes of individuals in the Five Black Category, seizing and burning items such as suits, cheongsams, books, oil paintings, photos, and diplomas. They also vandalized antique items, porcelain, and glassware. Mom's home fell victim to three raids. The first incursion was led by Red Guards from my mother's workplace, the second by those from my sister's school, Peiguang Middle School, and the third by Red Guards from my school, No. 62 Middle School. During the initial raid, the Red Guards from my mother's workplace stripped our house of my father's entire wardrobe, including coats, suits, shoes, and belts, leaving a conspicuous void in the front room. The Red Guards from my class methodically searched the homes of all Five Black Category students, including mine, leaving little behind. Among them was a fellow classmate who lived in the same alley as I did. Although we had been close friends since elementary school, this time, as a Red Guard wearing the distinctive armband, he joined the intrusion into our homes. The warmth in his familiar smile vanished from his tense face, as if he no longer recognized me. Unspoken questions lingered in the air; however, we, as junior high school students, seemed to have matured overnight. Without explicitly asking why, we tacitly distanced ourselves from each other. After completing their searches and before departing, the Red Guards affixed a couplet to the main entrance of the house: "Father is a hero, and son is a good man, father is a reactionary and son is a bastard," with a horizontal band reading "Fear of Devils." Those white couplets hanging in the air bore an ominous aura. Two other families upstairs shared the same entrance with us. One of them, an elderly dock worker and member of the proletariat, defiantly tore down the entire couplet after the Red Guards left, since he knew that the Red Guards were powerless to harm him.

In order to bring down his number one political rival, Liu Shaoqi, Mao first used the Red Guards and then encouraged the rebels to rise up and fight brutally against the cadres who had been in power in the past. In order to build up his "family reign," he did not hesitate to destroy the "party reign." After the crazy wave of beatings, smashing, and looting passed, the central Cultural Revolution team demanded that the target of the revolution be directed at the establishment. After all, the ultimate goal of the Cultural Revolution was for Mao's family to recapture power from Liu Shaoqi. So, the veteran cadres stepped aside, and the rebels took over. Our class master teacher Xu Guangyu became the leader of the faculty rebel group in No. 62 Middle School. Xu Guangyu was in his thirties, and his appearance made people not want to see him a second time. He had thin hair and yellow teeth. He had bad breath and stuttered when he opened his mouth. He always wore a stern face and appeared to be serious all the time. A pair of small eyes behind his thick lenses was like flashlights searching for boys. When he saw a girl, his face fell, and the hissing saliva dropped down his mouth. He said "in addition, in addition" a lot, in the manner other people say "you know, you know." Anything followed by "in addition" was not good news to boy students. We all hated him. One boy gave him a nickname, "Huai You." It means "bad addition." Because he stuttered and couldn't pronounce the word "hai" (which means "in addition"), he replaced it with "huai" (meaning "bad"). Xu's strategy in managing the class was to use girls to watch boys. He made sure that all the boys and girls shared a desk. The girls could be relied on to report to him everything their desk mates did wrong: Did the boy talk in class? Misbehave? Cheat? He called the girls in to see him one-on-one. He touched the girl's thigh when no one was in the office. Xu Guangyu was not married, but he had an unconcealed affair with a female colleague. Once, he and Mrs. Wang, a married woman in the same office, went to book a room in a hotel in Nanxiang, a suburb of Shanghai. The hotel manager sensed something suspicious and called the police. They were detained by the police and punished by the school administration.

Many of the activists who joined the rebellion had experienced oppression from the established authorities in the past. The Cultural Revolution served as a platform for them to express their personal grievances. Upon closer examination, the rebels did have misbehavior records. Some argue that a revolution can be seen as a celebration for troublemakers. As Marx and Engels stated in their Communist Manifesto, "The proletarians have nothing to lose but their chains. They have a world to win." Xu Guangyu, having faced punishment and suppression, was a natural rebel. However, he differed from other rebels as he came from a red family, with parents who were cadres that accompanied the Communist army down south. With a background rooted in communism, Xu Guangyu was destined for significance. The changing times propelled him to a prominent position at No. 62 Middle School. Taking advantage of the rebellion, my mother seized the opportunity to address the stage, accusing the school's former leaders of persecuting her, including allegations of ransacking her home. She sought her former boss's intervention for her rehabilitation and the return of confiscated belongings. My mother displayed great cunning in exploiting the situation. Nevertheless, she overlooked the fact that, despite the chaos of the movement, someone in the Black Five Category could not transcend their lower status in this Communist country. Consequently, she was swiftly instructed to cease teaching, with the new punishment of cleaning all of the school's toilets.

The Cultural Revolution, stretching beyond two years, has evolved from criticism of the Five Black Categories to targeting those in power. Consequently, mass organizations have engaged in conflicts, transitioning from civil strife to armed confrontations, leaving the duration uncertain. Government activity has dwindled, factories stand idle, and stores grapple with severe shortages. On campuses, rubbish heaps clutter the landscape, while classrooms lie in disarray, with broken desks and chairs piled up, rendering them impassable. As revolutionary fervor diminished and fatigue set in, a subset of individuals adopted a resistance tactic known as "decoupling and lying down," earning them the moniker "carefree sects." Shen Guoshu, son of Big Aunt, belonged to this group as a college student, while I, a junior high school student, also embraced this carefree mentality. Shen Guoshu and his friends welcomed my inclusion in their circle. Amidst the chaos of Red Guards' destruction and home raids targeting liberals, Western novels, magazines, and picture albums—rarely seen in public before—became accessible. Our preferred reading materials included translated works from the Republic of China era and classical literature from Britain, the United States, France, and Russia. Many of us encountered these books for the first time, eagerly absorbing their contents like dry sponges meeting water. The circulation of these books among us was swift and widespread.

The writers of the 19th century stand out not only for their literary prowess but also for being profound thinkers and philosophers. They vehemently criticized the hypocrisy, ugliness, and evil prevalent in society while offering readers glimpses of goodness, kindness, and beauty. Their language was steeped in philosophy, reflecting the crystallization of human wisdom. These novels became a gateway to a vast intellectual landscape, expanding my perspective, transcending the constraints of time and space, and revealing facets of life previously unseen. In "Les Misérables," the characters—the priest, the convict, and the police sergeant—radiated with the brilliance of humanity. Their displays of compassion, mercy, and justice left an indelible mark. "Human Comedy" resonated deeply with my personal experiences, demonstrating that even in distant France, the harshness of the world and familial coldness echoed familiar themes. Amid the war between three emperors in "War and Peace," artillery thundered relentlessly, yet the emperor remained unharmed. The battlegrounds were strewn with the corpses of peasants' children, portraying a poignant and powerful reality.

Oscar Wilde's notion of "art for art's sake" positioned him as a symbol of aestheticism in 19th-century Western literature. Beyond crafting numerous intricate and splendid golden sentences, Wilde dedicated his life to the pursuit of ultimate beauty, earning him the status of an artistic legend. His meticulous selection of words and sentences reflected a keen attention to richness and beauty. The continuous flow of various rhetorical devices and quick wit left readers with a lasting impression, a style highly revered in British culture at that time. In stark contrast, the language of Maugham and Hemingway differed significantly. Their brilliance lies in their ability to employ simple, concise, and melodious words to convey the complexity of the real world and the rich inner lives of their characters. Despite the simplicity of their writing styles, the conveyed meanings were profound. When I later visited the homes associated with Hemingway and Somerset Maugham, I discovered that their writing styles indeed mirrored the primitive simplicity of Key West and Tahiti. Wilde's beautiful essays, coupled with Hemingway's and Maugham's distinct writing styles, ignited my fascination for the English language and fueled my strong interest in learning it. In 1982, thanks to the recommendation of a friend at Anhui University, I had the opportunity to translate The Picture of Dorian Gray. The book was published by Anhui People's Publishing House in 1984, allowing me to realize a dream I had harbored since my teenage years.

Big Aunt's house concealed a secluded storage room, a covert sanctuary where Shen Guoshu, his friends, and I would gather. With tightly shut windows and drawn curtains, we clandestinely listened to black vinyl records. The collection primarily featured classical Western music—symphonies, sonatas, and the opening chapters of Suzhou Pingtan. In moments when words failed, music served as an invisible hand, reaching out to touch my soul. Books and music became wellsprings of ecstasy and solace, nurturing my compassion and empathy. More profoundly, they enabled me to transcend the material world, providing a spiritual refuge. Consequently, my life diverged from that of my peers. No longer afflicted by homesickness, books and music proved ample companions for me. Since the 1990s, my vacations have predominantly involved visits to Europe. I immersed myself in activities such as exploring the cemeteries of literary and musical luminaries I had encountered through the books of my youth, tracing their footsteps. I've visited Tolstoy's manor, Dostoyevsky's residence, Goethe's, Schiller's, and Bach's homes, as well as residences belonging to Hugo, Balzac, Shakespeare, Dickens, Andersen, Hemingway, and Somerset Maugham. Graveyards like those of Wilde, Molière, and Chopin also bore witness to my presence. In these places, I felt a connection between my heart and their souls. I explored grandiose sites like the Kremlin, the Hermitage, Versailles, and Fontainebleau. Within these majestic palaces, I couldn't help but envision mountains of bones and corpses.

By the summer of 1968, the nationwide power transition was nearing completion. The original objective of the Cultural Revolution was to remove those in power who were aligning with the capitalist path, and this mission had largely been accomplished. However, as various factions emerged among the rebel Red Guards in universities, internal conflicts escalated into factional wars, evolving even further into armed confrontations. Numerous places experienced bloodshed, resulting in casualties, and the normal order within colleges and universities disintegrated. This tumultuous situation drew the attention of Mao Zedong, who sought to rein in the rebellious Red Guards and restore stability. Mao's strategy involved dispatching propaganda teams comprised of factory workers to colleges and universities to quell the fighting among the Red Guards. However, Mao's decision faced resistance from the Red Guards. At Tsinghua University, there was an incident where Red Guards shot and wounded a member of a factory worker propaganda team. Enraged by this defiance, Mao Zedong took decisive action. On July 28, 1968, Mao Zedong, along with Lin Biao, Zhou Enlai, Chen Boda, Kang Sheng, and members of the Central Cultural Revolution Team, convened with the five major Red Guard leaders—Nie Yuanzi, Kuai Dafu, Tan Houlan, Han Aijing, and Wang Dabin. Mao engaged in a five-hour discussion, focusing on criticizing the Red Guards and urging them to adhere to orders. Following this conversation, the five Red Guard leaders found themselves trembling with fear, realizing they were in serious trouble.

By 1968, schools had remained closed for three years, creating a backlog of graduates from various educational levels. From universities and colleges to middle schools, both junior and high schools, there was a surplus of graduates for several years, and the question of their future was a pressing concern. Due to the Cultural Revolution's impact on enrollment and recruitment, the commercial and service industries were at a standstill, leaving urban junior high and high school students without avenues for higher education or job assignments. In 1968 alone, the backlog of graduates from the classes of 1966, 1967, and 1968 exceeded 4 million. This large cohort of graduates, many of whom were also Red Guards, had been involved in rebellious activities, including the destruction of the Four Olds and physical harm to their teachers. The carefree sect students, having missed schooling for three years, were now anxious and restless. Recognizing the social force of the Red Guards, Mao Zedong, and the Central Cultural Revolution Team understood the destabilizing potential posed by these graduates to society, the political system, and the Communist regime. It became imperative to disband and disperse this group across the country. With limited employment opportunities in the cities, Mao's call for parents to mobilize their children to leave for the countryside was essentially an emergency measure to avoid greater social unrest in major urban centers. While the key motive behind this "Sent down Youth" movement was reducing instability, its key impact on a generation of youth like myself was to enact a punitive measure against us. As the graduates departed from the urban centers, the Red Guard movement, characterized by violence and bloodshed, gradually receded from the historical stage. In the early days of the Cultural Revolution, the Red Guards served as Mao's enforcers. Even though it was at the direction of Mao's wife, Jiang Qing, to target figures like Liu Shaoqi and Peng Dehuai, they must be held accountable for their atrocities and acts of human evil. One example of such brutality was Han Aijing personally leading the extraction of confessions and assaulting Peng Dehuai, knocking him to the ground seven times. This resulted in severe injuries, including a broken forehead, fractured ribs on both sides, and serious lung injuries. None of the five leaders of the Red Guards in Beijing universities had favorable outcomes. Initially abandoned by Mao, they faced sentencing after the Cultural Revolution concluded.

Summer is typically the season when junior high school students apply for high schools or receive job assignments after graduation. However, in the summer of 1966, all schools were closed, and the usual student allocation procedures were suspended. The task of assigning work for the 1966 graduates was pushed to 1967. Among these graduates was my sister, Shenjie, who completed her studies at Peiguang Middle School in 1966. In the 1967 distribution plan, most students were assigned jobs in the city, while a few were sent to farms in the suburbs. As others prepared to embark on their new journeys, Shenjie found herself placed in the "pending for assignment" category, with no definite plans. I knew most of Shenjie's classmates, some of whom were our neighbors. Many of them hailed from non-red families. The question loomed: Why was she left behind when everyone else had been assigned? Shenjie had developed a habit of being self-centered and feeling self-important since childhood. However, the outside world proved to be different from home, and her personality wasn't always well-received. It became apparent that she couldn't always exploit everything around her. The delayed allocation may have seemed like a small prank, but for me, it marked a significant milestone. It set the tone for a lifelong dynamic between Mom, Shenjie, and me, influencing the course of our lives. The clock had started ticking on a new chapter.

In the summer of 1968, the school commenced the allocation of graduates from the Class of 1967, a class to which I belonged. Due to Shenjie being on the waiting list for distribution, both of us were slated for allocation simultaneously. The allocation plan for the Class of 1967 differed from the previous year, introducing the new policy known as the "four aspects." This policy encompassed assignments to urban units, suburban farms, frontier military reclamation farms, and poor villages in remote provinces. Before 1968, the prevalent model for sending individuals to rural areas involved farms. However, on December 21, 1968, Mao issued the "latest instruction," emphasizing the necessity for Educated Youths to undergo re-education in the countryside alongside poor and lower-middle peasants. This marked a shift in focus, making village settlement the elementary mode since the winter of 1968. As the term implies, village settlement involved placing individuals in small villages, where they earned a living through work points, much like local villagers. Village settlement meant joining a collective ownership system without the need for formalities such as political reviews, family background checks, and physical examinations. Importantly, there were no quota limits. The scale of village settlement, the number of families involved, the intensity of mobilization, and the profound impact both domestically and internationally were unprecedented. "Village settlement" thus acquired a special and significant meaning.

At the time, Shanghai's policy dictated that, for families with two children participating in the distribution, one could stay in Shanghai while the other had to leave. This policy seemed reasonable, prompting an immediate decision from my mom. She said to me, "Shenjie is not in good health, so you should go." Once the family made this decision, the graduation allocation team from No. 62 Middle School intervened at

Peiguang Middle School to coordinate. Fortunately, Peiguang Middle School agreed to halt the mobilization of Shenjie to the countryside, allowing her to remain on the waiting list for a city job allocation. The official responsibility for going to the countryside fell on my shoulders. The options for where to go were limited. Suburban farms, close to Shanghai with good living conditions and a salary, were highly sought after. However, considering my family background, this was not a feasible choice. Military reclamation farms in Heilongjiang and Yunnan presented potential military missions, making it unsuitable given my family background. The only viable option left was village settlement, with locations including Huaibei in Anhui Province and western Jiangxi Province. Several classmates, forced to choose a village settlement, leaned towards going to Huaibei. The parents discussed the possibility of going to the same place so that we could support each other. Regarding the departure date, many people wanted to delay and observe the situation. However, Mom's school added pressure by withholding her wages. Her monthly salary, originally ¥80, was reduced to Shanghai's minimum living allowance of ¥12 per person, totaling ¥48 for the entire family. The first group of people left Shanghai for Anhui on January 16, 1969. Since village settlements required the most effort to mobilize, the authorities launched a public campaign. The neighborhood party committee came to our house with much fanfare, beating gongs and drums, and affixed a red poster of "good news" on our door. On the day of our departure, we were paraded through the city on large buses. Each family received two platform tickets, allowing them to enter the train station to bid farewell to the departing passengers. A classmate who frequented our house asked Mom for a ticket, and she happily handed it over, relieved of the responsibility. As soon as I left, Mom's school promptly returned her previously withheld wages.

After the Chinese New Year of 1969, the allocation process for the Class of 1968 commenced with a new directive from Mao known as the "Supreme Instruction." The distribution plan for the 1968 class was labeled "thoroughly red," signaling a departure from the previous "Four Aspects." Under this new plan, there was no option to stay in the city, no allocation to farms, and village settlements became the sole choice. Chengquan, being part of the 1968 class, found himself with no alternative but to opt for village settlements. Interestingly, this policy change rendered Shenjie's previous "Pending for assignment" status invalid. Sometimes, Man proposes, but God disposes. What could Mom do? Given the circumstances, unlike Huaibei, where people eat rough grains, Jiangxi at least produces rice. Therefore, Mom decided that Shenjie and Chengquan would go to Jiangxi together. Before leaving, Mom repeatedly requested Chengquan to promise to take care of Shenjie, and whenever a positive opportunity presented itself, to step aside and do all he could to ensure Shenjie could take advantage of it.

3. Go up the Mountain and Go Down to the Village

Huaibei

The "Go up the Mountain, Down to the Village" movement took place between 1968 and 1978, primarily involving individuals known as "Educated Youths." This initiative aimed to relocate young people from urban areas to rural regions and lasted for over a decade, resulting in more than 16 million junior high and high school students being sent to rural parts of China. This group constituted over one-tenth of China's urban population and affected approximately half of the households in cities and towns during that period. The movement had significant consequences, depriving millions of young individuals of their right to receive basic education in junior high and high school and limiting their opportunities to pursue higher education. Swept along by fate and forced to go to the countryside, the sent-down "Educated Youths" were in fact a large group of young people who had lost their way, living at the very bottom of society. Only after leaving the rural areas could they regain a clear sense of identity: those recruited for factory work became workers, those admitted through enrollment became "worker–peasant–soldier college students", and those conscripted became members of the People's Liberation Army. Those who ultimately remained in the countryside, however, became a group of victims of the times, left with blurred identities.

Shanghai No. 62 Middle School, situated in the heart of the Huangpu District next to People's Square, held historical significance as a former British concession before 1949. The residents in this area were generally well-off, with most being from non-working-class families. The initial group of students who volunteered to go to the countryside was not genuine volunteers, as families faced pressure to comply. The withholding of our parents' wages served as a form of mild punishment. We departed from Shanghai under the escort of the school's worker propaganda team members. The destination for the students from No. 62 Middle School was Yong'an Commune in Suxian County, Anhui Province. Departure took place at a freight station in Pengpu, rather than the passenger terminal in Shanghai North Railway Station. On January 16, 1969, as the fully loaded train prepared to depart, the loudspeaker played "Sailing on the Sea Depends on the Helmsman," a popular song at the time, praising Mao. Unlike the usual joyous context, it conveyed a sense of impending doom. Both inside and outside the train, loud cries of sadness erupted. The scene felt surreal, like a dream. Despite the challenging circumstances, I found no reason to shed tears, as Shanghai was not my home, and leaving brought a sense of relief and a desire to get as far away as possible.

Anhui Province derives its name from the combination of Anqing Prefecture and Huizhou Prefecture, established during the Qing Dynasty and collectively referred to as Anhui. The character "Hui" (徽) encapsulates the essence of the region, representing its mountains, waterways, people, and rich cultural heritage. Geographically, Anhui is shaped by the Yangtze River and Huaihe River, which traverse through the mountains, dividing the province into three distinct regions from north to south. Southern Anhui, encompassing areas like Anqing and Huizhou, is situated along the Yangtze River, Xin'an River, and Huangshan (Yellow) Mountains. This region has historically been home to exceptional individuals. Moving north, the area between the Yangtze River and the Huaihe River is known as the Jianghuai region, while the region north of the Huaihe River is referred to as Huanghuai. There is a noticeable contrast between the prosperity in southern Anhui and the economic challenges in the north, in Huaibei. A Ming Dynasty folk poem, "Fengyang Flower Drums," vividly portrays these challenges: "Speaking of Fengyang, talking of Fengyang. Fengyang was originally a good place, but since the Emperor Zhu came to power, there have been nine years' worth of famine in ten years. There is a lot of land in Fengyang, but little harvest. As soon as the grain mills stopped, people ran away from famine. Fengyang girls only married out, and no brides entered Fengyang." Fengyang, on the south bank of the Huaihe River, still faces economic challenges. Huaibei, situated on the north bank, is even more impoverished.

The disadvantaged status of the Huaibei region can be attributed to various geographical and environmental factors. Positioned between the Huaihe River and the lower Yellow River, it is susceptible to frequent natural disasters. Over centuries, the construction of levees confined the Yellow River to a narrow course through the Huaibei region. Trapped within these embankments, the river deposited vast amounts of silt inside its channel rather than across the wider floodplain. As a result, the riverbed gradually rose higher than the surrounding land, creating the so-called "suspended river" (xuán hé) that characterizes the Yellow River in the Huaibei region. In addition to this threatening phenomenon, the lower river also undergoes frequent course changes, increasing the danger faced by areas along its banks, including Huaibei. The Huaihe River experiences less constant but still major disasters during heavy rains, minor disasters with light rains, and droughts in the absence of rainfall. The land in Huaibei is characterized by barrenness, with an abundance of saline-alkali and sandy soils. Even in areas with better sandy soil, water retention is notably poor. Locust infestations further compound the region's difficulties, leading to regional and large-scale plagues. Locust swarms are so dense that they obscure the sky and block the sun. Wherever they land, the sound of swallowing can be heard, leaving behind devastation akin to the peeling of skin from the earth. All green vegetation is swept away, leaving only bare tree trunks and soil in the wilderness. In addition to environmental challenges, adverse weather conditions pose significant hurdles for Huaibei. During critical months such as April and May, persistent southwesterly winds dry out the air and prematurely ripen wheat, reducing its yield. Subsequent weather events, such as rains in June, disrupt wheat harvesting and the planting of fall crops.

I encountered such conditions in June 1971, when continuous rain for over two weeks made it impossible to dry freshly sickled wheat grain. As a result, the wheat molded and sprouted in the field, making it difficult to extract flour and resulting in steamed buns that were sticky and hard to swallow. Legend has it that after Zhu Yuanzhang, founder of the Ming Dynasty, became emperor, he climbed Yunlong (Clouds and Dragon) Mountain in Xuzhou and remarked, "Barren mountains, bad water, shrews, and unruly men." Zhu Yuanzhang had a profound experience of Huaibei's wild mountains, dangerous waterways, and restless people.

In January 1969, our train journey took my fellow students and me through Nanjing and Bengbu, eventually arriving in Suxian early the next morning. At the train station square, some trucks were waiting to transport us to our designated communes. Upon my first glimpse of Suxian, the town appeared gloomy. Most of the houses lining the streets were simple adobe structures. The people, clad in black winter jackets, pants, and hats, made distinguishing between genders and age groups challenging. Yong'an Commune, where students from Shanghai No. 62 Middle School were placed, is situated 30 kilometers northwest of Suxian. It shares borders with Shicun to the east, Huigu to the south, Shunhe to the west, and Zhihe Township to the north. The truck journey along the mortar road took about two hours to reach Yong'an. I was assigned to the Qianxi production squad in front of Yelou village, along with another student, Shen Guanghua from Class 1. Our luggage was transported by a donkey cart provided by the village, and we followed on foot. Several young villagers, including production squad accountants Liu Yanqi and Li Zhenqiu, came to welcome and assist us. The distance wasn't too far, approximately 3.5 kilometers, and we covered it in about 45 minutes.

Seeing the Huaibei Plain for the first time was quite a sight. It stretched out so flat that I could see for miles. In the distance, the villages seemed like floating islands, sparsely dotted with trees. Liu Yanqi explained that Qianwang Village, where we were, is divided into two production squads, east and west. We belonged to the West, known as the Qianxi production squad. He gestured towards the village and mentioned that to the north of Qianwang was Yelou, to the east was Qiandong, to the west was West Lake, and to the south was South Lake. I was puzzled because these areas looked like fields, not lakes. Liu Yanqi clarified that the Huaihe River flooded every year, transforming all the crop fields into what locals called lakes. This naming convention stemmed from the regular inundation. I noticed ponds to the south of each village, and he explained that when constructing houses, villagers would fetch soil to build foundations, unintentionally creating artificial ponds. Consequently, the villages were built on elevated ground above the crop fields, providing protection to the houses during floods. As we journeyed further, I noticed a raised platform not far from the road, resembling the size of a village but devoid of trees or houses. Liu Yanqi cautioned me against approaching it, warning, "You could catch the plague," indicating that it was an abandoned village.

The tale of the deserted villages began in 1958 with the initiation of Mao's Great Leap Forward Movement. During this mass mobilization effort, people nationwide were urged to engage in steel production, leading to the collection of all available iron items and the clear-cutting of vast stretches of forest for fuel. Despite resulting in heaps of useless scrap metal, this misguided effort was celebrated with enthusiasm. On August 9, 1958, during Mao Zedong's inspection of Shandong Province, he proposed the establishment of people's communes. Subsequently, a nationwide campaign to form such communes was launched. Peasants were coerced into joining, losing the land they had acquired during the earlier land reform movement. They were compelled to surrender farm tools, livestock, and even furniture to the commune. Before the Communist Party, landowners rarely resorted to violence to seize the land of poor peasants. However, during the land reform movement, the Party compelled peasants to consistently use violence, setting a precedent that made them potential victims of violence themselves. When the state seized all land from peasants in the name of people's communes, the peasants were left voiceless. In a bid to impress their superiors, commune cadres exaggerated the success of the people's communes, engaging in false reporting of output known as "launching satellites." This deceitful reporting necessitated more grain to be handed over as taxes. Some production squads even surrendered seeds and still fell short of procurement requirements. Cadres went house to house like predators, searching for hidden grains and punishing anyone who dared to hide food. Families were prohibited from keeping food at home, and cooking pots were destroyed by cadres. Everyone, regardless of age, had to eat in public canteens. Initially stocked, these canteens soon devolved into chaos, offering only wild vegetables. Some managed to escape starvation by leaving for the city to beg for food. Those who relied on canteens lost the ability to move after five days of hunger. Resorting to desperate measures like peeling bark, digging up roots, and even consuming dirt and dead bodies, villages were depopulated one after another. Bodies were left unburied, and adobe houses crumbled into natural graves. After three years of famine, those who returned found their old villages transformed into tombs, compelling them to rebuild nearby. These dead villages stood like silent tombstones. During those years, military recruiters avoided Huaibei. Starvation in 1960 was labeled as "abnormal death," disqualifying a young man from joining the army if any family member had starved to death, AKA: died abnormally. This policy was not adopted out of sympathy for the surviving descendants, but because the PLA recognized and feared their potential enmity for the Communist Party.

According to the CCP's official records, about 40 million people died of starvation in China from 1959 to 1961 during a three-year famine. Surprisingly, the blame for the Great Famine wasn't placed on the CCP or Mao Zedong, but on "natural disasters" and cadres below the provincial level who had "deceived superiors" and "concealed corruption". In response, Mao re-emphasized the importance of "class struggle as the key" and initiated a socialist education movement. From February 11 to 28, 1963, the CCP held a working meeting in Beijing and decided to launch a socialist education movement, later known as the "Four Clean-Ups Movement" in rural areas and the "Five Antis Movement" in urban areas. The Four Clean-ups aimed to tidy up workers, accounts, assets, and storage, while the Five Antis targeted corruption, theft, extravagance, decentralization, and bureaucracy. The movement encouraged people to report each other, followed by a focus on class struggle education and fighting perceived enemies, ultimately leading to a reorganization of the party. On August 5, 1964, the Secretariat of the Central Committee established the "Four Clean-ups" and "Five Antis" headquarters, with Liu Shaoqi serving as the front-line commander. Displacing village cadres from leadership positions, Liu Shaoqi dispatched work teams to rural areas as replacements. In Yelou Village, I encountered a disabled man who used to hold a village leadership role. He faced accusations of hoarding extra food, misusing public property, and committing sexual assault during the Great Famine. Subsequently, the work team removed him from his position. In retaliation, an enraged crowd assaulted him, resulting in severe injuries that crippled his legs.

As Educated Youths, we received a settlement allowance of ¥210 per person, with ¥150 allocated to the production squad for house construction and ¥50 for purchasing small farm tools. Additionally, we were given ¥60 to buy grains, enough for half a year's food at ¥10 per month. In January, amid the winter chill, the cold weather made it impractical to construct an adobe house. The production squad arranged for Shen Guanghua and me to stay in a small kitchen hut instead. A typical villager's house consisted of three south-facing rooms—a central living room with a door and two side rooms. Often, there would be a small, untouched kitchen located in front of a bedroom, commonly referred to as the "pot house." These houses were constructed from adobe and thatch, with thick walls designed to withstand erosion from wind and rain. It typically took over half a year for a new house to dry completely. Due to a shortage of wood, having a panel door was a mark of good fortune, while windows were small holes in the wall filled with grass and sealed with mud in winter, yet opened during summer. Our pot house measured 3 steps long and 3 wide, totaling 9 square meters. Being newly built, the walls absorbed moisture during the day and frosted over at night. The settlement mode in the village differed from farm life; lacking support and cafeterias, we had to cook our meals. At our young age, we were incapable of truly taking care of ourselves, and we had no parents, relatives, or other adults to turn to for help, so our initial challenge was learning how to survive in this new environment.

On January 27th, 1969, a snowstorm struck. By the morning of the 28th, our tiny windowless pot house seemed to glow with light. Peeking out through the crack in the door frame, everything, sky and ground alike, was blanketed in white. This marked the beginning of a month-long period of continuous rain and snow, considered the largest snowfall since 1954—a warning from the heavens, forcing us to endure hunger and cold. Fetching water and cooking became daunting tasks as the village wells, mere holes in the ground, turned muddy and slippery, posing a constant risk of falling in. The firewood, soaked from the snow, posed challenges for starting a fire. Liu Yanqi and Li Zhenqiu frequently came to our aid, teaching us how to cook. The initial poverty we observed in Huaibei centered on food scarcity. It was common practice for villagers to beg for food during spring, but now the problem extended to the lack of fuel. Despite Huaibei being rich in coal mines, all of them were state-owned and provided no supply to the villagers. The effects of the Great Leap Forward movement and the Great Famine had left the region devoid of trees for miles. This reminded me of the famous Chinese tale of the "Seven Steps Verse." In the era of the Three Kingdoms, after the death of the famous warlord Cao Cao, his son, Cao Pi, became Emperor of the state of Wei. He then accused his brother, the brilliant poet Cao Zhi, of using ghostwriters to gain favor, and challenged him—on pain of death— to compose a poem on the spot, in the time it would take him to walk seven steps. Cao Zhi responded with the "Seven Steps Verse," lamenting the use of beanstalks to boil beans, reflecting their shared roots and tragic rivalry. Approximately 1,750 years later, lacking firewood and dry grass, we resorted to a method akin to the Seven Steps Verse—we used dried sweet potatoes to cook dried sweet potatoes. The pot contained dried sweet potatoes, and beneath it, we burned dried sweet potatoes as fuel.

The snow-covered Huaibei Plain evoked the imagery of the losers of the Russian February Revolution being exiled to Siberia. When we, the Educated Youths, first arrived, a pervasive sense of helplessness enveloped us, with challenges particularly pronounced for the young women among us. The young women from Shanghai, with their beauty and grace, seemed vulnerable, akin to sheep entering a tiger's den. In Xiaoliuzhuang (Little Liu's) Village, the party secretary had a mentally challenged son, whom no local girl was willing to marry. The secretary locked a Shanghainese girl up and physically assaulted her. His son then raped her. In January 2022, the Western news media drew attention to the "Chain Woman" case, revealing a woman who had endured multiple instances of abuse and trafficking in Huankou Town, Feng County, Xuzhou City of Jiangsu Province. However, similar incidents had occurred as early as 1969 in Suxian County, not far from Xuzhou. Regrettably, the mistreatment of young women was not uncommon throughout the country. The central government classified this as "sabotaging the movement of Go up the Mountain, Down to the Village" and mandated that all local governments take strict measures to address it. Perpetrators of such crimes were to be apprehended and imprisoned, with severe cases potentially resulting in a death sentence. Villagers colloquially referred to female Educated Youths as "high-voltage wires," indicating the high risks associated with them.

Huaibei farmers toiled strenuously, plowing, sowing, weeding, and harvesting by hand with sickles and hoes, using methods that had remained largely unchanged for one thousand years. Without large animals, they relied on human power to pull plows for field cultivation. A typical farmer's home contained minimal wooden furniture—a bed frame, a small, low table, and a rolling pin for noodle-making. Electricity was unavailable, prompting villagers to fashion makeshift kerosene lamps from empty ink bottles. Before long, the ceilings and walls of the rooms became covered with black smoke marks. The only semblance of modern life was a cable radio broadcasting the voice of Chairman Mao's Party Central Committee twice daily. We, the Educated Youths, earned work points comparable to farmers and received yearly dividends based on these points. Daily work points varied; a robust young farmer earned 10 points, a woman 8, and teenagers like us earned 8 as well. Each work point was valued at 2 to 3 cents in Chinese currency (RMB). I earned ¥0.24 working in the fields from sunrise to sunset. Grain rations were distributed per person, and settlements at year-end favored families with more children rather than those earning more work points. As a single person, I accumulated more work points than needed for rations, hoping to convert them into cash. Unfortunately, those in debt faced difficulties obtaining cash for repayment, rendering everyone's hard work throughout the year somewhat futile. Under the "socialist system," slacking off became a common occurrence. The Huaibei land, eroded by the Yellow and Huaihe Rivers over millennia, was extremely barren. Severe fertilizer shortages resulted in meager wheat yields on sandy and mortar soil, requiring 25 kilograms of seeds per acre but yielding only 50 kilograms in autumn. The planned economy system dictated that only wheat could serve as tax grain, with communes deciding crops for each production squad. The peasants, now Commune members, lacked the freedom to choose what to plant and faced restrictions on cultivating cash crops and raising certain livestock. Violations incurred punishment, known as "cutting off the tail of capitalism."

One day, I witnessed a villager planting a small patch of sesame seeds in his palm-sized yard. My roommate Shen Guanghua and I were intrigued, as sesame seeds were a rarity in Shanghai. Lacking a yard, we seized the opportunity to use a small piece of wasteland. We had heard that sesame did not require weeding or watering. Clearing the narrow wasteland along both sides of a ditch, we planted the seeds. True to what we had heard, the sesame plants flourished and grew abundantly. When autumn arrived, we were pleasantly surprised to harvest over ten kilograms of white sesame seeds. In addition to our sesame venture, I also learned the art of refining cottonseed oil. Since the government neither provided peasants with cooking oil nor allowed them to grow oil crops like soybeans or peanuts, ingenious farmers found ways to extract oil from cotton seeds. The process involved pressing the seeds to obtain raw oil, mixing a specific ratio of water and caustic soda in a pot, and gradually heating it to dissolve the caustic soda. The pressed raw cottonseed oil was then added to the pot, where impurities in the oil slowly precipitated. After separating, the clear, refined cottonseed oil could be scooped out and used for cooking. I found a small tin bucket, extracted and refined enough cottonseed oil to fill it up, and then set it aside to bring home. Additionally, our production squad engaged in making vermicelli from dried sweet potatoes. Villagers had the opportunity to trade dried sweet potatoes for this vermicelli. When I returned to Shanghai at the end of 1969 for the Chinese New Year, I brought back vermicelli, sesame seeds, and cottonseed oil. The sweet potato vermicelli, thicker and softer than the kind made from mung beans, was especially appreciated by my Grandma. I gifted her a sizable bag. Later, after the Chinese New Year, my siblings Shenjie and Chengquan took the remaining cottonseed oil and sesame seeds to Jiangxi.

In 1969, the worker propaganda team from Shanghai No. 62 Middle School made multiple visits to Yong'an Commune to engage with the Educated Youths. The commune organized meetings with the Educated Youths, aiming to provide re-education. During one such session, elderly impoverished peasants, who had endured significant hardships and harbored deep resentment toward the old society, were invited to share their personal experiences. At the commencement of the presentation, everyone recited a quotation from Chairman Mao emphasizing the necessity for Educated Youths to undergo re-education from poor and lower-middle peasants. Several washbasins were placed in the vicinity, each containing a cluster of cereal grains that we were to consume later. These grains were intended to serve as a reminder of the challenging pre-communist era. However, an old, poor peasant, gazing at the cornbread, tearfully exclaimed, "Life in 1960 was truly tough! If we had cornbread like this, perhaps fewer people would have starved." This revelation left us momentarily bewildered. Wasn't Huaibei liberated by the Communist Party in 1948? The commune officials sensed the discrepancy and swiftly ended the meeting, abruptly shutting down the re-education effort. The majority of peasants in Huaibei were illiterate and lacked formal education. The older generation struggled with numerical concepts and had a limited understanding of historical timelines. Expecting these individuals to re-educate the Educated Youths seemed impractical. Moreover, the commune cadres were themselves young, lacking knowledge about the Republic of China era. Their own experiences were shaped by the challenges of the Great Famine, and they were survivors of that period. However, they knew that discussing the events of 1960 was strictly prohibited. Following this incident, the commune never summoned us again to hear the recollections of sorrowful memories from old, poor peasants, nor did they attempt further "re-education."

The peasants in Huaibei faced severe poverty and lacked education, yet the local cadres compelled them to engage in daily political study. The study material primarily consisted of reading newspapers. In the summertime, the gatherings took place in an open-air patio outside a storage house. After dinner, the village leader repeatedly blew a whistle, prompting reluctant villagers to assemble. They squatted against the wall since small wooden stools were not available. In an era when urban residents received cloth coupons for purchasing clothes, little attention was given to the clothing needs of peasants. Most peasants wore self-woven homespun cloth, often dyed black. The homespun cloth was prone to damage from the summer heat and heavy perspiration. In the scorching daytime sun, peasants used gauze to shield themselves. As the sun set in the west, men would go bare-backed. Women who had given birth seemed to possess a certain freedom, appearing topless like men. The summer of 1969 marked my initial experience with the villagers. The sight of women with varying breast sizes and colors, openly exposed, left me speechless. During winter, villagers convened in the livestock house, the only structure in the production squad large enough for meetings. The space was crowded, and the air became thick with smoke as men incessantly smoked tobacco and spat. A woman breastfed a child with her arms open. As medical facilities were scarce in rural areas, and family planning had not yet begun, farmers believed that breastfeeding prevented pregnancy, so some children were breastfed until they were 2 or 3 years old. A young man looked at the nipples and flirted, "Let me touch them." The woman did not seem annoyed and responded with amusement, "I'll feed you after your brother is done." Laughter echoed, waking up a few elderly individuals who had dozed off during the political study session. With that, the session came to an end.

The political system of ancient China during the pre-Qin period was feudal. "Feudalism" refers to the practice of dividing land to establish states. The emperor would allocate lands outside of his directly controlled royal domain to vassal lords. These vassal lords could establish their own states and armies within their territories and had considerable autonomy. In 221 BC, Emperor Qin Shi Huang conquered the six other states, unifying all of China and establishing a centralized government. During the era of imperial autocracy, this centralization of power was limited to the realm of public authority, with governmental institutions established only up to the county level. The imperial court's intervention in civilian society and the lives of the people was very limited, with few instances of the emperor or the court proactively causing trouble for the populace. The phrase "the mountains are high, and the emperor is far away" reflects the vast freedom people enjoyed in their daily lives. People could easily find a secluded paradise to live a leisurely and carefree life. The populace had the freedom to relocate and choose their means of livelihood, and the gentry and scholars enjoyed the freedom of independent thought, adhering to moral principles rather than the emperor's commands. The people also had the freedom to transcend social classes: a farming family could become wealthy through hard work and frugality, and a poor scholar could achieve the dream of "fame on the golden list" through diligent study. However, a totalitarian system is different. It takes centralization to the extreme. The Chinese Communist Party's totalitarian rule is pervasive, with unprecedented intensity, pervasiveness, and penetration, interfering in every aspect of people's lives. The thorough politicization of society permeates every level of organization, reaching into every cell of society: every grassroots work unit, every community, neighborhood, village, and even every family. The Communist Party encourages people to inform on, betray, and attack each other, achieving complete control over society with no gaps. The people have lost all freedoms, and even the freedom of thought has been taken away. The power of life and death is entirely in the hands of party organizations at every level, turning everyone into modern slaves.

The extension of people's communes across the nation consolidated Communist Party control over the countryside. These communes were intricately tied to both the party and the government. Party secretaries held sway over the three levels of residential unity below the county: commune (township), production brigade (a group of villages), and production squad (an individual village). At the local village level, a party secretary wielded indisputable and absolute authority over everyone. Offending a branch secretary was akin to offending the entire system. There was no way to migrate and make a living elsewhere without a letter from the authority. Without an identity, a file, or a letter of introduction, an individual was practically a desperate fugitive. Even the last vestige of human agency, the ability to leave home and wander, has been stripped away, which is the cruelest offense against the vastness of the heavens and earth, and every spirited person.

Shen Guanghua came from a bourgeois family background, while the two of us, as members of the "Black Five Categories," carried the original sin. We could only accept fate and work doubly hard to reform ourselves. The house where Shen Guanghua and I lived was too small, with no space for cooking. So, we built an open-air earthen stove outside the wall of the house. When it rained, the earthen stove easily collapsed, making it difficult to boil water and cook a meal. The village's sanitation conditions were at the level of a primitive society. The toilets were dry pit latrines, and flies were everywhere. The well for drinking water was just a hole in the ground, without any fence or cover. When it rained, sewage flowed everywhere, making the well water unrecognizable. Intestinal diseases were common among villagers, and deaths were frequent. One night, Shen Guanghua suddenly started talking nonsense, fell asleep, and couldn't be awakened. I found him in a high fever with a foul smell in bed. Urgently, I sought out a barefoot doctor in the back village, known as "Mr. Fourth." He was one of the few literate individuals in the village, wearing glasses with lenses thick as bottle bottoms. Diagnosing Shen Guanghua with bacillary dysentery, Mr. Fourth administered streptomycin with a syringe. I shuddered at the thick mud on Mr. Fourth's glasses and under his fingernails. I didn't know if it was because the dosage of streptomycin was insufficient or if the illness was particularly severe, but Shen Guanghua remained unconscious for several days. His stool, laden with pus and blood, emitted a foul odor. I had to donate all my underwear for his use, changing them frequently. Unfavorable weather compounded the situation; the persistent rain made washing and drying the clothes a challenging task. Thankfully, after a week, Shen Guanghua began to recover, and I emerged from the ordeal unscathed.

When the Cultural Revolution began in 1966, schools nationwide were shut down for revolutionary purposes, and Suxian City was no exception. All schools in the city were closed, and teachers were relocated to rural areas. During the Republic of China era, the town's finest houses served as schools. However, the Communist Party had a different approach, recognizing only violence and power. Seizing the revolutionary opportunity, the county and regional governments took over the school buildings of No. 1 Middle School, No. 2 Middle School, and No. 1 Junior High School. These provincial key schools, highly respected and prominent before the Cultural Revolution, lost their locations, and their teachers were sent to rural schools in communes. In the summer of 1970, as rural schools began to reopen, Yong'an Commune Middle School, initially a junior high school, received a group of high school teachers transferred from the city. This allowed the school to offer high school programs for the first time. It was announced that all junior high school graduates could apply with a recommendation from the village party agent, subject to approval by the commune education team and Yong'an Middle School. Most applicants were local youths, with a few coming from Suxian City. I was the only Educated Youth from Shanghai who applied. However, I faced rejection from the village party secretary, Liu Zhengji. Liu Zhengji explained, "Many children of our poor and lower-middle peasants lack the opportunity to attend high school. Why should this quota spot be given to him?" Fortunately, several teachers at Yong'an Middle School supported my application. These educators, who had worked at Suxian No. 2 Middle School and Fuliji High School before the

Cultural Revolution, were graduates of normal universities with solid academic backgrounds and teaching experience. Despite being master teachers, they faced family background issues. As all the middle schools in Suxian City were now closed, these teachers were uncertain of their return, so they considered Yong'an as their new hometown. Nevertheless, their salaries remained unchanged and were higher than those of commune cadres, allowing them to maintain a decent lifestyle. These "decentralized" teachers and the Educated Youths quickly developed a natural affinity, and we got to know each other. They encouraged me, saying, "Junior high school graduates should continue their studies in high school and lay a solid foundation for college."

Among the sent-down Educated Youths in Suxian County was a girl named Yin Li. She had completed the admission procedures and was looking forward to me becoming her classmate at Yong'an High School. I first met Yin Li in the spring of 1969 at Yong'an Bus Station. She was waiting at the station for a bus to the county seat. She wore a classically styled shirt with a blue floral print on a white background, had long braids, and bright eyes. She appeared to be a charming girl from southern Anhui. Upon seeing me, she approached and greeted me openly, "Are you an Educated Youth from Shanghai? I am from the county seat. I am in Little Xie's village now. Come visit me when you have time." A few days later, we met again at the Yong'an market, and Yin Li expressed her desire to visit Yelou village to see my place. Upon arriving at Qianwang Village, I discovered that everyone in the village knew Yin Li, referring to her as Xie Daofeng's daughter. Yin Li was amiable, enjoying conversations with the villagers and sharing laughter with them, which made her quite popular. A woman from the neighboring house helped me cook a meal for Yin Li. She stayed until after dark. In the Qiandong production squad of Qianwang Village, there was another girl named Wang Guangqin, also an Educated Youth from Suxian City, like Yin Li. Wang Guangqin knew Yin Li. Her father worked as the county commerce director in Suxian City, and her parents resided there. Despite growing up in the city, Wang Guangqin now lived in the village as an Educated Youth. She had grandparents and relatives in the village. She invited Yin Li to stay overnight at her house. Liu Yanqi informed me that Yin Li's father, Xie Daofeng, was no ordinary person. When he stamped his feet at home, the whole city would tremble. At the start of the Cultural Revolution, big-character posters proclaiming "Down with Xie Daofeng" and "Burn Xie Daofeng" were widespread in the city. However, Xie Daofeng swiftly reversed the situation and was back in charge.

The next time I encountered Yin Li was at the Yong'an fair, accompanied by her grandfather. Yin Li introduced me to him. He had silver hair and a beard, dressed in a white jacket and black pants, presenting a clean and tidy appearance. Yin Li invited me to visit Little Xie's with them, and her grandpa kindly offered to cook for us. As we walked, he turned to Yin Li and remarked, "Liu Chengmo is quite handsome!" This made Yin Li blush. Little Xie's was located north of Yong'an, just a half-hour's walk away. Soon, Yin Li's younger brothers joined us – the older one named Erhei and the younger one Sanhei. Sanhei bore a striking resemblance to Yin Li, with silky white skin. When Xie Daofeng faced adversity, being confined to a cowshed and denied the right to return home, there was no one to care for the children. Therefore, their grandfather brought them to his native village. Since Yin Li was already in the native village, he took care of them collectively. Erhei and Sanhei enjoyed their freedom at their grandfather's house, spending their days fishing and playing with dogs. Upon learning that Xie Daofeng had regained his leadership position, I hesitated and told Yin Li, "You come from a Communist Party family, and I belong to the Five Black categories. Perhaps we aren't suitable as friends." Yin Li responded, "Don't think that way. If my dad were still under scrutiny, I would be considered a child of a 'gangster' too." Her words convinced me that Yin Li was someone worth knowing. However, to my surprise, a few months of friendship with Yin Li resulted in a long-term disaster. Yin Li's father blocked all opportunities for me and suppressed me for nine years. I found myself trapped with no way out, and the most precious years of my life slipped away.

During the eight years of the Anti-Japanese War, Xie's village served as a base for guerrilla activities. Xie Daofeng served as a courier for the local communist guerrilla commander, Captain Yin, and eventually, he married Captain Yin's daughter. Together, they had two sons and two daughters. The sons took on the surname Xie, while the daughters adopted their mother's surname, Yin. Xie Daofeng held a bureau-level position in the Suxian Region Administration, not at the highest rank but still significant. As the saying goes, "A military camp may be stable, but the soldiers change frequently." In Suxian City, however, it turned out "The camp may be solid, but the leaders change frequently." Because Suxian was a financially challenged and isolated area, it was difficult to attract officials from other regions. Those who assumed key leadership roles, such as administrative commissioners and regional party committee secretaries, usually didn't stay in Suxian for long. However, Xie Daofeng was deeply rooted in the local landscape. He successively served as the director of various regional bureaus, including the Industrial Bureau and Labor Bureau. His wife also held a prominent position as the director of the Regional Industrial Supplies Bureau. Through years of managing offices and strategically placing trusted individuals in different departments, Xie Daofeng established a vast political network in Suxian. The organizational structure of the Communist Party, similar to that of criminal gangs, allowed those capable of forming alliances for personal gain to ascend in influence. Despite facing criticism for utilizing connections to secure positions for his associates, Xie Daofeng's power only grew stronger. Over time, he emerged as one of the most influential figures in the Suxian Regional administrative compound, wielding authority throughout the eight counties in the region.

Peasants in Huaibei have long labored from sunrise to sunset, with winter typically serving as the off-season. During this downtime, they found solace in enjoying local operas like the popular Flower Drum Opera and Sizhou Opera, particularly during the New Year festivities. Suxian City boasted its own dedicated Flower Drum Opera Troupe. However, with the establishment of people's communes, peasants lost the autonomy to plan their activities and control over their work schedules. The city party committee in Huaibei saw the off-season as an opportunity for water conservancy projects to transform this period into a productive one. In late 1969, Suxian City decided to excavate the Xinbian River, a project spanning multiple counties. I, along with fellow village residents, embarked on a day-long journey to the construction site. There, we built rudimentary triangular huts using five tree trunks covered with grass. We slept on damp ground, enduring winds that penetrated our humble shelters. The physically demanding task of moving wheelbarrows up the canal bank required considerable strength. Positioned at the front of the line, I pulled the wheelbarrow and helped load it. Cold, muddy water seeped into the bottom of the canal, and we worked over ten hours daily, soaked to the bone. Some participants developed severe arthritis, impeding their mobility. Digging the canal proved arduous, and many villagers would have preferred the comfort of their homes during the winter leisure if given the choice. As Educated Youths, our duty was to engage in the most challenging tasks to earn recommendations for job recruitment and eventually leave rural life. We were provided with three meals a day of steamed bread and noodles. However, the lack of meat and other provisions left my stomach empty within two hours of starting the strenuous digging.

In the early spring of 1970, Suxian's "Agricultural Learning from Dazhai" initiative introduced a new endeavor: well drilling. While the Xinbian River Project aimed to address flooding, drilling wells aimed to tackle drought. Yong'an Commune established a dedicated well-drilling team, with technicians working in shifts around the clock at the construction site. Continuous operation was necessary as muddy water settled quickly. To support the project, the commune improvised a workshop for manufacturing cement culverts used in constructing well walls. These culverts, measuring one meter in diameter, came in two types: solid and perforated. The drilling process followed specific steps. Initially, a pit approximately 2 meters in diameter was excavated on level ground. This pit was filled with water, and a two-story tripod equipped with a large pulley was erected above it. A cone-shaped hollow steel tank, connected to a cross lever, was suspended from the pulley. The tank's pointed cone featured two open scrapers, which, when turned while the lever was pushed, scraped mud into the tank as it descended. This scraping and lifting continued until the well reached a depth of nearly 15 meters, at which point the cement culvert could be laid. The depth of the soil layer, recorded during the steel tank's descent, determined whether it was a silt layer or a water outlet layer. Solid and perforated cement pipes, matching these layers, were laid accordingly. Once the culvert was in place, any gaps outside it were filled with gravel. At this stage, the culvert was a cavity filled with muddy water, necessitating immediate pumping. Only after clearing the muddy water could clean water enter. Failure to promptly flush out the well would result in the rapid settling of muddy water, rendering the well useless. This crucial step in the process is called "washing the well."

The well-drilling team was equipped with a water pump. Since Yong'an had no electricity, a diesel engine was provided to drive the water pump. The diesel engine was produced by a machinery factory in Suxian County. Originally, the factory did not have the technical capacity to produce diesel engines; they were products of the Great Leap Forward. The diesel engines were difficult to start and prone to frequent shutdowns. The machinery factory was far from the communes and lacked qualified technicians, making it impossible for them to effect repairs promptly. The technicians of the drilling team were at a loss, so they went to find the commune cadres. Everyone was at a loss and desperate. I had learned about four-stroke diesel engines in physics class and had seen models of diesel engines in the laboratory. This diesel engine came with several specialized tools and a user manual. I opened the manual, which contained maintenance methods and troubleshooting guidelines. I understood that the engine stalled because when the heat dissipation was too slow, the machine would overheat, and the piston would seize. The repair method involved opening the cylinder, replacing the damaged piston ring, adjusting the sealing of the piston ring, and then closing the cylinder. Upon opening the cylinder, I found severe carbon buildup on the cylinder wall, likely due to the wrong type of diesel fuel being used. I asked the technician what type of diesel he was using, and he said he didn't know. I cleaned the cylinder wall and followed the steps in the manual. I manually ignited the engine with the hand-operated lever, and the diesel engine suddenly started. The onlookers jumped up. The commune cadres were excited and pointed at me, saying, "Xiao Liu, from now on, you don't need to do anything else, just wash the well." Drilling the well required continuous pumping for at least 24 hours. I slept next to the new well at night. The production squad parked a cart by the well, and a bamboo mat was placed on top of the cart to form an arched shelter, which was my overnight accommodation. In the middle of the night, I enjoyed a bowl of egg noodles sent by the production squad as a midnight snack. Although my high-school application was rejected, I ended up working as a technician for a time.

In Anhui's administrative hierarchy, below the provincial level are regional administrations, and the Suxian Region encompasses eight counties. Below the county level are districts, followed by communes. At this time, Suxian County implemented the merger of districts and communes, with four small communes combined into one large commune directly under the county committee's leadership. The Yong'an Commune's area suddenly expanded fourfold, and the task of drilling wells increased accordingly. Some Educated Youths on the well-drilling team returned to their production squad because recruitment targeting Educated Youths began. The first batch of recruiting units included the Suxian County Tire Factory, Suxian County Silk Factory, brick and tile factories, cement plants, agricultural machinery factories, roasted chicken factories, department stores, food companies, the Dongfeng Hotel, and the People Restaurant, as well as the Huaibei Coal Mine and Luling Coal Mine. These units were all county-level small factories and service enterprises under collective ownership. The working environment was dirty and rudimentary. However, monthly wages could be collected, and meals were provided in the canteen. There was no need to farm, gather firewood, mill grain, or work in the fields. After paying for meals, one could save a little money each month, a world of difference compared to the days of toiling under the sun.

The first step in recruitment began with recommendations from the production brigade. Ye Lou production brigade originally had five Educated Youths from Shanghai No. 62 Middle School. Shen Guanghua and I were in the Qianxi squad, while three girls from our school were in the Ye Lou back village squad. Later, the back village of Yelou added a boy named Lin Qianghua. Lin Qianghua was transferred from a village named Little Liu's in another small commune. The Party secretary of that village was removed from office and investigated because of a scandal involving him and a female youth. All the Educated Youths in Liu Laozhuang were transferred out. Lin Qianghua was a few years older than us and a shady character. There were rumors that he had improper relations with the widows in the village. He formed a gang with two or three other Educated Youths, wandering around and stealing chickens and ducks from villagers. They broke into other Educated Youths' houses and stole money. My roommate Shen Guanghua came from a relatively well-off family and brought a large, high-end semiconductor radio, the kind that ordinary working-class families couldn't afford. One day, Lin Qianghua and his two accomplices barged into our room and snatched Shen Guanghua's semiconductor radio. It was Shen Guanghua's most valuable possession, and he was in tears over it. Lin Qianghua didn't care; he was used to such acts of theft. Most grassroots cadres in rural areas were second-rate village bullies. Lin Qianghua was good at flattering the cadres. He shared a bottle with them and called them brothers.

In 1970, the leadership of the commune was still in a state of chaos. At that time, the dominant faction was the rebel faction, with a leader named Zhang Hua. The former secretary of the commune, Chen Jiabei, was a member of the rebel faction and a close friend of Zhang Hua. Chen Jiabei's wife worked at the commune's post office. Since the arrival of the Educated Youths, the post office had been bustling with activity. Chen Jiabei got to know many Educated Youths at the post office. Chen Jiabei was nicknamed "Chen Mazhi" (pockmarked face). He liked to wear his hat crookedly and leer at the female Educated Youths with half-closed eyes. The recruitment process began, and Chen Jiabei got hold of the lucrative task of distributing recruitment forms. He was greedy and lustful. Whoever treated him to a good meal and alcohol, he would give them the recruitment form, regardless of whether they were even Educated Youths or not. The commune allocated recruitment quotas to each brigade, and our Ye Lou brigade only received one quota spot. Lin Qianghua saw other Educated Youths in our brigade as competitors and considered me his number one enemy. He was very interested in Yin Li. He became furious when Yin Li came to visit me at Ye Lou. He told me, "A political enemy is worse than a romantic rival." He spread rumors among the brigade cadres, saying, "Liu Chengmo associates with Yin Li just for promotion." Lin Qianghua took the opportunity to repair semiconductor radios for the unscrupulous former Yong'an Commune secretary Chen Jiabei to get close to him, and gave Chen Jiabei the semiconductor radio he had stolen from Shen Guanghua. Birds of a feather flock together, and the two quickly developed a close relationship. Lin Qianghua spoke ill of me to Chen Jiabei, stigmatizing my relationship with Yin Li, to satisfy Chen Jiabei's dark psyche and further his own ambition. Despite his own problematic family background, Lin Qianghua secured the only quota spot allocated to Ye Lou. None of the five Educated Youth originally stationed at Ye Lou managed to get a job in the first wave of recruitment. Lin Qianghua was the first to leave Ye Lou. However, the county leather factory that recruited him was quite undesirable. In name, it was a factory, but in reality, it was just a small workshop emitting a foul odor. There was another Educated Youth in Ye Lou named Gao Jinsong. He was sent down from Suxian City. He didn't look like an Educated Youth; he seemed more like a grown man. His mother was a teacher who received a government salary, looking old and haggard. I heard his father was suppressed. Gao Jinsong pestered Chen Jiabei every day and drank with him, and eventually, he got recruited to the Huaibei coal mine. I knew he got a recruitment form from Chen Jiabei, but I didn't know how he managed to get approval through the county labor bureau. Several years later, when I visited my friend at the mine, I met Gao Jinsong's mother. She told me that she had spent all her life savings to secure that job for her son.

As part of the recruitment process, Educated Youths had to undergo family background and political reviews, commonly referred to as "Zhengshen," which was the abbreviation for political review. During Mao's era, political review was a mandatory process for individuals with a middle school education or above. This involved scrutinizing various aspects of an individual's background to ensure alignment with the prevailing political ideology. In the urban areas of Shanghai at that time, students had to undergo a political review of their family and social relationships before graduating from middle school. They filled out a political review form, which was then placed in their student file. This file was kept at their work or study unit or the police station with jurisdiction for their household registration. Approximately six months before graduation, the school dispatched representatives to the workplaces of each student's parents. By reviewing personnel files, they documented information related to family background, personal history, political beliefs, family members, major social relationships, records of awards and punishments, and any previous political review conclusions or other noteworthy details. Any issues requiring clarification were submitted to the unit for verification before the note was officially signed and stamped with an official seal.

Once both parents' materials were complete, the political examiner filled out the form, and the new political review note became an integral part of the student's file. If an immediate family member was found to have been sentenced to death, detained, or subjected to other legal measures, additional investigation was necessary, often requiring a copy of the court decision. The political review form became an indispensable component of student files during that period. After graduation, whether the students were assigned to the countryside or given a job, their files continued to follow them like a ghost and often haunted them like a nightmare, influencing their destiny. Before recruiting a student, a hiring unit had to review the student's file, accepting them only after they had successfully passed the political review. The process was thorough and carried significant weight in determining an individual's opportunities and standing in society.

Through the political review, the Communist Party implemented strict class identification and classified management of the population. Occasionally, the Party referred to children in the Five Black Categories as "educable children," a term that carried derogatory connotations.

These "educable children" were not handicapped in the traditional sense; they were not mentally retarded, emotionally disturbed, or physically impaired. Instead, they were individuals who were politically and socially disregarded by the Party. This demeaning label became a burden for those labeled as such, akin to a scarlet letter to wear and a cross to bear. It cast a lingering dark cloud over the lives of hundreds of millions of "political pariahs." This discriminatory practice finds its roots in historical examples such as India's caste system, complete with its untouchables, and Hitler's Jewish blood theory. It represents an ancient form of discrimination where an individual, through no fault of their own, is deprived of equal opportunities for further education, military service, job recruitment, and more, simply because of their birth. What makes this discrimination particularly distressing is its all-encompassing pervasiveness, reaching into the minutiae of daily life and burdening every party involved with an imposed political original sin. As time keeps passing, it may become difficult for future historians to fully examine the darkest moments of life that have remained submerged over the years. The relentless pace of human progress may inadvertently overlook the innocent lives trampled by iron boots, but the impact remains indelibly engraved in the daily lives of those deemed "educable children."

Policies may be fixed, but the individuals responsible for their implementation often exhibit flexibility. Zhang Hua and Chen Jiabei, in particular, demonstrated a willingness to deviate from established policies. Among the Educated Youths, some were more audacious, precocious, and willing to engage in bribery or trading sexual favors to obtain job recruitment forms. At the time, such practices were a byproduct of the system in place throughout China, but Chen Jiabei's own audacity and recklessness were bound to shorten his good days. He had his adversaries, those who envied him. Anonymous letters were sent to the county revolutionary committee, which began organzing a work team for investigation. This in turn led to Chen Jiabei being suspended pending review. Zhang Hua, due to excessive alcohol consumption, suddenly dropped dead before the county's investigative team arrived. As mentioned above, the incidents involving Zhang Hua and Chen Jiabei were not isolated cases. A written report revealed that in 1972, in a county in Anhui Province, Educated Youths had the opportunity to be recommended for university admission for the first time. Tens of thousands of Educated Youths in the county engaged in a large-scale competition, with only 70 individuals ultimately being selected. During the school selection physical exams, it was shockingly discovered that none of the female youths were virgins. This was not very unusual at the time, and there can be little doubt that it was due to those female youths either offering or being asked by a party member in charge of the student assessment process to trade their virginity for college acceptance.

In the summer of 1970, the well-digging team was assigned to the Lu Lake brigade. Initially, there were three boys and three girls who joined the brigade. Among the girls, Xu Yueying and Ren Yizhen were high school students from No.62 Middle School. Zhu Huifen was a junior high school student. Just a few months later, Ren Yizhen left Lu Lake and got married in a rural area near Changzhou, in Southern Jiangsu Province. This was a place of abundance, with much better living conditions than Huaibei. It's said that she and her groom hadn't even met before; the marriage was arranged by their parents. On the day she left, a young man from Changzhou came to Lu Lake to take Ren Yizhen away. He seemed quite decent. Xu Yueying's father was a Kuomintang major general, and he went to Taiwan in 1949. Xu Yueying was the youngest child, still a toddler at the time, and her aunt acted as her nanny. When the general's family left the mainland, the aunt forcibly took her off the plane, fearing that her own economic support would be cut off once the family was gone. Little did they know, Taiwan and the mainland would be separated for decades after that parting. Xu Yueying was no longer young; her prospects of promotion were slim. She married an accountant from the Lu Lake production brigade, who had graduated from Suxian No.1 Middle School. He returned to his hometown in Lu Lake with his parents after his father was labeled as right-wing. The young man had also worked on well-digging. During breaks, while other young people chatted aimlessly and cracked dirty jokes, he always quietly read a book. Unfortunately, Xu Yueying's husband passed away from illness in the

1990s. She had to raise several children on her own, which was not easy. Later, Xu Yueying worked at Yong'an Elementary School as a teacher until retirement. In the 1980s, when the mainland opened up to the outside world, Xu Yueying's parents had already passed away. Her siblings had never met her and had settled in the United States. In the 1990s, they returned according to their parents' wishes to find Xu Yueying. Meeting their youngest sister and hearing about her experiences, they couldn't help but feel deeply saddened by her life story.

The three boys who settled in Lu Lake were classmates at No. 62 Middle School. While Liu Gengnian and Wu Chongfang had already left for Huaibei No. 8 Mine and Suxian Tire Factory, respectively, Shi Taihua remained. I stayed at Shi Taihua's house during the well-drilling team's time at Lu Lake. The distance from Lu Lake to Little Xie's village was less than one mile, about a 20-minute walk. Yin Li, attending school in Yong'an during the day, returned to Little Xie's in the afternoon. During breaks from the well-drilling team, I had the opportunity to meet with Yin Li. Yin Li shared a passion for reading and writing, having published some short articles in local newspapers. As the second batch of Educated Youth recruitment unfolded, the units included state-owned factories and enterprises at regional and provincial levels, such as steel plants, fertilizer plants, meat processing plants, regional food plants, and Provincial Construction Company No. 3, responsible for building a thermal power plant in Huaibei City. Yin Li received a notice to report to the Suxian Bus Station. On the evening she received the notice, Yin Li and I walked hand in hand along a ditch beside an unpaved road to Suxian City. The water in the ditch flowed quietly, and the sorghum leaves rustled. Later at night, an auspicious time for love and reunion, Yin Li turned around, placed my hand on her chest, and rested her face on my chest. Her cheeks were warm, lips soft, and nipples erect. Her hair carried the faint scent of sandalwood soap, and her eyes sparkled brighter than the stars. Whispering, she suggested we go inside. As we approached the door, the flickering light of a kerosene lamp caught my eye, and I looked up to see a full moon crossing the sea of clouds. The moon emerged, and the sky suddenly illuminated, depicting the beautiful scenery of a wedding night when a scholar achieved top status. In an instant, the moon was swallowed by boundless dark clouds. I stopped, and my palms grew cold. Yin Li asked, "What are you thinking?" I replied, "Is there a bright future awaiting us?" Yin Li stopped and turned around, gazing at me silently, as if time had come to a standstill. I asked her what she was thinking, and she said, with a mist in her eyes, "Is it true that immortal Chang´e in the moon palace really has a jade rabbit to ease her loneliness?"

The next day, Yin Li came to Lu Lake to spend time with me. She quickly struck up a friendship with Shi Taihua, and the book she brought along was a favorite among everyone. These were translated European and American novels from the Republic of China era, popular among Educated Youth from Shanghai and Suxian City. While novels were in demand, Yin Li had a preference for children's literature, which suited her simple and joyful personality. After the schools in Suxian City were closed, the library was left abandoned. Many books found their way into society, with some still held by former teachers and students. Despite our extremely frugal material circumstances and the monotony of our daily lives, the presence of books offered solace. Even amidst hunger and cold, the enchanting tales provided a temporary escape from the harsh realities of life. On dreary, rainy days, immersing ourselves in books became a form of spiritual refuge—a safe harbor readily available.

Somerset Maugham wisely stated, "To acquire the habit of reading is to construct for yourself a refuge from almost all the miseries of life." Reading indeed provides a shelter that allows me to detach myself from reality, offering a respite from life's hardships. In the words of Zhang Henshui, China's preeminent popular novelist of the nineteen-thirties and forties, "With books, there is hope. With books, the road will stretch under your feet." For me, books were akin to a distant beam of light in a dark night, momentarily illuminating life and infusing it with hope. Books served as my guide, directing me toward exploration and revealing that, though distant, another world existed on this earth. In the face of life's tempestuous winds, books shelter. Regardless of how wronged I felt, they had the power to calm me, encouraging thoughtful contemplation of my path forward. Within the pages of a book, I always found a reflection of myself. Gradually, I came to understand that life was a sea of suffering. When the waves of life overturned the ship, causing panic and despair, I realized I wasn't alone in experiencing inner turmoil. Loneliness faded away, and I began to release my regrets. Life presented challenges to everyone, but as long as I was willing to read, there was always a book that could alleviate the pain. In Moments of anxiety and unease, reading served as a soothing balm for my mind. In times of helplessness, books became my most reliable guides. Regardless of the challenges I faced, reading consistently offered me inner strength. People who embrace reading are not easily defeated; they find resilience and fortitude within the pages of a good book.

Books, beyond being a refuge in life, serve as the habitat of the soul. In Moments of maverick thinking, I found kindred spirits within the pages of books; when feeling out of place, resonance echoed through the words on the paper. In a world where people could reject and make life miserable, books never did. When abandoned and denied, books became like old friends, offering spiritual companionship. As Victor Hugo put it, "To learn to read is to light a fire; every syllable that is spelled out is a spark." Reading helped me break free from the confines of reality and appreciate the vastness of time and space. My soul, within this expansive journey, was slowly infiltrated and nourished, allowing me to become a better version of myself. With books as companions, I no longer needed to be anxious, impetuous, or lonely. They opened a window for me to observe various aspects of life and explore the colorful world. While reading books, I was simultaneously reading about myself and seeking my soul. Reading became a form of spiritual practice, enabling me to introspect and discover the essence of my being. Before becoming a writer, Somerset Maugham worked as a medical intern. After witnessing countless instances of life and death, he grappled with the question, "What is the meaning of human life?" Until one day, he found the answer, and it was in books. The answer lay in living for truth, goodness, and beauty. Reading provides people with a vehicle to escape the shackles of fate and pursue these enduring values.

One day, an Educated Youth named Zhang Tieniu visited Shi

Taihua's house in Lu Lake. Upon noticing a copy of "Red and Black" on my bedside, he said that he wanted to borrow it. I informed him about the waiting list, mentioning that he would have to wait for a few days. Zhang Tieniu stood out among the Shanghai Educated Youths due to his unique background. His father, originally a cadre from the Northern part of China, spoke a Northern dialect, setting him apart from the Shanghainese-speaking community. During the Cultural Revolution, his father was labeled a capitalist roader, transforming Zhang Tieniu into an overnight gangster child. Faced with the challenges of his new status, he found himself temporarily staying with the children of the Five Black Categories. Despite this, the inherent superiority and arrogance of being a cadre's child were evident. Often seen in an old military uniform, his eyes, framed by short-sighted glasses, conveyed a mix of anger and pride. Fully aware of the need to wait and the necessity of offering some tribute to the party, Zhang Tieniu observed his surroundings carefully, waiting for the opportune Moment. Having been exposed to such strategies since childhood, finding an opportunity was not a difficult task for him. In a world where surveillance and informing were low-cost means, Zhang Tieniu was adept at identifying and seizing opportunities.

Since the founding of the People's Republic of China, each movement has required the establishment of a model figure, and the Educated Youth movement was no exception. Figures like Xing Yanzi in Tianjin, Hou Jun in Beijing, and Dong Jiageng in Jiangsu gained prominence. The arrival of Shanghai Educated Youths in Suxian marked a historic event, and identifying a noteworthy model among them became crucial for the regional and county revolutionary committees. Among the Educated Youths in Yong'an Commune, few had a red family background, making Zhang Tieniu stand out. To be a role model, one not only needed a good background but also commendable deeds. While some deeds could be fabricated, they couldn't be entirely baseless. Recognizing an opportunity, Zhang Tieniu promptly reported to commune leaders that I—Liu Chengmo—was circulating pornographic novels, framing it as a new trend in class struggle among the Educated Youths. The commune cadres were pleased with Zhang Tieniu's active cooperation. A commune cadre said, "Just hearing Zhang Tieniu's name makes me excited. Tieniu is a tractor and represents agricultural mechanization. Who doesn't like Tieniu in the People's Commune?" In 1971, Zhang Tieniu quickly joined the party, swiftly became a member of the county party committee, and was eventually promoted to the position of the Secretary of the Party Committee of Langan Commune. His transformation from a youth in need of re-education to a leader with real power was remarkable. Concerning Liu Chengmo, some cadres suggested organizing an Educated Youth meeting to openly criticize him. However, during the investigation, it was discovered that the book in question bore the seal of the Suxian No. 1 Middle School Library, confirming that it had been passed to me by Yin Li. When the incident involved Xie Daofeng's daughter, commune cadres applied the brakes, stating that it was inappropriate to publicly criticize an Educated Youth as it might negatively impact the Party's policy of "Go up the Mountain, Down to the Village."

When I was summoned by the commune for criticism, Yin Li had already started working at Suxian Bus Station—an enviable position. During that time, the two most coveted professions for ordinary people were those associated with stethoscopes and steering wheels. Medical and transportation roles represented the scarcest social resources. Being a driver not only provided substantial extra income but also offered various benefits. Working at a bus station meant having the privilege to buy bus tickets, a significant favor in high demand. After Yin Li began working at the bus station, I paid her a visit. She shared with me that He Guangyao was once again pursuing her. He Guangyao, a schoolmate from her junior high school, was one year her senior. Despite Yin Li's lack of interest, He Guangyao persistently pursued her. While others among the Educated Youths went to the countryside, He Guangyao enlisted in the military. Given that his father was a policeman, he had no trouble passing the political review. While returning home for a visit, He Guangyao came to the bus station to see Yin Li. She said that He Guangyao had a short temper. He threw a mug on the ground when Yin Li merely smiled at a coworker. Yin Li declared, "I am not his girlfriend. No one in our family likes him. Who does he think he is?" Yin Li's parents shared her sentiment, finding He Guangyao distasteful and, as the son of a local policeman, beneath their social status.

The northwest wind blew across the sky, prompting farmers to don cotton clothes with a grass rope tied around their waists. They believed a single rope was more sufficient than an extra layer of cotton. I tried it myself and found it reasonable; we all ended up looking like beggars. As the well-digging came to a halt when the water in the well began to freeze. All completed wells were left unused due to the lack of funds from the commune and production brigade to purchase pumps. The silt inside the wells gradually settled, rendering them all useless. A new initiative emerged in the agricultural movement, inspired by Dazhai's model. The county party committee issued a directive to all communes, urging the widespread adoption of Pesticide 920. This pesticide, essentially a crude form of gibberellin, held potential benefits for plant growth stimulation. Initially valued during the Great Leap Forward Movement, gibberellins were now reintroduced on a larger scale, with hopes of achieving agricultural miracles, improving livestock breeding, fostering forestry seedlings, and even impacting medical services and health care. Given the poor soil quality of the Huaibei Plain, particularly the deficiency in fertilizers, Pesticide 920 was viewed with high expectations. Superiors emphasized the immediate popularization of 920 through "simplified methods." The production process involved inoculating the gibberellin in a glass test tube, cultivating the fungus in a culture medium, and then transplanting it into bran for mass production.

Yong'an Middle School, equipped with a basic chemistry laboratory, became the designated location for the pharmaceutical factory. This factory was also considered Yongan Middle School's school-run facility. I, along with Shen Guanghua and Zhu Zongren—a local junior high school graduate orphan—were chosen to work on this project. Ning Chuanzhong, responsible for schools and Educated Youths with the Standing Committee of the Yong'an Commune Revolutionary Committee, sought to relocate me and Shen Guanghua to Yong'an Middle School. However, the village party secretary, Liu Zhengji, was reluctant to cooperate, citing concerns about work points and grain rations. Upset by this contradiction, Ning Chuanzhong decided to transfer me out of Yelou. To ensure my sustenance, he provided a local certificate to purchase grain. Private teachers were paid based on village work points and state subsidies, with primary school teachers receiving ¥8 per month and middle school teachers ¥13. Since the factory was affiliated with Yong'an Middle School, I received a ¥13 subsidy. I didn't have a village to provide me with work points, so the school factory offered me an additional ¥13. After encountering obstacles at Yelou, Ning Chuanzhong did not pursue the arrangement for Shen Guanghua any further. Shen Guanghua was later offered a teaching position by Yelou Village Primary School. Shen Guanghua felt very troubled about not being able to go to Yong'an Middle School.

One spring day in 1971, Zhan Yumin traveled by bus from Suxian to Yong'an to visit me. Zhan Yumin, a high school student from Bengbu City, had a mature appearance, standing at 5'9" with dark skin, curly hair, a prominent nose bridge, and deep eye sockets. His mother and sister worked as teachers in Bengbu, while his father, a Kuomintang general, had relocated to Taiwan in 1949. Assigned to Zhangguang Village, near where I had first been assigned, Zhan Yumin and I became friends while working together on the well-drilling team and sharing books. During the Cultural Revolution, despite the decline of most industries, performance groups gained popularity. Individuals from the Black Five Categories, like us, could secure exceptions and employment in performance groups. Zhan Yumin's evident artistic talent, including a good appearance and voice, marked him as suitable material for acting. Wu Dezhi, a standing committee member overseeing culture and education on the County Revolutionary Committee, organized the compilation of a short Flower and Drum Opera titled "Youths and Fine Horses" for national performance participation. Praising Mao's May 7th Instructions and keeping pace with the revolutionary situation, the opera won the grand prize and caused a sensation in Suxian City. Consequently, the County Flower and Drum Troupe expanded, recruiting Zhan Yumin and Yang Meizhen, an Educated Youth from Shanghai. When Zhan Yumin arrived,

I was about to leave for Yelou to retrieve some belongings, as I still had a few pieces of clothing there. Zhan Yumin suggested, "Let's go together and visit Shen Guanghua." Upon reaching Yelou Primary School, Principal Liu Xiu informed us that Shen Guanghua was not present, surprising us both. Did he have a class to teach? Liu Xiu added, "I find it strange too. Look, the clothes he wants to wash are still soaking in the basin." Upon entering my house, I noticed that a pair of white basketball shoes was missing. Failing to locate Shen Guanghua, Zhan Yumin and I had no choice but to return to Yong'an. Soon after, Zhan Yumin was recruited by the Hefei City Performance Troupe and left Suxian.

A few days later, two police officers came to Yong'an Middle School and visited me, inquiring whether Shen Guanghua had bid farewell and disclosed his destination before departing. They also went to Hefei and asked Zhan Yumin the same questions. Neither of us had any knowledge about his plans. The police officers then revealed that Shen Guanghua was currently detained in the West Gate, referring to the No. 3 Provincial Prison in the West Gate, Suxian City, characterized by high walls topped with barbed wire. According to the police, Shen Guanghua had been arrested in Shenzhen. After the Communist Party took control, Shenzhen experienced four major waves of mass exodus to Hong Kong, one of which occurred in 1972, involving Educated Youth. However, this information wasn't widely reported in newspapers, so at that time, many were unaware of these events. Given Shen Guanghua's family background—his father being a prosperous businessman in Shanghai with relatives in Hong Kong—it's conceivable that he learned about the waves of escapes, prompting his impulsive journey to Shenzhen.

The 920 Pharmaceutical Factory at Yong'an Middle School was short-lived. Expanding production required large quantities of bran, which presented challenges when the peasants did not have enough to feed their pigs. Thus, the school-run factory had to change its focus. Mr. Shi Xinbiao, a senior teacher at Yong'an Middle School, was undergoing a political background check at the time, so he was prohibited from teaching. Instead, he was assigned to work in the school-run factory. Originally from Henan Province, Mr. Shi brought a hand-operated tablet press machine to the school. Leveraging his knowledge of traditional Chinese medicine, he guided students in using the machine to produce herbal medicine tablets and honey-coated pills. Malaria was widespread in Huaibei, and the prescription drug quinine was both expensive and scarce. Recognizing the medicinal properties of the herb Bupleurum in treating malaria, I initiated the trial production of Bupleurum intramuscular injection. This involved soaking and boiling dried Bupleurum angustifolia in a high-pressure tank, steaming the herb, and extracting a liquid essence. Using a medical hollow latex catheter, I connected the tank to a condenser, allowing the steam to cool and return to liquid form. The distilled Bupleurum liquid was then sealed in 2 ml ampoules using a jet alcohol lamp. The final step was labeling the ampoules. I engraved "Bupleurum Injection 2ml" on a piece of wax paper, applied dark blue ink under it, rolled the ampoule gently on the wax paper, and printed the label on the ampoule bottle. Though the production process wasn't overly complex, creating an injectable product required meticulous attention to sterilization. I managed the initial steps independently and enlisted students to help with labeling and packing. By the summer and autumn of 1972, when mosquitoes were abundant and malaria cases were high, the effectiveness of Bupleurum injection was confirmed through its use by numerous patients. The commune health clinic and neighboring communes' health clinics began purchasing the product. Additionally, since the commune health clinic lacked distilled water for intramuscular injection, I supplied them with 5 ml ampoules of distilled water. With these two products, the school-run factory survived and began turning a profit.

The operations of the school-run pharmaceutical factory required various consumables such as ampoules, alcohol lamps, and packaging boxes. To secure the ampoules, I sought assistance from one of my cousins working as a salesperson for a pharmaceutical company in Suzhou. He helped procure the needed supplies, and since the school-run factory operated informally without a business account or checkbook, I had to go to Suzhou to pay in cash. After picking up the goods, I had to personally check them in at the train station. While I was away on a business trip, Shen Guanghua sent me a postcard from prison. It read: "Everything is fine here in prison, except for the lack of daily necessities. Can you send me soap and toilet paper?" By the time I returned from the trip and saw the postcard, Shen Guanghua had already been released. He was escorted back to the Yelou production brigade by police from the No. 3 Prison. The police instructed the commune and village cadres: "The party's policy is to provide a way out for those who have made mistakes, and there must be no discrimination against Shen Guanghua, so as not to interfere with the 'Go up the Mountain, Down to the Village' movement." Before I went to Yelou, Shen Guanghua's mother accompanied him to Yong'an Middle School to see me. This was the first and only time I met Shen Guanghua's mother. As soon as she saw me, she began to accuse me: "You guys were roommates. When Shen Guanghua was in trouble, you ignored him. You didn't even bother to reply to his letter." She knew that I had been away on a business trip, so her accusations sounded baseless. I treated them to a meal, and after they finished lunch, they left. Not long after Shen Guanghua's mother left, someone from Yelou informed me that Shen Guanghua was acting strangely. They said he had been found rolling in a manure pit on a windy and rainy day, shouting: "Go to the countryside and get covered in mud." Liu Yanqi pulled him out of the pit and cleaned him up. Liu Yanqi later approached me to discuss the incident, mentioning that it didn't seem like genuine madness and that Shen Guanghua might have been pretending. In response, I said, "There's no need to determine the truth of such matters. What appears false often is true, and vice versa." Ning Chuanshu, the director of the Yong'an Commune Health Clinic, was a seasoned individual. He was the younger brother of Ning Chuanzhong, the commune standing committee member who transferred me to Yong'an Middle School. At the time, Ning Chuanshu's wife worked as a barefoot doctor in Yelou Village and sympathized with Shen Guanghua. Recognizing Shen Guanghua's intelligence, skills, and interest in medicine, Ning Chuanshu transferred him to the health clinic as a barefoot doctor. Later, he arranged for Shen Guanghua's sister to work at the clinic.

In 1971, colleges and universities nationwide initiated the

recruitment of students from diverse backgrounds, including workers, peasants, and soldiers. These students were selected based on their adherence to political ideology, good health, over three years of work experience, approximately 20 years of age, and education equivalent to junior high school or higher. This group also included Educated Youths in rural areas. The admission process involved a blend of mass recommendation, leadership approval, and school evaluation, omitting the need for exams. Worker, peasant, and soldier students were entrusted with the significant task of "attending, managing, and transforming universities with Mao Zedong Thought," earning them a favorable status in the era. In 1971, Suxian City received limited university enrollment quotas, which were not distributed to lower levels. Xi'an Jiaotong University had an available quota spot, which Xie Daofeng assigned to Yin Li. Upon Yin Li's arrival at Xi'an Jiaotong University, she encountered He Guangyao, who had been recommended by the Air Force two years earlier, during a period when Lin Biao (the brilliant Chinese Communist general, famed for decisive victories in the civil war that helped bring Mao Zedong to power, and who later rose to be Mao's chosen successor before his sudden and mysterious death in a 1971 plane crash) enjoyed popularity. The Air Force was associated with Lin Biao's son, Lin Liguo. He Guangyao appeared to have a promising future. He Guangyao and Yin Li crossed paths again at the university, leading to a renewed pursuit by He Guangyao. Yin Li once again rejected his advances. He Guangyao resorted to drinking kerosene in an apparent suicide attempt to put pressure on Yin Li. Drinking kerosene does not cause death, but the attempted suicide of an active-duty soldier caused a great shock at the school. This disruption in Yin Li's studies prompted the school to allow her to return home and take a semester-long break. During this period, Xie Daofeng mobilized various individuals, including Yin Li's former teachers, to persuade her to accept He Guangyao's proposal. Yin Li visited Yong'an to confide in me. She expressed her distress, asking, "Will you simply stand by and watch me enter into a marriage devoid of love?" In response, I explained, "The circumstances are beyond my control. Consider this: once you complete your college education and secure employment in the city with a government salary, my residence registration will still be in Yong'an. How could we possibly establish a home together? It simply wouldn't work."

Xie Daofeng was a local tyrant, and those who cared about me in Yong'an were genuinely worried: "You shouldn't mess with the Xie Daofeng family. They can be very dangerous." Indeed, Xie Daofeng was notorious for his ruthlessness, and many county officials were intimidated by him to a degree, with even more compliance seen among the Yong'an commune cadres. Among Xie Daofeng's children, Yin Li was the eldest. Although she could be bold and free-spirited outside, she was afraid of her father at home. Erhei, on the other hand, was honest and obedient. Sanhei was rebellious for a while and refused to listen to his parents. Eventually, he moved out and didn't return home for a long time, causing great sadness to his mother. Sanhei liked to hang out with his good friend Wu Zheng, a Shanghai Educated Youth working at the steel plant. Xie Daofeng blamed Wu Zheng, accusing him of having a bad influence on Sanhei. In early 1976, after Premier Zhou passed away, the central government banned mourning activities. However, spontaneous memorial services were held in various places, including Xuefeng Park in Suxian, where Wu Zheng also participated. Xie Daofeng led a work team to the regional steel plant, using this as a pretext to label Wu Zheng as a current counter-revolutionary and have him arrested and imprisoned. Sanhei, in anger, threatened to kill his father with a knife, frightening Xie Daofeng so much that he didn't dare to return home for many days.

In the summer of 1973, Yin Li came to Yong'an to visit me again. She said her break from school was over, and next semester she would be interning at the Minhang Steam Turbine Power Plant in Shanghai with her classmates from the turbine department. She wanted to visit my mother while in Shanghai. I said it wasn't necessary, but she insisted and asked what Shanghai lacked and what she could bring for my mother. In those days, what wasn't lacking in Shanghai? I casually said, "Shanghai lacks rice." Unexpectedly, she actually carried ten kilograms of rice to Shanghai. When she arrived in Shanghai, Yin Li and another female classmate carried a bag of rice to my mother's house. My mother's indifferent demeanor made the two girls uncomfortable, so they hurriedly left. Yin Li's classmate was indignant and said, "You came all this way to bring her rice, and she treats you like this?" Yin Li's eyes turned red, tears welled up in her eyes, but didn't fall. Her classmate heard Yin Li say, "Liu Chengmo really has a miserable life!" In 1974, after graduating from Xi'an Jiaotong University, Yin Li returned to Suxian County and worked at the regional agricultural technical station. Finally, in 1975, Yin Li married He Guangyao. He Guangyao graduated two years earlier than Yin Li. By the time he returned to the Air Force, Lin Biao and Lin Liguo had already died in the shadowy "Lin Biao Incident" plane crash in Mongolia on September 13, 1971. The Air Force unit controlled by Lin Liguo was purged. He Guangyao returned to civilian life and went to work in a factory. Xie Daofeng's expectations were dashed. Nevertheless, it was better than being branded as a counter-revolutionary's family member. Later, He Guangyao got a job in personnel and used his minor authority to mingle with young women. He changed his attitude towards Yin Li, and incidents of domestic violence became frequent. After Suxian County was upgraded to a city, Yin Li served as the director of the Suzhou Municipal Women's Federation for many years. Her job was to protect women, but she couldn't protect herself. When Yin Li and He Guangyao finally divorced, they were both at retirement age.

The rise of the Cultural Revolution began with the Mao-Lin duet. It was Lin Biao who elevated Mao to the pedestal of worship. In 1966, Mao met with the Red Guards in Beijing eight times. On the tower of Tiananmen, the closely attached figures of Mao and Lin stood; on Tiananmen Square, an endless sea of red books rose, lashing Mao and Lin's future together. The Moment Lin Biao fell from grace was when Mao's image, theory, and reputation were completely shattered overnight. Criticizing "Lin the Traitor" while continuing the revolution was a difficult turn to make. During the criticism of Lin, his words resonated with the Educated Youths. For example, when Lin said, "Sending Educated Youths to the countryside is equivalent to a disguised labor camp." Lin also said, "We started the revolution for equality, fairness, and safety. After the revolution, we realized that these things don't exist. It's ridiculous." Many young people who were once full of revolutionary enthusiasm and ideals, even after being sent to the vast countryside by Mao, still could not forget the revolution. They began to be disillusioned with the purpose and means of the revolution, starting from Lin Biao's death, thus thoroughly reevaluating their views on leaders, the party, the country, the world, society, life, ideals, and reality. Some believe that China's reawakening began with Lin Biao's death. As Mao's close comrade-in-arms, designated successor, and deputy commander-in-chief, Lin Biao's divergence from Mao, the "great teacher, great leader, great commander-in-chief, and great helmsman," followed by his shadowy death, was his greatest contribution to China. It was during the criticism of Lin that I realized that the communist utopia simply did not exist. The road to utopia is paved with bones and skulls. The so-called path of revolution is nothing but a journey into a hellish maze. Mao visibly aged rapidly, and Lin's Little Red Book, the Four Glories, and every sweet blessing turned into merciless irony, piercing the CCP's heart like a thousand arrows. With Lin Biao's demise, Mao Zedong, Zhou Enlai, and the Cultural Revolution all began to come to an end.

The "revolution" was dead, and all that remained was maintenance. Everyone tacitly agreed to do things for their own good. Abandoning the facade of "revolution," commune leaders shamelessly exploited Educated Youths and their parents. In late 1971, Liu Beiru, a demoted cadre, arrived at Yong'an Commune. Hailing from Baizhuang, a village adjacent to Yong'an Town, Liu Beiru was known for his bold and assertive nature since his youth. Rumors circulated that he had fled after killing someone and then worked as a prison guard in a Kuomintang prison. With the arrival of the Communist Party, the need for prison guards persisted, and Liu Beiru retained his position. As the Cultural Revolution neared its end, the police and security system happened to be undergoing yet another round of vetting their personnel, and Liu Beiru grew understandably concerned about his personal history. Opting for early retirement, he returned home. During this period, a policy emerged that assigned downgraded cadres to oversee Educated Youths. Liu Beiru seized the opportunity and assumed control of the "5·7 team," responsible for managing Educated Youths. State-provided living expenses, wooden beds, and construction materials for housing were all distributed through the county's "Educated Youth Office" and the commune's "5·7 team." However, Liu Beiru misappropriated these funds and materials meant for the Educated Youths to curry favor with the commune cadres. Swiftly, he rose to fame within the commune.

Among the Educated Youths from Shanghai No. 62 Middle School, one individual stood out—Xu Weiguo. He was assigned to Baizhuang Village. In the years 1970 and 1971, some Educated Youths in the village secured jobs in Suxian City. However, Xu Weiguo, grappling with family issues, couldn't seize the opportunity to leave. His parents and siblings faced charges related to a family gangster crime, leading to sporadic incarcerations. By the end of 1971, Xu Weiguo's mother came to Yong'an. She hosted a banquet in Baizhuang to treat the villagers. Her charlatanism and Liu Beiru's style hit it off immediately, and Liu Beiru was overjoyed with her flirtations. Liu Beiru patted his chest upon her departure, "Don't worry about your son's promotion. Leave it to me." True to his word, Liu Beiru recommended Xu Weiguo to become the commune cafeteria manager. In his new role, Xu Weiguo exploited his position to control the food supply for the families of the commune leaders. The local butcher had to prioritize selling pork to Xu Weiguo before the store officially opened. The wives of commune cadres were effusive in their praise for Xu Weiguo. This pleased Liu Beiru immensely, observing the favorable reception of his recommendation.

Baizhuang, situated on the west side of Yong'an Middle School, brought Xu Weiguo to my attention as he frequently passed the school gate. Initially, I was puzzled about why Xu Weiguo considered me an adversary. It later became apparent that he had ulterior motives, harboring desires for several attractive girls at Yong'an Middle School. Unaware of his intentions, I neither collaborated with him nor provided opportunities. Adding to the complexity, there were some strikingly beautiful female Educated Youths in our commune. Seconded by Director Xie of the commune cultural station to a performance troupe, they formed connections with me. Additionally, girls from distant locations sought my assistance when they needed to travel to Shanghai to visit their families. Having walked miles from their production squad to Yong'an Town, they often couldn't catch the bus to Suxian on the same day, requiring an overnight stay in Yong'an. Xu Weiguo, despite feigning gentlemanly behavior, couldn't conceal his unsavory intentions. Consequently, no girls sought his help. His frustration peaked whenever I had a female visitor. In the words of Wilde, some people are very jealous, and excellent companions are unbearable for them. More than a century later, Wilde's acerbic wit remains relevant in resisting today's coarseness. Upon becoming Liu Beiru's confidant, Xu Weiguo heightened his manipulation, filling Liu Beiru's ears with disparaging remarks about me. He falsely claimed, "Liu Chengmo seeks the upper-level route. His affection for Xie Daofeng's daughter is a shortcut to promotion. In the '5·7 team,' he only has eyes for Standing Committee Ning Chuanzhong and looks down upon you."

After the Lin Biao incident in 1971, China's political landscape stagnated, casting a gloomy shadow on the future of the Educated Youth. Job opportunities in Huaibei had been suspended for three years, with only a scant number of limited quotas available each year. Faced with this grim reality, more Educated Youths resorted to desperate measures to escape the countryside. Some relinquished their first-night rights, while others feigned disabilities using fake prescriptions and incorrect medicines. In Shanjia Village, there was an Educated Youth from Shanghai named Zheng Suling. Petite and delicate, she found it challenging to adapt to the harsh life in Huaibei. Fearful of falling, she avoided fetching water from the well, couldn't endure the smoky heat of cooking on the adobe stove, and was averse to fieldwork. Zheng Suling's mother obtained a doctor's note in Shanghai, attesting to her daughter's poor health. With this note, Zheng Suling was entitled to request a return to Shanghai. However, when she approached Liu Beiru for an application form, he proposed a repugnant condition: sex. Liu Beiru's dirty face was so disgusting, but she missed the running water and gas stoves in Shanghai so much. Regrettably, after Zheng Suling gave in to Liu Beiru's demands, Liu Beiru continued to harass her and delayed the submission of her application for approval. Liu Beiru took advantage of Zheng Suling repeatedly. Tragically, a lamb had fallen into the tiger's mouth. It wasn't until Zheng Suling became pregnant that Liu Beiru realized there was trouble. Seeking a way out, he enlisted Xu Weiguo, giving him a letter of introduction and instructing him to secretly accompany Zheng Suling to the county hospital for an abortion. Xu Weiguo seized the opportunity to express his loyalty to Liu Beiru again. He said he would pretend to be Zheng Suling's boyfriend and accompany her to the hospital, ensuring that nobody would know this. After Xu Weiguo performed his favor for Liu Beiru, he used job recruitment as a bargaining chip to make a nice girl his wife to whom he had unrequitedly loved for many years. In the 1980s, Xu Weiguo ventured into reselling electrical appliances in Suxian City. However, deceived customers discovered his fraud and administered a thorough beating. While his life wasn't endangered, Xu Weiguo's physical mobility was impaired thereafter. Eventually returning to Shanghai, he succumbed to rectal cancer in his later years.

From 1964 to 1980, tens of millions of Educated Youths were sent to work in the mountains and countryside across China, with approximately half of them being female. Within this large group of female Educated Youths, there are no official statistics on those who suffered sexual assault from perpetrators commonly referred to as those who sabotaged the "Go up the Mountain, Down to the Village" movement. Some perpetrators faced legal consequences, including sentences and even execution, deemed fitting for their crimes. Unfortunately, due to the significant psychological and social pressure placed on young women who have lost their virginity, many female Educated Youths who experienced assault were then and still are reluctant to openly share their stories. Some of the perpetrators remain proud of their actions, while others will take their dark secret to their grave, but almost all share a sense of complacency, knowing they will never be made to pay for these crimes—at least not in this world, which it is safe to assume is the only one they believe exists. Additionally, some female Educated Youths who pursued higher education, joined the Communist Party, and achieved promotions despite being victims of assault, are even more hesitant to reveal the true extent of their traumatic experiences. Zheng Shuling's tragic ordeal is not an isolated case. Zhang Kangkang, a former Educated Youth turned author, once remarked, "After a transfer, even Sister Lin will fall." This statement reflects the harsh reality that even well-educated, intelligent, innocent, pure, and beautiful young women, akin to the character Lin Daiyu from Cao Xueqin's classic Chinese novel "Dream of the Red Chamber," were not immune to such incidents.

Among the Educated Youths in the countryside were the offspring of cadres. However, these individuals often found routes out of rural life through military service, recruitment work, promotions, or higher education. Even some of Deng Xiaoping's children had attended university before he returned to office. Shen Jianwen, an Educated Youth from Shanghai, belonged to this category as the son of cadre Shen Zhiyu. Shen Zhiyu had been part of the New Fourth Army and, after the Communist Party's ascent in 1949, served as the principal of the Shanghai Academy of Fine Arts and later as the director of the Shanghai Museum. Shen Jianwen's mother was a painter and school principal, and Suxian was her hometown. Consequently, Shen Jianwen, his sister Shen Jianhua, and several cousins arrived in Suxian together. In September 1969, less than a year after their arrival, Shen Jianwen was promoted to the county broadcast station. Standing at an impressive height of 1.8 meters/5 ft. 9 inches, he was considered one of the most stylish individuals in Suxian. Shen Jianwen rode a white streamlined civilian motorcycle imported from Japan, a rare sight in those days when bicycles and green military motorcycles were the norm. In the somber streets of Suxian City, Shen Jianwen stood out as a bright presence. Upon meeting Shen Jianwen, it was revealed that we shared the same birthdate in the same year and month. Jianwen proved to be a compassionate friend, often sharing food and even his dormitory bed with me. During winter nights, we would share a blanket for warmth.

At Jianwen's residence, I had the opportunity to meet his sister, Shen Jianhua. Jianhua's independent personality was striking, especially amidst the crowds of people from across the country praising and shouting, "Long live Chairman Mao." Her non-conformist attitude towards "receiving re-education from poor and lower-middle peasants" set her apart, making promotion seem unlikely for many years. Jianhua spent her days secluded in her small room, focusing on the study of oracle bones under the guidance of her father. After the conclusion of the Re-educating Youths Movement, she secured a position at the Provincial Museum. Subsequently, she became a student of Rao Zongyi, a master of Chinese studies, and later a researcher at the Institute of Chinese Culture at the Hong Kong Chinese University. People cross paths for a reason, and in Chinese culture, fate is believed to play a significant role. Jianhua eventually became one of my close friends. While at the county broadcast station, I also encountered Qin Zhen. Qin Zhen, a former college student at the Nanjing Institute of Aeronautics before the Cultural Revolution, was assigned a job in Suxian upon graduation. With a medium height and elegant demeanor, he, like Jianwen, showed great sympathy for my situation. At that time, Qin Zhen's fiancée held a prominent position, being highly regarded by some of the leaders of the Shanghai rebels—a renowned radical faction from the early days of the Cultural Revolution, responsible for the so-called "January Storm" which had overthrown the municipal government of Shanghai and declared the establishment of the "Shanghai People's Commune." This was done with initial support from Mao, but in a matter of days he and his inner circle grew warry of the potential threat posed to centralized authority and led the organizers to replace their "People's Commune" (modelled on the Paris Commune of 1871) with the "Shanghai Revolutionary Committee"—which was of course tied into and overseen by central Communist Party and state apparatus. So much for "grassroots revolutionary" movements in the People's Republic of China, which in this case, lasted for 19 days.

Qin Zhen's fiancée served as the party secretary of a county party committee in Jiangsu Province, wielding significant power. One day, she came to visit him, and Qin Zhen introduced us and encouraged her to help me. She wasted no time and asked me directly, "What is your family's problem?" I briefly explained the counter-revolutionary cloud my family had been living under since the arrest and imprisonment of my father and uncle years before. Without hesitation, she said if my file ever crossed her desk, rather than providing help, her only choice would be to literally throw it away. Qin Zhen appeared embarrassed, but I comforted him, saying, "Never mind, I've gotten used to it."

Among the Educated Youths from No. 62 Middle School, I had two best friends, Shi Taihua and Shi Mei'an. Shi Taihua's elder siblings were already working in Shanghai before 1968, so he and his younger brother had to leave the city. In the 1970 recruitment process, two of his roommates in the village got hired and left. However, he remained behind due to his family's peculiar issues. The circumstances surrounding his family sounded unusual. His father, Shi Jijie, shared the same first name, surname, and birthplace with a Kuomintang official in the Second Department of National Defense. Unfortunately, his father had passed away due to illness before the Cultural Revolution. His father's workplace was dissolved, and his files were transferred to a new unit, revealing a note that read: "Suspected spy." In reality, the other Shi Jijie had been arrested and imprisoned for espionage. Although this fact could be easily verified, nobody in the new unit knew his deceased father, and there was no interest in confirming whether a deceased person had been mistakenly branded as a suspect. However, passing a political review was a prerequisite for the recruitment of Educated Youth workers. The term "suspected" in his father's file became an obstacle to Shi Taihua's advancement. It was almost a rule in the Mao era that the shadows of the deceased hindered the futures of the living children. Educated Youths who failed to qualify for hiring faced a bleak future and struggled with depression. Jin Ruitang, a teacher at Yong'an Middle School, had family connections in the mining area of Huaibei City. He suggested that he could help us explore possibilities. However, the large-scale recruitment had ceased by 1972, and only a limited number of workers were being hired in the coal mines. But mining accidents were frequent, and local peasants were unwilling to work as miners due to the fear of death. Shi Taihua and I were desperate, feeling that our lives were not valued. During that summer vacation, we went to the Huaibei mining area to seek Jin Ruitang's assistance. He discovered that No. 6 Mine was currently not hiring. His acquaintances mentioned that even when hiring occurred, Educated Youths who failed the political review would not be accepted. Miners had access to blasting materials, and there was concern that we might cause trouble when working underground. As darkness fell, Shi Taihua and I had no choice but to spend the night under a large tree in front of Jin Ruitang's house.

In 1973, Deng Xiaoping was politically rehabilitated and restored to public life. He was made Vice Premier and a member of the CCP Central Committee. By then, the recommendation for university admission had been underway for four years. The State Council released the "Opinions on Enrollment Work in Higher Education Institutions in 1973," which emphasized the importance of academic attainment in addition to political qualifications. Besides grassroots recommendations, an academic examination including tests in mathematics, physics, and chemistry was to be conducted. During this time, Shi Taihua, on one hand, persisted in working in the fields, striving for recommendations from poor and middle peasants, and on the other, resumed studying textbooks he had abandoned for years. Without a desk or chair, he used a crude plank as a table and a large stone as a stool. Calculations required a draft paper, but there was only a small amount of writing paper brought from Shanghai. Hence, he first worked out problems with a pencil and then wrote them with a fountain pen. Since writing papers was insufficient, he would use blank spaces in the political study materials issued by the commune. Illumination for reading at night was scarce in rural areas, so he used a kerosene lamp. His lamp was particularly rudimentary, with a hole punched in the cap of a small bottle, into which a thin sheet of iron rolled into a tube was inserted, and the wick was made of twisted grass paper. Studying under the dim and flickering kerosene lamp at night caused his nostrils to blacken from the smoke and his eyes to water from the strain.

To save time cooking, he asked a neighbor, Mrs. Dai, to help make a stack of pancakes. He would then eat these pancakes and drink water, spending minimal time on meals. Shi Taihua performed well in the cultural examination and was assessed to have a high school level. He was eagerly anticipating the university admission that year. However, on July 19, 1973, the Liaoning Daily published a "thought-provoking answer sheet." On August 10, the People's Daily reprinted the full text, along with an editor's note. Zhang Tiesheng sparked an anti-examination trend and became the well-known "blank paper hero." The original admission plan was overturned, and exam scores were disregarded. Consequently, Shi Taihua failed to gain admission after successive layers of political screening. Following the college examination, Shi Taihua's health deteriorated, and he was afflicted with malaria and dysentery, falling seriously ill. Recognizing Shi Taihua's academic skills, the brigade made him an elementary teacher at the Lu Lake School.

In early 1975, the county sent Wan Lichao as the first Party secretary to Yong'an Commune, along with several trusted associates, including one named Wu Changmin. Wu Changmin had been stationed in Lu Lake and had good relations with the Educated Youths. Shi Taihua's older sister worked at a sewing machine wholesale department in Shanghai and could obtain sewing machine purchase vouchers. Shi Taihua helped Wu Changmin purchase a sewing machine. Shortly after taking office, Wan Lichao used the pretext of taking his wife for medical treatment along with Wu Changmin to Shanghai to visit the Educated Youths' parents. Liu Beiru recommended Xu Weiguo to accompany Wan Lichao to Shanghai. Upon arrival, they stayed at the Lushan Hotel on Tibet Middle Road. Xu Weiguo acted as a spy and gatekeeper. He provided intelligence to Wan Lichao on which Educated Youths' homes were worth visiting and which were not. When the Educated Youths' parents came to the hotel, they had to pass through Xu Weiguo first. Both my mother and Shi Taihua's mother were stopped by him. Later, Wu Changmin took Wan Lichao to Shi Taihua's home. My mother purchased a piece of nice piece of shirt fabric to give to Wan's wife. When Sheng Jie saw it, she remarked, "Such good fabric, you're not keeping it for yourself, but giving it away?" Later, my mother, Shi Taihua's mother, and many other parents of Educated Youths went to the train station to bid them farewell. Upon returning, my mother reported, "The luggage racks in half of the train car were filled with Secretary Wan's belongings. The fabric I gave didn't receive any attention." Inside the train, Wu Changmin took out a box of cookies. Wan Lichao asked, "Who sent these? Is this a joke?" Wu Changmin opened the package, and two brand-new Shanghai brand watches slid out. At that time, there were no counterfeit goods or cheap electronic watches. They were all genuine, mechanical movement watches with diamonds. A Shanghai brand all-steel shock-resistant watch cost ¥120, equivalent to five months of Wan Lichao's salary, and required dozens of industrial vouchers to purchase at that time. It was an extreme luxury item. Each watch had a name tag on it, belonging to a pair of siblings. When Wan Lichao returned to Yong'an, he instructed Liu Beiru to identify the siblings and immediately arrange for the girl to apply for medical leave to return to Shanghai and for the boy to be recruited to a factory in Suxian. It was a fair deal after all.

Lu Jiazhong, the secretary of the Luhu Brigade, was a disabled veteran who returned from the Korean War, known for his integrity and incorruptibility. Whenever there was an opportunity for promotion, he always strongly recommended Shi Taihua. At this time, Lu Jiazhong wanted to develop Shi Taihua into the Party. Party membership required political review, and Wu Changmin was sent to Shanghai for an external investigation by the commune party committee. Wu Changmin ignored all the messy and ambiguous contents in Shi Taihua's father's file. Shi Taihua was smoothly approved for Party membership. With the Party membership, even if there were problems in the family, it didn't matter anymore. In September, Shi Taihua was granted a quota spot and admitted to Shanghai University of Science and Technology, finally realizing his dream.

Shi Mei'an, another close friend of mine, had a family background similar to mine, with her father and uncle having faced imprisonment. Her uncle, Shi Jijie, was a senior official in the Second Department of National Defense, bearing the same name as Shi Taihua's father. She lived on Xinchang Road, close to my house. Her mother was an elementary school teacher, and she knew my mother. Shi Mei'an was a student at Xinchang Road No. 1 Primary School, where she was taught by my mother and was Shenjie's classmate. In 1978, Shi Mei'an and her sister were undergoing job allocation simultaneously. According to the policy at the time, one could stay in Shanghai, while the other had to leave. As Shi Mei'an's sister was a few years older, she remained in Shanghai, while Shi Mei'an went to Anhui. Shi Mei'an's sister did not marry until Shi Mei'an was promoted, and both she and their mother provided Shi Mei'an with significant financial support in an effort to build good relations with Suxian cadres. Originally assigned to Guacun Village on the outskirts of Yong'an town, Shi Mei'an, along with Xu Yiqian, was selected for the commune propaganda troupe for a few months. After the troupe was disbanded, they were reassigned to the Shanjia Brigade.

The year 1963 saw extreme rainfall and many severe flooding events throughout North China. At least 5,000 people died, and approximately 20 million were affected/displaced. The single most prominent story to emerge from this calamity was Mao's admonition throughout the following year, for "Agriculture to learn from Dazhai." In December 1964, this culminated with the Party Central Committee and State Council jointly issuing a directive institutionalizing Mao's slogan by making the mountain village of Dazhai in Xiyang County, Shanxi province, the national agricultural model, and the leader of its Production Brigade—Chen Yonggui—a national hero. The idea was to promote the dedication, resilience, and, above all else, self-reliance shown by Dazhai in the face of disaster. They did not call on the national or even provincial authorities to help them deal with their catastrophic flood. Instead, they dealt with it themselves. Or so the story went. In fact, the village received significant outside assistance, including significant state funds, outside labor brigades, replacement machinery, and priority allocation of seeds and fertilizer. It was then used as a stage-managed showcase for display to both the domestic audience and foreign delegations, and a decade later, in 1975, "model peasant leader" Chen Yonggui (despite limited education and no technical background) became Vice Premier of China. Following the death of Mao, the rise of Deng Xiaoping and implementation of his reforms, the slogan was abandoned, and in 1980, Chen Yonggui was dismissed. But by then, the agriculture sector of the entire nation had spent more than a decade trying to emulate a hollow myth.

One such example was in Anhui province, where, in an effort to learn from the revolutionary spirit and collectivist dedication of Dazhai, Song Peizhang, the Secretary of the Provincial Party Committee, established two models: Guozhuang Brigade in Xiao County and Shanjia Brigade in Suxian County. Jiang Guanghui, the secretary of Shanjia Brigade, was even taken to Beijing as a representative for the 10th National Congress of the CCP in 1973, where he had the honor of meeting Chairman Mao. Upon returning from Beijing, Jiang Guanghui, now a member of the Standing Committee of the county committee and the second secretary of the Yong'an Commune Party Committee, held significant influence. Wan Lichao, still the first secretary of the commune and a member of the county committee, had to report to Jiang Guanghui. Jiang Guanghui was supportive of the Educated Youths, and during the Spring Festival of 1974, Shi Mei'an took Jiang Guanghui's daughter to Shanghai for two months. During this time, I became acquainted with Jiang Guanghui's family. In 1974, the commune was granted a few highly limited enrollment quotas, and Jiang Guanghui secured two for the youth in Shanjia. The quota spot for Shanghai Medical College was given to Gu Meihong, who came from a worker's family, and that for Bengbu Medical College was given to Shi Mei'an as "an educable child."

Shi Mei'an trained in ballet when she was young and later in rhythmic gymnastics. In junior high school, she reached the level of a national athlete. Shi Mei'an had a graceful figure and a sweet smile. Before being sent down, she was recognized as the beauty of No. 62 Middle School. Because Shi Mei'an's family and my own were well acquainted, we became good friends after being sent down. Our close relationship aroused jealousy among several Educated Youths, two of whom were in the Shanjia Brigade. One was named Zhou Chaoguang, and the other was named Li Wei'er. They both belonged to a group that was constantly currying favor with Liu Beiru. Zhou Chaoguang's demeanor was somewhat elusive, with his constantly shifting eyes always assessing the situation. His expressions were unpredictable, making it difficult to discern the true meaning behind his words. Aligned with Liu Beiru, Zhou Chaoguang served as an informant, keeping Liu Beiru informed about the details of my interactions with Shi Mei'an and Jiang Guanghui in Sanjia Village. Liu Beiru rewarded Zhou Chaoguang for his successful information gathering by granting him a recruitment quota spot and securing him a job at a regional steel plant. Later, it was revealed that Zhou Chaoguang's promotion wasn't solely based on providing information. Liu Beiru didn't dole out rewards without getting something substantial in return. Zhou Chaoguang's family was very poor. His father was in prison, and his mother earned a living by hand-washing clothes for neighbors. The family's financial situation was very tight. His mother must have endured extreme hardship to earn some cash to offer a tribute to Liu Beiru. Only then did Zhou Chaoguang secure the job and leave Yong'an.

Less than a week after Zhou Chaoguang left Yong'an, shocking news arrived that he had drowned. The community was in disbelief, struggling to comprehend the sudden and tragic turn of events. Here's what happened: On a day when the temperature spiked unexpectedly, a group of newly recruited young workers found themselves in high spirits. During their lunch break, they headed to the ditch next to the steel plant to enjoy the breeze and take a swim. Among them was Zhou Chaoguang, a proficient swimmer. However, as they watched, Zhou Chaoguang dove into the water and never surfaced again. Initially, the group thought Zhou Chaoguang was playing a prank on them. As time passed without any sign of him, a sense of panic set in. They hurried back to the factory, calling for assistance and requesting long bamboo poles to aid in the rescue. It was then discovered that Zhou Chaoguang's lifeless body lay in a well within their sight. Although the water in the ditch wasn't deep, there were wells dug at intervals along the bottom. These wells, typically filled during the dry season, contained cold water and were surrounded by aquatic plants. Zhou Chaoguang had submerged into one of these wells, his body contorted, entwined with water plants. While his departure from Yong'an might have initially been viewed as positive news, the situation took a somber turn, transforming a joyous occasion into a funeral.

Li Wei'er, despite not being considered attractive among the female Educated Youths, managed to establish a close relationship with Liu

221

Beiru. Known to be an informant for Liu Beiru, other youths kept their distance from her, wary of her ability to observe and report on everything and everyone. In 1975, I left Yong'an Middle School and moved to Shanjia Brigade. Li Wei'er applied for the Communist Youth League and asked me to be her sponsor. Joining the league was evidence of good behavior, which was helpful for promotion. I understood her intentions. I refused her request because I had great disdain for snitching. I believed that snitching trampled on the bottom line of humanity. Informers had twisted souls, or at the very least weak ones. They betrayed others to benefit themselves. I couldn't endorse someone with such a despicable character. When Liu Beiru found out, he passed me a message saying I must help Li Wei'er join the league. Although Liu Beiru held power over every Educated Youth, I was stubborn and dared to say no. The benefits of snitching were obvious. Especially in an abnormal society during times of turmoil, informing was often a shortcut for shameless people to succeed. As expected, Li Wei'er failed to join the league but secured a job at the Suxian Silk Reeling Factory.

In February 1972, U.S. President Richard Nixon embarked on a historic seven-day visit to China, leading to the issuance of the renowned "Shanghai Communique" on February 28th of that year. This visit sparked a nationwide enthusiasm for learning English, and Yong'an Middle School responded by incorporating English classes into its curriculum. Lu Benxiao, an English teacher, had graduated from the English Department of Anhui University before the Cultural Revolution. Originally trained to work for the Ministry of Foreign Affairs in Beijing, the disruption caused by the Cultural Revolution led him to be assigned to his hometown, Suxian City. Lu Benxiao had been born and raised in Suxian City, and his family had remained there after he left for his education, so he was not unhappy to return. Having studied English for two years in junior high school and continued self-study, I became one of Lu Benxiao's enthusiastic students. He often tutored me, providing copies of "Beijing Review" for translation exercises to practice grammar and sentence structure. The school had a record player, and I used it to listen repeatedly to the English versions of Mao's "The Old Three

Articles," aligning my pronunciation with the recordings to improve my spoken English skills. In 1974, Lu Benxiao was transferred back to Suxian City, prompting our school to assign me to take over his English classes. Simultaneously, the school-run factory concluded its operations.

At Yong'an Middle School, the curriculum in mathematics, physics, and chemistry drew from pre-Cultural Revolution high school textbooks. There weren't many English classes, so I had plenty of free time to engage in independent study. Utilizing these textbooks, I immersed myself in the subjects, completing the attached homework and seeking guidance from the subject teachers. Fortunately, the teachers, including Jin Ruitang, Li Ming, and Li Yuming (who shared a dormitory room with me) were happy to answer my questions and review my assignments. Before the Cultural Revolution, Jin Ruitang and Li Yuming had taught in Fuliji High School, a key high school in Anhui Province. Both were government-employed public school teachers and had wives with rural household registrations. Li Yuming had previously served as the chairman of the physics department at Fuliji High School, while his wife worked as a private teacher at a junior high school in Yong'an Commune.

It must be noted that in late 20th-century China, "public" schools—meaning schools run and funded by the government—were generally higher quality than private schools. Teachers at these schools were government employees with secure salaries, benefits, and rigorous selection, giving them a relatively elite status in society. In contrast, private schools were often less well-funded, less prestigious, and their teachers were seen as more ordinary professionals. So unlike in the U.S., where private schools are often viewed as superior, in China at that time, the reverse was true.

Li Yuming corrected my physics homework. Liu Yuankai was an excellent math teacher. Sometimes I found time to attend his classes. There were also two language teachers whom I was very close to. One was named Wang Jipu, a brilliant graduate of Nanjing University, known for his intellect and warm-heartedness. He had been labeled as a rightist before graduation and was assigned to Fuliji in Anhui during the allocation process. The other was Qu Junling, who worked closely with commune cadres and often advocated on my behalf, speaking positively about me whenever possible.

Zhou Hualu and Liu Shulian were a married couple, both receiving salaries from the state. Zhou Hualu had previously served as the principal of Suxian No. 1 Junior High School before being forcibly transferred. They resided in Yong'an with their young daughter, while their two sons, of school age, remained in the city, taking care of themselves. Zhou Hualu and Liu Shulian worked six days a week in Yong'an, with only one day off on weekends. The demanding schedule made it difficult for them to visit their sons in Suxian regularly, making those years particularly challenging for the family. During winter vacations, Zhou Hualu and Liu Shulian would reunite with their sons in Suxian and celebrate the New Year together. Their residence was located across the street from a movie theater. In the winter of 1972, the North Korean film "Flower Girl" gained immense popularity, providing a welcome diversion from the monotony of the government-endorsed "eight model plays." Cinemas extended their hours, screening "Flower Girl" around the clock, and it became a cultural phenomenon. Zhou Hualu purchased movie tickets for me, inviting me to stay at his house, extending consideration and hospitality. Director Xie of the Yong'an Commune Cultural Station and his wife also offered friendship, hosting me for dinner at their house. Director Xie later returned to Suxian, and his position at the Cultural Station was assumed by Liu Keji, a gym teacher from Yong'an Middle School. The time I spent at Yong'an Middle School was the most tranquil period of my life up until then, despite having no chance to move out of the countryside. In his poem "Influence Life with Life," Tagore said, "Keep the goodness in your heart, because you don't know who would take advantage of your kindness, out of despair." While there may not be much worth remembering about China during that time, the kindness shown by those who supported me through adversity is cherished. Despite government discrimination, the compassion of individuals stood out. In the summer of 1975, the school issued me a high school diploma. Though the academic qualifications may not have held great value, the acquired knowledge was genuine. When the college entrance examination resumed in 1977, I was well-prepared and less nervous than most other candidates, thanks to the foundation laid during the time I was at Yong'an Middle School.

When school resumed in 1975 after the summer break, Xie Andui, who was not part of the school staff, unexpectedly arrived at the school as a barefoot party secretary (a CCP leader who was seen as working and living amongst the rural peasants, instead of behaving as a detached official). Initially, the commune's health clinic and middle school shared the same branch within the Party and did not have separate secretaries. Xie Andui, residing in Xie's, returned home two years ago after being demobilized from the army without securing employment. The teachers and principal at Yong'an Middle School were all qualified educators with a state salary, and there were also a few private teachers, like myself, receiving state subsidies. Xie Andui lacked the qualifications to be a teacher or a school administrator, making his appointment as our school leader a surprise to everyone. However, he had the support of Xie Daofeng. After his return, Xie Andui spent his time wandering around the commune compound and informing Xie Daofeng about what he heard. Seeing an opportunity, Xie Daofeng, needing a watchdog in his hometown, convinced the commune to create a job for Xie Andui. With Xie Daofeng as his backer, Xie Andui assumed his position with a high profile. During the first school staff meeting, Xie Andui declared, "Chairman Mao said that Wang Hongwen is qualified to be the vice chairman of the CCP because he has experience as a worker, a peasant, and a soldier. By the same token, I have done the same thing. Therefore, you have to be convinced." When Xie Andui joined Yong'an Middle School, his position was unofficial, and the state neither paid him a salary nor subsidized him. Facing the faculty and staff, he felt inferior due to his lack of qualifications and teaching abilities. To establish his authority, he relied on wielding the whip of class struggle, bullying teachers, and making promises to those who wanted to gain their own Party membership. For teachers who resisted, he subjected them to political reviews and family background checks, accusing them of being right-wingers who had escaped scrutiny in past movements. During this time, the county education department faced budget constraints, preventing the allocation of funds for office expenses. The school struggled to afford basic supplies such as paper, chalk, and repairs for blackboards and furniture. The school-run factory, the pearl in the palm of the school, generated income, and I, as the only adult in the factory, was responsible for its accounts. Upon Xie Andui's arrival, he ousted me and took over the account books. Subsequently, cash and items in the factory—including Chinese traditional herbal medicine and a large bucket of honey used to make honeysuckle balls—disappeared without explanation.

Xie Andui and Yin Li were relatives; he referred to her as his aunt. During Yin Li's visit to Yong'an Middle School to see me, Xie Andui appeared polite. However, his demeanor changed immediately after Yin Li departed. He knew that I was a thorn in the side of Xie Daofeng and couldn't wait to take some harmful action against me to please him. He said to me, "All Educated Youths are working hard in the field. Why do you think you're so special? You must go and get re-educated by the peasants. How dare you be Yin Li's boyfriend? A toad wants to eat swan meat! I've discussed it with Liu Beiru, and you will go to Lu Lake Educated Youth's Farm." The Lu Lake Educated Youth's Farm operated independently from production squads, falling under the direct management of the commune's 5•7 team—those in charge of "Reeducation through labor and study," with Liu Beiru at the helm. Liu Beiru considered the farm his private property and the Educated Youths his assets. Whenever Liu Beiru undertook projects at home, such as extending his house, he exploited the Educated Youths to transport stones, lime, and lumber for him. Liu Beiru consistently mistreated me, always trying to make things difficult. As a professional jailer with a dark mind, Liu Beiru enjoyed torturing people, just as Mao Zedong wrote, "To struggle with Heaven is boundless joy; to struggle with Earth is boundless joy; to struggle with people is boundless joy." They were essentially the same kind of person.

Choosing to relocate to Shanjia Brigade seemed like a more favorable option than Lu Lake Educated Youth's Farm. Jiang Guanghui, known for his fair treatment of Educated Youths, appeared to be a benevolent figure. Leveraging his influence, he secured promotion quotas for Shanghai Educated Youths in Shanjia, prioritizing their advancement. When I expressed my concerns to Jiang Guanghui, he welcomed my decision to move to Shanjia. He elaborated that, in light of the current circumstances, the Shanjia Brigade needed to add junior high school classes alongside its primary schools, and the infrastructure was already in place. Shanjia could offer me work points for grain rations. This arrangement should allow me to make a living without any problems. My responsibilities would include teaching physics, chemistry, and English, with two additional teachers assigned for reading and math. The warm reception extended by Shanjia Primary School's principal, Gao Shanci, and other faculty members was reassuring. Shanjia Brigade arranged assistance for my luggage. As the cart passed Baizhuang, Liu Beiru stood on the roadside, shouting, "Liu Chengmo, don't think you can make it by taking the upper-level route. Don't forget that this is the Communist Party's country. You can never take it out of my hands. You will never leave Yong'an in your life. I will let you know how powerful I am!" Liu Beiru had good reasons to speak with confidence because the backbone of the Communist Party's power rested on individuals like him from the lumpenproletariat.

When I arrived there, Shanjia Brigade had already gained recognition as a model, attracting visitors from across the province who sought to witness its success. Upon my arrival in Shanjia, Jiang Guanghui entrusted me not only with teaching but also with overseeing the Communist Youth League branch and the performance troupe. A loudspeaker was installed at the village office, and from then on, my living quarters also served as the broadcasting room. I also assisted visitors and news reporters requiring overnight accommodations. In the winter of 1975, the county party committee decided to hold a county-wide on-site conference on "Agriculture to learn from Dazhai" in Shanjia. At the western end of Shanjia Village, a row of brick bungalows was erected as a guest house for county party committee leaders. Wei Hongfu, the secretary of the county party committee—who had previously served as the political commissar of a PLA regiment under Anhui Province Party

Secretary Song Peizhang—frequented Shanjia and stayed at the guest house during the conference. Various departments and offices of the county government, along with the commune and county radio stations, cultural station, and teachers from Yong'an Middle School, collaborated to set up an open-air venue. A county propaganda team took charge of organizing and managing the conference. Li Yijun, an alumnus of the Fine Arts Department of East China Normal University, proved to be a talented artist. He created a sketch for me and later invited me to his home in Suxian, where his wife worked as an elementary school teacher. They extended their kindness to me graciously. To entertain conference participants in the evenings, Shanjia established a performance troupe, with Jiang Guanghui appointing me as the coordinator. He enlisted Educated Youths from other brigades for the troupe, including Gao Hong from Liu Wafand Brigade.

Li Wei'er relayed all the details regarding Jiang Guanghui's confidence in me and my activities in Shanjia to Liu Beiru, greatly angering him. Determined to cause more trouble for me, Liu Beiru seized an opportunity when two Educated Youths from Bengbu arrived in Shanjia. They asserted that the commune Communist Youth League had dispatched them to Shanjia to reform the Communist Youth League branch. The individuals involved in the event were Xie Bin and Tang Weidong. Xie Bin was assigned to his father's hometown, while Tang Weidong was assigned to Lu Lake. During the Civil War, Xie Bin's father, Xie Yifan, and mother, Zhang Fengzhi, both served as medical orderlies in the People's Liberation Army. They had no professional medical training, but were educated and literate and able to support professional medical staff. After the war, they were discharged and were assigned jobs by the CCP back in their hometown. Still later, the party appointed Xie Yifan president of Bengbu No. 3 People's Hospital, and his wife, Zhang Fengzhi, went to work in the laboratory department. Xie Yifan and Xie Daofeng were relatives within the same family. Despite this connection, Xie Daofeng held higher seniority than Xie Yifan. Given Xie Yifan's position, commune and county cadres frequently sought him out for urgent medical treatment, including Xie Daofeng and his people. Bengbu

No. 3 People's Hospital boasted superior medical services compared to Suxian County Hospital. Xie Bin received exceptional care in Yong'an due to his family background. Yin Li's sister, Yin Meng, also arrived at Xie's. Yin Meng was regarded as Xie Daofeng's princess and enjoyed special privileges in Yong'an. Tang Weidong, on the other hand, received support from a relative who held a position as a commune cadre.

In an era marked by continuous political movements, a campaign to rectify the party emerged. Upon Wan Lichao's arrival in Yong'an, he encountered a disordered situation in the commune office, characterized by incomplete files and a lack of information regarding the number of party members in the commune. Many branch secretaries in local villages were illiterate, lacking the ability to read or write. The initial step in rectifying the party involved establishing a file for each party member, compiling evidence of their party enrollment, and verifying their records of rewards and infractions. To aid in this endeavor, the Party Rectification Working Group enlisted the help of Xie Bin and Tang Weidong. Both individuals performed admirably, earning recognition from the working group for their efforts. Following the conclusion of the party rectification movement, the commune Communist Youth League sought their continued assistance in organizing the files for the commune Communist Youth League. Upon learning of this, Liu Beiru approached Xie Bin and urged him to prioritize scrutiny of the Shanjia Brigade. He argued that if their task was to rectify the League branch, the primary focus should be on none other than me, Liu Chengmo, whom he labeled as a counter-revolutionary unfit to lead the League branch. Xie Bin and Tang Weidong spent several days in Shanjia, engaging with Jiang Guanghui, party members, schoolteachers, and Educated Youths. After a thorough investigation, they found no evidence against me. When they reported back to Liu Beiru, they affirmed that Jiang Guanghui had indeed designated Liu Chengmo as the leader of the Communist Youth League branch in Shanjia, and they found no reason to take issue with that decision. However, Jiang Guanghui clarified that the position of Secretary of the Communist Youth League branch was still officially vacant, and filling it was open for further discussion. At that point, Liu Beiru had no choice but to cease pressing the matter further.

I was brought into the Communist Youth League while teaching at Yong'an Middle School. In China, teachers have long been expected to embody moral integrity and serve as examples for their students. My conduct at the school left little room for reproach, so the secretary of the commune's CYL branch singled me out as someone worth recruiting. In its efforts to tighten its grip on the younger generation, the Communist Party allowed CYL branches at the grassroots level to admit a token number of youths from the "Five Black Categories"—a gesture meant to showcase the regime's supposed "leniency." For those of us with such backgrounds, to apply for membership on our own would have been nothing but self-inflicted humiliation. But once the organization set its gaze on you, there was no declining—only dutiful thanks and compliance. Despite its outward appearance as an honor, CYL membership conferred no privilege. The age limits of membership from fourteen to twenty-eight were strictly enforced—once overage, one had to withdraw. But what was far stricter during my own years of membership was the loss of personal freedom. After joining, I found myself under closer watch, not less. Regular attendance at political meetings became mandatory. I was expected to report my thoughts, submit to criticism from fellow members, and accept the organization's constant scrutiny.

My recruitment into the Communist Youth League gave me two very different but equally memorable shocks. First, I was shocked to be asked to join, since people with politically undesirable family backgrounds like mine were supposed to be kept outside the League. Second, after joining, I was shocked to find that I gained no benefit at all, and the only change was that I came under even stricter surveillance. Recruitment into the "organs of the party" could be a blessing or a curse, be it small fry like the Youth League or big fish like the Communist Party itself. Take my uncle Bao Ting as an example: as a party member, he survived countless close calls on the battlefield and made it through the war alive, only to be later accused of being a "class enemy who had snuck into the Party." As a result, he was unjustly imprisoned for twenty years.

One day, I was taken by surprise when two unexpected visitors arrived on bicycles, each with two little roosters tied to the handlebars. To my amazement, the visitors turned out to be Erhei and Sanhei, Yin Li's two younger brothers, who had recently been discharged from the army and returned home. Erhei had been assigned to an agricultural machinery factory, while Sanhei had found a position in a printing factory. Drawing on his experience as a cook in the army, Erhei promptly showcased his culinary skills by preparing a delicious chicken dish. It had been quite some time since I had last seen them, back when they were not yet old enough to be considered Educated Youths in Xie's. Now, both had grown into adults and secured employment. Despite the passage of years, they still remembered me! At that time, the journey from Suxian to Yong'an covered a 35-kilometer pebble road, and the bus ride took about two hours under good weather conditions. Their decision to make the long bicycle ride to see me was truly heartwarming, and I deeply appreciated their friendship.

Liu Beiru's initial intention was to send Xie Bin to create trouble for me. Surprisingly, after Xie Bin and I crossed paths, we forged a strong and enduring friendship. Despite being the son of a cadre, Xie Bin displayed none of the typical arrogance or entitlement often associated with that background. Instead, he chose to refrain from leveraging his family connections and diligently worked to carve out his own path. Renowned for his physical prowess, Xie Bin exhibited remarkable resilience during the harsh winter months, loading soil into carts at the bottom of Xinbian River clad only in shorts and a vest, covered in mud and water. During the summer, he engaged in the challenging task of spraying pesticides in cotton fields, where the bollworm had developed resistance, making eradication difficult. Resourceful and committed, Xie Bin delved into relevant magazines for new insights and ingeniously modified the sprayer. He opted for ultra-low-volume, high-speed sprinklers that efficiently dispensed concentrated pesticides directly onto cotton leaves, enhancing both labor and insecticide efficiency. However, the cost of his dedication was high. In an era when highly toxic organophosphate pesticides like Parathion (formulation 1605) and Demeton (formulation 1059) were prevalent, Xie Bin sacrificed his health.

He battled anemia for the rest of his life, contending with persistently low white and red blood cell counts, which severely compromised his immune system.

By the end of 1975, Xie Bin and I were nominated by our brigades and the commune to attend the Advanced Educated Youth Congress in Suxian. While being designated as a representative of "Advanced Educated Youths" sounded impressive, in reality, it offered little practical benefit. During that era, social mobility primarily hinged on securing a coveted city job or gaining entry into the Communist Party. Given his family background and exemplary conduct, Xie Bin was qualified to join the party. However, an unexpected turn of events unfolded. At this time, Yin Meng, who had arrived alongside Xie Bin and worked as a private teacher at the same Elementary School, also applied for party membership. Yin Meng, indulged by Xie Daofeng, spent more time in their home in Suxian City than in Yong'an. Despite not meeting the required credits for party membership, Yin Meng's application was swiftly approved by the commune party committee, while Xie Bin's was rejected. Xie Bin was told he needed to do more to prove himself. The true reason behind this decision soon became evident – Xie Daofeng's influence. Unwilling to see anyone, even his close relatives, on equal footing with his children, Xie Daofeng's favoritism was blatant. This incident incensed Xie Bin. Previously, Xie Daofeng had brought numerous people to Bengbu, and Xie Bin's parents not only arranged medical treatment for them but also provided for their food and lodging. Now, not only did Xie Daofeng refuse to provide help, but he went out of his way to obstruct Xie Bin's upward trajectory. During the congress in Suxian, Xie Bin asked me to accompany him to visit Xie Daofeng, out of respect for his seniority. Xie Daofeng resided in a communal apartment building in the compound designated for regional committee cadres, with several rooms at his disposal. Having sent his sons to the army to avoid working in the fields, they were now discharged from the military and had jobs in the city. When we visited, Xie Daofeng summoned his children to join us, exclaiming, "Look at Xie Bin and Liu Chengmo. They are representatives of advanced educated youths. How glorious they are! You must learn from them..." Disheartened by the hypocrisy of his words, Xie Bin left in anger, remarking, "Xie Daofeng brought all his children back to the city. We are trapped in the countryside. It's so hypocritical for him to say this to us."

Despite being Communists, Xie Bin's parents demonstrated immense compassion and care, not only for their own children but also for others in need. This generosity was evident in their assistance to Gu Zhuoxin's children. Gu Zhuoxin was the deputy director of the State Council Planning Commission before the Cultural Revolution. Once that tumultuous period began, Gu Zhuoxin endured prolonged imprisonment, and his family faced dispersal. With their future bleak in Liaoning Province, Gu Zhuoxin's children sought aid from their parents' former subordinates, traveling all the way south. Unfortunately, many veteran cadres were unable or unwilling to offer them protection during that turbulent period. In this desperate situation, Gu Zhuoxin's children found solace in Xie Yifan and Zhang Fengzhi. Despite being strangers, Xie Yifan and Zhang Fengzhi generously extended their support, facilitating their relocation to Anhui to escape Liaoning's grip and assisting them in establishing a new life. By 1977, under the leadership of Deng Xiaoping, Wan Li and Gu Zhuoxin assumed prominent roles in Anhui. Wan Li became the first secretary of the provincial party committee, while Gu Zhuoxin served as the second secretary. During Xie Bin's studies in the Physics Department of Anhui University in Hefei from 1978 to 1982, Gu Zhuoxin frequently invited him to Daoxianglou as a weekend guest.

Upon hearing about me from Xie Bin and Yin Li, Xie Bin's parents expressed deep concern for my situation. They generously invited me to visit Bengbu and stay with them for a few days. Zhang Fengzhi told me she was Yin Li's sister-in-law and that they talked about everything. Zhang Fengzhi said, "We all know that you are a good person. Yin Li came to me and cried many times before she got married. She said she was unwilling to give in. She dreamt of building a family with you. Unfortunately, the world operates in ways beyond our control. Nevertheless, I'll find a way to assist you. I'll find you a girlfriend." Zhang

Fengzhi was fast-talking and very enthusiastic. She gave the impression that whatever she said she would do would be accomplished, and that nothing was impossible for her. And in fact, later on, she did stay true to her word by setting me up on a date with a girl for me at Bengbu Medical College and making the introductions. Zhang Fengzhi comforted me, saying, "So what that you have a bad family background? My father was a big landowner in Sichuan, but I was able to get past it. The problem is that your personal enemies in Suxian, Liu Beiru, and Xie Daofeng, are too powerful for you to navigate past. You must leave. The only way for you to do more than barely survive is to leave Suxian. I will find a place to accept you near Bengbu."

Mao's death in 1976 ushered in a period of uncertainty, with widespread apprehension about the stability of the central government. Newspaper reports echoed this sentiment with statements like, "We will proceed according to established guidelines," reflecting the lack of clarity regarding the country's future direction. The lingering effects of the Cultural Revolution only added to the ambiguity, and there were no immediate, visible shifts in governance. Economic issues and poverty remained largely unaddressed, with job opportunities in urban areas becoming increasingly scarce, leading to a virtual halt in hiring. Following my relocation to Shanjia in 1975, my visits to Yong'an Middle School became sporadic. One day, Liu Jiling, the accountant of Yong'an Middle School, extended an invitation to his home for dinner. Liu Jiling's wife was a teacher at Yong'an Elementary School, and they lived in the school's attached housing. Despite residing in a rural area, they held urban residence registration, and they received state salaries and commercial grain rations, placing them in the upper echelons of Yong'an society. Liu Jiling's nickname was "Liu Yunzi" (meaning "lightheaded") because he drank too much. Under his surface foolishness, he harbored a malevolent disposition and faced punishment for corruption. The couple had six children—five daughters and one son, with the youngest being their only son. During a period of decentralization, the first three daughters became Educated Youths, resulting in a shift in their household registrations from urban residents to rural commune members. The second eldest child, Liu Feng, exhibited a cunning and snobbish demeanor. She managed to avoid working in the fields and was a private teacher at Yong'an Elementary School.

The arrival of Shanghai educated-youths brought a fresh perspective to the people of Suxian. Ma Hengfeng, a mid-level cadre at Shanghai Changning District Central Hospital and a native of Yong'an, quickly became a sought-after figure for those in Suxian grappling with serious illnesses. For the people of Huaibei, Shanghai seemed distant and mysterious, and any association with it symbolized a higher social status. During my tenure at Yong'an Middle School, Liu Jiling's wife, Liu Zhenling, required surgery and opted to seek treatment in Shanghai. Before her departure, she approached several Shanghai educated youths for their home addresses, expressing her eagerness to visit them and satisfy her curiosity about life in Shanghai. Accompanied by Liu Feng, her second child, they visited several families of Educated Youths in Shanghai and were particularly impressed by my mother's living conditions. My mother resided alone on the entire ground floor of a townhouse, a stark contrast to the cramped living spaces of some families spanning three generations. Liu Zhenling assured my mother that she intended to be her friend, patting her chest to emphasize her sincerity: "With us in Yong'an, you don't have to worry about Chengmo." Upon their return to Yong'an, Liu Feng frequently visited the middle school to see me, addressing me as "Brother Chengmo." However, rumors soon began to circulate, alleging an affair between Liu Feng and me. One day, Liu Feng invited me to dinner at her father's house. During this visit, Liu Jiling requested my assistance in procuring a Shanghai brand watch. I explained my inability to obtain an industrial coupon for the purchase. Eventually, Shi Taihua stepped in and helped him acquire the watch. Subsequently, Liu Zhenling asked my mother to purchase a Butterfly Brand sewing machine for her. When that didn't work, and she realized she couldn't exploit any advantages from my mother, she promptly distanced herself from me.

I was surprised when Liu Jiling visited Shanjia to see me and extended yet another dinner invitation to his house. It soon became apparent that Liu Jiling had a favor to ask. He had three daughters who were Educated Youths, all eagerly anticipating promotions. With opportunities for advancement scarce, he sought a favorable spot for them, and Shanjia emerged as the preferred choice due to its priority in recruitment quotas. Liu Jiling requested my assistance in connecting him with Jiang Guanghui, expressing his desire to relocate his family to Shanjia. Knowing that Jiang Guanghui held me in high regard, he implored, "I'd like to move my family to Shanjia. I know Jiang Guanghui likes you. Please take me to his house. I'll build a house on my own, at no cost to Shanjia. Liu Feng and her mother are both teachers, offering two teachers to Shanjia School for free. Shanjia has nothing to lose." He then added with apparent sincerity, "Let me share a secret with you; my brother is Liu Beiru's son-in-law. Liu Beiru and I are close relatives. I can help you establish a good relationship with Liu Beiru. What Liu Beiru desires is just respect from Educated Youths. You've never visited his home, never made any effort to please him. This is the problem. Listen, he enjoys wine, and I'll get you a bottle of Kouzi wine. Present it to Liu Beiru, make him smile, and all the clouds will dissipate."

Two days later, Liu Jiling came to Shanjia, and I accompanied him to meet Jiang Guanghui. During this period, Shanjia was actively engaged in construction, focusing on building one-story row houses. In Huaibei, peasants' houses typically had adobe walls and thatched roofs, but Shanjia Village aimed to showcase a socialist new countryside and became a focal point in the province. To achieve this, it was decided to construct two rows of brick houses on both sides of the main road through the village. Shanjia received a Jiefang Brand truck and a Dongfanghong Brand tractor for construction purposes. These vehicles traveled to a quarry 20 kilometers away to collect stones for the house foundations. The commune operated a brick and tile factory, providing Shanjia with bricks and tiles on credit. However, the availability of wood for construction was under state control. Liu Jiling, being resourceful, proposed a solution to Jiang Guanghui: "I work part-time as the accountant for the commune 5•7 Team. Many Educated Youths in Yongan don't have beds. The county Educated Youth Office recently allocated funds and wood quotas for Educated Youths. If you need money or wood quotas, just let me know." Soon after, Liu Jiling's family moved to Shanjia and became one of the first to move into one of the newly constructed brick houses. Not long after, the county silk reeling factory temporarily lifted its hiring freeze with a limited number of positions for a limited time. This information was not publicly announced in Yong'an. Liu Li, Liu Jiling's eldest daughter, secured a job and left quietly.

After Liu Jiling settled in Shanjia, he helped me buy a bottle of Kouzi wine. I visited Liu Beiru's house accordingly. Liu Beiru took the bottle and dryly laughed a few times, leaving the atmosphere awkward. Unsure of what to say, I promptly left. The following month, a meeting of Educated Youths was convened by the commune's 5•7 team. During the gathering, Liu Beiru placed the bottle of wine on the table, loudly proclaiming, "Liu Chengmo comes from a counter-revolutionary family. He has always been unwilling to accept re-education from poor and lower-middle peasants. He likes to take the upper-class route and corrupt cadres with food and drink. Look! This is the wine he gave me." The meeting took place in an open-air space within the commune compound, and the words uttered by Liu Beiru were audible to passersby, including commune cadres. It appeared that Liu Beiru had chosen an inopportune Moment to publicly criticize me. In December 1972, Li Qinglin, a primary school teacher in Putian, Fujian, wrote to Mao Zedong, expressing concerns about his son Li Liangmo, an Educated Youth, facing hardships with insufficient food, inability to afford daily necessities, and medical treatment expenses. Despite Li Qinglin having been classified as a rightist in 1957, Mao personally responded with a letter that read: "Sending you ¥300 to help with your lack of food problem. There are many similar situations around the country, for which we must find comprehensive solutions." This incident led to adjustments in central government policies for Educated Youths, including subsidies for living difficulties and severe punishments for local cadres mistreating Educated Youths. Given this context, Liu Beiru's criticism of an Educated Youth for "eating and drinking too much and corrupting the cadres" seemed absurd, especially when all the Educated Youths were grappling with food scarcity.

A few days later, Jiang Guanghui asked me what I had done to upset Liu Beiru. I said that I had been fooled by Liu Jiling. Jiang Guanghui chuckled and remarked, "Liu Jiling is a messed-up person." He disclosed that Wan Lichao had discussed the issue with Liu Beiru, expressing disagreement with publicly criticizing an Educated Youth. Wan Lichao clarified that the commune party committee had no prior knowledge of the meeting and emphasized the political sensitivity surrounding Communist Party cadres. Acknowledging that no cadre was entirely immune to corruption, Wan Lichao was concerned that Liu Beiru's accusations against me could attract the attention of higher authorities, potentially causing trouble for many people in the commune. Wan Lichao promptly addressed Liu Beiru: "You're aware that People's Daily published Chairman Mao's letter to Li Qinglin. We must support Chairman Mao's 'Go up the Mountain, Down to the Village' movement and take care of the Educated Youths. Be careful not to bring negative impacts to the 'Go up the Mountain, Down to the Village' movement. Remember, the Educated Youths are like a high-voltage line." When Wan Lichao mentioned the term "high-voltage line," Liu Beiru visibly tensed, realizing the potential consequences of his actions. Faced with the risk of exposure regarding the pregnancy incident, Liu Beiru promptly applied for resignation, citing health reasons. Wan Lichao happily appointed another retired cadre, Lao Li, to replace Liu Beiru as the leader of the 5•7 team.

Soon after, Shanjia received another recruitment quota. When Liu Jiling and his family arrived at Shanjia, he promptly secured one quota for his daughter, Liu Li. Many people deemed this unfair, believing it should have been given to a more long-term Educated Youth who'd been waiting for years for such an opportunity. However, considering the recent criticism against me, Jiang Guanghui thought it might not be the right time for me to take the quota. Undeterred, Liu Jiling began frequenting dinners and drinks with Jiang Guanghui, attempting to sway his decisions. Meanwhile, Liu Zhenling sought to seduce Jiang Guanghui's godfather, who worked as a barefoot doctor at the brigade health clinic. This enraged Jiang Guanghui's godmother, who publicly confronted Liu Zhenling for attempting to steal her man. Amidst this chaos, Liu Jiling managed to obtain another recruitment form from Jiang Guanghui at dinner one night. Within the Liu Jiling family, it was decided that Liu Yan, the third child, would benefit from this opportunity. The second eldest child, Liu Feng, who worked as a private teacher, could afford to wait. Liu Yan, however, bore the brunt of household chores and fieldwork; her status was akin to a servant in the family hierarchy. Neglected by her parents, Liu Yan's anticipation of a positive change was profound. Tragically, Liu Yan's hopes were dashed when Liu Feng quietly took the recruitment form meant for her. In despair, Liu Yan threw herself down a narrow well shaft, rendering rescue efforts challenging due to its small diameter. Villagers scrambled to find suitable tools for a rescue attempt, but their lack of supplies due to poverty limited their options. By the time they fashioned together enough ropes to reach her, it was too late—Liu Yan's body had already stiffened. As the scripture in Matthew Chapter 10, Verse 36 reminds us: "A man's enemies will be those within his own household."

In 1980, while I was studying at Anhui Normal University, an event was organized jointly by Anhui Normal University and Anhui Mechanical and Electrical Vocational School. As the Director of the Arts and Entertainment Department of the Student Union at Anhui Normal University, I presided over the event. During the gathering, I unexpectedly encountered Liu Juan, the fourth child of Liu Jiling, among the students from the vocational school. Having taught at Yong'an Middle School, I remembered Liu Juan as one of my former students. However, her reaction indicated discomfort upon seeing me. Liu Juan explained that her father, Liu Jiling, was aware of my presence in Wuhu and had instructed her not to meet or talk to me. I reassured her, saying, "Thanks for letting me know. No problem." I then walked away from the situation. Subsequently, I heard from sources in Suxian that Liu Jiling had suffered several strokes, resulting in symptoms such as crooked eyes and mouth, dribbling saliva, and unsteady walking.

Conscience is an inherent aspect of human nature that guides individuals to recognize the necessity of curbing the potential harm caused by the darker elements of their own character. Consequently, societies establish laws and universally accepted norms to maintain order and protect individuals from the negative consequences of unchecked malevolence. When an individual disregards these rules, allowing their more animalistic instincts to prevail and violate the principles of civilized society, they not only cause harm to others but also risk losing touch with their humanity, violating the principles of civilized society, and causing harm to others. Betraying or snitching on others to advance one's own interests crosses a fundamental line in human morality. Not only does it harm those being betrayed, but it also inflicts damage upon the betrayer's own soul. The idea of retribution has deep roots, with historical and literary examples emphasizing how wrongdoing will ultimately lead to consequences for the wrongdoer. If the Old Testament concept of justice being an eye for an eye and a tooth for a tooth is promoted and embraced, then it follows that the majority of people will do their best to avoid behaving in ways that will make them the object of such retribution. As early as ancient Greece, the central idea of its drama reveals that evil deeds will be punished, and human beings cannot escape their fate, nor can they escape the pursuit of a vengeful god. But Zhou Chaoguang, who drowned, Liu Yan, who jumped into a well, Liu Jiling, who suffered from cerebral infarction, Xu Weiguo, who suffered from rectal cancer, and Li Wei'er, who suffered from breast cancer, could any or all of these harsh fates be classified as just?

In the summer of 1976, Jiang Guanghui informed me about a recruitment opportunity. Jiang Guanghui said to me, "Huaibei No. 3 Construction Company is coming to Suxian to recruit workers. We get only 7 quota slots in the entire county. So each of the county committee's standing committee members takes one. They say that I am at the grassroots level, so they give me two. I see that you and Gao Hong have been here for so many years. I would like to let you go this time." Huaibei No. 3 Construction Company, officially known as Anhui Province No. 3 Construction Engineering Company, was engaged in constructing a thermal power plant in Huaibei City. This construction site, named

Huaibei 307, fell under the Anhui Provincial Electric Power Construction Bureau. As a provincial-level entity, the company offered superior working conditions and benefits compared to regional and county units. Gao Hong was stationed in the Liu Wafang Brigade. She was a talented actress and spent some time with the Shanjia art troupe. Jiang Guanghui valued her contributions enough to provide this opportunity for her as well as me.

When Liu Beiru held office in the commune 5•7 team, more than a hundred Educated Youths had to cater to his whims. Wherever he went, he was surrounded by sycophants, ready to curry favor with him. Like a decaying carcass attracting flies, he could pick and choose those willing to devote themselves to him. The allure of power was so strong that even after his departure, he maintained connections with the county's 5•7 team. When Liu Jiling informed him that I had filled out the recruitment form, he promptly rushed to Suxian and spoke to the contact person in charge of recruitment at the County Labor Bureau. He emphasized that my family background was the darkest in the entire Yong'an Commune. Both my father and uncle had been imprisoned, and my own behavior was deemed problematic. Director Xie Daofeng of the regional labor bureau had expressed reservations about me, stating that I should not be promoted. This placed the county labor bureau in a difficult position. Since all candidates, including myself, had been recommended by the Standing Committee of the County Party Committee, they couldn't easily reject my application or request a replacement. However, Xie Daofeng's reservation added a layer of complexity. To navigate this situation, seeking instructions from Xie Daofeng seemed like the most viable solution.

Sanhei was Xie Daofeng's younger son. Sanhei had a girlfriend named Xiaodai, who was a Shanghai educated-youth. Xiaodai and Sanhei appeared to be a good match. They were both tall and had fair skin. They looked very energetic and beautiful. Xiaodai was promoted to a job in the city and worked at Dongfeng Restaurant. Xie Daofeng sent Yin Meng to the restaurant to find out about Xiaodai's behavior and requested the restaurant manager to pass Xiaodai's file to him for review. Xiaodai and

Sanhei were furious, and in the aftermath, Sanhei stayed away from home for half a year. Sanhei was his mother's favorite, and she felt very depressed after not seeing him for so long. When Sanhei heard that my recruitment form had been submitted to the county Labor Bureau, he went home to see his father. His mother suffered from severe eye disease and injured her foot in those days. Hearing Sanhei's voice, she was so happy and staggered her way out. Sanhei told her, "Chengmo's job recruitment form has been submitted to the county labor bureau. I want to notify father and ask him to take care of it." His mother replied: "Okay, okay." The recruitment process was quick. The recruiter of a company needed to cover a few counties. They could not wait. As soon as the recruiter left, the process was over. A few days later, the county labor bureau informed the commune that my job application was not approved. Lao Li and Jiang Guanghui were surprised to hear this. They told me in detail how Liu Beiru went to the County Labor Bureau to make trouble for me. The county labor bureau did try to find Xie Daofeng for instructions. The regional labor bureau office responded that they could not get in touch with Xie Daofeng because he was on a business trip. I know Sanhei had good intentions to help me. However, we were too naive. It was so easy for Xie Daofeng to play a game with a young man like me. Two days later, I met Gao Hong at Yong'an. Her production squad sent someone to help transport her luggage to Yong'an Bus Station. Gao Hong was very surprised and saddened by the turn of events. I said, "It's unexpected. It's a pity that I wasted a precious quota slot."

Losing this opportunity left me feeling utterly defeated. Gazing up at the sky, I pondered Oscar Wilde's words: "We are all in the gutter, but some of us are looking at the stars." I also reflected on Somerset Maugham's sentiment in *The Moon and Sixpence*: "There were sixpence all over the ground, but he looked up and saw the moon." In this analogy, sixpence symbolizes the mundane aspects of everyday life, while the moon represents our inner aspirations and dreams. The conflict between our dreams and the reality we face is a timeless theme. We all strive to discover our true selves and realize our deepest desires. So, when would I find my own moon?

In 1977, rumors spread that the central government was considering reinstating the college entrance examination, igniting excitement among Educated Youths. Many began seeking pre-Cultural Revolution textbooks to prepare for the possible exams. Meanwhile, the crucial wheat harvest season commenced on June 1st in Suxian, prompting commune cadres to prioritize supervising wheat collection for tax purposes. For villagers, the harvest's yield determined their sustenance for the year, with any surplus after taxes serving as their staple grain until the next harvest. Throughout the rest of the year, they relied on whole grains like sorghum and dried sweet potatoes to stave off hunger. Schools observed a two-week break during the wheat harvest from late May to early June, followed by summer vacation in July and August. During this period, I traveled to Suxian for a two-week stay. Generously, Sanhei offered me his room equipped with a record player in the printing factory, allowing me to listen to English reading records. Amidst this, Yin Meng approached me for math tutoring. I suggested she seek help from Yin Li, who had graduated from Xian Jiaotong University, one of the most prestigious science and technology institutions in the country. However, Yin Meng expressed reluctance, stating that Yin Li lacked proficiency in solving quadratic equations of one variable.

After my visit to Suxian, I traveled to Huaibei to meet with Liu Gengnian first and then Gao Hong while continuing my exam preparations. Despite their demanding jobs as miners in No. 8 Mine, they and many other Educated Youths there were also engaged in exam preparations. The work in the mines was hazardous, with frequent injuries and fatalities. On one occasion, Liu Gengnian took me down the mine on a railcar, providing me with a firsthand experience of the challenging conditions. Miners lay on their backs, slowly advancing with basic tools like pickaxes and shovels, confined in a space reminiscent of a coffin, surrounded closely by coal and rock. Wherever the miner's lamp shone, the air was filled with sparkling coal dust, blackening the nostrils within Moments. Despite the seriousness of their work, Liu Gengnian's humorous and entertaining personality shone through. He even took sick leave to spend more time with me during my visit. On our way to a medical clinic, he playfully pretended to experience a stomachache, bending down and holding his stomach with a frown. After obtaining a sick note from the doctor, he ran out laughing, unfazed by the risk of being caught. Liu Gengnian had a close brush with death when a steel cable pulling the railcar in the tunnel suddenly snapped and ricocheted against the tunnel wall. Although coal dust flew everywhere and hit him in the face, he miraculously avoided being struck by the steel cable, which likely would have been fatal. Despite the dangers, Liu Gengnian's determination paid off when he successfully passed the college entrance exams in 1978, gaining admission to the Physics Department of Huaibei Coal Mine Normal University. After graduating, he was fortunate enough to secure a well-deserved teaching position in Shanghai.

On August 4, 1977, a significant development occurred for all of China and the "Educated Youth" in particular: the restoration of the college entrance examination system throughout the country. A symposium was held at the Beijing Hotel, where 33 experts and scholars from the Academy of Sciences system and universities across the country gathered. During this event, Wen Yuankai, a teaching assistant at the University of Science and Technology of China, proposed a plan for the college entrance examination, featuring the principles of "voluntary application, leadership approval, strict examination, and merit-based admission." Deng Xiaoping, recognizing the issues caused by excessive "leadership approval" in the past, remarked that the second item, "leadership approval," could be removed. In the Mao era, numerous Educated Youths were stuck because they could not get "leadership approval." In fact, that process was tantamount to passing through the gates of hell. How many leaders were kind enough to provide a young man with their approval for free? When recommending workers, peasants, and soldiers to attend college, if the candidate was very good and capable, with high test scores, but a village leader, a commune leader, or a unit leader disliked him, then all the efforts the aspiring applicant had made were a waste, and they could go nowhere. By eliminating leadership approval from the college application process, Deng Xiaoping removed a huge mountain that had been weighing on the Educated Youth for years.

From then on, every student in China could legitimately spend time preparing for the exams. In many developed countries, equal access to education has a history as a basic human right. In China, Mao took away all the basic rights of the people. Now this one vital right returned to us, though still with some qualifiers. In addition, we were told that we must thank Deng Xiaoping and the party. While Deng's pragmatic decisions often had a positive impact on individuals seeking education, it's important to note that his restoration of the college entrance examination—like all his actions—was driven by his desire to save the party, not by concern for the "Five Black Category" youths. Throughout both the early and later phases of his leadership career, Deng was merciless in suppressing people. He was a key architect of the anti-rightist movement in 1957, and it was Deng who ordered the Tiananmen massacre in 1989.

The official announcement by the State Council on October 12, 1977, declaring the resumption of the college entrance examination, marked a significant turning point in China's history. The new policy of "voluntary application and merit-based admission" breathed new life into millions of individuals seeking educational opportunities. The announcement made waves across various media outlets, including the Central People's Broadcasting Station on October 21. It was like a sudden burst of spring, raising blossoms on thousands of pear trees overnight. This policy change symbolized a historic shift, as political oppression based on family class origin gradually faded into the past. The removal of this historical barrier opened doors for millions of "educable children," representing a significant step toward realizing Confucius' idea of "education without distinction" from two millennia ago and steering back towards the relatively fair imperial examinations of a thousand years ago. This transformative move triggered the thunderous unlocking of countless desperate hearts, releasing the pent-up aspirations of individuals across the country. The college entrance examination became a pathway for class mobility that had been stagnant for decades, offering a chance for thousands to change their destiny through hard work. The reform allowed eager souls to pursue a brighter future, contributing to a rebirth of youthful energy across the vast and ancient land.

The period between the announcement of the new policy and the specific date of the first new college entrance examination in December 1977 spanned approximately two months. During this time, qualified candidates were eager to study intensely, striving to alter their destinies. Xie Bin, Tang Weidong, and I arranged to meet at Yong'an Middle School every night for joint study sessions. After an early dinner, I would cover the 1.5-kilometer distance to reach Yong'an Middle School. On the way, I often crossed paths with Jiang Guanghui, who worked in Yong'an during the day and returned to Shanjia in the evenings. During a villagers' meeting, Jiang Guanghui teased me, "Agriculture Learn from Dazhai. If we had Liu Chengmo's drive in taking the college entrance examination, we would have succeeded in improving our crop yield long ago." In the 1977 examination, all levels of higher education institutions, including colleges, junior colleges, and technical secondary schools, used the same single test. The type of school to which a candidate would gain admission was determined based on their test scores. Candidates could apply for their preferred subject and major, and take the appropriate test, either for liberal arts or science and technology, with additional tests available for foreign languages if requested. I applied for a foreign language major in English, while Xie Bin and Tang Weidong applied for science majors. Our focus in preparation was on subjects like mathematics, physics, and chemistry. Review materials were scarce, so we made use of whatever resources we could find. Two weeks before the exam, I received notice from the county college exam office that foreign languages were categorized as liberal arts. Consequently, I had to pass exams in liberal arts first before taking a foreign language exam. During 1977 and 1978, liberal arts majors were also required to take the math test, so I devoted some time to reviewing math. However, liberal arts subjects did not include physics and chemistry tests, but rather history and geography. In a rush, I started studying history and geography materials. Fortunately for me, these subjects focused on so-called "dead knowledge"—inert facts and figures which I could read and memorize. When the exam date arrived, the county college exam office realized there had been a misunderstanding, and I could have taken either liberal arts or science exams, plus a foreign language test. Unfortunately, it was too late to make another change, so with my mere two weeks' worth of preparation, I proceeded to take the liberal arts exams.

In 1977, the age limit for applicants was extended to thirty years old. However, institutes of foreign languages only accepted those under the age of 25. Being just over 25 years old, I could only apply for a foreign language major at a normal university. My college choices included East China Normal University in Shanghai, Anhui University in Hefei, Anhui Normal University in Wuhu, and Suxian Normal College. Despite the policy for resuming the college entrance examination, including the requirement of "political review," which supposedly focused on the candidate's behavior rather than family background or class theory, there were still many hidden areas of discrimination. Institutions like the Military Industrial School and the Diplomatic Academy reserved spots for the children of communist cadres in power. Knowing this, I chose not to bother with applying to them. Although the 1977 College Entrance Examination admission documents stated that the main consideration was the candidate's behavior and that family background should not be an obstacle to admission, in practice, the injustices and false accusations from the founding of the People's Republic of China and those during the "Cultural Revolution" remained unaddressed. Many examiners leaned towards the left, and their mindset remained in the era of the Cultural Revolution. Candidates and their parents harbored lingering fears. In the first year of implementation, the policy directive to focus on the candidate's own behavior alone and disregard their family background was not fully enforced. One day before the exam, Xie Bin, Tang Weidong, and I arrived in Suxian City, sleeping side by side on the floor. The next day, we queued to enter the examination room with our admission tickets. On December 10, 1977, I took the Chinese language test in the morning and the history and geography test in the afternoon. The following day, there was a math test in the morning and a politics test in the afternoon. The exam papers, including Chinese language, Mathematics, History, and Geography, seemed to be at a junior high school level, which was

247

somewhat disappointing. However, the English test paper was intriguing. In addition to some Chinese revolutionary slogans in English, it featured English grammar, sentence structure, and reading comprehension. The 1977 college entrance examination marked the end of an eleven-year suspension, with middle school graduates from the classes of 1966 to 1977 and some high-performing high school students from the class of 1978 competing against each other. This resulted in 13 years of applicants entering the examination rooms in 1977. The nationwide number of test-takers was 5.7 million, of which 272,971 were admitted. With a ratio of 21:1, the acceptance rate was 4.8%, making it the lowest admission rate in the history of higher education in China.

After returning to Shanjia, I received a notice for an English oral test. Three teachers from different universities—representatives from East China Normal University, Anhui University, and Anhui Normal University—came to Suxian County to conduct the examinations. During the oral test, we were given a short English article and a few minutes to prepare. We then entered the examination room one by one to meet with the examiners. When it was my turn, a teacher instructed me to read the short article aloud and then translate it into Chinese. After I finished, Mr. Feng from East China Normal University said, "We're staying at the Coal Ministry Guest Hotel. I'd like to invite you to come see us this evening. We want to ask you a few more questions. Please don't tell the other candidates." At that time, the county and regional guest houses were quite run-down, but the Coal Ministry Guest Hotel was considered the most upscale. In the evening, I went to the hotel as invited. They asked me where I learned English and what English books I had read. I mentioned that I had read English versions of "Beijing Review," "China Daily," and Mao's Three Old Articles. I also mentioned that I could recite a bit of the Three Old Articles. They encouraged me to recite, and I started with "Serving the People." I had listened to English recordings of these articles numerous times and was able to mimic the announcer's tone and intonation perfectly. The three teachers, all Russian majors with shortcomings in English listening and speaking skills, seemed shocked by my performance. Mr. Feng signaled me to stop and then said, "I can tell you that your total score in liberal arts exceeds the admission cutoff score for national key universities. You scored 103 points in the English test, the highest among all candidates in Suxian County. I really want to take you with me. But East China Normal University is a national key school, and there's no way for me to take your file. If I took it, it would be rejected by the school anyway." I replied, "I understand." A teacher from Anhui University expressed a similar sentiment, explaining that while Anhui University was not a national key school, the Department of Foreign Languages was dedicated to training cadres for the Ministry of Foreign Affairs, and so he couldn't take my file either. However, Mr. Liu Yunkuan from Anhui Normal University said, "Anhui Normal University trains elementary and secondary school teachers. I can take your file." Amidst the grateful cheers of "Hello Xiaoping!" echoing in the news, despite my first class test score, due to my "counter-revolutionary" family background, I was admitted to a third-class college.

In January 1978, I received an admission notice from Anhui Normal University. At the end of February, I bid farewell to Jiang Guanghui and my colleagues at Shanjia School. Nearly ten years had passed since I arrived in Yong'an, and it was time to move on. As the saying goes, all rivers flow eastward, and there's no need to look back. Before departing, Mr. Zhou Hualu gave me a letter to deliver to Zhu Choumei at Anhui Normal University. Zhou Hualu shared that Zhu Choumei, born in poverty in Huaibei, faced hardships during his junior high school years, lacking even basic necessities like shoes. Zhou Hualu, as the principal of the school, took good care of Zhu Choumei and expressed confidence that Zhu would look out for me at the university. The night before my departure, many people came to see me off. I was among the first batch of "Educated Youths" sent to Suxian and the last batch to leave. Over nine years had passed, and my time in Yong'an had come to an end. Time flies, and my youth has flowed out like running water. When I left, some of the Educated Youths fortunate enough to have been reassigned to Suxian were already married with children, their futures clearly mapped out, while I was a bachelor just beginning. At Dongfeng Hotel, a structure built by Shanghai Educated Youths, friends gathered to bid me farewell.

Yin Li was also present, and when asked why she hadn't had a child yet, she humorously shared that she and He Guangyao had been married for three years but hadn't spent three weeks together. Everyone laughed, amused by her candidness.

Decades later, some former "sent-down youth" began saying they had "no regrets" about that part of their lives. I find this hard to believe. Our best years were wasted, and many suffered scars that can never fully heal. What is there to look back on with pride? Half a century after the "sent-down youth movement," a wave of people and cultural works— backed by the CCP—started to glorify those years of hardship. Yet the Party itself has admitted that the Cultural Revolution was an "unprecedented catastrophe." In truth, the suffering of the Chinese people did not begin or end with the Cultural Revolution, but it has been a constant under Communist rule. Given that reality, celebrating hardship—while it contradicts common sense—makes perfect sense as propaganda for the current regime. The reasons behind this are not hard to see. On the one hand, it comes from a long tradition in Chinese culture that values power above all. For centuries, people have accepted the idea that "winners are kings, losers are outlaws." As a result, many have learned to submit to authority, believing it is the safest choice—and sometimes hoping to gain small advantages from it. On the other hand, decades of authoritarian rule have forced people to live with situations that make no sense, until the abnormal comes to feel normal. Over time, this sort of rule and the dynamics it creates have shaped generations to become more selfish, shortsighted, and indifferent—ready to ignore the law, blur right and wrong, and act without compassion.

The following day, I boarded a southbound train and visited Xie Bin's parents in Bengbu, where I stayed for a few days. Xie Yifan welcomed me at the station, and their home radiated with joy, celebrating both Xie Bin's and my college admissions. Zhang Fengzhi's happiness was palpable, her smile seemingly endless. Coincidentally, it was January 15th on the Chinese lunar calendar, the Lantern Festival, which also happens to be my birthday. The five of us gathered around the table, crafting sweet dumplings to commemorate the festival and my special day.

In Xie Yifan's family, which comprised the couple, Xie Bin, and his sister Xie Jinsha, emotions ran high. Jinsha suddenly burst into tears, lamenting, "You're all going to college, and I'm being left behind." During the Cultural Revolution's onset, art troupes flourished, and Jinsha joined the Bengbu City Art Troupe as a ballet dancer, thus escaping being sent down to the village. However, as the Cultural Revolution waned, many troupes disbanded, leaving Jinsha adrift. Xie Yifan arranged for her to work in the laboratory department of Bengbu Medical College, where she grumbled about washing bottles all day. Xie Yifan countered, "What's wrong with washing bottles? Even medical school graduates do it. Why can't you?" Despite her initial tears, Jinsha persevered, passing exams the following year and gaining admission to the Foreign Languages Department of Anhui University in 1978. Later, Xie Yifan and Zhang Fengzhi credited me with influencing Xie Bin and Jinsha's college aspirations. Conversely, none of Xie Daofeng's children gained college admission, heightening Zhang Fengzhi's jubilation during those days.

On January 11, 1979, the CCP issued the "Decision on the Removal of Hats from Landowners and Rich Peasants and the Identity of Their Children." Official figures revealed that during the land reform of 1950, there were over 20 million landowners and over 60 million of their offspring. By the time this decree was enacted, only 4.4 million landowners remained, along with 20 million of their descendants. This stark reduction signifies a staggering loss of 70%, or 15.6 million lives, over the past three decades. These deaths occurred through various means, including execution by order of the dictatorship, mob violence, and imprisonment during the ravages of famine and the tumult of the Cultural Revolution. The vast majority were deprived of fundamental rights such as education, employment, love, marriage, and the autonomy to shape their destinies. I count myself fortunate to have survived and departed Suxian in 1978. I am a survivor. However, despite the opening of university doors to me, it did not signify the establishment of justice and equity. My status merely progressed from "unsuitable for admission" to "suitable for admission to a third-class college only." I denounce that era! I denounce the figure lying in the crystal coffin and his collaborators!

I denounce the Party!

What is justice? John Rawls (1921~2002), an American political philosopher, encapsulated his thoughts succinctly in his "Justice as Fairness" theory, which holds: "Only when you shed your own identity can you truly grasp the essence of justice." He employed the theoretical device of a "veil of ignorance" to explain his ideas. Standing behind this metaphorical veil, one could be the wealthiest individual or the most marginalised in society, devoid of any knowledge about their position. If you deem justice to be the redistribution of wealth, envisioning a world where the rich are stripped of their possessions, you might reconsider once the veil is lifted and you discover yourself to be someone like Warren Buffett. Similarly, if you subscribe to the notion of familial inheritance determining virtue or vice, believing that a father's status dictates his son's character, the revelation of being born into a stigmatised lineage could evoke profound despair. Applying this concept to societal matters such as resource allocation, educational opportunities, housing, employment, and healthcare, it becomes apparent that utopian socialism and communism fail to embody justice. Justice transcends mere egalitarianism—it involves recognising the diversity of individual talents, upholding private property rights, and ensuring equitable participation in free competition. If blind loyalty to political ideologies and unquestioning adherence to party principles are a matter of course, then once the "veil of ignorance" is removed, you may regret it when you find that you are a pregnant woman lying on the operating table bleeding heavily, facing a group of communist doctors whose only professional qualifications are their devout political beliefs and family backgrounds. At that point, you may regret having been an active advocate supporting "identity theory," "blood theory," and "class struggle."

Jiangxi

On March 5, 1969, my brother Chengquan and sister ShenJie arrived at the Xiashijing Production Squad of the Fangyuan Brigade in Tianbao Commune, Yifeng County. Nestled in the remote mountains of western Jiangxi Province, Yifeng County posed transportation challenges. To reach the production squad, they first had to traverse a 1-kilometer mountain road from the Educated Youth Center. Then, a further 1.5 kilometers of rugged terrain awaited them on the way to the brigade. From there, a 14-kilometer gravel road led to the commune, where a daily shuttle bus offered transportation to the county town. Beyond that lay a day's journey by bus to Nanchang, the capital of Jiangxi Province, followed by a 16-hour train ride to Shanghai.

The production squad allocated an abandoned ancestral hall to accommodate a group of 10 Educated Youths from Shanghai. Upon arrival, they were met with grim conditions: the rooms were dimly lit, with damp walls and muddy floors. Each room contained nothing but a simple bed board. Some of the girls, shocked by the stark reality, burst into tears, feeling deceived by their teachers' promises of adequate amenities and good food. A stream flowed behind the ancestral hall, contributing to the pervasive dampness. As the days passed, mold grew on handkerchiefs left in pockets, and the lack of firewood necessitated frequent trips into the forest to gather dry branches and bamboo, where one girl suffered a painful wasp bite on her head. Swarms of mosquitoes plagued the area. You caught them when you were blinking. Rainfall occurred every few days, and regardless of weather conditions, fieldwork was mandatory. Even during winter, when thin ice covered the paddy fields, the youths were expected to continue their labor. The swampy fields, dotted with hidden springs, posed challenges for both humans and oxen alike. During rice transplanting, colorful leeches infested the area, leaving painful triangular wounds that bled profusely. By the end of the transplanting season, Chengquan discovered over 100 small wounds on his legs. While plowing the fields, a cold water snake slithered past one girl's leg, prompting her to scream in terror.

By the end of 1969, all 10 Educated Youths were eager to return home for the New Year. However, rather than announcing their departure collectively, they opted for a more discreet approach by fabricating medical excuses for two of the group. Lao Tao, from the village office, provided them with medical passes to facilitate their departure. Under the cover of night, they quietly left their homes, maintaining a careful distance from each other and avoiding the village office. Carrying local goods and a few live chickens, they reached the bus station by 5 o'clock in the morning. Unfortunately, their plans hit a snag when the bus they intended to take broke down, with no backup options available that day. Noticing a reclamation farm nearby, they sought assistance from Lao Zhou, a Shanghainese resident who had relocated to the area in 1958. Lao Zhou helped them secure transportation by connecting them with a truck bound for Yichun, which was scheduled to transport timber that day. Fortunately, the truck driver agreed to take them along. Yichun was two stations beyond Nanchang, requiring them to pay a small additional fee for the train ticket. Despite the setback, they managed to board the train on the same day, making progress towards their journey home.

Chengquan, Shenjie, and seven other youths spent two uneasy months in Shanghai and returned to Jiangxi in March 1970. They brought back supplies like cottonseed oil, fried rice flour, dried radish, and sesame seeds. Due to a lack of supplementary food, the rice ration remained insufficient. However, the addition of a barrel of cottonseed oil significantly improved their quality of life. Upon arriving in Nanchang, they hurried to the bus station and luckily secured tickets to Yifeng County for the next day. For an overnight stay at the guest house of Nanchang Medical College, they paid ¥0.80 per person. As they lay down to rest, a group of militiamen armed with rifles entered, driving all passengers out of the room for individual interrogations. Those without passes suffered beatings, with some sustaining head injuries. Fortunately, two members in Chengquan's group had passes, and everyone possessed the next day's bus tickets, so the militiamen left them unharmed. Arriving in Yifeng County the following afternoon, they discovered that bus tickets to Tianbao Commune for the next day were sold out. Waving down a tractor on the road, the driver kindly assisted them with their luggage. They walked 22 kilometers to Songxi village to meet the driver and then traversed an additional 8 kilometers along the mountain road to reach the production squad.

Nine out of the ten Educated Youths went to Shanghai to celebrate the New Year, leaving only Wang Huili behind. As the only Communist Youth League member in the household, Wang Huili aspired to advance politically and join the Party, a process requiring a sponsor. Xue Xiu, a party member and clerk in the brigade office, held some power due to his possession of the official seal, making him a convenient ally. Wang Huili spent the New Year alone in the production squad, which was very convenient for her to be close to Xue Xiu. Later, she simply moved into the brigade office. Upon the return of other Educated Youths after the Chinese New Year, Wang Huili was frequently seen crying, and her growing belly became noticeable. During the intensified "Go up the Mountain, Down to the Village" movement of 1969 and 1970, aimed at cracking down on those hindering the movement, severe consequences were meted out, including imprisonment and execution. When the commune investigated Wang Huili's pregnancy, Xue Xiu, frightened, knelt. The investigation team talked to Wang Huili and told her not to feel any shame and to hold nothing back. They wanted to know if she had been raped by Xue Xiu. The investigation team said they would protect her privacy and transfer her away from Jiangxi, to Anhui or some other province. Wang Huili said the sex had been consensual and never changed her story. The investigation team was disappointed and Xue Xiu was saved. Subsequently, despite facing opposition from Wang Huili's parents, she and Xue Xiu got married. After the birth of their daughter, Wang Huili's parents eventually accepted the marriage. The girl was raised by her grandmother in Shanghai. In October 1978, the National Work Conference on the "Go up the Mountain, Down to the Village" movement decided to conclude the movement and find employment for Educated Youths. Post-1979, most Educated Youths gradually returned to cities. Wang Huili secured a job in the commune's supply and marketing cooperative, while Xue Xiu worked in the commune's finance and taxation office. Their second daughter was raised by them in Tianbao Commune. As the two daughters grew up—one in Tianbao, the other in Shanghai—they were completely different; the girl in Shanghai was an urban sophisticate, while the girl in Tianbao was a country bumpkin. It became difficult to imagine they were biological sisters.

At the outset of the Cultural Revolution, in the province of Jiangxi, a man named Cheng Shiqing wielded significant power. Having risen to the rank of brigadier general in 1955, when the tumultuous era of the Cultural Revolution began, Cheng assumed the role of political commissar of the 26th Army. He held multiple key positions, serving as director of the Jiangxi Provincial Revolutionary Committee and first secretary of the Jiangxi Provincial Party Committee. Simultaneously, he served as deputy political commissar of the Fuzhou Military Region and political commissar of the Jiangxi Provincial Military Region. Aligned with and sponsored by Lin Biao—China's preeminent general and a prominent political official at the time—Cheng Shiqing secured a position as a member of the Ninth Central Committee at the Ninth National Congress. Under Cheng Shiqing's leadership, cadres who were not aligned with his faction were expelled from Nanchang and relocated to the countryside, including personnel from the provincial police department, Xinhua Bookstore, and democratic parties. Together with Educated Youth, these individuals formed the 5•7 Army. The expelled cadres assigned to rural areas still received state salaries and were excused from fieldwork duties, and instead were tasked with managing the Educated Youths. Employing military-style organization, production squads were collectively termed "squads," while the commune level was designated as a "company." A reassigned cadre named Lao Chen assumed the responsibility of overseeing the Educated Youth's households and took pride in their exceptional performance. The busiest time in Jiangxi's rural areas was the double rush season, demanding peasants to complete both harvesting and planting within a few days. During this period, my brother Chengquan and another boy toiled continuously for 30 hours in the paddy fields, breaking a record in the double rush season. Lao Chen commended their hard work and exemplary behavior to the commune and county, leading to county-wide cable broadcasts and recognition as model, advanced Educated Youths. After laboring in the paddy fields for 30 hours, Chengquan observed the waters of a stream shimmering like a rainbow in an oil painting on his way back to the village. The excessive fatigue from these two days resulted in Chengquan's severe visual impairment, a condition that persisted throughout his lifetime.

The company commander of the 5·7 Army in Tianbao Commune was Lao Jiang, with Cao Chengyu— affectionately referred to as Lao Cao—serving as the political instructor. In 1969, Lao Jiang visited Shanghai to meet the parents of the Educated Youths. He noticed that all three of my mother's children were gone. He expressed sympathy to my mother. Lao Jiang promised that if there was an opportunity, he would facilitate the transfer of either Chengquan or Shenjie out of the village. My mother invited Lao Jiang to dinner and asked if there was anything he needed. Lao Jiang mentioned a kerosene stove, a commodity not readily available in the market at the time. My mother had a colleague whose husband worked in a factory and was capable of fabricating a kerosene stove. In a period when many workers were idle due to the lack of production in factories, it was common for individuals to use factory tools for personal projects, such as crafting a sofa or making a floor lamp. My mother asked her colleague for help. The kerosene stove he built for her met Lao Jiang's urgent need. He wrote to my mother to express his gratitude. In the early spring of 1971, Lao Cao attended a meeting in the village where my brother, Chengquan, and my sister Shenjie had been sent. It was already midnight when the meeting ended. The moon rose high, and the temperature dropped. Everybody was hungry. Shenjie had some sesame seeds I brought to Shanghai for the New Year. She used the sesame seeds and sugar to make a bowl of sweet rice dumplings for Lao Cao. This simple yet thoughtful midnight snack not only warmed Lao Cao's stomach but also touched his heart.

On September 13, 1971, Lin Biao tragically died in a plane crash in Mongolia. For almost two years, there was no official mention, let alone explanation, of what had occurred; all newspapers stopped printing his name, his wall-posters were taken down, and he was edited out of textbooks. Immediately after the crash, highly-restrictred internal notices were circulated to upper-level cadres, branding Lin as the leader of a "counter-revolutionary clique"—but it took almost two years before an official narrative was presented to the public, portraying Lin Biao as having fled in panic after attempting to stage a failed coup against Mao and the Communist Party, which led to his destruction. Following the "Lin Biao Incident," Cheng Shiqing lost power in 1972. His leadership position in Jiangxi Province was assumed by Jiang Weiqing, who had served as the first secretary of the Jiangsu Provincial Party Committee before the Cultural Revolution. With these changes, cadres who had been sidelined by Cheng Shiqing regained their positions in Nanchang. Among them was Cao Chengyu, who had previously served as the chief of staff of the Provincial Police Department before the Cultural Revolution. The police system was a critical government department characterized by exclusive organization, secrecy, and internal loyalty. Cao Chengyu was well-connected, and his extensive network reached every corner of the province.

In the 1970s, the recruitmen in Tianbao Commune was only by small county factories. Then, in 1971, provincial workplaces started coming. One such workplace, publicly known as 6911 but internally referred to as the Transportation Department of the Provincial Construction and Engineering Bureau, came to Tianbao Commune. The Transportation Department was allocated 5 quotas for Educated Youths from Tianbao Commune. My brother Chengquan was considered an outstanding candidate, and the commune recommended him to the recruiter, Dai Yingen. Dai Yingen had his own agenda, aiming to secure one of the recruitment quotas for his wife, who resided in another commune. Because this would necessitate assistance from the Tianbao Commune, Dai Yingen accepted all the Educated Youths recommended by them without questioning. Thus, he did not bother to scrutinize Chengquan's file or try to find faults in his family background. The Transportation Department, with over 100 trucks and a motor vehicle garage, was strategically located between the city and the airport. Initially headed by a military representative with ties to Lin Biao, the unit went through changes after Lin Biao's death. The director was arrested, military representatives withdrew, and Zhou Keyun, former commissioner of the provincial police department before the Cultural Revolution, took over the Provincial Construction Committee. Zhou Keyun and Cao Chengyu both came from the same region in Northeast China and came down to

Jiangxi together. Zhou Keyun was Cao Chengyu's boss before the Cultural Revolution, and has now become his boss again. Following these changes, the Transportation Department was renamed Jiangxi Construction Machinery Factory.

In April 1972, Zhou Keyun appointed Lao Cao as the head of the machinery factory, bringing joy to the five Educated Youths recruited from Tianbao Commune. To express their enthusiasm, they welcomed Lao Cao at his residence in Nanchang and assisted him in unloading the truck and moving in his furniture. Chengquan received a letter from Mom, instructing him to build a good relationship with Lao Cao so that our sister Shenjie could also be recruited to the same factory. During this time, Lao Li, Lao Cao's wife, was pregnant. Chengquan took the initiative to visit Lao Li's house every Sunday, helping with household chores, purchasing rice and oil, cleaning the house, and fixing things. When Zhou Keyun was reinstated, Cao Chengyu chose to stay at the Construction Machinery Factory rather than return to the police department. The factory was located in Nanchang County, adjacent to Bayi Commune. As a significant enterprise in Jiangxi Province, the Provincial Construction Machinery Factory brought various benefits to Bayi Commune, making them particularly fond of Lao Cao. In the summer of 1972, Lao Cao arranged for Shenjie to move to Bayi Commune, and by the end of the year, he sent drivers to Tianbao Commune to bring Shenjie to the factory. Upon Shenjie's transfer, Lao Cao informed the commune leaders that Shenjie was his goddaughter. Chengquan and Shenjie affectionately called Lao Cao and Lao Li dad and mom, resulting in the commune cadres viewing Shenjie with special favor, providing her with various privileges. Nanchang County, situated on a plain with many dry fields, offered a notable improvement in working conditions for Shenjie. No longer immersed in leech-infested paddy fields, she could wear long pants and shoes while working. She lived with two other female Educated Youths in the village office located on the other side of the wall from the machinery factory. Thanks to family connections, these other two young women only rarely had to show up for work. Shenjie had her meals in the factory's canteen, eliminating the need to climb up the mountain to chop firewood. After dinner each day, Chengquan would carry a mast lantern to escort her to the village office. On Sundays, she often joined Chengquan to cook for Lao Cao and Lao Li, building a strong bond with Lao Cao, who grew quite fond of her. Once, when Lao Cao went on a business trip to Hainan, he bought a pearl necklace for each of his daughters, and one for Shenjie as well.

Starting in 1973, a variety of factors combined to create an unofficial but still wide-ranging hiring freeze throughout much of China. Jiangxi province was no exception and so had only a limited number of annual promotion quota slots available for college admissions. These slots were exclusively reserved for factory-level cadres at or above the division level. Lao Cao shared his plan for Shenjie with Mom, explaining that Shenjie's time in Bayi Commune was a stepping stone. He hoped to find an opportunity for her to attend a vocational technical school the following year. The de facto job recruitment freeze plunged many Educated Youths into despair. Tragically, two girls in Tianbao Commune experienced mental breakdowns, initially leading villagers to believe they were intentionally feigning—until they witnessed them eating feces. Lao Cao's wife, Lao Li, served as the director of the Jiangxi Provincial Complete Equipment Management Bureau. She had met Lao Jiang when both were at Tianbao Commune. After Lao Cao returned to Nanchang, Lao Jiang went back to his hometown in Wannian. Lao Cao and Lao Li raised four daughters, and their eldest, Xiao Ying, faced some health issues. In 1974, when Lao Jiang visited Nanchang, Lao Li asked him to inquire if Chengquan would be interested in marrying Xiao Ying. Chengquan declined, expressing disinterest. Lao Jiang did not want Chengquan to have any stress, so he did not pass this reply on to Lao Li. Lao Li was left puzzled for many years over why Lao Jiang left without saying goodbye.

On August 25, 1968, the Central Committee of the CCP, the State Council, the Central Military Commission, and the Central Cultural Revolution Committee jointly issued the "Notice on Sending Worker's Propaganda Teams to Schools." The next day, on August 26, an article signed by Yao Wenyuan titled "The Working Class Must Lead Everything" was published in the "People's Daily," announcing Mao

Zedong's latest instructions: "To achieve the proletarian education revolution, we must have the leadership of the working class... The worker's propaganda team must stay in the school for a long time, participate in all tasks of struggle, criticism, and reform in schools, and always lead the school. In rural areas, schools should be managed by the poor and lower-middle peasants, the most reliable allies of the working class." The nationwide deployment of worker propaganda teams commenced rapidly. In a single week after September 5, Shanghai selected 31,000 industrial workers to work in 513 middle schools and 129 primary schools across the city. In August 1968, Xinchang Road No. 1 Primary School also hosted a worker propaganda team. This team consisted of personnel from the Shanghai Municipal Public Transport Company, responsible for maintaining the city's trolleybus lines. The trolleybus yard was located at the southeast corner of Xinchang Road and Beijing Road West, very close to Xinchang Road No. 1 Primary School. All members of the worker propaganda team were party members and seasoned workers. Master Li, the captain, was a knowledgeable senior worker. Shao Xuewen, a team member, had lost his wife to cancer and harbored romantic feelings for my mother. Master Li played a role in fostering a relationship between Shao Xuewen and my mother.

Shao Xuewen, originally from northern Jiangsu Province, had come to Shanghai pulling a rickshaw and working as a coolie when he was young. His first wife, a factory worker, had passed away, and he considered himself fortunate to have found a teacher to become his second wife. Shao Xuewen had five children, with the eldest daughter already married, and the second being a mentally retarded son. The third child, Baozhen, could be sent to an Anhui village. But because of her good family background, she was sent to Chongming Farm in the Shanghai suburb instead. The fourth child was a son, and the fifth was a little girl. Living with his three children in a small room, Shao Xuewen—once he started his relationship with my mother—would visit her every day after work. My mother always found tasks for him to do and even sent him to her third aunt to perform heavier house chores for her, causing him to return home late at night. Bao Qin, Shao Xuewen's youngest child, recalled feeling like an orphan, as her mother had passed away, and she rarely saw her father throughout the day. From my mother's perspective, the "big red political umbrella" she would gain from marrying a CCP member was what she needed politically, but economically, she did not want to bear the burden of Shao Xuewen's intellectually disabled son. So, she made a prenuptial agreement with him before agreeing to marry. They would both remain financially independent after marriage. Despite facing party punishment for marrying a woman with severe political problems, Shao Xuewen was protected by Lao Li, preventing any serious consequences, except for the revocation of his overseas assignment to Tanzania in 1973.

My mother's second husband, Shao Xuewen, whom I called uncle, came into my life during the Spring Festival. It was the first time I met him, and he gave me ¥10 as a gift when my Mom wasn't looking. The following day, my Mom angrily confronted me: "Uncle gave you ¥10. Why didn't you tell me?" I responded, "You keep complaining about joint pains. You said you wanted to buy a set of chlorinated fiber-cotton blend thermal underwear, but you couldn't find it in Shanghai. I have sent the money to Yaoyuan, a cousin in Suzhou, to buy one for you." Mom paused for a Moment, her voice softened a bit, and she said, "If you take Uncle's money, you have to let me know." The sweater arrived shortly after, and she didn't say anything about it. Throughout the ten years I spent in the countryside, Mom never sent me a penny or a parcel. I didn't expect anything from her, and I didn't want to take anything from her. I had been abandoned by her since birth, and I had grown accustomed to it. Despite her efforts to belittle me, I remained a proud child, much to her frustration.

The "Go up the Mountain, down to the village" model was in large part driven by the central government's awareness of the growing problem of youth unemployment and unrest in China's big cities, resulting from the same government's own failed economic policies. By removing vast numbers of high school-age youths from those cities, Mao and his lieutenants found a way to relieve pressure on China's major urban economies without having to actually improve or expand them.

Indeed, the only thing they had to expand was human suffering. In the 1970s, the country gradually permitted Educated Youths to return to urban areas through various means, including job recruitment, college admissions, health excuses, job replacement, being an only child, having no children around, and so forth. While some methods required political review and family background checks, others were exempt and did not necessitate recommendations and extensive scrutiny. Options such as health excuses, replacing a retired parent, being an only child, and having no child around did not involve a rigorous approval process. Some parents chose early retirement to facilitate their child's return from a remote village to the city, eliciting envy from their peers. However, my mother, who had never sacrificed the slightest of her interests for anyone, did not consider early retirement for the sake of her child. The option of "being an only child" did not apply in our family. We had two alternatives: "no child around" and health excuses. A strategic approach was for both Shenjie and me to return to Shanghai, with me leveraging the "no child around" category and Shenjie later utilizing health excuses. Mom consistently emphasized Shenjie's poor health. While it was relatively straightforward to consult a doctor in Shanghai and obtain a medical certificate for Shenjie, the challenging part was obtaining approval from the county Educated Youth office. Shenjie was Lao Cao's favorite, making it easy for her to secure approval. Nonetheless, Mom chose to pursue the "no child around" approach to facilitate Shenjie's return, leaving me to stay in the countryside.

At the end of 1973, my mother obtained an application form for Shenjie, but I noticed that neither Chengquan nor Shenjie returned to Shanghai for the 1974 Chinese New Year. This was a departure from our usual family routine. This change puzzled me. Historically, Shenjie had always been the first to return home and the last to leave. One evening, while my mother was preparing vegetables in the kitchen, I approached her with my concerns: "Some of the Educated Youths in my commune have begun returning to Shanghai under the 'no child around' policy. Why hasn't Shenjie come back yet? We need to discuss this." My question caught her off guard, and it took her a moment to collect her thoughts.

Finally, she replied, "Alright, I'll write another letter to encourage her to return." My mother lived on the first floor of our house, while the Zhang family occupied the pavilion on the second floor. Mr. Zhang worked as a dock worker, and as he aged, his employer reassigned him to work in a public bathroom for dock workers. Gong Guiying, Mr. Zhang's wife and a member of the neighborhood security committee, wielded considerable influence in our neighborhood due to her favorable family background and close ties with the sub-district party branch secretary. She often overshadowed the neighborhood committee secretary in decision-making. Displeased with my mother's preference for Shenjie, Gong Guiying approached me one day: "Your mother submitted an application form to us. All the other neighbors want their sons back, but your mother wants her daughter back. It's not fair to you. If you want to return, I'll provide you with another form to fill out. I'll disregard your sister's application." My friends Fen Jianguo and Longlong shared their concerns with me as well. I explained to them, "Who wouldn't want to return to Shanghai? However, given our family's notorious reputation in the neighborhood, engaging in a conflict over Shenjie and Mom would only escalate matters. It would turn into a spectacle for the neighbors. If both Shenjie and I could return, it would be worth fighting for. Since that's not possible, I'd rather remain in the countryside." Gong Guiying responded, "This decision is crucial; you must think carefully about it."

In those days, household registration often came at a steep price, leading to disputes between siblings and old friends over opportunities like returning to Shanghai. In our commune, there were instances of violent conflicts between siblings. Privacy was virtually nonexistent, and many family matters became public knowledge within the neighborhood. Feng Jianguo, my classmate and neighbor, lived just a few doors away from my mother's house. His wife Awu remarked, "Chengmo, there are many things I can tolerate, but not this, definitely not. This is a matter of survival. You need to consider it carefully." I replied, "Honestly, I don't want to endure my mother's cold demeanor every day. Once Shenjie returns, I'll be the only one left in the countryside. I trust they'll appreciate my sacrifice and do something to help me in return." However, I was mistaken. My sacrifices and efforts went unnoticed and unacknowledged. The indifference of my mother and sister had no bounds. In 1967, during the graduation allocation period, I left Shanghai to allow Shenjie to remain. Yet now, she disregarded my rights without a word. She assumed everything would go her way. Even if she possessed the entire world, she wouldn't appreciate it. In her eyes, the world revolved around her, and she felt entitled to everything, showing little regard for others. When the 1974 celebration of the Chinese New Year ended, I chose not to confront my mother about this and quietly left home, returning to Anhui.

In the *Liyu Xia* chapter of *The Teachings of Mencius*, Mencius said, "The difference between humans and beasts is very slight." He believed that the distinction between humans and animals is minimal. In meeting the basic needs of survival, humans are no different from other living creatures; what truly makes a person human is the divine quality that transcends mere existence. Once this divine nature is lost, a person is reduced to nothing more than animal instinct. Confucianism calls this divine quality "conscience," holding that one who loses conscience becomes indistinguishable from beasts. Western philosophers such as Aristotle (384~322 B.C.) and Immanuel Kant (1724~1804) referred to this divine quality as "reason." The Confucian concept of "conscience" closely resembles what Kant called "reason." For human beings, the pursuit of material satisfaction alone is not enough, for we also have spiritual needs. True spiritual happiness arises from genuine care for and respect of others. If one seeks profit through deceit and/or exploitation of others for their own selfish gain, not only will one fail to earn others' respect, but they will also be haunted by guilt at a subconscious level— thus making true inner peace and spiritual fulfillment impossible.

In the spring of 1974, soon after my departure, Shenjie quietly returned to Shanghai. Upon arrival, she shed many tears, unable to accept our mother's second marriage. She confronted Mom, asking, "You mentioned you wanted to get married because you needed someone to look after you. So, why did you choose to do this when you were certain I would be returning home?" Mom replied, "Yes, you can care for me, but you can't help me escape the stigma of being a counter-revolutionary spouse." Shenjie was temporarily assigned to the task of excavating air-raid shelters while awaiting a permanent job placement. Several months elapsed, yet nothing changed on that front. One day, Lao Cao arrived in Shanghai, and he was distressed to see Shenjie returning home from work, covered in mud. Lao Cao said, "Shenjie, please take me to the district's party committee office." Upon their arrival, Lao Cao presented his identification and offered, "If you require any assistance in Jiangxi, please do not hesitate to inform me." Many families in our residential district had children in Jiangxi, including some cadres. One of the cadres mentioned that his daughter, Ah Hua, had applied for a medical excuse. She had applied to the county's Educated Youth Office some time ago but had not received any response. Lao Cao assured him, "I happen to know the county party secretary, and I will write a note to him. He will take care of it." Lao Cao said, "I would like to ask you a favor. I would like to request that you prioritize finding a job for Shenjie as soon as possible." The district cadre began bargaining with Lao Cao. He asked Lao Cao for help for two youths. Lao Cao said, "No problems. I can help if you grant Shenjie the privilege of selecting a job she likes before the job list becomes accessible to everyone else." After Lao Cao left, Shenjie was called in to choose her job. Shenjie got to choose between working in collective-owned units and state-owned units. State-owned units offered better wages and benefits. Shenjie, of course, picked the best one: the assembly workshop of Shanghai No. 2 Watch Factory. The assembly workshop was temperature-controlled, and workers there wore white lab coats. Such good working conditions were very rare in Shanghai. In the summer of 1974, she began working at the factory and enjoyed the comfort of an air-conditioned room. When she got home, she asked our mother if it had been hot, because she worked in an air-conditioned room the whole day, so she had no idea. She took a portrait photo wearing a white lab coat, and her joy was beyond words. In 1975, Shenjie got married. She decided not to inform her brothers of the wedding date. This decision was made because Shanghainese people might look down on her when they found out that her brothers lived outside of Shanghai, especially considering that one of them (me) lived in a village that was

266

considered lower in status. Shenjie and the groom did not want the brothers to attend the wedding. But they didn't forget to ask for a cash gift afterward.

On the afternoon of March 17, 1975, Hua Guofeng, the Chairman of the Chinese Communist Party and Premier of the State Council at that time, announced an amnesty for the last batch of Kuomintang (Nationalist) war criminals during a meeting of the National People's Congress Standing Committee. The amnesty aimed to release these individuals from custody and reintegrate them into society: "A total of 293 war criminals were released under this amnesty. This group included 219 Chiang Kai-shek officers, 21 party and government personnel, and 50 spies; 2 puppet Manchukuo war criminals and 1 puppet Mongolian war criminal. At this point, all war criminals in custody have been dealt with." He said: "The amnesty was aligned with the spirit of Chairman Mao's instructions and involved granting citizenship rights, providing job opportunities for those capable of working, offering medical care for the sick, and taking care of those unable to work. It also allows those who want to go to Taiwan the opportunity to do so, with travel expenses provided. Those who want to come back after their trip to Taiwan are welcome back. At the time they are released, each person will be given new clothes and ¥100 of pocket money, and they will be gathered in Beijing for a welcome party. The party and state leaders will meet them and invite them to a banquet. Then they will be provided a chance to visit and study different places in our New China." On the 19th, "People's Daily" announced the amnesty decision, and my father, Bao Zuxian, was on the list of those granted amnesty. Bao Zuxian wished to go to Shanghai for a family reunion. However, my mother Liu Hairong and my sister Liu Shenjie both stated that they had already drawn clear boundaries with Bao Zuxian and refused to accept him. As a result, arrangements for Bao Zuxian's whereabouts were temporarily suspended.

In the Chinese New Year of 1976, Mom told me as soon as I arrived home that Lao Cao was waiting for me to meet him. He had just finished a meeting in Beijing and was passing through Shanghai on his way back to Nanchang. He and Lao Li were staying at the Peace Hotel. I had heard a lot about Lao Cao. I knew that he was a good man. He was fond of Chengquan and Shenjie, considering them his godson and goddaughter and letting everyone know about it. After Chengquan's promotion, there were no openings for young women for quite some time. During that period, Lao Cao was assigned to lead Chengquan's factory. This factory was a large enterprise, and the neighboring commune benefited significantly from the factory, including access to electricity, water, transportation, and more. Lao Cao made considerable efforts to relocate Shenjie from a remote mountain area to the commune next to the factory. He informed the commune and village leaders that she was his goddaughter, and Shenjie enjoyed certain privileges in the commune as a result. Before long, Shenjie returned to Shanghai, and Lao Cao traveled to Shanghai to assist her in finding the best possible job. My Mom felt indebted to Lao Cao and believed that she must do something to repay his kindness.

However, I didn't see any reason for me to get involved in this matter. Why should I go and meet them? The situation unfolded as follows: Lao Cao and Lao Li had four daughters, but no sons. They had a strong affection for Chengquan and hoped that he would marry their eldest daughter, Xiao Ying. However, Chengquan expressed that he had no romantic interest in Xiao Ying. In my mother's words, "Xiao Ying has some health issues and is a little bit slow. Initially, Lao Cao wanted Chengquan to become his son-in-law. But Chengquan has a good job in a state-owned factory and does not want to marry someone with special needs. You've been in Anhui for many years and are hopeless. If you were to become Lao Cao's son-in-law, it could resolve all of your problems." I replied that I had no interest in meeting Lao Cao. My mother insisted, saying, "That's not an option. I've already made arrangements to meet with Lao Cao and Lao Li. I must keep my word. You need to see them tomorrow. Let me share something with you. They have a deep fondness for Chengquan, and they've heard that you're even more promising than he is. They can't wait to meet you. Additionally, I have a plan to use their suite for a bath tomorrow." I said, "The truth is you want to sacrifice me to pay off your debts." Mom responded, "Isn't it beneficial for everyone?"

In an attempt to save face, my mother accompanied me to the Peace Hotel the following day. Upon entering Lao Cao's room, she stated, "You two can talk; I'll take a bath." Historically, Shanghai women regarded it as a luxury to rent a hotel room and enjoy a warm bath during the winter. It was also a status symbol for them. Lao Cao and Lao Li proved to be open-minded and pleasant individuals. Observing my lack of interest in marrying one of their daughters, they changed the topic of conversation. I remained there for a little while and then said goodbye.

I used to ponder why, throughout China's millennia-long history, there endured such a stark division between those wielding power, likened to sickles, and those consigned to the margins, akin to leeks. It seemed as though one group was born into privilege while another was destined to be perpetual victims. Adding to the perplexity was the audacious assertion by those wielding the power that their right to subjugate should persist unchanged for generations. I struggled to comprehend how such injustice could endure. Eventually, I came to realize that a significant number of exceedingly selfish individuals existed in China, much like my mother. They were willing to sacrifice the well-being of millions for their own selfish gains without hesitation. Essentially, my mother contributed to laying the foundation of the Chinese Communist Party, albeit not as an official member. After all, the family serves as the smallest building block of society, shaping the character of society at large. Once, I penned a letter to my mother, conveying, "You often lament being a victim, attributing your hardships to Mao Zedong. I want to stress that within our family, you are the Mao Zedong." In China, it is the countless "little Mao Zedongs" who collectively mold the image of great national leaders like Mao Zedong. Many years have elapsed since Mao's passing, yet as long as these "little Mao Zedongs" endure, the potential for another all-powerful tyrant to emerge in China persists.

My second encounter with Lao Cao unfolded in the summer of 1982. My newlywed wife, Rui Yin, and I embarked on a train journey from Shanghai to Xiamen to meet her parents, with a brief stop to see my brother in Nanchang for a few days. Chengquan was employed in

Nanchang at the time. Generously, Lao Cao and Lao Li offered us their master bedroom, warmly welcoming us to stay. Although my second uncle, Liu Zhonghou, deputy secretary of the Jiangxi Provincial Party Committee, resided in Nanchang in a larger house on Jingwei Road, I appreciated Lao Cao's sincere hospitality and chose to stay at his home for two days. The third occasion I had the pleasure of meeting Lao Cao occurred during the summer of 2000. I was recommended to the Ministry of Education in Beijing for a lecture tour by the Chinese Consulate General in New York. A close friend of Chengquan, Huang Zhaohui, an editor at the Jiangxi Publishing House, warmly welcomed us and accompanied Chengquan and me on a tour of the Jinggang Mountains. At that time, Lao Cao was seriously ill, but he still brought his family to the hotel to attend the gathering.

In 1977, Liu Zhonghou, the son of Grandma Lan, received a transfer from the central government to assume the role of Deputy Minister of Education. Before the Cultural Revolution, Liu Zhonghou had served as the Secretary for the Yancheng Regional Committee in Jiangsu Province and gained recognition for his significant contributions to agriculture, earning praise from Premier Zhou Enlai. However, he was inexperienced in education. At the Ministry of Education, he held the lowest position among the deputy ministers, essentially a sidelined role. The rank of deputy minister in Beijing was considered a minor official position. Both Zhonghou's mother-in-law and Grandma Lan lived in their household, leading to significant expenses due to the large household size. Zhonghou's wife complained about the poor living conditions in Beijing. Before the Cultural Revolution, Jiang Weiqing was the Secretary of the Jiangsu Provincial Committee, and Liu Zhonghou was Jiang Weiqing's favorite subordinate. When Jiang Weiqing was transferred to Jiangxi as the Secretary of the Provincial Committee, he did not bring his own people. The seven deputy secretaries had strong factions, severely hindering Jiang Weiqing's work. Deng Xiaoping promised three promotions and three demotions. In December 1978, among the three deputy secretaries transferred in, Liu Zhonghou was the closest to him. Jiang Weiqing entrusted Liu Zhonghou with the responsibility of managing the Political and Legal Affairs Committee and agriculture, making him the most powerful figure among the deputy secretaries. Jiang Weiqing also recommended to the central government that, after his retirement, Liu Zhonghou should take over his position to govern Jiangxi.

Liu Zhonghou occupied a prominent position in Nanchang, where his family resided in a luxurious single-family villa equipped with amenities like a chauffeur, secretary, and attendant. The convenience of having daily essentials delivered to their doorstep contributed to my aunt's contentment with her life in Nanchang. However, during Liu Zhonghou's tenure, Lao Cao faced a period of misfortune. After three local deputy secretaries were reassigned from Nanchang, Jiang Weiqing initiated a reform campaign targeting their subordinates. Fan Fei, Lao Cao's superior and the director of the Provincial Construction Committee, became ensnared in this effort. In 1975, Lao Cao was transferred to the Construction Committee to serve as the office director under Fan Fei's supervision. However, when Fan Fei fell out of favor, Lao Cao was implicated and subsequently removed from his position. Concerned for Lao Cao's family's safety, the factory's security department arranged for Chengquan to stay at Lao Cao's residence as a security guard for two weeks. Throughout this period, Chengquan staunchly defended Lao Cao's actions in front of Uncle Zhonghou, emphasizing that even if Fan Fei had erred, Lao Cao was not complicit and should not have been dismissed. In response, Liu Zhonghou remarked, "After reviewing the documents, it seems there may have been some irregularities with Fan Fei." As Lao Cao found himself unemployed and at home daily, the need for a housekeeper diminished. Chengquan recommended the housekeeper to Uncle Zhonghou's wife, fostering a strong rapport between them. During this time, Chengquan regularly alternated between visits to Uncle Zhonghou's and Lao Cao's residences every weekend.

In 1982, following Jiang Weiqing's completion of the reorganization at the departmental level, he began to assign roles to cadres below that level. Liu Zhonghou frequently heard others praise Lao Cao for his reliability and competence. Consequently, he entrusted Lao Cao with a significant responsibility: overseeing the preparation of the Jiangxi Province Political and Judicial Cadre School. Upon assuming his role, Lao Cao arranged for the Personnel Department to temporarily assign Chengquan to the school. The purpose was to lay the groundwork for transitioning Chengquan's employment status from that of a worker to that of a cadre in the future. Lao Cao played a pivotal role in initiating and developing this school from its inception, achieving noteworthy results. Liu Zhonghou expressed deep satisfaction with Lao Cao's contributions. After the finalization of the school's establishment, Lao Cao was appointed as the head of the Jiangxi Province Political and Judicial School. Liu Zhonghou subsequently invited Lao Cao to his house to provide an overview of his work, fostering a closer relationship between them. This marked Lao Cao's return to the political and legal arena after his time in the Construction Committee.

In the summer of 1983, I spent my vacation in Shanghai. During that time, my mother received a letter from Uncle Liu Shaohou in Beijing. Liu Shaohou and Liu Zhonghou are half-brothers. Uncle Shaohou had worked at the Ministry of Electronics Industry for an extended period and held some influence due to his connection with Minister Wang Guangying. There was a factory in Wuxi under Shaohou's supervision, and he was assisting Chengquan in transferring from Nanchang to Wuxi. The purpose of this letter was to inform my mother and Chengquan that the necessary hurdles had been cleared, allowing Chengquan to proceed with the transfer. I was elated for Chengquan, but my mother appeared troubled. It turned out that Lao Cao had come to Shanghai during that time and inquired about the progress of Chengquan's work transfer. If there was no hope for the transfer, he proposed promoting Chengquan to a cadre job in Jiangxi, relocating him from the suburbs to Nanchang city, and providing him with housing. My mother informed Lao Cao that the prospects for Chengquan's transfer were bleak. She said to me, "It has been a long time since Chengquan initiated the transfer process, and it hasn't been successful. I simply told Lao Cao to let it go. Shaohou's letter arrived at an inopportune time. How can I explain this to Lao Cao? I won't let Chengquan know about this letter." It appeared that my mother was willing to sacrifice Chengquan's years of effort and aspirations simply to avoid changing her stance. I disagreed and told her, "Lao Cao genuinely cares for Chengquan. If Chengquan truly doesn't want to stay in Jiangxi, Lao Cao won't force him to stay. You can hide the letter for a while, but you can't hide it forever." I suggested that my mom give the letter to Lao Cao and see what he says. After some contemplation, my mother agreed, saying, "It seems like there are no other options." The next day, my mother went to see Lao Cao. She felt uneasy when she left but returned feeling relaxed. She told me, "You were right. Lao Cao read the letter with a big smile. He said he would deliver the letter to Chengquan and assured me not to worry. He asked me to leave this matter to him and his godson." China's household registration system is a crucial aspect of the government's control over its citizens. Transferring residency was a notoriously cumbersome process. With Lao Cao's assistance, Chengquan's household registration was eventually transferred out of Jiangxi.

In 1985, Chengquan was finally transferred to Wuxi and took up residence in our grandma's old house at No. 35 Cotton Lane. In 1984, Lao Cao moved to Nanjing for a new position as the deputy director of the Jiangxi Provincial Office in Jiangsu. During one of his trips to Wuxi for a meeting, he made a special visit to Cotton Lane to see Chengquan. Meanwhile, Shenjie had married and started a family in Shanghai, leading to a more settled life. Lao Cao became less important to her, and she began to distance herself from him. In 1996, Lao Cao's youngest daughter, Xiao Qing, got married. Shenjie expressed reluctance to buy a gift or engage with the celebration. She confided in Chengquan, saying, "You're more familiar with Lao Cao and his family, given my limited interactions with them. I prefer not to become more involved." Chengquan was later transferred from Wuxi to Shanghai, where he continued to maintain a close relationship with Lao Cao. In the autumn of 2002, Lao Cao's health deteriorated significantly, requiring dialysis every few days. With both our parents having passed away, Chengquan invited Lao Cao and Lao Li to come to Shanghai and stay at the house on Xinchang Road. This location was convenient as it was close to Changzheng Hospital, where Lao Cao could receive proper medical care. Chengquan also extended an invitation for Lao Cao to dine at the New Jinjiang Hotel revolving restaurant. However, though also invited to attend, Shenjie did not show up, revealing her capacity to be fiercely passionate when necessary and ice-cold when not, a trait shared by both mother and daughter. In 2007, Chengquan immigrated to the United States, and sadly, Lao Cao passed away in 2008. In 2010, Chengquan returned to China to visit Lao Li in Nanchang and pay his respects at Lao Cao's grave. Eventually, in 2020, Lao Li also passed away in Nanchang.

4. At Anhui Normal University

At the end of February 1978, after celebrating the Lantern Festival at Xie Bin's home, I stayed in Hefei for a few days to visit my old well-digging friend, Zhan Yumin. At that time, Zhan Yumin was working in the Hefei Municipal Cultural Troupe. Then, I took a train from Hefei to Wuhu. At that time, I needed to take a ferry at Yuxikou Pier on the north bank of the Yangtze River. There was a lively atmosphere at the entrance of Anhui Normal University. At that time, the last two batches of Worker, Peasant, and Soldier students were still in school. The freshmen carried their bedding and thermos flasks to register at the freshmen reception station and were escorted to the dormitories by senior students. In our English department, Class 77 had three English classes and one Russian class, each with about twenty students. Our Class 2 was considered the top class. Two months after entering the university, the department organized exams. After the exams, students were reorganized into fast and slow classes based on their scores. I remained in the top class. The teaching resources in the English department of Anhui Normal University for Class 77 were very limited. The entire class had copies of just one textbook, the resource room was empty, and there were only one or two English dictionaries available. Except for Professor Wu Ningkun and Professor Zhang Chunjiang, none of the English department faculty had ever stepped out of the country. They had never spoken to foreigners, and their English proficiency was woefully lacking. Despite the poor learning conditions, the enthusiasm of our Class 77 college students for learning was truly astonishing. We were like crops encountering a timely rain after a long drought; we could immerse ourselves all night in self-study sessions. Due to a lack of teaching materials and guidance, some of us simply resorted to memorizing English dictionaries to expand our vocabulary.

Professor Wu Ningkun was from Yangzhou. He attended the Department of Foreign Languages at Southwest Associated University from 1939 to 1941, but later interrupted his studies to volunteer as an interpreter for the Flying Tigers (the First American Volunteer Group of the Republic of China Air Force). In 1946, Wu Ningkun studied at Manchester College in Indiana, USA, and two years later pursued a Ph.D. in English and American Literature at the University of Chicago. During his time in Chicago, he met future prominent Chinese figures in literature and science, including Zhao Luorui, Zhou Jueliang, Zha Liangzheng (Mu Dan), Lee Jong-Dao, Yang Zhenning, and others. In 1951, Wu Ningkun received an urgent telegram from President Lu Zhiwei of Yenching University inviting him to teach there. In mid-July 1951, Wu Ningkun abandoned his half-completed doctoral dissertation. He boarded the cruise ship President Cleveland in San Francisco and sailed towards the "new China" he longed for. Lee Jong-Dao, an alumnus of the University of Chicago, helped with his luggage and saw him off at the pier. Wu Ningkun asked Lee Jong-Dao, "Why don't you go back to work for the new China?" Lee Jong-Dao replied with a smile, "I don't want to have my brain washed." The then 25-years-old Lee Jong-Dao turned out to be far more politically astute than the then 31-year-old Wu Ningkun. Hu Shih, the prominent Chinese liberal intellectual and one-time diplomat, rejected Mao and the CCP's own rejection of freedom and left the mainland, first for the USA and later for Taiwan. Even at a young age, Lee Jong-Dao similarly foresaw the tragedy of being brainwashed. Some intellectuals who remained in mainland China were successfully brainwashed, striving to align themselves with the party and losing their independent spirit and freedom of thought. Those who did not embrace their own brainwashing faced inhumane humiliation and hardships, and their notable achievements, often as pioneers in their fields, were completely erased.

Upon Wu Ningkun's return to his homeland after an eight-year absence, Zhao Luorui (Lucy), the head of the Department of Western Languages at Yanjing University, personally welcomed him at the Beijing Front Gate station. Filled with confidence, Zhao aspired to enhance Yenching's English professor lineup and establish an outstanding English program modeled after the English department at the University of Chicago. However, just two weeks after Wu Ningkun arrived at Yanjing, he found himself subjected to brainwashing. Assigned to teach the history of English literature from a Marxist-Leninist perspective, Wu Ningkun improvised, incorporating concepts like "class struggle" without a proper understanding of the Chinese Communist perspective. He became both a recipient and a practitioner of the brainwashing process, impacting not only himself but also his students. Before Wu Ningkun could consolidate his position on the faculty, in November 1951, the "Three Anti-campaigns" unfolded, leading to the dissolution of Yanjing University, which was merged into other institutions. Zhao Luorui, the education visionary, saw her efforts to build an ivory tower crumble. It was she who had encouraged Wu Ningkun to abandon his incomplete doctoral dissertation and travel thousands of miles back to China. Now found herself in a situation where she could only watch helplessly as he suffered at the hands of others. He was transferred to Nankai University, and the future seemed distressingly uncertain. In 1955, during a mobilization meeting of the Campaign to Supress Counterrevolutionaries, Wu Ningkun was declared the school's top "hidden counter-revolutionary" and the leader of a counter-revolutionary group by the Faculty of the Literature College of Nankai University. Subsequently, in 1957, he was labeled a "bourgeois rightist" and an "extreme rightist," resulting in dismissal from his job and a sentence to reeducation through labor. His journey led him to Beijing's Half-step Bridge Prison, the Beidahuang Wilderness, and eventually the Qinghe Farm between Tianjin and Tangshan. During the Three Years' Famine Period (1959~1961), Wu Ningkun faced extreme hardship. His uncle managed to send him a packet of pancakes. A cellmate named Mr. Liu asked him for a piece of pancake. Wu Ningkun gave him a piece, and in return, Mr. Liu insisted on writing him an IOU. Wu Ningkun saw the calligraphy was very beautiful and asked Mr. Liu to write a scroll for him later. A few months after this, Wu Ningkun received orders to go to the corner of the farm and dig a pit. After the pit was dug, a skinny horse arrived pulling a flatbed cart with a body covered by a straw mattress on it. He opened the mattress and saw that it was the same Mr. Liu he had shared his pancake with. In 1961, Wu Ningkun's sister visited him and described seeing him in his deteriorating condition: "His face was bloodless, his whole body swollen, staggering, and on the brink of death. The two siblings were speechless, unsure if they would see each other again." Wu Ningkun's misfortune extended to his family, with his daughter Wu Yimao (Emily) enduring hardships during countryside re-education. The family's financial struggles were so severe that Yimao had no shoes to wear. Her teachers wouldn't allow her to enter the classroom simply because she was barefoot.

In 1957, while Wu Ningkun faced expulsion from public office and labor reeducation as an "extreme rightist," his schoolmate, Lee Jong-Dao, had already achieved the distinction of becoming the youngest full professor in the 200-year history of Columbia University. That same year, Lee Jong-Dao was awarded the Nobel Prize together with his fellow Chinese expatriate scientist and research partner, Yang Zhenning. On June 30, 1961, Wu Ningkun was released on medical parole and began teaching at Anhui University the following year. However, with the onset of the Cultural Revolution, Wu Ningkun faced criticism and confinement in the "bullpen." Subsequently, he lost his job benefits, and the entire family was sent to labor in a village. In May 1979, Wu Ningkun returned to Beijing to undergo "right-wing" correction procedures at his original unit, the Institute of International Relations. In October of the same year, upon learning that Lee Jong-Dao had returned to China to lecture, Wu Ningkun hastened to visit his old schoolmate at the Beijing Hotel. After 28 years of separation, their reunion took place, and during their conversation about their respective experiences, Lee Jong-Dao displayed no particular interest in or sympathy for his old friend's suffering. Wu Ningkun had a sudden realization, recognizing the profound disparity between their lives: "We live in two completely different worlds, between which there is an insurmountable gap... He lives happily and securely in the 'fortress of American imperialism,' and now even more so with the laurels of a 'patriotic scientist'! He resides in a luxury hotel, enjoys limousine service, and meets with senior national leaders, while I, follow the 'Party's call' and returned from afar, only to be treated as a 'public enemy of the people'..."

At the beginning of 1974, the government permitted Wu Ningkun and his wife, Mrs. Li Yikai, to leave the labor village and return to Anhui University, but the school refused to accept them. Instead, they came to Anhui Normal University in Wuhu. The university arranged for their accommodation inside an old chapel. The small chapel originally had seven narrow stained-glass windows, which are now partitioned into seven small compartments with reed mats. The close quarters made any movement easily audible between the two walls of the cubicles. Their immediate neighbor, Shen Shiliang's family, assumed the role of constant surveillance, acting as sitting police to monitor Wu Ningkun's family around the clock. They meticulously recorded every word, action, and visitor, reporting it diligently. Shen Shiliang's son even resorted to hurling insults over the wall and, at times, dumping sewage and fecal water in front of their entrance. In 1975, Xia Peiran, serving at the United Nations, visited Beijing as Zhou Enlai's state guest of honor. His wife, Wang Yu, proposed a visit to Wuhu to see her uncle Wu Ningkun. In response, Anhui Normal University swiftly increased Wu Ningkun's salary and relocated his family overnight to a place with living conditions better than the cramped reed mat cubicle.

In 1979, Wu Ningkun and his wife, along with their youngest child Yicun, were transferred back to the Beijing Institute of International Relations. I enrolled at Anhui Normal University in 1978, and our paths crossed for a little over a year. Professor Wu didn't teach our class of '77; I never had the chance to meet him. However, I was classmates with his son, Wu Yiding, and daughter, Wu Yimao. Wu Yiding, a non-registered student in my class, sat at the desk in front of mine. In the 1977 college entrance exam, Wu Yiding's test scores were exceptional, ranking among the highest in the province and surpassing the admissions cutoff scores for major national universities. However, due to concerns about his family's political background, his file was set aside during the admissions process. It wasn't until the end of the admissions process that someone rediscovered his file and hastily admitted him to Fuyang Normal College, an annex of Anhui Normal University. Fuyang and Suxian Counties are neighboring regions in Huaibei. Fuyang, even more impoverished and remote than Suxian, had student dormitories without doors, using straw curtains for protection against rain and snow. While other families celebrated their children's university admissions, the Wu Ningxun family closed their door to mourn. Wu Yiding attended our class for two years before leaving for the United States in 1980. Wu Yimo followed suit, going to the USA to study in 1981. They eventually emerged from the sea of suffering, experiencing a rebirth like the Phoenix.

Wu Ningkun retired from the Beijing Institute of International Relations in 1991. He and his wife then left mainland China to settle in the U.S. In early 1993, Wu Ningkun's memoir, "A Single Tear," was published in English in New York. The memoir documents the personal experiences of three generations of the Wu family over several decades in mainland China and caused a sensation in the English-speaking world. In June of the same year, it was released in London, followed by Japanese, Korean, and Swedish editions. However, powerful figures at the Beijing Institute of International Relations disagreed with certain contents of the book. They sent individuals to force open the door of Wu Ningkun's empty house in Beijing, removed their personal belongings, and then the school reclaimed their housing. In July 1993, the retirement pay of Wu Ningkun and his wife was suspended. The Institute of International Relations also pressured the Commercial Press, through the Ministry of State Security, to instruct the editor-in-chief of its magazine, English World, to apologize for publishing and distributing an article about "A Single Tear" in issue No. 2/93 and for publishing excerpts from the book. The Institute further demanded the removal of Wu Ningkun from the magazine's editorial board and the cessation of sales of that particular magazine issue. In response to these actions, Wu Ningkun, while in the United States, wrote numerous letters to the leadership of the Institute, seeking a resolution, but received no reply for many years. In 1999, Wu Ningkun wrote to Zhu Rongji, the Premier of the State Council, during his visit to the United States, to address the matter. At the end of the year, the Chinese Embassy in Washington, D.C., notified Wu Ningkun that the Institute of International Relations had decided to reinstate the retired salary of the couple, effective January 2001. However, the Institute refused to reimburse them from July 1993 to December 1999. In July 2002, the Chinese edition of "A Single Tear" was published in Taipei by Vista Publishing. In 2007, a new, updated Chinese edition was released in Taipei by Asian Culture Publishing Co., Ltd., featuring a foreword by Yu Ying-Shih, who, though he lived and worked in the United States, was arguably the world's preeminent scholar of Chinese history and thought. Please translate the above into Chinese. In 2006, the English edition of Wu Emily's memoir, "A Feather in the Storm," was published in the U.S. Fortunately, all three of Wu Ningkun's children are living and working in the United States. His sister, Wu Ninghui, was also labeled a "rightist" in 1957. After she retired, she and her husband migrated to the United States. Her three children settled in the United States, too. The tyranny of the Communist Party of China has been beyond its reach. I had many interactions with them in the U.S. Wu Ningkun passed away on August 10, 2019, at the age of 99 in suburban Washington, D.C. On August 22, I attended a memorial service for him at a church in Virginia.

Professor Zhang Chunjiang, a figure ten years senior to Professor Wu Ningkun, pursued sociology studies in the United States. He served as a sociology professor at Hujiang University（University of Shanghai） for many years, even holding a position on the university's board of trustees in 1949. In 1952, during the reorganization of higher education institutions, Hujiang University, as a Christian university, was closed, and sociology was classified as a "pseudo-science of the bourgeoisie." Consequently, Professor Zhang was assigned to Anhui Normal University, not as a professor, but as an English teacher without a title, with a monthly salary of ¥66.50, equivalent to that of a teaching assistant. Whenever there was a political movement, he was arrested and sent to a labor camp, only to be released after the movement ended. This happened three times. Professor Zhang was a devout Christian Baptist who endured countless injustices without complaint. After each release, he tirelessly devoted himself to serving his beloved country with the same innocent enthusiasm, doing his utmost to help students and colleagues. Typing was not his primary job, but whenever he had free time, he went to the typing room to help. For decades of selfless dedication, he never received any recognition, nor did he expect any rewards. After the Cultural Revolution, Professor Zhang Chunjiang's "miscarriages of justice" were finally rectified, and he regained his original title and salary as a professor. This elderly man, nearing the age of seventy, became even more spirited, devoting himself wholeheartedly to English teaching. He harbored no resentment towards those who had wronged him in the past. Professor Zhang Chunjiang taught us the Extensive Reading Course for the three classes of the 1977 Grade. He spoke impeccable American English and was the only teacher in the department who spoke English consistently during the class. His wife, Zhou Hejun, also studied in the United States and was a piano professor in the Art Department of Anhui Normal University. Professor Zhang Chunjiang sincerely cared about our academic progress. When I applied to American universities, he wrote me a letter of recommendation. Wu Ningkun, reflecting on Zhang Chunjiang, aptly remarked, "Professor Zhang Chunjiang was truly like a river of spring water that flowed through the lives of an unknown number of people during a long, harsh winter. In his dedication to half a century at Anhui Normal University, he was a living legend on the university campus. He is also a living, wordless condemnation of those who ruined most of his life and took advantage of his talents and patriotic fervor."

After settling in at Anhui Normal University, I sought out Zhu Choumei. Finding him was straightforward. He served as a member of the Party Committee's Standing Committee and as Minister of Propaganda at Anhui University. His wife was the head of the Chemistry

Department. Both were graduates of the Chemistry Department at Anhui Normal University and opted to stay on after completing their studies. Despite lacking a privileged family background, Zhu Choumei exhibited remarkable wisdom, seeming naturally suited to official responsibilities. I located Zhu Choumei's residence and delivered Zhou Huaru's letter to him. He warmly welcomed me, saying, "I oversee student affairs at the Party Committee. You're in the student union. Feel free to visit me whenever you like." Zhu Choumei's mother showed particular kindness upon learning that I came from Huaibei. Zhu Choumei had three daughters, with the eldest, Xiaoping, approaching college age. In the following days, Zhu Choumei approached me and said, "Your scores on the college entrance examination are outstanding. I'd like to ask you to tutor my daughter and help her prepare." I agreed and began tutoring Xiaoping five times a week. I was overjoyed when Xiaoping was admitted to Anhui University the following year.

On New Year's Day in 1979, the Standing Committee of the National People's Congress (NPC) issued the Letter to Compatriots in Taiwan. The establishment of diplomatic relations between China and the U.S. that same year created a favorable international environment for the potential peaceful reunification of mainland China and Taiwan. During his visit to the U.S. in January 1979, Deng Xiaoping expressed hope for a peaceful resolution to the Taiwan issue, explicitly stating, "We will no longer use the expression 'liberation of Taiwan'; as long as Taiwan returns to the motherland, we will respect the reality and the existing system there." On September 30, 1981, Chairman Ye Jianying of the NPC issued nine proposals for work on Taiwan, famously known as "Ye's Nine Articles." Subsequently, on October 9, 1981, Hu Yaobang, as the head of the CCP Central Committee, extended an invitation to Chiang Ching-kuo and others to visit the mainland and his hometown. In July 1982, Deng Yingchao, who led the Group of the CCP's Work on Taiwan, came across an article by Chiang Ching-kuo in Taiwan, expressing homesickness and memories of his father, Chiang Kai-shek. Deng Yingchao promptly convened a meeting of the Taiwan Working Group, suggesting that Liao Chengzhi, the deputy leader of the group, should write an open letter to

Chiang Ching-kuo, Liao Chengzhi's fellow schoolmate at Sun Yat-sen University in Moscow. Liao Chengzhi's open letter marked a significant step in the CCP's work on Taiwan, aligning with the directives of the Central Committee and Deng Xiaoping.

From Liao Chengzhi's open letter until October 1986, Shen Cheng, Chiang Ching-kuo's secret envoy, made three trips northward. Shen Cheng, a retired major general who previously served as a staff officer in Chiang Ching-kuo's entourage in the Reserve Cadre Bureau of the Ministry of National Defense, carried out covert missions on Chiang Ching-kuo's behalf. Acting under the guise of a Hong Kong businessman, he delivered messages across the Strait, with explicit instructions from Chiang Ching-kuo during his later visits to accelerate communication with the top leadership on the mainland. Shen Cheng had the unique opportunity to meet with top CCP leaders, including Ye Jianying, Deng Yingchao, Yang Shangkun, Deng Xiaoping, and others. On March 19, 1987, Shen Cheng returned to Taipei and personally handed a letter from Chinese President Yang Shangkun to Chiang Ching-kuo. After reading Yang Shangkun's letter repeatedly, Chiang Ching-kuo, on March 25, 1987, summoned Shen Cheng to a meeting in his study at Cihu. He expressed his belief in the sincerity of the CCP and stated that reciprocal negotiations at the central level of the two parties were feasible. Consequently, in the second half of 1987, Chiang Ching-kuo initiated the establishment of the mainland work steering group in the Central Committee of the Kuomintang. He also announced the opening of family visits to the mainland and the lifting of martial law in Taiwan. On December 7, 1987, Chiang Ching-kuo informed Shen Cheng that the Central Committee of the Kuomintang would discuss candidates for negotiations in Beijing in early January. The two sides of the strait were on the path toward renewed engagement between the Kuomintang and the CCP. However, history took an unforeseen turn. On January 8, 1988, Chiang Ching-kuo unexpectedly passed away due to hemoptysis. The plan for contacting and communicating with the mainland, held in Chiang Ching-kuo's mind, could not be executed as intended.

From 1979 onward, the CCP initiated a significant United Front campaign engaging Chiang Ching-kuo, impacting individuals like my father. In 1981, during my senior year at Anhui Normal University, Zhu Choumei approached me with news that someone from the Ministry of Public Security in Beijing had arrived. The government had discovered that my father, Bao Zuxian, had close relatives and real estate in his hometown of Baoshan, Shanghai. If Bao Zuxian agreed, the government proposed settling his household registration in Baoshan and returning the real estate under his name. This government offer was driven by renewed attention on my father due to Chiang Ching-kuo's associates in Taiwan, particularly those from his inner circle during the formation of Sanmin Youth Corps. My father had been a member of this circle during his time with Sanmin Youth Corps. Representatives from the Ministry of Public Security requested that I meet with my father to discuss the details of his settlement in Baoshan. Simultaneously, they urged me to encourage my father to write a letter to Chiang Ching-kuo to join the United Front chorus. Zhu Choumei explained that the Ministry of Public Security had left my father's address and had tasked him with mobilizing me to write letters to and visit him.

Following the instructions of the Ministry of Public Security, I penned my first letter to my father, addressing it to Xindang Middle School in Xiangshui County, Jiangsu Province. Xindang Middle School catered to the children of Huanghai Farm's staff, located in the north of Jiangsu Province. Formerly a labor reform farm housing "war criminals" awaiting resettlement after amnesty, it had been renamed a state farm, and the workers' status changed to that of farm workers. Although nominally free with jobs and salaries, they lacked true freedom, were unable to communicate with the outside world, or leave the farm without authorization. My father, seemingly excited about the government's arrangements, was cooperative and even flattered by the request to write to Chiang Ching-kuo. However, complications arose in specifying the household registration. My mother and sister lived at No. 122, Lane 340, Xinchang Road, which had been part of the British Concession before 1949. The property owners were foreigners, and when my father married, he paid a deposit in gold bars to the sublease landlord and then paid monthly rent. After my father's imprisonment, my mother took over the household. When he was pardoned in 1975, complications persisted because both my mother and sister refused to accept him back to the house on Xinchang Road. In the Baoshan ancestral house, my father still had property in his name. The government suggested that household registration could be realized in Baoshan. At that time, Baoshan was a suburb of Shanghai, with living conditions not as favorable as those in the city, making it uncertain whether my father was willing to move there.

Before the summer vacation of '81, I informed my mother of my plan to see my father. In response, my mother wrote back and requested that I wait for her in Nanjing because she wanted to go with me. Despite her request, I decided to proceed alone to northern Jiangsu. From the age of four months, I had been taken to Wuxi by my grandmother, where I was raised until the age of four before returning to Shanghai. During this time, my father had already left for Nanjing, and I had no recollection of him. At Xindang Middle School, it was the first time we met as father and son. My father and his colleagues, former cellmates, had a gleam of delight in their eyes upon my arrival. They were aware that the day of my father's departure from the farm was approaching, and he would soon be able to lead a normal life outside. I observed their clothing, which consisted of the same kind of dull-colored civilian clothes worn by ordinary people. However, what caught my attention was their feet— none of them wore socks, instead opting for bare feet in a pair of black rubber-soled liberation shoes with green uppers, similar to uniforms, making them very conspicuous. They all maintained a formal demeanor, eyes cast down, avoiding eye contact, and moving with minimal noise, surprisingly silent.

Upon returning from northern Jiangsu, I reunited with my mother at Uncle Yihou's house in Nanjing. I was aware that many relatives sought to curry favor with Liu Zhonghou during his tenure as the deputy secretary of the provincial party committee in Jiangxi. However, I was unaware that Mom had recently visited Nanchang. It was in the summer of '81 when Liu Zhonghou's family had yet to arrive, and he was residing at the provincial party committee's guest house. Meanwhile, my mother stayed at Lao Cao's house and went to visit Liu Zhonghou. He appeared amiable and invited her to the theater that evening. Following the play, he instructed his chauffeur to drive her back to Lao Cao's residence. Known for maintaining a clear boundary between public and private affairs, Liu Zhonghou never allowed his family members to ride in his car. My mother considered the ride in Zhonghou's vehicle a significant favor, a story she recounted frequently among relatives. Upon my mother's arrival in Nanjing after I visited my father, she appeared uncertain about her next steps. Uncle Yihou suggested she send a telegram to my brother Chengquan regarding "mother's illness, urging him to quickly come to Nanjing." Chengquan was puzzled by the telegram, as he had just said goodbye to Mom following her visit, at which time she'd been fine. Upon reaching Nanjing, he discovered that Mom needed him to accompany her to Huanghai Farm. She faced challenges as her accommodation in Shanghai belonged to our father, Bao Zuxian, and she held tens of thousands of RMB that rightfully belonged to him. The state intended to find a residence for Bao Zuxian, prompting the question: Should she return the house and money to him? Both the house and the money were vital to her, and she was unwilling to let go. Negotiating with Bao Zuxian was necessary, but as Shao Xuewen's wife, meeting him alone posed difficulties. She realized she couldn't compel me to cooperate with her. Fortunately, she could rely on Chengquan's presence. Upon arriving at Huanghai Farm, she left Chengquan outside, closed the door, and engaged in a three-day private conversation with our father, her ex-husband.

During the Spring Festival of '82, while I was in Shanghai, two individuals from the court approached me to discuss a matter. They stated, "Your mom has filed for divorce from Shao Xuewen. As the eldest son and a college graduate, we would like to hear your opinion." In response, I expressed, "As a child, I certainly want my parents to find happiness in their senior years. I was unaware of Mom's marriage to Shao Xuewen at the time, but I can see that he is a good man." After the court representatives left, my mom approached me and said, "I've been scared all my life. I hope you can understand me." To this, I replied, "I completely understand you, but understanding does not necessarily mean approval."

The Class of '77 comprised mostly mature students with social experience, including party members and the children of county party secretaries. In life, many believe that aligning with influential figures is the key to advancement. Upon entering the school, some astute students immediately sought the favor of department heads, and many of these ranking instructors actively embraced the opportunity to groom such willingly obedient individuals. There were three classes in the English major, each supervised by a different class advisor. Zhang Cheng and Ji Juyuan were influential within the department, while Shen Shiliang, though academically weaker, aimed to achieve the title of associate professor, desperately seeking the support of colleagues and leaders. During joint examinations at the end of the semester, all tests were set by Ji Juyuan, who was known for his resourcefulness. Ji Juyuan, facing personal challenges with his wife's illness, favored a female student in his class who was a party member, granting her special treatment during testing. A school magazine article later highlighted Ji Juyuan's apparent success in transforming a slow class into high performers in a short period. The department celebrated Ji Juyuan's achievements, leading to a pay raise and promotion. However, students in the class reported Ji Juyuan for leaking test questions and unfairly favoring certain students. The school launched an investigation, but the department refused to cooperate. Ultimately, Ji Juyuan faced no consequences, while the whistleblower experienced silent punishment, highlighting the unspoken dynamics within the Communist Party where addressing problems takes a backseat to silencing those who report them.

In the foreign languages department, the power dynamics were shaped by Secretary Wang Lingchi and Deputy Secretary Chen Qinle. Chen Qinle, hailing from a cadre family, harbored a sense of entitlement and openly exhibited hostility toward first-generation cadres like Zhu Choumei. He believed that only the second generation of Reds deserved leadership positions, suggesting that Zhu Choumei should step down. Due to my frequent visits to Zhu Choumei's home while tutoring his daughter, I became a target of Chen Qinle's scrutiny. The school held an annual selection of "merit students" based on exceptional academic performance, and those with solid but not exceptional grades who also happened to be student union cadres could be chosen as "outstanding cadres." This designation was seen as a consolation prize. When I was nominated as a candidate for "outstanding cadre" by the department, Zhu Choumei opposed downgrading me to this category, arguing that my performance met the requirements for merit students. When Zhu Choumei awarded me one of the medals for "merit students," Chen Qinle's bias against me deepened. By the time I realized that I had unwittingly become embroiled in the power struggle between Zhu Choumei and Chen Qinle, it was already too late.

When the time came for graduate placement job assignments in early '82, the students' disappointment was palpable. The favorable options for placements were limited, with most graduates ending up in county middle schools. Among us were several children of the university staff, local students with influential connections, and favorites of Zhang Cheng and Ji Juyuan, who claimed almost all the popular quota slots, leaving little for the rest of my class. Our homeroom teacher, Shen Shiliang, was eager to please Zhang Cheng and Ji Juyuan, so to gain their favor, he readily sacrificed opportunities for deserving students who lacked powerful connections. Non-local students, especially those from Shanghai, found themselves at the very bottom of the list, with no one to advocate for them. In the placement process, a unit called "Guandian Forestry School" emerged, notable for its remote location. None of the students were willing to sign up for this unfamiliar destination. Guandian, as later revealed, was a small railway station situated between Mingguang and Chu County, with the forestry vocational school nestled in a ravine about an hour's walk east from the town. Lacking transportation to the town or train station, it was an unattractive choice. This placement fell on my shoulders. Accustomed to the social status of being "the last in line," there was no way for me to escape being at the mercy of the powers that be in this land.

5. After College

Among the graduates of the '77 and '78 classes of Anhui Normal University, corresponding to the '82 and '83 graduating years, some returned to Shanghai. During this period, there was a policy of repatriation in Shanghai: When parents retired, their children's household registration from outside Shanghai could be transferred back, and the children would be assigned to work units based on their specific circumstances. Those with a teaching degree were often assigned to teach in urban schools. A friend from the Art Department of the Class of '77 returned to Shanghai after graduation, taking advantage of the repatriation policy for his parents. He was assigned to work in an elementary school on Datong Road, which was close to Xinchan Road, where my mom lived. Chen Yuebo, a teacher from my mother's school, retired at that time, and her daughter returned to Shanghai to take her place. My mother's decision to retire in 1982 was kept a secret from me. She managed to conceal this information since I spent only a few days a year in Shanghai. She decided to allow Baozhen, the daughter of her now soon-to-be second ex-husband, to take her place. The decision had several motives. Firstly, it was for her own benefit. It allowed her to exclude me from the house one more time, relieving her of any concern that I might claim a share in it. Secondly, it served as a form of compensation to Shao Xuewen as she was asking him for a divorce. Additionally, this move aimed to silence Shao Xuewen's complaints. More than once, he told my mother, "Chengmo is a good person. It's unfair that he hasn't had a chance to return to Shanghai." He asked my mother, "Why didn't Chengmo come back when everyone else's sons did?" Mom gave him the reason: "I had no choice. Shenjie threatened me that she would jump into the Huangpu River if I didn't choose her." Shao Xuewen went to confront my sister Shenjie, and Shenjie flatly denied it, saying, "I did no such thing." The third aspect was to benefit Shao Xuewen's daughter, Baozhen. Since my mother had enabled her to return to Shanghai from the Chongming farm, Baozhen was significantly indebted to her. From then on, Baozhen regularly brought generous gifts to honor my mother during various festivals, and my mother relished being the benefactor.

In early '82, as my future wife Rui Yin began teaching at Chuzhou Teachers' College, at the same time, I began teaching at Guandian Forestry School. Six months later, when we tied the knot, we had an abundance of love, but our financial situation was modest. Mom handed me ¥600, saying, "Grandma left ¥2,400. Now that my eldest son is getting married, we can split it up, one for each of the four of us." When Shenjie got married, Mom gave her a sum of money as a wedding gift. A few years after I, when Chengquan got married, Mom also gave him some money. However, I received nothing from her except grandma's money. During summer and winter vacations, when Rui Yin and I stayed in Shanghai, Mom asked us for money to cover our meal expenses. Upon receiving the money, she would jest, "You are good at paying for your meals. Shenjie is supposed to come back to take care of me, but in reality, who knows who takes care of whom? Financially, I have subsidized household expenses for years. When I was sick, she had a good time with her family in the front room. Only Shao Xuewen took care of me." I responded, "If you are content helping her out, don't complain; if you are unhappy, you do not have to pay." Mom often intentionally treated her children differently, using it as a reason for Shenjie to reciprocate in the future. However, she failed to grasp that repaying a favor is built on the foundation of fairness. Attempting to win hearts and minds by subverting justice was entirely illogical. Eventually, this became evident, but she did not realize it until the very last moment of her life.

Even more disheartening is that we are not the only family left without a normal kinship structure amid the stormy winds of the revolution. Even within the families of CCP cadres, the situation is dismal. Writer Lao Gui was born into a family of high-level intellectuals. His father, Ma Jianmin, was a high-ranking official in the CCP's literature and education department, and his mother, Yang Mo, was a well-known writer. When Lao Gui wrote, he dared to defy the traditional admonitions of "keeping the secrets of the honored one" and "the son should not speak of his father's faults," portraying his father, mother, and himself as ordinary people. In Lao Gui's depiction, Yang Mo's treatment of her own children reached astonishing levels of hard-heartedness, violence, selfishness, and lack of sympathy. During the Three-Year Famine Period, "My parents bought a lot of high-class candies, high-class snacks, and high-priced nutritional supplements, but these treats were kept in their room for their enjoyment only. They locked the door when they went out and did not allow their children to touch them..." "My brother, like me, couldn't get enough to eat when he came home. He voluntarily handed over food stamps every time he came home, helping his parents with chores even when sick, yet he was still scolded constantly." Ma Jianmin demanded that his own daughter pay for food stamps with money when she came home to eat, counting pennies. Ma Jianmin, with a short temper, often physically abused Lao Gui. When Yang Mo beat Lao Gui, Ma Jianmin was on the sidelines, fueling the fire. It is these families, devoid of affection, that collectively contribute to forming a society devoid of humanity, which serves as the social foundation for the development of the CCP's brutal Party culture.

On June 5, 1982, Rui Yin and I hosted a wedding banquet at the Xinya Restaurant in Shanghai, inviting some relatives and friends. Rui Yin's parents, working at Xiamen University, couldn't attend. We went to Xiamen for our honeymoon. Arriving at Xiamen train station, we coincidentally saw Rui Yin's father picking up two American guests— Prof. Jing Yunjing from Ohio State University and one of his students, a white girl. Prof. Jing, a college classmate of Rui Yin's father, was invited by Rui Yin's father to lecture at Xiamen University. China had just opened up in 1982, and Prof. Jing was a pioneer in academic exchanges between the U.S. and China. Prof. Jing mentioned his assistance to several Chinese students studying in the U.S. and kindly offered me sponsorship. He sent me application materials for U.S. universities upon his return. In the fall of '82, I received a letter from Prof. Jing along with an I-134 Form. Reviewing U.S. university application guidelines, I realized I needed to pay an application fee for each application, usually around $60. With my monthly salary of less than ¥60 RMB and a black-market exchange rate of ten RMB for one U.S. dollar, I couldn't afford the fee. Fortunately, the University of Iowa allowed a waiver. In 1982, a teacher at Anhui University was editing a series of books titled "Pastoral Symphony." Kindly, he offered Rui Yin and me the opportunity to translate Oscar Wilde's novel, The Picture of Dorian Gray. Published by Anhui People's Publishing in 1984, we were paid two thousand RMB, a significant sum equivalent to a college graduate's salary for four years. In 1985, Rui Yin used the money to purchase a plane ticket to the United States. Before that, when I bought my ticket to the U.S. in '84, I had depleted our savings down to the last penny.

At the beginning of 1983, Guandian Forestry School received unexpected news—it was approved to relocate to Hefei, the capital of Anhui province. Initially, the predecessor of the Guandian Forestry School was the Hefei Forestry School, situated on Dashushan Mountain in the western suburb of Hefei. During the Cultural Revolution, Hefei Forestry School moved down to Guandian, as its original site was taken over by an artillery unit. During the early 80s, the central government made efforts to revitalize education and restore all the schools shut down in the Cultural Revolution. The artillery unit reluctantly returned the site to the school. The full relocation of the school wasn't completed until the fall of '83. During my stroll in the streets of Hefei, I unexpectedly encountered Zhu Choumei. I knew that Zhu Choumei was promoted to the president of the university after I graduated. I inquired, "President Zhu, are you on a business trip in Hefei?" He responded, "No, I am working in Hefei. Come to see me at the Education Department when you have time." A few days later, I visited the Education Department and discovered that Zhu Choumei held the position of commissioner and Party secretary of the Education Department. I also reconnected with two friends from the '77 class of Anhui Normal University Student Union—Chen Xin, the Director of the Studies Department, and Huang Yuanfang, the Director of the Propaganda Department. Both held division-level positions in the Education Department. It was a pleasant reunion with old friends. Zhu Choumei informed me that his family had relocated to Hefei and invited me to visit his new home.

When I visited Shanghai in the summer of 1983, my father had already settled on Xinchang Road. Unbeknownst to me, my parents never remarried, a fact that Shenjie and Chengquan were aware of and had been instructed not to disclose to me. Upon my father's return to Shanghai, he was assigned to work as an accountant in a police station in the Huangpu district. Expressing my concern, I said, "The people in the police station are the same people who arrested and guarded you. How can you bear it when you have to see them every day and work with them? You are old. You should have retired long ago." He responded, "The people in the police station are courteous to me. If I don't go to work, the police station can't function." I chuckled, saying, "You shouldn't take yourself so seriously." He explained, "All the daily cash transactions in the police station require two keys to open the safe simultaneously. The chief holds one key, and I hold the other." I joked, "You're the only Kuomintang among Communists in the police station. How can they trust you?" He replied, "The Communists are shrewd. They insist that one key must be held by the Kuomintang. If both keys are in the hands of the Communists, all the cash inside the safe will disappear."

My daughter was born in May 1983 in Shanghai. As Rui Yin and I were living in different towns, making it challenging to raise a child, Rui Yin's parents took on the responsibility of caring for her in Xiamen. Now that I am in Hefei, I am eager to transfer Rui Yin to Hefei, allowing our family to be together. The Anhui Provincial College of Education, a university in Hefei under the immediate supervision of the Department of Education, was previously a junior college but had recently been upgraded to a four-year college. Zhu Choumei's wife was already working at the college, and she introduced me to the head of the foreign language department. The head of the department mentioned a shortage of English teachers and informed me that most teachers were in the Russian major, with the only new teacher being Guo Beibei, a graduate of the Class of '78 from Anhui Normal University. Guo Beibei told him, "Liu Chengmo and Rui Yin from the class of '77 had very good grades." The head of the department invited Rui Yin and me to give a demonstration lesson. All the teachers of the Foreign Languages Department and several college leaders attended our demo lessons. The feedback was excellent, prompting the college to send letters to our respective schools requesting a transfer. Principal Fang of the Forestry School was cooperative, stating, "You have your future, and I won't stand in the way. It is okay if you want to leave. I can request another college graduate next year." However, Chuzhou Teacher's College was reluctant to release Rui Yin. The school's control over its employees was comprehensive, ranging from professional evaluations and salary increases to opportunities for continuing education, job transfers, bonuses, and housing allocations. Ms. Feng, in charge of Chuzhou Teachers' College as a vice president, managed female teachers with strict oversight, like a mother-in-law to her daughter-in-law, who were all her enemies in her eyes. When new teachers arrived, she would invite herself and inspect their dormitories, evaluating everything from furniture to personal belongings. She took the college as her private asset. She would not be happy before using the power in her hand to the extreme. Zhu Choumei brought the director of HR of the Education Department with him to Chuzhou to discuss the mobilization of Rui Yin. Ms. Feng said, "I understand that the Provincial Education College is short of teachers, but my school is even shorter. There are so many couples separated from each other. I can't help Rui Yin at this time." Zhu Choumei promised to assign more college graduates to Chuzhou Teachers' College next year. Despite his efforts, Feng remained firm in her decision. Chuzhou Teacher's College was under the supervision of the Chuzhou Regional Party committee, not the Department of Education, making it challenging for Zhu Choumei to secure the transfer. The principal of the teacher's college was concurrently held by Secretary Ma of the Chuzhou Regional Party committee. He seldom appeared on the campus of the teacher's college. When Secretary Ma came, I observed that Feng was capable of putting on a smile for him.

In the autumn of '83, I received an acceptance letter from the admissions office of the University of Iowa Graduate School, halting my plan to transfer to the Provincial College of Education. At that time, the policy for self-funded overseas students mandated two years of work after college graduation before going abroad. Having commenced employment in early '82, by the start of '84, I had fulfilled the requisite two years and became eligible to apply for a passport to travel abroad. The fall semester at the University of Iowa commenced at the end of August. In May '84, I visited the Education Department to catch up with friends. Commissioner Zhu queried, "Why are you still here?" I replied, "I'm awaiting my passport." Commissioner Zhu retorted, "Do you think you can acquire passports merely by waiting?" This statement puzzled me, but to avoid offending Commissioner Zhu, I refrained from seeking clarification. He handed me a note addressed to the labor camp director. Although curious as to why my passport involved the labor camp, I opted not to question Zhu. Upon entering the Public Security Department building, I encountered a group of people playing poker in the lobby, all bareback without police uniforms, yelling like a band of bandits. The policeman escorting me shouted, "Director Hu, someone's looking for you!" I presented Commissioner Zhu's note to Director Hu, who nonchalantly said, "Oh, it's a note from Commissioner Zhu. Got it, go away." The following day, the Public Security Office contacted the Forestry School, informing me that my passport was ready for pickup.

Upon reaching the U.S. Consulate General in Shanghai, the visa hall was impeccably clean and surprisingly empty. I submitted my passport and I-20 form, and before long, the visa officer exclaimed, "Congratulations! Come get your visa this afternoon." Born into humble circumstances, I held aspirations to elevate myself and refused to easily relinquish my dreams. A new chapter of my life began! In the summer of '84, I took a flight from Hongqiao Airport, bidding farewell to the land that had been a source of curses for 32 years. While times may change, as long as my feet tread upon this soil, my status as a third-class pariah remains unshakable. The ruling class employs every means to fortify class solidarity, ensuring their offspring continue to wield power. This, indeed, is the non-negotiable core interest of the CCP. While my wife Rui Yin's grandfather Ying Chengyi was still alive, he imparted these words to me: "Chengmo, you must go overseas." I fully grasped the profoundly wise meaning behind his statement. My grandfather-in-law, Ying Chengyi, was a 1923 University of Wisconsin graduate and former dean of the law school at Shanghai Fudan University during the Republican period, and possessed keen insight.

My father kept his promise to write to Chiang Ching-kuo. In the 1980s, the "Three Directs" (Direct Mail, Direct Trade, Direct Flights) were not yet established between the mainland and Taiwan. Mails had to be forwarded through a third country. I came to the U.S. to study in '84, bringing my father's letter with me, which I then mailed from the U.S. to my Great Uncle, Bao Eryi, in Taipei. Subsequently, Bao Eryi forwarded it to Chiang Ching-kuo. Bao Eryi (1921~1990) was my father's uncle, a year younger than my father. They grew up together and attended junior high school in Wusong, maintaining a close friendship. Bao Eryi graduated from the Department of Accounting at Fudan University in 1943, excelling as an assistant professor there. He pursued graduate studies at George Washington University in the U.S.A. After arriving in Taiwan in January 1947, he served as a professor at Soochow University from 1960 to 1988. He concurrently held positions as the head of the Department of Accounting and the Director of the Graduate School of Accounting from August 1973 to July 1978. Additionally, he was a professor and Dean of the College of Business at Tunghai University in Taiwan from 1978 to 1981. He held academic positions, including professor, department head, and examiner for master's and doctoral degrees at National Taiwan University, National Political Science University, National Chiao Tung University, and Fu Jen Catholic University in Taiwan. A notable figure in Taiwan, Bao Eryi, had connections with Chiang Ching-kuo. In 1998, when I visited Taiwan with my daughter, Bao Eryi had already passed away. I visited the apartment in Taipei where he had lived, which was vacant and still in his wife's name. He had a son, Bao Daxian, who taught at Columbia University in New York. I heard that Bao Eryi's wife lived with him in New York. During that time, I also resided in New York and attempted to contact Bao Daxian several times, but received no response.

After I departed from China, Rui Yin resided and worked alone in Chuzhou, while our daughter remained in Xiamen. Rui Yin's younger brother, a Xiamen University graduate from the class of '77, was assigned a job in Beijing in '82. During that period, there existed a policy allowing parents without their children nearby to retrieve them. Xiamen University forwarded a request to Chuzhou Teachers' College on behalf of Rui Yin. Vice President Feng's response was dismissive: "I am only aware of issues arising from separated couples. It is not my concern to assist you when your parents are without a child around. Isn't your husband in the United States? Go ahead and join him." Such callousness and arrogance were characteristic of many Communist Party cadres, ingrained in party culture with little room for deviation.

During my time in Iowa, I encountered Dr. Olson, a medical school professor. Dr. Olson, along with his wife and two daughters, resided in a spacious house. He employed two students to assist with household chores: one for weekly cleaning and me for ironing his laundry. In November of '84, Dr. Olson graciously invited me to join with his family for my first Thanksgiving in the United States. He remarked that prolonged separation of spouses was uncommon in America. Dr. Olson offered to sponsor Rui Yin to facilitate her enrollment at the University of Iowa. With the assistance of Dr. Olson's I-134 form, Rui Yin applied to the University of Iowa Graduate School and swiftly received Form I-20 for admission. To apply for a passport from the police department, Rui Yin required a letter of introduction from the teacher's college. The school rejected her. No reason was given; power is arrogant. Mao once asserted that the Communist Party operated above the law, a sentiment reflected in this bureaucratic obstruction. However, in the spring of 1985, a breakthrough occurred with the issuance of a red-mandate directive by the government: citizens seeking to travel abroad for personal reasons could now obtain passports directly from the police department without organizational endorsement. Capitalizing on this opportunity, Rui Yin secured her passport.

China operates a distinctive system known as the household registration system, overseen by specialized household registration police. Notably, only three countries worldwide utilize such a system: China, North Korea, and Benin in Africa. Moreover, North Korea and Benin have drawn inspiration from China's household registration system.

Initially, this system curtails individuals' freedom of movement and then distributes essential commodities required for daily life solely based on their registered location. For instance, grain tickets were essential for purchasing rice, cloth tickets for clothes, and specific tickets for sugar, oil, soap, and toilet paper. The household registration system served as a potent instrument for government control over the populace, evolving into a lifeline for individuals. Children's registration was tied to their mothers, and those leaving the country would have their household registration suspended or canceled.

When my wife Rui Yin ventured abroad, her household registration was canceled, raising questions about our daughter Luoluo's registration. A practical solution emerged: Luoluo would relocate to Xiamen with her grandmother. According to the registration relocation process, the Xiamen Police Department required a release certificate from the Chuzhou County Police Department to transfer Luoluo's registration to Xiamen. However, obtaining this certificate proved arduous. The Chuzhou County Police Department insisted that Luoluo's account remained within the collective registration of Chuzhou Teachers' College, demanding a letter of introduction from the college's administrative office before separating Luoluo's account from the collective registration. The administrative office's response was dismissive, stating, "The school seal is not something available to you just because you need it." This epitomized the absurdity and irrationality of the authoritarian system, showcasing one of the main characteristics of the CCP government bureaucracy: a lack of space for reasoning. In the summer of 1985, my brother Chengquan arrived in Chuzhou to aid Rui Yin in the relocation process. Working at the "Jiangxi Provincial Political and Judicial Cadre School" in Nanchang, Chengquan visited the Chuzhou County Police Department in a police uniform with proper identification. Upon noticing Chengquan's credentials from the Jiangxi Provincial Police Department, the household registration police became polite and cooperative. Chengquan explained the situation, and the police officer, choosing to categorize it as an "outward move" which—unlike the arrival of a new resident—did not necessarily require additional approval from higher authorities, facilitated the process.

I arrived at the University of Iowa in August 1984 with only $200 in my pocket. That year, there were 40 international students from mainland China at the University of Iowa, most of whom were publicly funded and older, with only a few self-funded individuals. For self-funded students, the initial challenge was financial survival. Fortunately, we were able to secure sponsors, a prerequisite for obtaining a visa, from friends and relatives. We agreed with our sponsors that we would never ask them for money. Thus, upon my arrival in Iowa City, I immediately began searching for employment. I juggled several jobs simultaneously, working in the laundry plant at the university hospital, the student cafeteria, the university library, and at Professor Olson's house. Additionally, I took on odd jobs like mowing lawns, cleaning gardens, and shoveling snow on campus during winter. I became known at Iowa as the "King of Part-Time Jobs." In the fall of 1985, Rui Yin joined me at the University of Iowa to study Actuarial Science and Statistics, earning her Master's Degree in '87. I transferred to New York in 1985 and earned a Master of Science in Special and Bilingual Education from Hunter College of the City University of New York in 1991, a Doctor of Philosophy from New York University in 1996, and a Master of Educational Administration from Long Island University in 2001. I received full scholarships for all three degrees and was honored with the New York State Award for Outstanding Graduate Student of the Year. In the United States, the pathway of social mobility is open. Despite discrimination and feelings of inferiority in my home country, I was given a fair chance to compete and realize my potential in the United States. My experience is not isolated; many self-funded students who came to the U.S. in the 1980s shared similar journeys.

From 1987 to 1990, I served as a high school teacher, after which I transitioned to the role of an educational evaluator for the Committee of Special Education in the New York City School District 24. Beginning in 2005 until my retirement in 2018, I worked for the New York State Education Department as a School Improvement Specialist. The nature of my work closely resembled that of a school inspector in the Chinese school system. In my capacity, I monitored, inspected, and evaluated the quality of teaching and learning in school districts and schools, aligning with federal and state education laws and regulations. At the start of each school year, I formulated a plan to enhance the quality of education in the schools under my responsibility, setting goals for various student groups in their main subjects by the end of the year. I collaborated with principals and assistant principals to establish a systematic and effective teaching approach. Additionally, I provided in-service training for new teachers, assisted school administrators in tracking student test scores, and assessed the quality of teaching and learning. At the conclusion of the school year, I assessed the school leadership team's implementation of the annual plan, identified gaps against the set goals, analyzed data to identify underachievers and skill deficiencies, and provided recommendations in the annual plan summary for effective teaching methods to improve target students' performance in the following year. Schools showing significant progress received substantial bonuses for the principal, assistant principals, and the school as a whole. Conversely, for schools significantly lagging behind, the State Department of Education could decide to revoke the school's license due to serious leadership failures, complete breakdowns in teaching and learning activities, or declining student performance on state standardized tests and graduation rates for three consecutive years. In cases of school closure, students would be redirected to other schools, and both the principal and teachers would be demobilized. My work hours at the Education Department were from 8 am to 4 pm. From 4 to 7 pm and during holidays, I held a part-time position as a certificate specialist in the Division of Human Resources of the New York City Department of Education. In this role, I evaluated applicants' transcripts, reviewed their qualifications for induction, and guided them in applying for various levels of teaching certifications.

My favorite aspect of working in the U.S. is the positive and supportive relationships within the office. Colleagues and supervisors communicate politely, trust one another, and maintain a relaxed and happy atmosphere. Unlike in China, there is no constant need to be on guard. When I initially entered the school system, my spoken English was limited, I lacked the required credentials, and I had no work experience in the United States. However, my supervisor and many colleagues sincerely and enthusiastically assisted me without reservation. In 1992, I faced a crucial decision about whether to pursue a doctoral program at New York University (NYU), having been recommended by Hunter College. NYU is renowned and is listed as one of the 25 New Ivy League schools in the U.S. In the 2018 "U.S. News" Magazine, NYU is ranked 30th overall in the U.S., and in the 2017 "Center for Worldwide University Rankings" (CWUR), it holds the 22nd position globally among universities. By 2016, NYU had produced 36 Nobel Prize winners, ranking 19th worldwide and 12th in the United States. The university boasts more than 30 Pulitzer Prize winners, 30 Academy Award winners, 19 Medal of the American Academy of Sciences, and numerous Abel Prize, Emmy Award, and Tony Award winners. Additionally, NYU is ranked 18th in the annual Global CEO Alma Mater rankings and 8th in the total number of famous alumni in the United States. The list of distinguished alumni includes Alan Greenspan, John Kennedy Jr., Ma Ying-jeou, Eric Chu, Ang Lee, Anne Hathaway, Angelina Jolie, Lady Gaga, Oliver Stone, and Spike Lee. Entering NYU is a dream that proves challenging for many American students due to its stringent academic requirements and a competitive acceptance rate of about 13%. Graduating from NYU is even more daunting, with a graduation rate of approximately 85%. The prestige and academic excellence associated with NYU make it a highly coveted institution.

NYU extended a gesture of special favor by offering me a fellowship for a research position contingent on my commitment to carrying a full course load each semester as a full-time student. This posed a significant challenge for me, given the demanding nature of my studies and the need to support my family, requiring simultaneous work and study. Uncertain of my ability to navigate these demands, my supervisor, upon learning of my situation, provided encouragement. She shared, "I applied to NYU the other year and didn't even receive an acceptance letter. How can you give up now that you've even secured a fellowship?" She advocated on my behalf with my coworkers and allowed me to carve out some time at work to study. Upon earning my degree and advancing in my position, my coworkers acknowledged my hard work and were supportive, stating, "You have been working so hard. You deserve it." This positive and supportive atmosphere contrasts sharply with certain individuals encountered in China: he hates you if you are better than him; he steps on you if you are not as good as him. Hu Shih once criticized a kind of national inferiority among the Chinese people. He said, "The greatest evil of human nature is to hate you for what you have and laugh at you for what you don't have, to dislike you for being poor and fear you for being rich." Reflecting on initial encounters, the practice of measuring each other's status and worth to determine a power dynamic is prevalent: to kneel or to be kneelt upon. Ji Xianlin (1911~2009), a Chinese Indologist, linguist, paleographer, historian, and writer, said, "Years later, I woke up and finally discovered a universal truth: in the system of public services, every unit is dominated by shameless villains, and decent people are always in the minority and powerless. The masses are blind and snobbish, and seldom side with the virtuous." I didn't encounter anyone like that at my workplace in the US. If I had to return to work in China, I would certainly not thrive in such relationships.

Working in the New York public education system granted me ample holidays and vacations, affording me the flexibility to make guest appearances in organizations beyond the system. Columbia University's Teachers' College housed a "China Education Center" in the 1990s, specializing in training Chinese college administrators, provincial and municipal education administrators. I delivered lectures there on multiple occasions and issued trainees certificates of completion on behalf of Columbia University. Furthermore, professors from various institutions, such as the State University of New York at New Paltz, the City College of the City University of New York, and Pace University in downtown New York, invited me to give guest lectures. In 2001, I obtained state approval to establish an educational consulting company, JCB of Glen Cove Inc. The name "JCB" incorporates my initials, while Glen Cove represents the company's Long Island, New York location. The escalating prevalence of autism in the U.S. over the past two decades has fueled a surge in demand for services. In 2000, one child in every 2,500 had autism; by 2018, this ratio had escalated to one in every 68. Clinical signs typically manifest around 18 months of age, emphasizing the critical importance of early intervention, with optimal outcomes observed before the age of 5. New York State law mandates that parents and pediatricians promptly refer children with suspected developmental issues to the appropriate educational agency. Neglecting this obligation can lead to serious legal repercussions. The New York State public education system offers free education from age 3 through 21. The considerable demand for services for children under 3 has spurred the emergence of private schools and education management companies. Despite the Department of Health providing generous compensation for teachers serving autistic children to conduct evaluations and services, there was a shortage of teacher resources for some time. To bridge this gap, private schools recruited teachers internationally, including from China. These schools facilitated the training of newly recruited teachers, assisted in obtaining special education teaching licenses, and provided green cards for permanent residence. Licensed teachers are mandated to undergo a specified number of hours of in-service continuing education annually to continue working with children and their parents. The primary focus of my educational consulting company was to train new teachers, offer in-service programs for private special schools and educational agencies, and evaluate and screen children with autism. Additionally, I guided parents in supporting their children with special needs.

Beginning in the late 1990s with China's opening up, the country embarked on a period of significant growth and development, marking its most prosperous three decades. This era also coincided with the peak of positive U.S.-China relations. Throughout this period, I actively participated in various exchanges and initiatives. I had the privilege of hosting numerous visiting Chinese education delegations in New York, ranging from representatives of the Ministry of Education's Division of Public Education to delegations from various provinces and universities. During this time, I had the opportunity to meet with Hu Jintao and Wen

Jiabao on three occasions at the Waldorf Astoria Hotel in New York. In return, I was part of a delegation of American educators that visited China, organized by the College Board. In 1990, I played a role in facilitating a significant collaboration by introducing Yong'an Middle School in Suxian County, a grassroots institution, to the Zigen Foundation in New York. The Zigen Foundation included Yong'an Middle School in its funding program. Subsequently, the foundation provided financial support to assist the school in setting up a library and enhancing its science and chemistry laboratories.

In New York State, teachers nominated for tenure must hold U.S. citizenship. When I began teaching in 1987, the New York City Department of Education initiated the green card application process on my behalf, and in 1993, I completed the immigrant naturalization process, becoming a U.S. citizen. The first thing I did was to revert my last name to "Bao" on my U.S. passport, ending the "Liu" phase from 1966 to 1993. In 1990, my mother informed me that my father, Shao Xuewen, and she had decided to purchase a cemetery in Wuxi. Shenjie communicated that the cost would be shared among the three children, and I sent a lump sum to cover the expense. When my mother expressed her desire to install a flush toilet, bathtub, and water heater in the house, I provided the necessary funds. In 1996, Shenjie and Chengquan sought my assistance in applying for immigration to America. I covered the $100 application filing fees for each of them and instructed them to pass on the funds to our parents instead of repaying me. From leaving home at 16 until departing China at 32, I received a total of ¥240 RMB from my mother, amounting to a monthly allowance of ¥10 during my last two years of college. Since joining the New York City Department of Education in 1987, I have consistently sent money to support my parents' daily expenses. At the time, my mother's monthly salary was ¥80 RMB, and I provided a monthly subsidy of $50 USD (with the exchange rate of $1 USD = ¥7~10 RMB), exceeding her salary. Initially, the checks were made out in my father's name, but later—at my mother's request—they were issued in her name, as she objected to his using the money for stock speculation.

Entering the 1990s, as economic reforms deepened, China saw the rapid rise of a new class of private entrepreneurs. General Secretary Jiang Zemin then announced the lifting of the "party ban," allowing capitalists to join the Communist Party. The Party that once proudly declared itself the "vanguard of the proletariat" now began presenting itself as a party of "all the people." However, this move was not motivated by any intention to promote political democratization. Instead, it was designed to bring the fast-growing private economic sector firmly under the Party's control, binding entrepreneurs' interests tightly to the Party's direction and preventing the emergence of an economically powerful elite independent of the political system. Although private entrepreneurs were allowed to join the Party, this did not grant them access to real political power. They were incorporated mainly into the United Front system, functioning more as symbolic tokens of inclusiveness than as participants in core decision-making. The purpose of bringing them in was always to manage and control them, not to share power with them. Whenever political needs arise, these entrepreneurs may be asked to comply, withdraw, or sacrifice. Should they be deemed "uncooperative" or unwilling to "align with the Party Center," they can quickly be recast—from "representatives of advanced productive forces" into "gangsters" or "criminal elements." Within such a structure, their assets can be seized, their companies taken over, their reputations destroyed. Even their personal freedom—sometimes their very existence—can evaporate without meaningful recourse.

In 1994, my mother asked me to go to Shanghai to celebrate her 70th birthday. Accompanied by Rui Yin and our daughter Luoluo, who now had the English name Flora, I returned to China, bearing gifts for everybody in the family and presenting my mother with a cash gift of $1,000 USD. In the same year, my mother asked me to buy an apartment in Shanghai, stating, "It's eventually yours if you buy a property in Shanghai. But Shenjie and I can live there first." Mom's residence was far from modest; in fact, her dwelling in Chengxingli garnered envy and attention from neighbors in the entire lane for many years. On the other hand, I was responsible for mortgage payments in New York and was unable to fulfill her request, leading to resentment from Mom and Shenjie. Mom informed me that Shenjie had become an upstanding member of the Communist Party, which surprised me. Seeking confirmation, I approached Shenjie in person and questioned, "Growing up, we were treated as counter-revolutionary children. How could you join the Party?" She explained, "Our unit was facing a significant layoff, and being a Party member could potentially shield me from being the first to be laid off." Despite Shenjie's affiliation with the Communist Party, the Shanghai No. 2 Watch Factory eventually shut down completely, and her party membership did not secure her job. Communists, by rule, profess allegiance to communism, yet they exhibit a pragmatic approach. They visit the Jade Buddha Temple to burn the first incense on Chinese New Year's Day and attend Mass at the Catholic Church on Christmas. As long as they can use it for their own purposes, they will not spare anything.

In the summer of 1994, Rui Yin and I spent a few days in Shanghai before heading to Wuhu to reconnect with our old schoolmates. At that time, Heng Xiaojun, who had returned from his graduate studies in England, was leading the Foreign Language Department. Heng was a talented individual with a high IQ and a high level of emotional intelligence. Another classmate who remained at the university was Associate Professor Ouyang Junling. During our visit, Professor Zhang Chunjiang was still alive, and Ouyang accompanied us to see him. We also saw our good friends Liang Jianfeng and Jiao Xiaoyu, a couple who both graduated from the Art Department, with Liang majoring in voice and Jiao in piano. During my tenure as the head of the Arts and Entertainment Department of the student union, Liang Jianfeng served as the deputy director, fostering many interactions between us. Jiao Xiaoyu's mother, Ms. Wang, a piano professor in the art department, showed me special favor and took the initiative of introducing me to a girlfriend. Nothing was more important than securing a good position, AKA: job, and finding a suitable partner, but all through the 1960s, 70s, and to a large degree even the 80s, there was little to no "social life" in China. So, if someone was willing to help me get a good job or introduce me to a potential spouse, it was the greatest kindness possible, deserving of memory and mention.

After graduation, Jiao Xiaoyu worked at the university teaching piano, while Liang Jianfeng was assigned to the Chuzhou School of Education. As both Liang Jianfeng and Rui Yin were in Chuzhou, our interactions increased. When we met in 1994, Liang Jianfeng had already been transferred to Wuhu, where he became the principal of the elementary school affiliated with Anhui Normal University, excelling in his role due to his exceptional interpersonal skills. In the 1990s, the couple moved to Shenzhen to establish a successful music school. Leaving Wuhu, we proceeded to Hefei and stayed at the home of a classmate. Before I visited China in 1994, I received a letter from Commissioner Zhu Choumei, expressing his wish to visit the United States. Tragically, he fell ill with cancer and passed away prematurely. In Hefei, we visited Zhu Choumei's home, met his wife, and paid our respects to his portrait. All three of his daughters were present on that occasion. Additionally, I visited an old friend, Zhan Yumin, in Hefei, and another colleague and old friend, Qian Zhili, at the Hefei Forestry School in Dashushan.

Parting ways in Hefei, Rui Yin headed to Tongling, while I made my way to Suxian County. During my stay in Bengbu, I visited Xie Yifan and Zhang Fengzhi. Xie Bin and his wife had moved to the U.S. a year after I did, both earning master's degrees, securing stable jobs, and welcoming a son. Xie Yifan and Zhang Fengzhi were thrilled to be grandparents and eagerly anticipated my visit for a good chat. Unexpectedly, upon my arrival at Xie Yifan's house, I found Yin Li and Xie Daofeng waiting for me. Xie Daofeng said, "Sanhei is currently in the Czech Republic and is in a difficult situation. For the sake of our past friendship, please lend him a hand." I agreed to discuss it with Xie Bin and then contact Sanhei. We wrote to Sanhei, inviting him to come to the United States, but he showed no interest. The following day, Xie Daofeng returned, this time accompanied by a young man from Bengbu Medical College, Dr. Wang. Xie Daofeng explained that Dr. Wang had done an exemplary job treating Yin Li's mother's eyes and aspired to pursue further study in the United States. Xie Daofeng urged me to help fulfill Dr. Wang's wish. Zhang Fengzhi, consistently disapproving of Xie Daofeng's actions, expressed her frustration. She said, "It's not easy for Chengmo and me to meet. We want to talk, but you come and take up our time. Remember how you treated Chengmo back then. How dare you approach him now?" Ignoring her, Xie Daofeng persisted, saying, "You go to Suxian County, and I'll arrange for the regional governor to meet you." However, I declined, "That's not necessary. I do not know him. Why should I see him?" Being received by the governor is an honor for someone like Xie Daofeng, who worships power. For me, it's akin to putting legs on a snake.

Upon arriving in Suxian, Zhou Hualu picked me up at the train station. After a brief rest at the hotel, Zhou Hualu took me to his home. He served as the principal of the No. 2 Middle School in Suxian, and his house was located in a spacious and tidy bungalow within the school campus. Seeing his wife, Liu Shulian, brought me great joy. We reminisced about our days at Yong'an Middle School and shared a poignant reflection. That day, I also met Liu Shulian's relatives who had come from Taiwan. The No. 2 Middle School was a provincial key middle school with an impressive campus. Zhu Choumei had visited many times, and the Education Department generously allocated funds to the school. Several teachers from the original Yong'an Middle School had been transferred back to work in the city. I hosted a banquet in Suxian for almost all the original teachers from Yong'an Middle School. They told me that my tumultuous life experiences had made me a legendary figure in Suxian. Their students regarded me as an inspirational role model. What I wanted to tell them then was, and still remains: "Here in China, the political system determines a person's fate, and this is the primary factor. Personal struggle and character play a secondary role." "An authoritarian society turns people into ghosts, while a free society can turn ghosts into people," and I am proof of this.

In the country where I was born, I was heavily discriminated against and considered a pariah who would never rise. It was only in the United States that I had the opportunity to earn a PhD from a top university, realize my potential, achieve academic and career success, and stand tall and proud as a dignified human being. The next day, Zhou Hualu, along with the director and secretary of the Suxian County Education

Department, accompanied me to Yong'an. I inspected the newly established library at Yong'an Middle School. It was unforgettable; during the darkest period of my life, colleagues from Yong'an Middle School and Shanjia School supported me in adversity, comforted me in a remote land, and respected me in times of trouble. When I visited Yelou and Shanjia, the local residents, including two generations of my fellow villagers, still remembered me. When I saw that Liu Yanqi and his wife were living in a thatched shed after their house caught fire, I left them some money to help in their time of need.

In 1995, my college bunkmate Heng Xiaojun, with whom I shared a bunk bed in the same dormitory room for four years, was appointed as the Education Consul at the Consulate General of China in New York. The Education Section Counselor was Lu Tiecheng (Mr. Lu returned to China to become the president of Sichuan Union University at the end of his term). They informed me that they had sent my published articles in the U.S. back to Beijing, where Minister of Education Chen Zhili read them with keen interest. They urged me to return to China to introduce the theories and practices of education reform in the U.S. In '96, '98, and 2000, I took advantage of my summer vacations to travel to Beijing, Shanghai, Hefei, Huaibei, and Xiamen to deliver lectures and participate in academic exchange seminars. In 1996, I visited East China Normal University in Shanghai, engaging in discussions with professors and researchers at the Institute of International and Comparative Education. I met Mr. Feng, who had conducted English oral tests in Suxian in '78. I remarked, "Although East China Normal University didn't accept me as a student in 1978, it's incredible to meet you as a visiting scholar here today." In 1998, I was invited by Mr. Zhuang Yiqun, Secretary of the Party Committee of the National Advanced Academy of Education Administration in Beijing, to deliver a lecture. I accompanied my daughter to stay at Changping and Tsinghua University in Beijing for a few days before traveling south to Suxian. Mr. Zhu, the director of the Suxian City Education Commission, and his team welcomed me at the municipal government building entrance. The secretary-general of the municipal government, a female cadre, greeted me, acknowledging, "You are a legend in Suxian. We all know the story of Yin Li and you. Yin Li is now the director of the Women's Federation of our city." Yin Li then visited me, saying, "The city government has arranged car services for you. I won't accompany you to Yong'an. It may save a lot of gossip." Two days later, the director of the Huaibei City Education Committee personally came to Suxian to escort me to Huaibei. Afterward, I took my daughter to visit the ancestral village of the Bao family, Tongyue, in Shexian, Huizhou.

In mid-August 1998, I gathered my parents and the entire family at Meilongzhen Restaurant in Shanghai to celebrate my father's birthday in advance. Towards the end of the month, as I was preparing to depart from Shanghai, my father fell seriously ill with a severe cold and had to call for an ambulance. Since childhood, he had one underdeveloped lung and had previously battled tuberculosis, resulting in compromised lung function. Despite this, when the ambulance arrived at 10:00 a.m., he managed to slowly walk out of the alleyway and get into the van on his own. Upon reaching the hospital, the doctor attempted to assist his lungs with oxygen through a tube, but his alveoli had already lost their function. Sadly, he passed away at 1:00 p.m. Just a few days before this incident, he had ridden his bicycle from Xinchang Road to Huangpi Road, crossing People's Square to the police station to collect his paycheck. My father's sudden demise occurred at the age of 78 (1920~1998), just before I was set to leave for home. Was it an arrangement from the heavens? I rebooked my air ticket, delaying my trip to the United States by a week. I hosted a memorial service for my father at Longhua Cemetery, where I met my father's two brothers for the first time. In 1998, following my father's death, the memorial service incurred a cost of ¥8,000 RMB. Shenjie managed the accounts and revealed that the gift money she received was also ¥8,000 RMB. A dispute arose as my mother insisted that the gift money belonged to her, asserting that the children should cover the costs. I proposed contributing ¥6,000 RMB, with Shenjie and Chengquan each contributing ¥1,000 RMB, which helped ease the situation.

In 1999, my mother, born in 1924, passed away at the age of 75. At the time of her death, she left behind US$7,000, representing the remaining balance from the years I had been financially supporting her, and ¥40,000 RMB. During the 70s and 80s, she held ¥60,000 RMB when the median monthly income for an elementary school teacher was ¥60 RMB. This amount of ¥60,000 RMB was equivalent to ¥1,000 RMB per month (83 years) of a teacher's salary. However, by 1999, the year of her passing, the value of the RMB had sharply declined. The median monthly income for an elementary school teacher had risen to ¥5,000 RMB. As a result, ¥40,000 RMB was now only equivalent to 8 months' salary. In 2000, my daughter and I returned to China to bury my parents' ashes in the Qinglongshan Cemetery in Wuxi, a choice they had made long ago and for which I had purchased the plot. It was only then that my brother Chengquan revealed to me that my parents had never remarried, a decision primarily made by my mother. Despite having divorced Shao Xuewen, she decided against remarrying, fearing potential political campaigns and the risk of being labeled a counter-revolutionary spouse once again.

In the summer of 2000, I delivered a lecture at the Basic Education Division of the Ministry of Education in Xidan, Beijing. I then took a train down to Suxian. Many of my old friends had retired. I hosted a banquet for most of my colleagues and acquaintances from the former Yong'an Middle School, including Ning Chuanzhong, Ning Chuanshu, and Jiang Guanghui. In 2000, Xie Yifan and Zhang Fengzhi travelled to Shanghai to apply for visas to visit Xie Bin in the U.S. I was eagerly looking forward to welcoming them in New York. However, Zhang Fengzhi tragically passed away due to a heart attack in Shanghai. In 2004, Xie Yifan also left us. In 2010, Yin Li and Yin Meng accompanied me to Bengbu to visit the graves of Xie Yifan and Zhang Fengzhi and pay my respects to them. Yin Li later retired as the deputy director of the Suxian City People's Congress. Around the year 2000, several of my articles were published by various universities and professional journals in China, including "Perspectives on American Education: The Experiences and Reflections of 20 Chinese American Ph.Ds.," published by Peking University Press, as well as contributions to journals such as Fudan

Education, Journal of Foreign Education Studies of East China Normal University, Shanghai Education, English Teaching and Research Notes, and Exploring Education Development.

After dedicating thirty years of my career to New York, the period leading up to my retirement involved extensive travel across the United States and overseas in search of an ideal retirement destination. In 2015, Rui Yin and I decided on a retirement location in Washington State. Stretching over 2,500 miles along the west coast of the Pacific Ocean, the Cascadian bioregion extends from the Copper River in Southern Alaska to Cape Mendocino, approximately 200 miles north of San Francisco, and eastward to the Yellowstone Caldera and continental divide. It stands as the largest temperate rainforest on earth. Washington State lies in the heart of the Cascade Range. Shielded by the Rocky Mountains, it is spared from the cold air of Canadian winters, resulting in infrequent occurrences of snow and ice. The state's high latitude ensures the absence of summer heat waves and minimizes mosquito presence. Washington boasts relative immunity to natural disasters, lacking the tornadoes of the U.S. Great Plains, the annual typhoons of the southeastern states, or the recurring droughts and fires of California. The rainy season, lasting from October to April, typically brings showers, drizzles, or sun showers, with rare instances of torrential rain. Locals eschew umbrellas on rainy days, relying on jacket hoods instead. Washington earned the moniker "The Evergreen State." In the seasonal rainforest zone, prominent tree species include Douglas fir, western red cedar, Sitka spruce, and western hemlock. Douglas fir and red cedar trees boast sturdy trunks, reaching heights of a few dozen meters to over 100 meters and living up to 3,500 years. The Cascade Range features numerous peaks formed by volcanic activity, with Mt. Rainier (14,411 ft.) standing as one of the highest peaks. It is also the tallest mountain in the continental United States, covered in perpetual snow and ice. Our chosen retirement community lies northwest of Mt. Rainier National Park in Tehaleh, a term derived from the native American language Chinook Jargon meaning "highlands" or "the land above," situated at around 600+ ft. above sea level. To reach Tehaleh from Sea-Tac Airport, one drives southeast for approximately 50 minutes through the Puyallup River Valley, which sits at about 40 ft. above sea level, ascending more than 600 ft. above sea level until reaching the small town of Bonney Lake. From Bonney Lake, a ten-minute drive south leads to Tehaleh.

When we initially arrived in Tehaleh during the winter of 2015, the community comprised just over a hundred one-family houses. During our three-day stay in a model house surrounded by a lush forest, the air was so rich with oxygen that it resembled an oxygen bar. Tehaleh is organized into seven small communities constructed by seven distinct contractors, including Trilogy, a 55+ resort-style community. In 2016, we purchased a lot at Trilogy and collaborated with a designer to select a model and building materials. Shea Homes served as the contractor, completing the house by the end of 2017. In March 2020, we engaged a moving company to transport our furniture and belongings in a container truck across the U.S. to Trilogy. By 2020, Tehaleh had seen the construction of 3,000 single-family, garden-house-style residential homes. An additional 3,000 homes were planned for the south side, where the land had already been leveled. The prevalence of new construction in Tehaleh has led to its reputation as an upscale residential area, attracting those with stable jobs and financial security. Given the affluence of its residents, Tehaleh has become known as an upscale residential enclave in Washington State. The West Coast states, including California, Oregon, and Washington, are all considered "blue states," with Democratic strongholds in cities like San Francisco, Portland, and Seattle. During the Black Lives Matter protests and contemporaneous smash-and-grab robbery sprees in the summer of 2020, Trilogy remained untouched by the protests or the crime sprees. The community, home to a significant number of retirees, including veterans from the Coast Guard, Army, Navy, and Air Force, boasts residents with a strong belief in the right to bear arms. Gun ownership is seen as integral to America's constitutional democratic republic. In Washington State, obtaining a gun and ammunition is straightforward; a driver's license is sufficient, and the process is relatively inexpensive. Gun stores in the area often include shooting ranges for marksmanship practice. Those protest movements and rogue thugs are afraid of guns. Even powerful politicians are wary of the impact of a single bullet. The Trilogy community's residents are mainly veterans and retirees from Boeing, Amazon, Microsoft, and other professionals, including judges, engineers, doctors, nurses, accountants, professors, and teachers.

Tehaleh was meticulously planned from the ground up, granting the freedom to design street alignments, residential neighborhoods, schools, parks, and commercial service areas. Just outside The Post, Tehaleh's information center, one encounters outdoor fireplaces, fire pits, and outdoor furniture. The main road leading out of Tehaleh serves as a direct path ascending towards the main peak of Mount Rainier, resembling a passageway to heaven. Behind The Post, the glistening glaciers at the tip of Mount Olympus in Olympic National Park come into view. Mount Rainier, adorned with 25 large glaciers, gives rise to the Puyallup River, which meanders south of Tehaleh. The surroundings boast glaciers, snow-capped mountains, forests, and meadows untainted by pollution. The river valley, rich with volcanic ash deposits, forms fertile land that yields the freshest vegetables and fruits. Orchards, nourished by snow water, produce renowned watermelons, apples, cherries, strawberries, blackberries, and raspberries that are celebrated throughout the United States. Beyond the window of my cottage, lush greenery graces the landscape year-round, with blossoming flowers in spring, and stepping out the door leads to a forest trail. The air, especially after a light rain, feels akin to an oxygen bar. Gazing upward, the towering Ten Thousand Years of Snow Mountain enhances the scenic panorama. Driving along the highway often reveals the clouds in the river valley, creating an indistinct yet enchanting sight. I cherish Tehaleh, considering this place my home. Life here is characterized by tranquility and safety, a sense of freedom and abundance, and the pride of being a respectful American citizen.

If the path is impassable, ride on a raft afloat on the sea. Those who have gone through hunger cherish food; those who have gone through suffering cherish the ordinary. I value the ordinary life after leaving China. Albert Einstein made a statement in a speech on February 7, 1933, at the

California Institute of Technology in Pasadena, California, USA. This was shortly after Adolf Hitler came to power in Germany, and Einstein, who was of Jewish descent, was deeply concerned about the rise of anti-Semitism and the erosion of political freedoms in his home country. He said: "As long as I have a choice, I would like to live only in a country that is politically free, tolerant, and where all men are equal before the law. Freedom of speech and freedom to express political opinions in writing are also part of political freedom, and respect for personal beliefs is part of tolerance. None of these conditions currently exists in Germany." Similarly, I choose to live in the United States because China lacks the conditions to maintain independent individuality and liberated thought." The conditions to be a normal citizen do not exist in China. The 18th-century British philosopher, historian, and economist David Hume proposed the three principles of modern civilization: stable possession of property, transfer by consent, and adherence to contracts, which have been labeled as "Hume's three principles." In the Republic of China, people were honest. Although freedom in the Republican era was limited, it was, after all, better than any dynasty in the prior two thousand years. To be patriotic, I can love the Republic of China before 1949. In the future, I would love a democratic constitutional republic like post-World War II Germany and Japan, where people no longer blindly worship obedience to power, and where power is confined. The dominant idea of the modern concept of the state is that sovereignty resides in the people. If the sovereignty of a state is not in the hands of the people, the existence of the state loses its legitimacy. In this context, it is worth pondering what constitutes "love of country." What kind of "country" do we love? Today's China is not worthy of my love.

In China, the government consigned me to a third-rate university. In the United States, I had the opportunity to earn a doctorate from a first-class university. In China, a "socialist" country, the individual is subjugated to the state, and private property can be seized arbitrarily. The planned economy serves to cement social classes and close off avenues of upward mobility, ultimately —and ironically—consolidating the power of the ruling class. Even if one encounters an opportunity to ascend the social ladder, numerous obstacles emerge, and thousands of Liu Beirus and Xie Daofengs will appear and stand in the way, hindering progress. All efforts prove futile. In China, there are millions of people like me, full of frustration and with no hope of ever rising above it. In the United States, a "capitalist" country, the relationship between the individual and the state is contractual. The market economy provides a platform for free competition, and private property is held sacred. Individual independence of thought and freedom of speech are safeguarded. Individuals have the chance to explore their potential and abilities, with each effort leading to a potential reward. It becomes possible to transcend class boundaries and achieve self-fulfillment. Abraham Lincoln, Bill Clinton, and Barack Obama all emerged from families at the bottom of the social hierarchy, rising through personal struggle and effort to become president of the United States. Such a journey is inconceivable in an authoritarian country like China. This exemplifies the disparity in systems and the power inherent in the system.

Which system do you prefer? I respect every person's choice. My choice is to be an American citizen. Over the years, I have been hailed as a patriotic Chinese at one time and a traitor to China at another. I am neither. I love some individuals in that country. But it is impossible for me to love that country. I have lived in that country for thirty years. Please give me a reason why I should love it. Calling me a traitor to China? You flatter me. I don't have so much as a tile over my head or an inch of land under my feet in China. What do I have to sell out? In China, only those in power have the privilege of betraying the country. The ones with the most power are, of course, the Great Leaders. I've been away from China for more than 40 years. What is home? Peace of mind is home. It doesn't matter where I was born, but where I am treated as a human being. That country doesn't deserve to be my motherland, and I don't need a motherland. Wherever there is freedom, that is my homeland.

Appendix I

The Specter of Communism

"What has always made the state a hell on earth has been precisely that man has tried to make it his heaven."

— *Friedrich Hayek's "The Road to Serfdom"*

"A specter is haunting Europe—the specter of communism." This is the famous opening line of "The Communist Manifesto." First published in London on February 24, 1848, it was the first major work to take the view that all of humanity was divided by class struggle. In the 19th century, significant advancements were made in the natural sciences. British biologist Charles Robert Darwin (1809~1882) published "On the Origin of Species" in 1859. In this groundbreaking work, he introduced the theory of biological evolution, centered on natural selection and the concept of "survival of the fittest," which gained widespread acceptance. Marx incorporated Darwin's theory into his analysis of historical processes, particularly in relation to class struggles. He posited the inevitability of social system development, delineating stages from primitive society through slave, feudal, capitalist, to communist societies. Although neither Marx nor Engels was a scientist in any empirical or experimental sense, their followers nonetheless designated this doctrine as "scientific communism." However, the subsequent 150 years of communist movement history reveal a lack of empirical evidence supporting this theory. Moreover, it stands in stark contrast to historical realities, rendering it fundamentally unscientific and erroneous.

The Communist Manifesto espouses a utopian vision of equality and prosperity for all. However, achieving this ideal necessitates the establishment of a dictatorship of the proletariat, involving the deprivation of freedom for some and the elimination of others. Karl

Marx and Friedrich Engels meticulously outlined their perspectives in the Manifesto, emphasizing the "abolition of private ownership" and the concept of "class struggle." Marx entrusted the Communists with the mission of overthrowing the bourgeoisie, seizing power for the proletariat, and ultimately realizing communism, which they saw as the pinnacle in human social development. The debate arises: should private ownership be abolished or safeguarded? According to Scottish Enlightenment philosophers David Hume (1711~1776), Adam Smith (1723~1790), and Adam Ferguson (1723~1816), the acknowledgment of property rights marked the genesis of human civilization and established its boundaries. Without this boundary, civilized people would become barbarians. With the concept of property rights comes moral and legal responsibility.

Property serves as a crucible for fostering personal responsibility, integrity, education, and freedom of thought and action. It endows individuals with rights and underpins law, politics, morality, and the arts, constituting the cornerstone of society. The protection of property rights makes a civilized society, with its degree of civilization measured by the extent of such protection. The establishment of the property rights system was the beginning of the civilized way of human cooperation. One of the most important features of a civilized society is the clear boundary between "yours" (property, rights, freedoms, etc.) and "mine" (property, rights, freedoms, etc.) as defined by custom and law. Respect for property rights is the dividing line between civilized people and barbarians. The paradigm of "what is mine is mine, and what is yours is mine" rejects the paradigm of justice for the paradigm of barbaric banditry. Occupying the fruits of other people's labor without compensation is definitely not the behavior of civilized people. In modern society, only criminals of various types do not respect the property rights of others. To outlaw the property rights of citizens is to steal the property of others. Only barbaric nations spared no effort to outlaw the property rights of their citizens. Without the right to property and economic freedom, the poor will never have the opportunity to become rich.

John Locke (August 29, 1632 ~ October 28, 1704), the English philosopher and physician, is widely regarded as one of the most influential Enlightenment thinkers and commonly known as the "father of liberalism." He emphasized that as humanity transitioned from the state of nature to organized society, certain rights must be relinquished to the government through a social contract. However, Locke asserted that three fundamental human rights—the right to life, the property right, and the right to liberty—were inalienable and could not be surrendered. Locke believed that the purpose of government's existence was not to pursue the vested interests of the government, but for the public welfare. The public welfare requires safeguarding the life, property, and liberty of the citizens, which the government must not violate in the name of others. Locke established a criterion for identifying tyranny, asserting that it occurs when the government exceeds its legal authority and places itself above the law. This form of tyranny, characterized by arbitrary decrees and disregard for the rule of law, jeopardizes the protection of life, property, and freedom for all citizens. Under such oppressive conditions, individuals can at best only endure, lacking the ability to truly thrive. According to Locke, the progression of human civilization is marked by the retreat of tyranny from the historical stage, paving the way for greater freedom, justice, and societal advancement. Only when the government abides by the law can society be harmonious, stable, and prosperous. The tyranny of "calling a deer a horse and changing decrees overnight" deprived everyone of the protection of life and property, and made freedom naturally impossible. Under tyranny, one can only survive. The proof of the progress of human civilization is the withdrawal of tyranny from the stage of history.

The Communist Manifesto heralded "class struggle" as the central tenet of the Communist Party's agenda. According to Marx's vision, the proletariat's seizure of power and the establishment of proletarian dictatorship should first take place in the developed industrialized capitalist nations. Marx asserted that the working class, being the most organized, disciplined, and progressive, was duty-bound to assume leadership. However, a scrutiny of Communist Party leaders, including Marx, Engels, Lenin, Mao, Liu, Zhou, and Deng, reveals not a single individual hailing from the working class. Marx's prediction of a violent proletarian overthrow of the bourgeoisie and the subsequent establishment of a socialist state governed by the dictatorship of the proletariat in developed capitalist nations proved erroneous. Reality contradicted Marx's forecast. The red regimes, born out of violent upheavals in the Soviet Union, China, Vietnam, and Cuba, all emerged from agrarian societies with underdeveloped capitalism and a limited working class. Marx anticipated the ascension of workers in the political realm, yet the sole workers' party to rise was the Nazi Party under Hitler. Notably, the full name of the Nazi Party was the National Socialist German Workers' Party, National-Sozialistische Deutsche Arbeiterpartei (NSDAP), which underscored its purported allegiance to the working class.

If the theory of Marxism is flawed, then its "revolutionary" implementation leads inevitably to malevolence. The cost of endeavors aimed at realizing the utopia of communism was staggeringly high. In rural areas, the establishment of communes transformed the state into a massive landowner, abruptly stripping peasants of their land and relegating them to state-controlled sharecropping. In urban centers, state enterprises supplanted private businesses, and planned economies superseded market economies. Despite Marxist sociology asserting that the state serves its populace without conflict of interest, the practical reality unfolded differently. A new ruling class swiftly emerged from the ranks of state officials, fundamentally altering the "party as vanguard" concept purporting to usher in a new era. The Communist Party had no choice but to install this new class, on which it depended to consolidate its power. Stéphane Courtois (November 25, 1947~), a French historian, university professor, and director of research at the French National Center for Scientific Research at the 10th University of Paris, estimated in the Black Book of Communism that: Crime, Terror and Repression in communist regimes caused the deaths of 85 million to 100 million individuals worldwide, roughly equal to the combined casualties of both World Wars. Those who survived also paid a terrible price. To achieve national unanimity and unanimity of opinion, communist countries use high-handed means to banish, imprison, or deprive of the right to speak those who do not agree with them. Those who do not agree with them are often smart, capable, and far-sighted. Thus, there is a reverse elimination effect. Those who are mediocre and/or incompetent, those who are uncommitted, can survive. On the contrary, those who are visionary, loyal, and selfless are unable to survive. In this way, the communist countries lost their outstanding talents and became correspondingly weak.

After the Second World War, the socialist bloc emerged across Europe and Asia, comprising 12 socialist nations led by the USSR. This bloc grew to include the USSR, Poland, East Germany, Czechoslovakia, Hungary, Romania, Bulgaria, Albania, China, Mongolia, North Korea, Vietnam, Cambodia, Laos, and Cuba. But in late 1962, after a protracted period of rising tensions, China and the Soviet Union split, creating the greatest breach in the history of "Proletarian Internationalism." More than a quarter-century would pass before the world's two biggest communist powers restored diplomatic relations in May 1989—but only two and a half years later, in December 1991, the Soviet Union ceased to exist. Subsequently, the nations of Eastern Europe transitioned to constitutional democracies. As of 2025, only China, Cuba, Laos, and Vietnam remain as avowedly Communist countries.

As early as 1957, Milovan Đilas (1911~1995), a prominent Yugoslav Communist theorist and political leader, raised a fundamental challenge to the legitimacy of Communist rule in his seminal work The New Class. He advanced a sharp and subversive argument: in Communist states, although the capitalist class in the traditional sense had been eliminated, it was replaced by a new ruling group—the "new class." This "new class" was not founded on private ownership of property, but rather on its monopoly over the party and state apparatus, the system of planned economic allocation, and ideological resources, through which it secured institutionalized privileges. By controlling access to positions, rationed goods, housing, education, and information, it generated de facto class differentiation within societies that proclaimed themselves classless. Such a structure, Đilas argued, betrayed socialism's original promise of equality and emancipation, transforming it instead into a system of bureaucratic domination. Ðilas further predicted that this system, increasingly rigid and steadily eroding its own social legitimacy, would inevitably descend into crisis and eventual collapse. The New Class is widely regarded as one of the most powerful internal critiques of socialism during the Cold War. Its analysis profoundly shaped understandings of power structures in the Soviet and Eastern European systems and provided an important theoretical resource for subsequent institutional reflections in Eastern Europe and the Soviet Union.

The failure of communist practices has been starkly evident, with Marxist theory being repudiated both in theory and practice, notably in Russia. However, China persists in its adherence to Marxism, as renouncing it would undermine the Chinese Communist Party's legitimacy. Despite waning belief in the utopia of communism among party members, the CCP clings to this ideological banner. Nevertheless, as Chiang Ching-kuo remarked, "There is no permanent ruling party," signaling the inevitability of the CCP's eventual exit from the stage of history. The era characterized by the use of violence and bloodshed to pursue utopian ideals is drawing to a close. The dawn of "Farewell to Revolution" is upon us. Just as the Berlin Wall fell overnight on November 9, 1989, and the Soviet Union collapsed in December 1991, the countdown to the demise of the remaining national governments still waving the flag of "communist revolution"—that meat grinder which has consumed countless lives, tens of millions of them in China—has commenced. Let the evil of communism, born from hell, return from whence it came!

Appendix II

In the Name of Revolution

The term "revolution" typically carries a positive connotation, symbolizing progress in a nation's political structure, economic success, and/or moral enlightenment. Britain's bloodless "Glorious Revolution" exemplifies this notion. However, do subsequent violent upheavals, such as the French Revolution, the October Revolution, which resulted in the creation of the Soviet Union, and the Chinese Communist Party's Red Revolution, truly deserve the title of "revolution"? Are they worthy of the laurels associated with the term? Revolution is such a stirring word that makes one's heart pound and one's blood boil. The sad truth is that most of the time, revolution is a carnival for the rabble. A group of marginalized social figures, who were originally silent and not worth mentioning, with their superior strong-armed and gangster tactics, turned over like salted fish and floated up like dregs in the torrent of the muddy revolution, and became popular. However, when we lift the bright coat of the revolution, we see that by the light of the sun, it mostly consists of white bones and blood stains. Revolution, how many crimes have been committed in your name? Why do people like to kill? It is because force is the easiest way to terminate an opponent. But you cannot unwind the bow, and once the brutality begins, it is very difficult to stop the process. Once physical destruction has become the primary means, then dictatorship and violence can never adjust or refrain from continuing down these dark paths. To stop violence is to send the violent to the guillotine. The use of violence to eliminate one's opponents inevitably leads to the abuse of violence, because the revolution, with its innate bloodthirsty instincts, devours its opponents and then returns to devour the revolutionaries and their own sons and daughters. Tyranny causes revolutions, and revolutions produce tyrants, and so on and so forth. In

China, from the first major peasant uprising against the Qin Dynasty in 209 B.C. to the Communist Revolution, this meat grinder has never ceased to pulverize the spirit and flesh of the Chinese people.

Peng Baishan (1910~1968) joined the Party in 1931, joined the New Fourth Army in 1937, and became the head of the propaganda department of the Shanghai Municipal Committee of the Chinese Communist Party (CCP) in 1952. He was later labeled a Hu Feng counter-revolutionary and died tragically during the Cultural Revolution. Film director and author Peng Xiaolian (June 26, 1953 ~ June 19, 2019) recorded her father Peng Baishan's words in her article After My Father's Accident: "The War of Liberation was just a few years ago, and it's still fresh in my mind. Under the command of General Su Yu, I fought with Commander Pi in the Huaihai Campaign and crossed the Yangtze River. But in the blink of an eye, the guns have turned on me. In this last quiet shout, you can hear his rage at the injustice of his circumstance, but, beyond that, you can sense his voice getting lower and lower, until it finally falls silent. He said no more. He said nothing. He gradually realized that no one could save him. No one could speak. Even his legendary former commander, the brilliant General Su Yu, at this moment, must remain silent. Perhaps in the last days of his life, Pang Baishan realized that "revolution is a meat grinder."

1. The British Glorious Revolution

To trace the origin of modern revolutions, we must start with the "Glorious Revolution" in 1688. At the start of the 17th century, England was ruled by the Stuart dynasty. This changed during the tumultuously eventful two decades encompassing the Civil Wars, Commonwealth, and Protectorate (1642~1659), but in 1660 the Restoration returned the Stuarts to the monarchy. While not absolute, the English throne still wielded substantial political power, though it did so amid continuing constitutional and religious tensions—until two events in June 1688 precipitated the "Glorious Revolution." The first was the Seven Bishops' Incident, and the second was the birth of James Francis Edward Stuart, heir apparent to his father, King James II. The Seven Bishops' Incident occurred when James II ordered the Church of England's chaplains to read the Declaration of Indulgence from their pulpits, granting religious freedom and tolerance to Catholics and non-Anglican Protestants. This was seen by much of the country as at best a slap in the face of the Anglican Church and at worst the latest and most unabashed step on the path to restoring Roman Catholicism as England's official religion and transferring the levers of power to a Catholic dynasty aligned with France. Seven bishops of the Church of England petitioned the King, requesting exemptions, and James II had them all arrested. The second event that same month was the birth of King James II's son, James Edward Stuart, Prince of Wales and heir to the throne, which gave the current king a clear successor who, it could be reasonably assumed, would carry on his father's approach to English religion and politics.

Together, these two events initiated a political crisis in England that resulted in what became known almost immediately after it had occurred as The Glorious Revolution. With the majority of English society at large fearing a return of Catholic power and potential civil strife or even renewed civil war, the ruling class reached out to King James II's daughter, Mary, and her husband, the Dutch ruler, Prince William III of Orange, offering to depose James and enthrone William as the next King of England—and William and Mary accepted the offer.

On November 15, 1688, William's army landed in England with little resistance. James had so alienated himself that his council, his daughters, and his army generals all defected to William. James himself appeared to be weak and without judgment at this time. Since the tide had turned, he threw everything away and fled to France. By fleeing, James in effect deposed himself. The throne of England was changed with relatively little death and destruction, so the English people took pride in the event and called it the "Glorious Revolution"—a name which emphasized its honorable, largely bloodless, and successful nature.

The Glorious Revolution of 1688 marked a pivotal moment in history—a largely peaceful transfer of political power at the national level and a constitutional realignment and shift in national governance (the new king was invited to take the throne, replacing the old king, by Parliament, which represented the people). It's true, there were a few skirmishes in England, the Battle of the Boyne (July 11, 1690) and the Williamite War (March 1689 ~ October 1691) in Ireland, and the of Jacobite Risings and Rebellions in Scotland, but those conflicts represented post-facto resistance to the Revolution, not parts of the event itself—which remains far less violent than any comparable national political upheaval in Europe up until that time, and most since. And though the Glorious Revolution was driven by social, political, and religious dynamics, its aftermath established the foundations for a true constitutional monarchy, wherein parliamentary authority surpassed that of the monarch. The subsequent solidification of the two-party system in the United Kingdom post-1688 reverberated not only throughout British history but also left an indelible mark on the political landscapes of many European nations and the United States. In 1689, the passage of the Bill of Rights by the British Parliament curtailed the monarch's powers, laying the foundation for a constitutional government where the monarch reigned but did not rule, gradually transferring administrative authority from the monarch to the parliament. Towards the end of the 19th century, as Chinese reformers advocated for change, they often looked to the British democratic political system as a model worth emulating.

Queen Elizabeth II passed away on September 8, 2022, at Balmoral Castle in Scotland. On September 11th, her casket was transferred from Balmoral Castle to the Palace of Holyrood Palace. I was aboard a cruise ship when the Queen's procession crossed the bridge into Edinburgh. The following day, September 12th, saw Elizabeth II's coffin make its way along the Royal Mile in the Old Town, from Holyrood Palace to St. Giles' Cathedral, where the ceremony unfolded. At 10:00 a.m., I joined the throngs lining the Royal Mile, amid a sea of British flags, awaiting the funeral procession. As the Queen's coffin and four of her children passed by, mere meters away, I sensed a profound affection from the crowd—not just for the Queen as an individual, but for the British system itself. This system, rooted in the covenant of the Glorious Revolution of 1688, has endured for over three centuries. The Crown and the people of the

United Kingdom have honored this compact to the present day. This enduring commitment has provided stability, enabling the maintenance of law and order, and fostering peace and prosperity for the populace.

2. French Revolution

The peaceful transition from monarchy to constitutional government in Britain was facilitated by the presence of a parliament comprising landowners with bourgeois characteristics, aligning it with democratic ideals. Unlike Britain, where an elite upper class composed of both aristocracy and bourgeoisie acted as a counterbalance to monarchical absolutism, the French monarchy effectively neutralized such opposition. Consequently, when revolution erupted, curtailing monarchical power proved ineffective, leaving the elimination of monarchy as the sole viable solution. This marked a stark contrast to the Glorious Revolution in England. In this context, the French monarchy, as noted by the French thinker and historian Alexis-Charles-Henri Clérel de Tocqueville (1805~1859), became its own gravedigger.

During Louis XIV's fifty-four-year reign (1661~1715), the consolidation of royal authority reached its zenith. Politically, Louis XIV concentrated all power in his own hands, famously declaring, "I am the state." He pursued an authoritarian approach toward the nobility, curtailed the High Court of Paris's authority to critique royal decrees, and dismissed the need for convening the king's councils. Louis XIV established a baroque autocracy in France, with himself at its core. In the latter years of his reign, extensive military campaigns depleted the French treasury, plunging the economy into debt and near-bankruptcy. Consequently, he resorted to increasing tax burdens on peasants. According to Tocqueville, heavy taxation, along with Louis XIV's weakening of noble power and the disenchantment of politically disenfranchised citizens, constituted the political, social, and economic catalysts for the French Revolution of 1789.

Louis outlived both his son and his oldest grandson, so it was his great-grandson who ascended the throne as Louis XV. Throughout Louis

XV's reign (1715~1774), public dissatisfaction with the monarchy grew, leading to persistent criticism of the king's rule. This discontent helped fuel the Enlightenment Movement, which produced influential thinkers such as Voltaire (1694~1778), Montesquieu (1689~1755), Rousseau (1712~1778), and Diderot (1713~1784), whose ideas promoting natural human rights, constitutional monarchy, the separation of powers, and the sovereignty of the people gained momentum. Before the revolution, French society was divided into three classes: the First Estate (the clergy), the Second Estate (the nobility), and the Third Estate (the commoners).

On May 5, 1789, King Louis XVI (August 23, 1754 ~ January 21, 1793) convened a meeting of the estates at the Palace of Versailles, seeking to impose increased taxes on the third estate to address the government's financial crisis. The third estate delegates rejected this proposal, deeming it unlawful. Instead, they demanded a constitution to curb the king's power and implement reforms. Confronted with escalating social tensions, Louis XVI expected the Estates-General (a national assembly) to address the issue. The third estate narrowly won the vote by 17 votes, Louis XVI reneged on his promise and insisted on imposing taxes. On June 17, 1789, the third estate deputies proclaimed the establishment of a parliament and asserted that the king lacked the authority to veto the National Assembly's resolutions. The National Assembly, renamed the Constituent Assembly on July 9, called for a constitution to limit the king's powers. Recognizing the threat to his authority, Louis XVI dissolved the National Assembly, declared it illegal, and invalidated all its resolutions. He then mobilized his army in an effort to disband the Assembly and arrest its representatives. News of these actions sparked outrage in Paris, leading to the eruption of a long-simmering revolution.

In the eastern part of Paris, there was the Bastille Square. The Bastille was 100 feet high, with thick walls and eight towers. Fifteen cannons were mounted on it, and hundreds of barrels of gunpowder and countless shells were piled up beside the cannons. More than twice as tall as most buildings in Paris, it looked down on the city like a bird of prey circling above. Most of the famous figures who dared to oppose the monarchy were imprisoned here, including Voltaire twice. On July 14, 1789, the Bastille, a symbol of French autocracy, was conquered by the crowd, a date which later became a national holiday in France. On December 2, 1792, Maximilien de Robespierre (May 6, 1758 ~ July 28, 1794), the supreme leader of the Jacobin Dictatorship of the French Revolution, delivered a famous speech at the National Assembly, "Opinions on the Sentencing of Louis XVI," in which he argued that since the Revolution essentially concerned the sovereignty of the people, a Revolution could not coexist with a king, and thus, he reached his famous conclusion that Louis must die, so that the Revolution could live. On January 21, 1793, in the Place de la Révolution in Paris, Louis XVI was executed by a guillotine of his own design. On that day, Louis XVI was first dragged out and paraded, then tied up and laid flat on the guillotine. At this time, Louis XVI did not behave as his usual cowardly self but instead showed the majesty of a king. According to Alexandre Dumas's account, the king looked solemn and not the least bit timid, which was in no way in line with his widely publicized insecure and withdrawn character. In the final moments, Louis XVI changed his clothes without fuss and said goodbye to the crowd. He shouted to the gathered French people: "I die innocent of all the crimes of which I have been charged. I pardon those who brought about my death, and I pray that the blood you are about to shed may never be required of France…" The audience, numbering over 20,000, was silent. Louis XVI was then executed.

Nine months later, Queen Marie Antoinette (November 2, 1755 ~ October 16, 1793) was also guillotined. Even before her execution, the queen showed great grace and kindness. Her last words for her children, who would soon be orphans, were: "Never take revenge for what has been done to us." She asked God to forgive her and all her enemies. Early that morning, the queen changed into a clean white dress, tied her hands behind her back, and rode to the execution ground in a prison carriage. Before lying down on the execution platform, the queen accidentally stepped on the shoes of the executioner, and she whispered, with a small, dignified bow, "Pardon me, sir, I didn't mean to." Those were her last words. Then she fell to the guillotine. After the beheading, a man bent down with a basin to catch the flow of blood from the top of the queen's neck; the executioner held up the queen's severed head and displayed it to the crowd. Cruelty in human nature is ubiquitous and does not discriminate based on social class; often, the lower the class, the more barbaric the methods employed. Throughout European history, three kings faced execution: Charles I (King of England, executed in 1649 after the English Civil War), Louis XVI (King of France, executed in 1793 during the French Revolution), and Nicholas II (Emperor of the Russian Empire, executed by the Soviet government in 1918).

Louis XVI's youngest child was a son, Louis-Charles, had already been in prison for one year when he was separated from his mother, Marie Antoinette, and placed into solitary confinement at age eight. His older brother Louis-Joseph had died of tuberculosis 40 days before the storming of the Bastille. Now, with his father also dead, he was de facto King of France, and many Jacobins considered him a direct threat to the Revolutionary Republican government. He was ordered to undergo "Republican Reeducation," which consisted of being isolated and psychologically abused. This abuse also included being encouraged—and sometimes even forced—to consume alcohol at age eight. Then he was coached and pressured into signing false statements accusing his mother of incest. The statements were used to add the charge of incest against his mother, Marie Antoinette, when she was tried by the Revolutionary Tribunal, operating under the government of the National Convention. At her two-day trial, the dethroned Queen of France argued so convincingly against the obviously false charge that the prosecutors ended up dropping it. Nonetheless, she was convicted of high treason for "conspiring with foreign governments against the people of France" and executed, as noted above. Her now orphaned son, Louis-Charles, continued to suffer alone in prison, with virtually no human contact and a complete lack of medical care. This went on until the fall of Robespierre, the self-styled "Incorruptible Messiah of Virtue" and author of the most extreme crimes of "The Terror," the most extreme era in post-Revolution France. But when officials finally came to inspect the now nine-year-old

Louis-Charles, it was too late. They found him severely malnourished, physically stunted, and covered in sores. He was likely suffering from tuberculosis, worsened by neglect. Despite diligent medical attention, Louis-Charles died less than a year later, on June 8, 1795, at age ten.

His older sister, Marie-Therese Charlotte, fared slightly better at the hands of revolutionary France, but not much. She inherited her mother, Marie Antoinette's beauty, earning her the moniker, "the Rose of France." Marie spent her childhood in the Palace of Versailles, sheltered from the hardships of life. But at the tender age of fifteen, she was arrested and imprisoned with the rest of her family in the Temple Tower (a massive Medieval keep built in the late 13th Century for the Knights Templar) by revolutionaries, forever altering her fate. Following her father's execution, she was isolated and subjected to callous interrogations. She was intimidated, threatened, and psychologically abused. Her jailers also tried to extract corroborative testimony from her regarding the false accusation of her mother having committed incest with her little brother, but she held fast and refused. After her mother's execution, she endured a mercilessly prolonged solitary confinement, until—on the eve of her seventeenth birthday—she was finally released and transferred to the custody of the Habsburg Monarchy in Austria (her mother's family) in exchange for French prisoners held by the Austrians.

After the fall of the Bourbon Dynasty, the revolutionaries established the First French Republic (1792~1804), with the highest authority known as the "National Convention," presided over by the aforementioned brilliant lawyer-turned-radical revolutionary leader, Maximilien Robespierre. But despite the appearance of solidity, the First French Republic was rife with factions, each advocating different political views, leading to sharp conflicts. Robespierre led the Jacobin Faction, and his dictatorial rule became known as the "Jacobin Dictatorship" or the "Reign of Terror." On April 5, 1794, Robespierre, along with his supporters, guillotined 35-year-old Georges Danton, a fellow Jacobin with differing political views. The notorious Law of 22 Prairial (the 10th of June in the second year of the Republic) dramatically intensified the terror. In the eight months before the decree, Paris was already witnessing an average of 32 executions per week. However, between the decree and Robespierre's subsequent fall on July 27, the weekly executions skyrocketed to a horrifying 196. The proportion of the former "Aristocrat" classes among those executed was already very small, amounting to only 16.5% of the dead in June, and dropping to 5% in July. The rest were the bourgeoisie, the military, the officials, and especially the underclass, who accounted for more than 40% of the sans culottes or "men without breeches" – the popular contemporary term for the common people of France. Robespierre's brutal suppression of dissident revolutionaries and political factions blatantly violated the principles enshrined in the Declaration of Human Rights and contradicted the democratic ideals he professed. On July 27, 1794 (the 9th day of the month of Thermidor in the second year of the Republic according to the new French calendar), the Thermidorian Reaction culminated in the overthrow of Robespierre by the Thermidorianists. Having staunchly advocated for the execution of King Louis XVI, Robespierre himself met the same fate at the guillotine a year later, executed by his former comrades in the revolution.

On November 9, 1799 (the 18th day of Brumaire in the year VIII of the Republic), Napoleon Bonaparte (August 15, 1769 ~ May 5, 1821) orchestrated a coup d'état, overthrowing the Directory's rule and seizing power as one-third of the trio that then formed the Consulate government, with him as First Consul. Five years later, on December 2, 1804, he had himself crowned at Notre Dame Cathedral in Paris, assuming the title Emperor of the French and establishing a dictatorship. With Napoleon's ascension to Emperor, the revolutionary era came to an end. In 1814, following Napoleon's first abdication, Louis XVI's younger brother, the Count of Provence, exiled in England, returned to France and assumed the title of King Louis XVIII, with support from anti-Napoleonic allies and elements of Napoleon's former army. Louis XVIII (Louis-Stanislas-Xavier, November 17, 1755 ~ September 16, 1824) became the seventh monarch of the Bourbon dynasty in France and the first king (1814~1824) after the restoration of the Bourbon dynasty.

Returning to Princess Marie-Thérèse Charlotte, in 1799, while residing with her extended royal family as guests of the Tsar of Russia in modern-day Latvia, she married—at the strong urging of her uncle, Louis XVIII, the King of France in exile—her first cousin, Louis-Antoine, Duke of Angoulême. More than a decade later, Marie-Thérèse became pregnant for the first and only time, but tragically lost the child by miscarriage. When Napoleon abdicated in 1814, she returned with the restored Royal Family to France and spent time visiting the sites where her parents and little brother, Louis Charles, had died. She saw to the exhuming of the King and Queen's bodies from the cemetery where many victims of the revolution's guillotine had been hastily buried, and their reinternment in the Basilica of Saint Denis, the royal cemetery of France, on January 21, 1815—the 22nd anniversary of her father's execution.

Two months later, Charlotte was in Bordeaux when Napoleon Bonaparte returned to France, quickly raised an army, and took control of much of the country. While her uncle, the king, fled Paris for Belgium, she refused to leave Bordeaux and convinced the army garrison there to defend her, though they refused to march out and start a civil war with Napoleon's troops. When Napoleon's troops arrived with orders to arrest her, believing her cause lost, she agreed to leave, sparing the city needless death and destruction. Her conduct at Bordeaux impressed even her enemies, as Napoleon himself was said to have remarked that she alone of all the Bourbons showed resolve. After Napoleon's second, final, defeat, Charlotte returned to Paris and is recorded on multiple occasions of intervening to urge clemency on tribunals pronouncing sentence upon individuals who had been directly or indirectly involved in her harsh captivity and mistreatment.

Almost all those who pursued radical social change after 1789—from Marx and Engels to Karl Liebknecht (August 13, 1871 ~ January 15, 1919) to Lenin and Stalin—consciously invoked the French Revolution as their inspiration. They proudly identified themselves as its heirs, imbuing the term "revolution" with positive connotations. However, what were the outcomes of the French Revolution? Following Louis XVI's execution in 1793, France witnessed Napoleon's rise to power, followed by a tumultuous period of civil unrest and warfare. After paying a heavy toll in human lives, France circled back to the Bourbons in 1814, embracing authoritarian rule once more. The French Revolution succeeded due to a widespread wave of popular uprisings. However, these popular revolts failed to dismantle autocracy; instead, they merely replaced the king's autocracy with a new form. The revolution's fundamental flaw lay in its lack of compromise and tolerance. Marked by inflexibility and exclusion, even fellow revolutionaries resorted to violence when disagreements arose. This internal discord intensified, leading to extreme measures and ultimately resulting in the guillotine becoming the Revolution's enduring symbol.

In the spring of 1994, I made my inaugural journey to France. On a damp morning, I ventured to Père Lachaise Cemetery in the 20th arrondissement of Paris. It stands as the premier garden cemetery in the city, sprawling across an expanse exceeding 430,000 square meters. Nestled within the cemetery's 76th division, in the northeast corner of Père Lachaise Cemetery, lies a weathered gray brick wall. Bullet holes mar its surface, telling a tale of strife and struggle. Adorning this wall is a solemn gray-white marble slab, bearing three elegantly simple lines in gilded French: "AUX MORTS DE LA COMMUNE—21-28 MAI 1871" (To the Dead of the Commune, 21-28 May, 1871). This is the renowned Wall of the Communards. The Communards were mostly Parisian National Guardsmen, along with workers and radical republicans who, in the immediate aftermath of France's shocking defeat in the Franco-Prussian War, took up arms to resist the authority of the newly-formed Third Republic's government at Versailles, which they saw as conservative, illegitimate, and hostile to social reform and "true republicanism."

From March to May 1871, the Paris Commune governed the capital before being crushed during the "Bloody Week," culminating in mass summary executions by government troops of any Communard captured with a weapon. The last such battlefield execution took place at the cemetery wall. Here, 166 Communards (19 officers and 147 men) met their demise, marking the end of what the Marxists, Socialists, and

Communists would celebrate as the first attempt in history by the working class to directly seize state power. As a brief yet tragic revolutionary experiment, it lasted only seventy-two days (March 18 ~ May 28, 1871) and resulted in the death of 15,000 to 20,000 mostly Communards but also civilians and government troops.

Two days after the fall of the Commune, on May 30, 1871, Karl Marx gave his address, later published as a pamphlet titled "On the Civil War in France," to the General Council of the International Workingmen's Association (also known as the First International) in London. In it, he praised virtually all radical actions taken by the Commune while it ruled Paris, including shutting down Catholic churches and banning public religious instruction; transferring control of workshops and factories from owners and operators to workmen; and the execution of the Archbishop of Paris, Georges Darboy, together with approximately 60 to 100 other hostages, mostly police and priests. Twenty years later, in his introduction to the new edition commemorating the 20th anniversary of the Commune, Marx's fellow radical theorist and co-author of "The Communist Manifesto," Friedrich Engels, wrote: "*Of late, the Social-Democratic philistine has once more been filled with wholesome terror at the words: Dictatorship of the Proletariat. Well and good, gentlemen, do you want to know what this dictatorship looks like? Look at the Paris Commune. That was the Dictatorship of the Proletariat.*" How sadly right the future would prove him to be.

3. Soviet Union

The ideal of communism necessitates societal equality, envisioning a world devoid of class distinctions where every individual is on equal footing. Its origins trace back to ancient Greece, notably articulated in "The Republic" by the ancient Greek philosopher Plato (428 BC ~ 347 BC). Despite sporadic efforts throughout history to realize this ideal, the first large-scale experiment unfolded in Russia from 1917 to 1991.

On February 18 (*on the Old Style Julian calendar then in use in Russia/March 3 on the New Style Gregorian calendar used by the rest of Europe*),

Russian industrial workers initiated strikes due to food shortages and deteriorating factory conditions. Subsequently, unrest spread across the country, culminating in a democratic revolution that saw the spontaneous overthrow of tsarist autocracy. The February Revolution of 1917 led to Tsar Nicholas II's abdication, followed by the establishment of a provisional government led by those favoring a "Bourgeois Revolution" to put Russia on a path towards Western constitutional democracy, allied with members of the "Soviets" (workers councils) who favored socialism. Lenin, then in Swiss exile, endeavored to return to Russia immediately, but the ongoing World War posed significant obstacles, as travel through enemy territories was perilous. On April 3, 1917, Lenin and fellow political exiles received assistance from the German Foreign Office and Military Intelligence, facilitating their return to Petrograd via Germany. Lenin had formulated a socialist coup plan in Switzerland, which garnered staunch support from Kaiser Wilhelm II and the German General Staff. Recognizing Lenin's potential to destabilize Russia, the Kaiser permitted his passage through Germany en route to Sweden and then Finland, eventually enabling his return to Russia. As early as 1915, Lenin had begun receiving funding from German authorities, totaling 26 million marks by the end of 1917 alone. Relying on German support, Lenin clandestinely mobilized his organization, procured weaponry, organized armed forces, and orchestrated his return to Russia, buoyed by a substantial financial backing of 50 million gold marks (equivalent to over 9 tons of gold). The October Coup of November 7, 1917 (October 25 in the Julian calendar), saw the overthrow of the Russian Provisional Government and the establishment of the Soviet regime. In 1918, Lenin negotiated peace with Germany, resulting in the Treaty of Brest-Litovsk, which entailed significant territorial concessions in Russia and Ukraine. These lands were ceded permanently per the terms of the treaty. However, the tides turned later in World War I, leading to the collapse of the German army and the unexpected return of these territories to Russia. Lenin's revolution undoubtedly relied on support from hostile foreign powers. Despite Tsar Nicholas II's relatively lenient treatment of Lenin (during his time as a political prisoner in Siberia, he was never tortured or even forced to perform physical labor, and during his time as a political exile abroad, he was never targeted for assassination), Lenin ordered the brutal execution of Tsar Nicholas and his entire family.

Following the "October Revolution," Lenin swiftly advocated for the convening of elections to establish a Constituent Assembly. However, the election outcome proved disappointing for him, with the Bolsheviks securing only 163 out of 703 seats, rendering them a minority lacking broad support from the Russian populace. Faced with this setback, Lenin resorted to force. In 1918, he illegally dissolved the Constituent Assembly, sparking widespread opposition among workers. Demonstrations erupted in Petrograd and Moscow, drawing tens of thousands of participants. Bolshevik troops quelled these peaceful protests with gunfire, staining the streets with the blood of workers. The All-Russian Railways, Russia's largest industrial union, declared a political strike in protest of the assembly's dissolution, garnering support from numerous other unions. Yet, the Soviet Communist Party brutally suppressed the strike, banning non-Bolshevik-controlled unions and employing force to quash dissent. Throughout the spring of 1919, workers staged multiple strikes across Russian cities, demanding equitable food rations, an end to communist privileges, freedom of expression, and fair elections. These protests were met with ruthless repression by the Cheka (the first version of Soviet secret police), marked by arbitrary arrests and deadly shootings.

In the summer of 1918, Russia faced a severe food shortage amid the civil war. To address this pressing issue, Lenin dispatched Stalin to the city of Tsaritsyn in the Volga Valley, a region traditionally known as Russia's breadbasket. Faced with reluctance from farmers to sell grain to the government at low prices, the authorities resorted to forceful seizure. The new Soviet government in Moscow armed unemployed urban residents, forming a formidable grain collection force tasked with procuring the so-called "surplus grain" from various locales. This was one of many ruthless policies officially adopted under Lenin's direction during the Russian Civil War, which he would later refer to collectively as "War Communism." These included but were not limited to: criminal arrest and punishment, including execution based on class membership alone;

the creation of labor camps; forced deportation; hostage-taking; the sanctioning of extra-judicial execution; the rejection of legal restraint as a principle; and the violent seizure of grain. But the measures Stalin pursued during his pursuit of grain in Tsaritsyn from late May 1918 to early February 1919 escalated the violence even further, up to and including the mass executions of multiple categories of the population, including large numbers of peasants, members of the Cossack ethnic minority, captured White Russian officers and soldiers, merchants accused of "speculating" to profit from the Red Army.

One year later in 1920, in Tambov Province—another of Russia's richest agricultural regions—over 50,000 farmers organized a self-defense force to resist forced grain requisition and engaged in armed conflict with more than 100,000 Red Army troops under the command of the notably young and bold General Mikhail Tukhachevsky, only 27 at the time, who rose to fame in the Western press as the "Red Napoleon." Even under the arguably brilliant leadership of Tukhachevsky, the fighting dragged on until June 1921, when Leon Trotsky, the Soviet "Commissar of War," instructed Tukhachevsky to employ poison gas and incendiary tactics, transforming vast swathes of Tambov into uninhabitable zones. During the suppression of the peasant uprising in Tambov Province, the lowest estimates are 50,000 peasants killed, 50,000 peasants imprisoned, and 20,000 peasants exiled. With an overall population at the time of 2.5 to 3 million people, meaning a minimum of almost 5% of the population was permanently removed from the province one way or another. It's worth noting that both the Red Napoleon, Tukhachevsky, and the "War Commissar" Trotsky ended up dead at the orders of their old comrade Stalin. Tukhachevsky was executed by a firing squad in Moscow during the Great Purge in 1937, while Trotsky was assassinated in Mexico City in 1940 by the NKVD (Soviet secret police successor to the Cheka), the secret police.

On September 5, 1918, Lenin issued the directive to establish the first special labor camp on the Solovetsky Islands, a grim facility intended for the imprisonment, torture, and execution of political dissidents and opponents of the fledgling Soviet regime, particularly those who resisted the October coup. Subsequently, the Soviet Communist Party constructed additional labor camps across various locations, laying the groundwork for the infamous Gulag Archipelago that came to define Stalin's era. "Gulag" is an acronym for "Main Administration of Corrective Labor Camps" in Russian. Throughout Stalin's reign, amidst relentless purges and intensified state repression, the proliferation of "Gulags" expanded across the Soviet Union. By the time of Stalin's death in 1953, the Gulag system had reached its zenith, with 170 camps scattered across the nation, resembling an "archipelago" of suffering. Renowned Russian Nobel laureate Aleksandr Isayevich Solzhenitsyn (December 11, 1918 ~ August 3, 2008) himself fell victim to this brutal regime, serving an eight-year sentence for daring to criticize Stalin. In 1973, he published "The Gulag Archipelago" in Paris, a harrowing exposé depicting the appalling conditions within the labor camps. Solzhenitsyn meticulously cataloged 31 torture methods employed, ranging from psychological torment to physical annihilation, all employed to extract confessions. The relentless use of multiple punishments simultaneously by the secret police sapped prisoners of their physical vigor and shattered their mental resilience, ensuring compliance. Within the labor camps, inmates endured starvation, inadequate clothing, and had to perform high-intensity physical labor for twelve to sixteen hours a day in the ice and snow. Violent deaths were tragically commonplace. Many entire families were sent to the Gulag. Some husbands served prison terms, and their wives were exiled. Even 80-year-olds were not spared. Victims of the Gulag spanned the spectrum from high-ranking party officials and military leaders to ordinary citizens, religious figures, professionals, and laborers, encompassing all facets of society. Conservative estimates suggest that over 500,000 prisoners perished in Soviet labor camps between 1930 and 1940 alone.

The Gulag system was finally done away with in 1960. Russian state media outlets revealed in 2013 that over 15 million individuals had been sentenced to Gulag camps, with more than 1.5 million dying before release. While the creation of concentration camps is generally ascribed to Nazi Germany, Soviet Russia's labor camps not only served as a blueprint for similar institutions in other communist regimes but also attracted the interest of Hitler, who dispatched the Gestapo to study and emulate the Soviet model.

In the Soviet Union, domestic policies were marked by ruthless authoritarianism, resulting in widespread suffering and abnormal deaths for tens of millions of Soviet citizens through events like the Great Purge, Great Famine, and Great Suppression. In the treatment of its own general population, as opposed to ethnic/religious minority "others," the Soviet Union's level of cruelty surpassed that of Nazi Germany, Fascist Italy, and Imperial Japan. From 1927 to 1928, Stalin forcibly implemented the collective farm movement, targeting Ukrainian peasants who were often labeled as kulaks—overly-prosperous "exploitive" peasants—and relocated to Siberia and other regions. On one front, the state enforced compulsory expropriation, seizing grain and food from rural areas and exporting it in exchange for Western machinery and equipment to fuel Soviet industrialization. Concurrently, the government enacted stringent measures to eliminate affluent peasants, triggering widespread dissatisfaction among farmers. Many chose to slaughter and sell their livestock rather than join collective farms, leading to a decline in agricultural output and grain shortages. Data from the Soviet Union's agricultural collectivization period (1928~1934) revealed a 7.8% drop in total cereal output, juxtaposed with a staggering 150% increase in state purchases during the same period. This dire situation culminated in severe famine across regions such as Ukraine, the North Caucasus, the Volga region, Kazakhstan, and Siberia. In the winter of 1932~1933, despite crop failures in Ukraine, the party zealously seized grain from farmers for export, utilizing the military to prevent escape. The Soviet Union's grain exports to Europe peaked during this time, even as millions faced starvation. Resistance was met with harsh reprisals, and numerous incidents of cannibalism and "ethnic cleansing by starvation" occurred. It's estimated that six to seven million people perished in this man-made catastrophe. From the Soviet Union to China and now North Korea, famine remains a tragic hallmark of communist history, forever intertwined with the trajectory of the communist movement.

In the 1930s, the Soviet Union initiated the "Great Purge," a ruthless campaign targeting perceived "enemies of the people" within its ranks. The human toll of this purge is staggering, with at least 700,000 individuals falling victim to it. According to Professor Xu Tianxin of Peking University, in his article "The Great Purge of the Soviet Union in the 1930s," an alarming 1,108 out of the 1,966 delegates who attended the 17th Congress of the Communist Party of the Soviet Union (Bolsheviks) were arrested on charges of counter-revolutionary crimes. Similarly, out of the 139 Central Committee members and alternate members elected at the congress, a staggering 80% were arrested and subsequently executed. Stalin's grip on power was ruthless, as evidenced by the fate of the highest echelons of the Soviet leadership. Among the last seven members of the Politburo during Lenin's lifetime, Stalin orchestrated the execution of the other five, leaving only Lenin untouched. Between 1919 and 1935, 31 members of the Politburo were elected, of whom 20 met a grim end. The Red Army also bore the brunt of this purge. Notable casualties included three of the five Soviet marshals, fifteen out of sixteen group army commanders and deputy commanders, sixty out of sixty-seven army commanders, and 199 division commanders. Additionally, all four senior Air Force generals, all six Navy admirals, and nine out of fifteen Navy lieutenant generals faced persecution. A staggering 35,000 military officers, out of 80,000, were subjected to various forms of persecution ranging from expulsion from the army to death sentences.

The Great Purge spared no social class, but   intellectuals, farmers, clergy, technical professionals, and ethnic minorities   bore the brunt of Stalin's ruthless policies. The targeting of intellectual, religious, technological, educational, academic, literary, and artistic circles took precedence over even the military and political spheres. From 1937 to 1938, nearly all churches were shuttered, dealing a devastating blow to pastors and clergy. A staggering 165,200 clergy members were arrested for practicing their faith, with 106,800 of them executed by firing squad. During the height of the Great Terror, from 1937 to 1938, the Soviet secret police arrested 1,548,366 individuals suspected of "anti-Soviet activities," resulting in the execution of 681,692 people, making up just over 44% of those arrested—an average of 1,000 executions per day. Those fortunate enough to survive often faced harsh sentences, condemned to toil in labor camps. To put this in perspective, during the eighty-five years from 1825 to 1910 under the tsarist regime, only 3,932 political prisoners were sentenced to death in Russia. By 1941, when Nazi Germany invaded the Soviet Union, there were a staggering 2.35 million prisoners held in Soviet concentration camps. On the eve of the Soviet Union's dissolution in June 1991, Chairman of the Soviet KGB Nikolai Vasilyevich Kryuchkov (1924~2007) announced that approximately 4.2 million people had been suppressed by the Soviet regime from 1920 to 1953, with over 2 million of them targeted during the infamous "Great Purge" of 1937~1938. However, Alexander Nikolayevich Yakovlev (December 2, 1923 ~ October 18, 2005), who led Boris Yeltsin's commission for the rehabilitation of victims of Soviet political repression, suggested a much higher figure. In a 2000 interview with reporters, Yakovlev estimated that Stalin's suppression had affected around 20 million people, if not more.

On August 23, 1939, Vyacheslav Molotov, the Soviet Union's People's Commissar for Foreign Affairs, signed the Non-Aggression Pact with Joachim von Ribbentrop, the Foreign Minister of Nazi Germany. Numerous historical records suggest that the start of World War II in Europe was instigated through a collaboration between Stalin and Hitler. In the early stages of the conflict, both leaders engaged in a symbiotic relationship, leveraging each other's strengths. There were instances of cooperation between the Soviet Union and Nazi Germany, including joint military parades under the Nazi flag. The Soviet Union's complicity extended to deporting Jews to Nazi-controlled territories and collaborating with Germany to partition Poland. Stalin even granted the Nazis access to a naval base near Murmansk, facilitating Hitler's subsequent invasion of Norway. In December 1939, Soviet and Nazi officers convened to discuss the war's progress, expressing mutual satisfaction and optimistic projections for the future. Soviet Prime Minister Molotov's visit to Berlin to discuss postwar arrangements further underscores this collaboration, with other Soviet delegates being entertained by Goebbels. Moreover, the Soviet Union served as a crucial resource supplier to the Nazi war machine, providing significant quantities of oil, iron ore, building materials, and grain to sustain the German army. One of the most chilling episodes of Soviet complicity was the Katyn massacre, where 21,768 Polish prisoners of war, comprising Poland's military and technological elite, were executed between April and May 1940 in the Katyn Forest near Smolensk, Russia. Although Soviet officials vehemently denied involvement, in 1989, Soviet scholars confirmed Joseph Stalin's orchestration of the massacre. Subsequently, in 1990, General Secretary Mikhail Gorbachev acknowledged the Soviet People's Commissariat for Internal Affairs (NKVD)'s responsibility for the atrocity. The Katyn massacre marked the first large-scale atrocity of World War II, with the Nazis later following suit in their own atrocities.

The ideologies of Nazism and Communism share common roots, both advocating for the ruthless elimination of human lives in pursuit of creating an ideal society. While the Nazis focused on race, considering their self-styled "Aryan" nation superior and seeking to eradicate "inferior" nations like the Jewish people, the Soviet Union centered its ideology on class struggle, believing in the violent elimination of opposing classes within a class-based society. Both doctrines espouse cruelty, emerging from a similar mold evident in their propaganda, methods, and conduct. The similarities between Nazi and Soviet propaganda posters are striking, blurring the lines between originality and imitation. Similarly, military parades in both regimes featured uniformity and precision, with the resounding sound of boots striking the ground evoking equal measures of fear. In fact, in Asia, we are not unfamiliar with these. The military parades in Beijing and Pyongyang always echo the same voices as those of the Nazi Soviet Union.

In the summer of 2006, my family and I embarked on a two-week journey to Russia, and I revisited St. Petersburg in 2012. During our visit, we observed that Lenin and Stalin had been pulled down from the altar by the government and the people. In the garden outside of Moscow's famous red brick city walls, Lenin and Stalin, played by clowns, solicited tourists to take photos. One of the highlights of our trip was exploring Moscow's Novodevichy Cemetery, the resting place of over 27,000 prominent figures, including poets, writers, musicians, political leaders, and scientists. Among the notable graves, we first encountered Anton Chekhov's (1860~1904) tomb. Not far from the tomb of Wang Ming (Van Miny, May 23, 1904 ~ March 27, 1974), an early leader of the Chinese Communist Party, was the resting site of Nikita Khrushchev (April 15, 1894 ~ September 11, 1971). Khrushchev's black and white tombstone seemingly offered an impartial assessment of his achievements and shortcomings. Subsequently, Boris Yeltsin (February 1, 1931 ~ April 23, 2007) and Mikhail Gorbachev (March 2, 1931 ~ August 30, 2022) were also laid to rest here.

Venturing 50 to 200 kilometers northeast of Moscow, we explored the "Golden Ring," a collection of eight ancient towns renowned for their historical significance. These towns, adorned with majestic landmarks such as the Kremlin, monasteries, and onion-domed cathedrals, exude the timeless charm of Russian architecture spanning from the 12th to the 18th century. Surrounded by picturesque countryside, these towns captivated us with their serene beauty. Our journey also led us to Yasnaya Polyana (Bright Glade), the former estate of the renowned writer Leo Tolstoy. It is located 12 kilometers southwest of the town of Tula and 200 kilometers from Moscow. Tolstoy lived and died here and penned his masterpieces "War and Peace" and "Anna Karenina" in this house. The Yasnaya Polyana estate covers approximately 1,600 hectares (4,000 acres) of dense virgin forest and a series of four serene ponds. In Tolstoy's day, about 350 farmers lived and worked here. Entering the gate of the manor, a flat avenue of birch trees leads to Tolstoy's former residence. When we visited, countless horses were grazing in the fields on both sides of the road. Tolstoy's grave is tucked away in a peaceful patch of greenery not far behind his former residence.

One night in November 1910, Tolstoy could no longer stand his wife's endless complaints and long-running anger, so he quietly sneaked out of the house alone. The 82-year-old man could not withstand the severe cold of the Russian winter. On November 20, he passed away at a small train station. I can imagine Tolstoy's despair. He ran away from home to die. The travel agency that handled our visa application and accommodated us throughout the entire journey was said to often host ministerial-level diplomatic missions and travel groups. However, after we set off, the driver and tour guide still couldn't figure out the specific location of the manor and took a lot of unnecessary steps. Upon arrival, I found the square before the manor deserted, hinting at a disconnect between modern Russians and their historical heritage.

In St. Petersburg, we explored the Smolny Palace, once a prestigious boarding school for aristocratic girls and later transformed into the headquarters of the Bolshevik Central Committee and the Petrograd Soviet. Trotsky and Lenin directed the October Revolution from here. While Lenin statues are scarce in present-day Russia, one remains prominently displayed in the school's front yard, a reminder of its revolutionary past. Additionally, we visited the Fyodor Mikhailovich Dostoevsky (November 11, 1821 ~ February 9, 1881) Literary Memorial Museum in St. Petersburg, located in the apartment where the acclaimed author lived and created his seminal works. Despite its significance, the museum attracted few visitors, reflecting modern society's rapid pace and dwindling interest in recent history. Perhaps those literary giants of their time were out of touch with the lifestyle and culture of the thousands of serfs on the vast Russian land.

4. Hungary

In 2014, I had the opportunity to visit Budapest for the first time. As the former capital of Austria-Hungary, Budapest's cityscape resonates with the grandeur of imperial architecture, reflecting the rich history of a significant nation. Throughout the Soviet era, Hungary stood out as a beacon of liberalism and fashionability among its satellite counterparts, serving as a gateway for the socialist bloc to the Western world. Today, Hungary's contemplation of its authoritarian past sets it apart from other nations, with the depth of this introspection vividly portrayed in institutions like the House of Terror Museum. Situated at 60 Andrássy Avenue (Andrássy út) in Budapest, the House of Terror Museum occupies a prominent location along this beautiful tree-lined boulevard, often likened to the Champs-Elysées of Budapest. Andrássy Avenue stretches from the wide "Heroes' Square" in the northeast to the iconic St. Stephen's Cathedral in the southwest. The boulevard's northern stretch boasts a collection of foreign embassies and museums housed within classical mansions, while the southern section is adorned with international luxury boutiques. The House of Terror Museum stands as a poignant memorial where narratives of prosperity and tragedy intersect, providing visitors with a somber yet insightful glimpse into Hungary's tumultuous history. Just a 20-minute walk from both Heroes' Square and St. Stephen's Cathedral, it remains a compelling destination for those seeking to delve into the complexities of the past.

The House of Terror Memorial, a three-story edifice, stands as a solemn witness to the harrowing chapters of fascist Nazism and communism, serving as a poignant tribute to the victims of two dark and tumultuous periods in Hungarian history. During the brief tenure of Nazi rule, 60 Andrássy Avenue served as the nerve center for the political police, where the notorious Arrow Cross Party orchestrated sinister plots and subjected detainees to unspeakable torment. After the Soviets "liberated" Hungary, the Hungarian Communist Party repurposed 60 Andrássy Avenue and expanded its footprint by annexing neighboring structures, transforming it into the headquarters of the State Security Service (AVH) and the Soviet government's State Security Service (KGB). Today, the building's facade bears witness to its solemn purpose, adorned with a circular arrangement of white porcelain plates, each bordered in black and bearing the simple portrait of an individual who perished during these tumultuous times. As one strolls along the avenue, these haunting visages silently bear witness to the tragic toll exacted, with many commemorating the volunteers who met their demise at the hands of Soviet forces during the 1956 uprising. In stark contrast to its surroundings, the building's somber gray exterior, accented by a bold black frame, commands attention. Atop the structure, metal plates with

Skeletonized Letters encircle the roof, casting a solemn shadow over the memorial below. Upon entering the museum, visitors are greeted by two marble monuments: a black obelisk on the left adorned with the Arrow Cross emblem symbolizing the Nazis, and a red counterpart on the right featuring a five-pointed star representing the Communist Party. Beneath these intricate symbols, Hungarian inscriptions solemnly declare "In Memory of the Victims of Nazi Terror" and "In Memory of the Victims of Communist Terror," serving as enduring reminders of the atrocities committed and lives lost during Hungary's darkest hours.

Upon stepping through the main entrance of the museum, visitors encounter a diverging tunnel, leading to two distinct exhibition areas. One section meticulously documents the harrowing era of Nazi German rule, while the other vividly portrays the tumultuous aftermath of Soviet dominance over Hungary. While the Nazi puppet regime of Szálasi Ferenc (January 6, 1897 ~ March 12, 1946) endured for only a brief span, the grip of the Hungarian Communist regime endured for four decades, thus commanding a significantly larger portion of the museum's space dedicated to recounting its horrors. As visitors venture into the House of Horrors exhibition, they are greeted by a spacious atrium adorned with a formidable tank stationed below, serving as a stark reminder of the oppressive machinery that once loomed over the populace. Alongside, a solemn wall of black-and-white photographs stands, each frame bearing the faces of victims and the enduring legacies of their shattered families. The museum's narrative unfolds chronologically, guiding visitors through a curated journey, each room offering poignant insights into the tumultuous chapters of Hungary's past.

In the initial room on the second floor, positioned to the right upon entering, a sizable projection screen dominates the space, illuminating the wartime developments of World War II, illustrating Hungary's precarious position amidst adversarial forces. Inside the room, two rows of screens, totaling eight in number, stand back-to-back. The innermost quartet vividly portrays the brutal atrocities committed by German Nazis within Hungarian borders during WWII, while the outer screens depict the relentless onslaught of the Soviet Red Army, capturing scenes of mass killings and the grim aftermath of corpses piled high on hillsides, a haunting tableau of carnage. Echoing through the room, impassioned speeches from Soviet and Nazi commanders resonate, their voices akin to voracious black holes consuming countless lives. Yet, it was the culmination of the exhibition journey that left an indelible mark on my psyche. As visitors congregated in groups, they were ushered into an elevator, its interior adorned with a television screen broadcasting the agonizing torture endured by victims within these very walls. Slowly, the elevator descended, each moment of the descent punctuated by the grim imagery unfolding on screen. As the doors slid open, the chilling sight of the cold execution table greeted us, its presence delivering a visceral shock that lingered long after. The first floor of the basement retains many of the cells from that time, which are eerily dark and narrow. A cell of about 9 square meters in size had to be filled with at least a dozen people, and there were also single-occupancy cells so small that it was difficult to even squat down.

In 1944, following the defeat of the Germans, Hungary fell under Soviet occupation, becoming a satellite state of the Soviet Union. Although Hungary was annexed by the Soviet Union and was no longer free, it never stopped fighting for national liberation. As the victor of the war, the Soviet Union plundered Hungary unscrupulously, which made the people of Hungary suffer, and their safety was not guaranteed. The turning point came in 1956, from October 23 to November 4, when the "Hungarian Spring" uprising erupted. Initially dubbed the 1956 Hungarian Counter-Revolutionary Rebellion by the Soviet Union and its allies on the Eastern Front, it was later renamed the 1956 Hungarian Uprising after the collapse of the Soviet Union. This seminal event marked the first significant challenge to Soviet hegemony in Europe post-World War II. The Hungarian Revolution began with a student protest on October 23rd. The protests began to spread, and thousands of people marched to the parliament building in the center of Budapest. At the same time, some students entered a radio station and demanded that it broadcast their demands. These students were arrested, and when the demonstrators outside the radio station demanded the release of the students, they were attacked by the secret police of the National Security Service inside the building, resulting in many deaths and injuries, and this incident became the spark for the revolution.

As the revolution unfolded, the Hungarian government collapsed, and political prisoners were released. Tens of thousands of Hungarians armed themselves and fought against the secret police and the Soviet army. At the same time, the Hungarian people formed "Workers' Committees" to seize the power of the Hungarian Communist Party and demanded political reforms. To stabilize the situation, Imre Nagy (June 7, 1896 ~ June 16, 1958) formed a new government, dissolved the former Communist Party, and prepared for free elections. On October 30, 1956, the Red Army withdrew from Budapest, the Soviet government expressed its willingness to negotiate the withdrawal of Soviet forces from all of Hungary, and peace was restored.

That same day at Budapest's Köztársaság tér (Republic Square), after a rumor spread that the State Protective Authority's (AVH) secret police had shot anti-communist demonstrators, armed protestors attacked members of the AVH standing guard outside the Hungarian Communist Party headquarters building, killing 20 of them, along with the head of the party's Budapest Committee, Imre Mező. Though the leaders of the Hungarian Revolution condemned the attack and asked the protestors to cease and desist from mob violence, in a matter of hours, news of the incident and images of the dead communists were turned into propaganda all over the Soviet Union. At about the same time as the attack occurred, Prime Minister Nagy met with the Soviet ambassador (and future General Secretary of the U.S.S.R.) Yuri Andropov, and told him that geopolitical neutrality was now a long-term objective of the Hungarian People's Republic, and in the short-term, he planned to withdraw his country from the Warsaw Pact. The virtually simultaneous developments of the deadly attack outside Hungarian Communist Party headquarters and the "official" delivery of Hungary's plan to leave the Soviet Bloc convinced Kruschev to invade and suppress the uprising with overwhelming force. He feared not doing so risked making him look weak, both at home and abroad, as well as the possibility of a "Domino

Effect" that could hollow out the Soviet "sphere of influence" in Eastern Europe. At this point, on October 31, Kruschev received encouragement to invade and suppress the "counter-revolutionary" uprising in Hungary from Liu Shaoqi, Deputy Chairman of the CCP, who happened to be in Moscow to celebrate the 39th anniversary of the October Revolution. Liu also passed on Mao Zedong's personal support for military intervention and Mao's advice that "unleashing violence now would prevent larger wars later."

Consequently, on November 4, 1956, Soviet troops launched a brutal incursion into Budapest and other parts of Hungary, unleashing a wave of bloodshed and terror. In the ensuing chaos, Nagy's government collapsed, prompting Nagy and 15 of his supporters to seek refuge in the Yugoslav Embassy. Despite valiant resistance from some Hungarians until November 10th, the outcome was bleak. Over the thirteen days from October 23 to November 4, the toll was staggering: 7,800 lives lost, 12,000 wounded, over 30,000 persecuted, and hundreds of revolutionary figures arrested and executed. Desperate to escape the tyranny, over 200,000 fled to the West, while 47,000 sought exile in the United States. Following the suppression of the revolution, a brutal crackdown ensued, marked by mass arrests, coerced confessions, and torture. In the name of "pacification," innocent Hungarians faced execution at the hands of Soviet forces, among them Imre Nagy, a revered symbol of Hungarian freedom and progress, who was executed for treason by the Soviet puppet-government of his own country on June 16, 1958. Notably, a newspaper on display within the showroom depicted Zhou Enlai riding in a Soviet tank, documenting crimes committed during January 16–17, 1957, when Zhou Enlai led a Chinese Party and government delegation to Budapest and took part in directing the suppression of Hungarian demonstrators. As I gazed upon the walls adorned with newspapers from that tumultuous era, the echoes of Nazi and Soviet propaganda blaring from the loudspeakers filled me with a familiar dread. The chilling parallels with the ruthless persecution of "counter-revolutionaries" during China's Cultural Revolution evoke a profound sense of empathy and solidarity with the victims of oppression.

For the subsequent three decades, discourse surrounding the revolution remained stifled in Hungary. It wasn't until 1988 that the widows of victims and Erzsébet Nagy (April 13, 1927 ~ January 29, 2008), daughter of Imre Nagy, established the "Historical Justice Committee." Their aim was to demand the vindication of all revolutionaries and the restoration of their honor. On March 15, 1989, during the Hungarian Youth Day, a large-scale event was held in front of the statue of Sándor Petőfi (1823~1849), the Hungarian poet and liberal revolutionary. The public called for the rehabilitation of the Hungarian Revolution, demanded the withdrawal of Soviet troops, opposed the one-party system, and advocated for freedom of speech, press, and religion. On June 16, the 30th anniversary of Imre Nagy's execution, another demonstration took place, calling for the rehabilitation of the Hungarian Revolution. Nagy's remains, which had been secretly buried, were recovered and given a formal state funeral, reinterred in the national cemetery with 300,000 people attending the memorial and burial, recognizing him as a national hero of Hungary.

During the upheaval in Eastern Europe in 1989, the country was renamed the "Third Republic of Hungary." The democratic government of the Republic of Hungary overturned the "counter-revolutionary" label imposed by the previous communist regime on the "Hungarian Uprising," officially recognizing it as the "1956 Revolution." Legislation was passed to designate October 23 each year as Republic Day. The new government announced the abandonment of the socialist system, significantly amended the constitution, abolished the one-party system, and implemented a multi-party system. In 1990, the Hungarian Democratic Forum, a major conservative opposition group, secured victory, marking the first peaceful transition of power between political parties. Hungary joined NATO in 1999, followed by accession to the European Union in 2004 and membership in the Schengen Convention in 2007. In 2014, the Hungarian government sentenced Biszku Béla (September 13, 1921 ~ March 31, 2016), the former government's second most powerful figure, to five years and six months in prison for his role in suppressing the Hungarian Revolutionary War. This marked the first trial of a high-ranking official from the Communist Party regime in Hungary.

On the eve of the Soviet Union's dissolution on December 26, 1991, a significant gesture was included in the preamble to the Treaty on Bilateral Relations signed by Hungary and the Soviet Union. Gorbachev, representing the Soviet Union, and Yeltsin, representing Russia, formally apologized for the Soviet Union's actions in Hungary in 1956. The House of Terror Memorial, inaugurated on February 24, 2002, stands on the former site of the Secret Police Command, serving as a poignant testament to the hard-fought triumph of democracy. Uniquely, the Hungarian people have chosen to memorialize the atrocities committed by both the Nazis and the Communists within the same structure, aptly labeling it the "House of Terror," which serves as a testament, reflection, critique, and judgment of history.

5. China

During World War I, with the strong support of the Kaiser of the enemy country, Lenin rushed back to Russia with Germany's gold mark to overthrow his own government, seize power, and establish the Communist Party of the Soviet Union. The founding of the Chinese Communist Party (CCP) was an egg laid by Soviet Russia. In 1917, when the Soviet Union was just founded, it took advantage of China's membership of the Third International to "export revolution." In April 1920, the Comintern dispatched Representative Grigori Votinsky (April 17, 1893 ~ June 11, 1953) to China to establish a communist group. He first met with Li Dazhao (October 29, 1889 ~ April 28, 1927), a cofounder of the Chinese Communist Party and mentor of Mao Zedong in Beijing. He later contacted Chen Duxiu (October 8, 1879 ~ May 27, 1942), a Chinese revolutionary socialist, who co-founded the CCP with Li Dazhao in 1921, in Shanghai. He provided financial support to promote the establishment of the party in Shanghai and southern China. On the evening of July 23, 1921, Comintern representatives and Soviet intelligence agents Maring (May 14, 1883 ~

April 13, 1942), Nicolsky (February 10, 1889 ~ September 21, 1938) and 13 Chinese representatives secretly held the First National Congress of the CCP. The historic gathering took place at No. 106 Wangzhi Road (now No. 76 Xingye Road) in the French Concession in Shanghai. By 1922, the Central Committee of the CCP officially affirmed its status as a subordinate branch of the Comintern. Since its founding, the CCP has been an "imported product" attached to the Communist Party of the Soviet Union.

When the CCP was established in 1921, its founding members comprised several prominent professors and intellectuals. It would be unjust to assert that this initial cohort lacked ideals; indeed, they were earnestly grappling with China's destiny. However, with Mao Zedong's initiation of the "Ruffian Movement" in rural Hunan in 1926, the trajectory of the CCP began to veer towards a more ruthless path. Over time, the party's leadership underwent a transformation, gradually sidelining intellectuals in favor of individuals from society's margins. Their ranks included some who had spent time as bandits and others who spent time as unenthusiastic foreign students. In a functioning and healthy social order, such marginalized figures would find it challenging to ascend to positions of authority. In September 1927, when Mao Zedong first arrived in the Jinggang Mountains, he formed an alliance with Yuan Wencai and Wang Zuo, infamous green forest outlaws known for their criminal activities. Initially condemned as murderers and thieves, they found redemption under the banner of "justified rebellion" and "revolution," transforming their sordid past into a revolutionary narrative. On November 7, 1931, coinciding with the National Day of the Soviet Union, the CCP, under the guidance of the Soviet Communist Party and with Stalin's approval, established the "Chinese Soviet Republic" provisional government in Jiangxi, with Mao Zedong appointed as chairman. Even the name of the country mirrored that of the Soviet Union. From its inception, the CCP has been viewed as an anti-government terrorist organization nurtured by hostile foreign forces.

In the 1930s, the CCP was in its infancy, merely a spark that ignited a ruthless campaign. In April 1930, Mao Zedong branded dissenters within the party as "counterrevolutionaries," under the guise of the "AB Group." During the Kuomintang's Northern Expedition, a small right-wing faction known as the "Anti-Bolsheviks" (AB) emerged in Jiangxi, but it swiftly crumbled in April 1927 due to the onslaught from the mainstream Kuomintang faction. Mao capitalized on this defunct group as a pretext for his purges. The purported "Eliminating counter-revolution" was, in reality, Mao's method of eliminating dissent, targeting leading cadres of the Jiangxi Provincial Committee of the CCP and the Red Army who opposed him. Mao exhibited traits of arrogance, hot temper, stubbornness, and arbitrariness, alongside a strong desire for leadership. His approach was marked by cunning ruthlessness, resorting to suppression and retribution when faced with challenges. This tactic of purging dissidents through the pretext of countering counter-revolutionaries became a hallmark of Mao's rule. By October, over 1,000 out of 30,000 Communist Party members in southwest Jiangxi were accused of affiliation with the "AB Group" and summarily executed. A quarter of the Soviet government's personnel in southwestern Jiangxi were implicated in the "AB Group." Xu Xiangqian (November 8, 1901 ~ September 21, 1990) and He Long (March 22, 1896 ~ June 9, 1969) were Marshals of the People's Republic of China (PRC). According to Xu Xiangqian's "Review of History" and accounts from He Long and others, more than 100,000 Red Army soldiers fell victim to these purges. The Red 20th Army, encircled and annihilated by the Central Red Army, saw its designation revoked, with survivors absorbed into the Seventh Red Army. Over 700 individuals, including military commander Xiao Dapeng and political commissar Zeng Bingchun, were detained and subsequently executed as part of the AB regiment.

The Red Army departed the Soviet area in Jiangxi in 1934, reaching the Soviet region in northern Shanxi by 1936. In 1942, it initiated the Yan'an Rectification Movement alongside the "Rescue Movement." The rectification aimed to solidify Mao Zedong's preeminence within the Party Central Committee, granting him ultimate authority, known as "the final say," positioning him above previous general secretaries in the Politburo. Consequently, allegiance shifted from the Party to Mao, stifling dissenters both within and outside the party, whom Mao ruthlessly marginalized or eliminated. Leading the rectification team was Liu Shaoqi (Nov. 24, 1898 ~ Nov. 12, 1969, Chairman of the PRC 1959~68), with Kang Sheng (1898~1975, third vice-chairman of the CCP in 1973) as his key ally. During this period, over 15,000 individuals were branded as spies, many enduring secret executions or unjust deaths following torture for confessions. Prominent figures like Zhang Wentian (August 30, 1900 ~ July 1, 1976, a high-ranking leader of the CCP), Wang Jiaxiang (August 15, 1906 ~ January 25, 1974, a senior leaders of the CCP in its early stage), and Zhou Enlai (March 5, 1898 ~ Jan. 8, 1976, Chinese communist leader and premier of the PRC) were among those targeted. The rescue movement primarily targeted intellectuals who had defected to Yan'an. An illustrative case is that of Wang Shiwei, whose article "Wild Lily" led to his demise.

Mao's animosity towards intellectuals finds its origins in the May Fourth period, during his tenure as a junior administrator at Peking University Library. Despite his earlier prominence in Hunan, Mao's arrival in Beijing in the summer of 1918 relegated him to obscurity among the city's luminaries, leaving him feeling overlooked. Cai Yuanpei (1868~1940, the president of Peking University) intervened on his behalf, securing Mao a menial position in the library through Li Dazhao, the director. For approximately six months, Mao toiled in the library, earning a paltry monthly salary of 8 yuan, a stark contrast to the esteemed professors at Peking University who commanded 300 yuan per month. Mao's inability to seize opportunities for overseas study further accentuated his sense of alienation. In the eyes of those with international exposure, Mao was perceived as a rustic outsider, a sentiment that wounded his pride deeply. Throughout his rule, Mao seized every chance to exact vengeance on intellectuals, evident in his relentless targeting of them in various campaigns, including the "anti-rightist" movement. During the Cultural Revolution, he dispatched "worker propaganda teams" to oversee educational institutions and dispatched Educated Youths to rural areas for "re-education" by impoverished peasants.

During the Anti-Japanese War, the CCP's extensive foreign

propaganda efforts played a significant but misleading role. On July 4, 1943, Mao Zedong penned an editorial in Xinhua Daily, the CCP's official newspaper, titled "Ode to Democracy: Dedicated to the Independence Day of the United States." In it, Mao extolled the virtues of American democracy, expressing admiration for the country's perceived friendliness towards China and its democratic ethos. The article states: "Since we were young, we have felt that the United States is a particularly amiable country. We believe this is not only because it has not occupied Chinese land, nor has it launched an aggressive war against China; moreover, it has basically, the Chinese people's good impression of the United States stems from the democratic demeanor and broad-mindedness that emanates from the American national character." "The American people are good friends of the Chinese people. The goal of our party is to overthrow the Kuomintang dictatorship and establish an American-style democratic system so that the people of the country can enjoy the happiness brought by democracy. I believe that when the Chinese people fight for democracy, the American people will support us." This rhetoric served as a strategic move to vie with Chiang Kai-shek for power. Mao Zedong invented a scam called "New Democracy": promising land redistribution to farmers, intellectual freedom, industrial and commercial development, worker leadership, and a government modeled after Lincoln's and Roosevelt's ideals. However, Mao's promises proved illusory. Upon assuming power, he reneged on his pledges. Land reform was a facade, leaving farmers landless. Intellectuals faced forced transformation. Workers were prohibited from striking or forming unions. Property owners were coerced into "voluntarily" surrendering their assets. Ultimately, all Chinese citizens were bestowed with a "People's Republic" devoid of electoral rights.

The CCP won the civil war because it took advantage of the vast rural population of peasants. China's agricultural heritage spanning millennia laid the foundation for its peasant majority, comprising 88% of the 461 million-strong population in 1947. Recognizing peasants as a wellspring of recruits, the CCP initiated aggressive land reforms in its controlled territories. These reforms aimed not only to conscript peasants into the conflict but also to forge an unbreakable bond with the cause of communism, even at the cost of their lives. Qin Hui, a notable figure at Tsinghua University, underscored this strategy, elucidating that the crux of violent land reforms lay in coercing peasants to procure "Certificates of Investment." A very important condition for getting everyone to throw their lives and blood is to give you no way out. With the certificate of investment, you don't have to worry about not being able to get started. He said: Why should it be so bloody? Peasants·may not "spend their lives and blood" for a few acres of land, but if they can benefit from the Communist Party's victory, and their lives will be in danger if the Communist Party fails, then of course they will be highly mobilized easily. Therefore, we must carry out bloody land reform. Drawing from ancient wisdom. The CCP implemented Shang Yang's (390~338 BC, a statesman and reformer of the state of Qin) principle of "Remove the Strong" from the Book of Lord Shang: "If a country governs its good people by ruthless people, it will surely rule to the greatest strength." The land reform implemented the principles of Shang Yang's governance. Task forces for land reform empowered unsavory characters to seize control, employing deceit to manipulate the virtuous. Mao asserted that "where there is land, there are tyrants; where there are gentry, there are scoundrels." He classified landlords and affluent peasants, who had built their lives through hard work and agricultural labor, as class enemies to be eliminated. The "local tyrants and evil gentry" were dragged to mass gatherings for public trials and executions. The class relations in rural areas were artificially intensified, with directives from top to bottom that "every household smokes, every village sees red." Regarding the death toll from land reforms, scholars like John King Fairbank (1907~1991), an American sinologist and historian from Harvard University, estimated the numbers to exceed one million.

During the "Land Reform," the CCP mandated the classification of villagers into distinct social groups, singling out numerous landlords and affluent peasants to meet specified quotas, marking them as targets for persecution. Many were falsely implicated merely to meet quotas, while some who didn't originally qualify as landlords or rich peasants were unjustly elevated to such status. Essentially, the policy dictated that at least one individual must be executed as a deterrent. China's landscape was once steeped in civilization and decorum, with Confucian values of reverence for elders, care for the young, and mutual respect deeply ingrained. Rich and poor coexisted harmoniously, fostering orderly production and life. However, the land reform stripped rural elites of their land and possessions, eradicating China's agrarian aristocracy both politically and economically. This upheaval reshaped the social fabric and traditional culture of rural China, consolidating control over rural political power. The "Land Reform" artificially sowed seeds of animosity, dismantling the noble moral fabric of the Chinese nation and leaving profound scars on society. By elevating the pursuit of wealth and violence to a glorified "just cause," it eroded traditional moral values, fostering selfishness, discord, intrigue, and moral decay. In contemporary China, rampant materialism and unchecked desires prevail. Reflecting on its origins, "land reform" cannot escape culpability for this moral decline.

The CCP executed all rural elites during the "Land Reform" and then proceeded with the "Three Anti's and Five Anti's" campaign to systematically eliminate wealthy individuals in urban areas, instigating terror while seizing social wealth. In Shanghai alone, from January 25 to April 1, 1952, incomplete records indicate that 876 people resorted to suicide due to the onslaught of the movement. Among them, numerous capitalists chose to end their lives along with their families. By the end of 1952, the CCP declared the elimination of over 2.4 million "counterrevolutionaries." However, the actual death toll surpassed 5 million, representing nearly one percent of the population at the time. In 1955, another wave of purges targeted intellectuals in a renewed "Eliminating counterrevolution" campaign, resulting in the expulsion of over 1.3 million individuals. Given that the total number of intellectuals across the country was approximately 5 million, this meant that every four intellectuals faced expulsion. Those singled out during the counter-revolutionary movement were often targeted based on personal grievances perceived by their unit leaders. In the words of Lu Xun, they were accused of committing "abominable crimes." Both my father, Bao

Zuxian, and my uncle, Bao Ting, fell victim to this ruthless campaign.

In 1956, immediately following the "Eliminating counter-revolution" movement, the "anti-rightist" campaign commenced. Those who voiced grievances over errors during the suppression found themselves accused of undermining the movement, thus falling into the trap and being labeled as rightists. Expressing grievances or complaints was construed as an attack on the counter-revolutionary efforts, warranting classification as a rightist. In this context, the anti-rightist struggle served as the completion of the "Eliminating counter-revolution" drive. The anti-rightist campaign not only marked the conclusion of the "Eliminating counter-revolution" movement but also represented its further extension. One of the remote causes of the anti-rightist struggle was Mao Zedong's enduring bias and animosity towards intellectuals, which significantly shaped the fate of Chinese intellectuals thereafter. The second remote cause of the anti-rightist struggle was Mao Zedong's hostility towards the China Democratic League. As early as November 30, 1947, during a period when the Kuomintang still held considerable power and the war's outcome remained uncertain, Mao Zedong had signaled in a telegram to Stalin his intent to discard the Democrats' post-victory. Another recent cause of the anti-rightist movement stemmed from the enthusiastic response of the Chinese intellectual class to the Twentieth National Congress of the Communist Party of the Soviet Union and the events in Poland and Hungary, actions that greatly displeased Mao Zedong. Additionally, internal party disputes between factions advocating "anti-advances" and "anti-countermeasures" also fueled tensions. Mao believed that adopting anti-countermeasures would dampen the spirits of the 600 million populace, criticizing Zhou Enlai's approach as a "rightist attack," equating it to pushing comrades perilously close to the rightist edge, merely 50 meters away.

On April 28, 1956, Mao Zedong unveiled the policy of "letting a hundred flowers bloom and a hundred schools of thought contend" during an enlarged meeting of the Politburo, followed by its endorsement at the Supreme State Council on May 2. He fervently encouraged individuals both within and outside the party to contribute to the rectification of Communist Party movements. This served as Mao's precursor to the anti-rightist campaign. In March 1957, during the third plenary session of the second session of the Chinese People's Political Consultative Conference (CPPCC), under the persistent urging and incitement of CCP leaders led by Mao, the campaign was further intensified. After a brief period of unrest, Mao Zedong began to tighten the noose. On June 8, 1957, the People's Daily issued an editorial titled "Why is this?" signaling the commencement of the anti-rightist struggle. Hundreds of thousands of intellectuals responded to the Communist Party's call, aiding in rectifying reforms and expressing critiques of party organization. However, they were unexpectedly accused of challenging party leadership and aggressively undermining it, and thus branded as enemies.

Reflecting on the history of the anti-rightist struggle, observers often marvel at the authorities' fickleness, betrayal, and manipulation of power dynamics. Initially, Mao called upon people from all walks of life to assist in the party's rectification efforts, urging them to "reveal everything they knew and speak freely." However, these words swiftly evaporated as dissenting voices emerged, each dissenting individual suddenly cast as adversarial. By common standards, one cannot cultivate trust by oscillating between contradictory actions, flip-flopping orders, and reneging on promises. Yet, this pattern did not commence with the anti-rightist movement; it was a hallmark of Mao's lifelong approach: With a gun in hand, I am the gangster. Who should I fear?

On January 30, 1958, the "Regulations of the Central Committee of the CCP and the State Council on the Principles for Handling Rightists among State Salary Employees and Students of Colleges and Universities" were issued. The second provision of these regulations outlined six categories of punishment for addressing rightists among state-paid personnel. Most faced administrative penalties such as expulsion and relocation to rural labor camps. Many of my uncles from the Bao family and uncles and aunts from the Liu family bore the stigma of being labeled "rightists." Following the dismissal of my grandmother's nephew, Lu Puyun, from public office, his family relied on my grandmother and her brother, Lu Puhong, for sustenance over the decades. Furthermore, individuals who underperformed in the movement but escaped classification as rightists were also targeted and branded as "rightists who slipped through the net." My father-in-law, Professor Rui Hejiu, was a prominent example of a "rightist who slipped through the cracks" at Xiamen University and endured prolonged surveillance. Though he retained his job, he faced imprisonment and relocation to the countryside during the Cultural Revolution. Even the Central Committee of the CCP at the time lacked comprehensive data on the nationwide arrests of rightists. It wasn't until 1978, under the leadership of Hu Yaobang, who oversaw the "rightist correction" efforts as Minister of the Organization Department of the Central Committee of the CCP, that the true extent of the correction efforts came to light. The total number of corrected rightists exceeded 500,000, with a final tally of 552,877 individuals "corrected."

The impact of the anti-rightist struggle in history transcends the suffering endured by hundreds of thousands of rightists and their millions of family members; it marks a pivotal shift in the trajectory of government oppression in China. From this point onward, the emphasis shifted decisively to "taking class struggle as the key link" and paving the way for the "Cultural Revolution." The anti-rightist campaign, along with the critical "anti-countermeasures," laid the groundwork for Mao Zedong to realize his ambitions. Consequently, criticism of Mao, whether from within or outside the party, became unthinkable. Indeed, as Mao Zedong and Zhou Enlai asserted, the Great Leap Forward was a direct consequence of the anti-rightist struggle. Anyone who dared to voice concerns or offer criticisms risked being labeled as a rightist and silenced. Witnessing the fate of those recently branded as rightists, intellectuals and cadres not yet classified as such understandably remained silent. Proposals like backyard steelmaking, sparrow hunting, high-yield satellite fields, and free meals were met with no opposition, creating fertile ground for Mao Zedong to initiate the Great Leap Forward, plunging the Chinese people into an even deeper catastrophe.

One of Mao Zedong's driving forces behind the Great Leap

Forward was his desire to rival Khrushchev for leadership within the International Communist Movement. Mao aimed to engineer a monumental feat that would astonish the world, solidify China's status as a formidable nation, and bolster his leadership within the global communist movement. In 1957, China's steel output stood at 5.35 million tons. In June 1958, Mao summoned his part-time secretary Li Rui, Deputy Minister of Water and Power, and instructed him to double that output to 10.7 million tons for the year. When Li relayed Mao's directive to Wang Heshou, Minister of Metallurgy, on what Mao meant, Wang was taken aback but lacked the courage to confront Mao with the logistical challenges: the immense coal mining required, the construction of additional coke ovens, iron mines, and railway cars, as well as the sources for electricity and materials for steel-making furnaces. To meet the steel production targets, people resorted to extreme measures, even demolishing monuments to obtain bricks for furnace construction. However, ordinary bricks were ill-suited for refractory purposes, and makeshift earthen blast furnaces failed to reach the temperatures needed for proper iron smelting. Consequently, the nationwide effort to produce steel transformed into a mass campaign of melting down iron tools and pots. When iron ore proved scarce, people resorted to smashing iron items en masse, including copper washbasins and pots, to meet quotas. By year's end, the People's Daily announced the successful completion of the 10.7 million-ton steel production target. However, the actual usable steel, after excluding inferior local production, amounted to only about 8 million tons.

Amid Mao Zedong's fixation on steel production, he steered China toward yet another calamitous path: corporatization. To showcase the purported superiority of the people's communes, an alarming trend of exaggeration took hold. In June 1958, the "People's Daily" began publishing reports from various counties, featuring staggering figures: yields of 7,000, 10,000, 15,000, and even 37,000 jin in Hubei Province, while Anhui boasted a "miraculous" 43,000 jin per are (1 jin = 500 grams, 1 are = 0.1 acre）. The pinnacle of this exaggeration was epitomized by Huanjiang County in Guangxi Province, claiming a rice yield of 130,000 jin per are—a ludicrous record. Renowned scientist Qian Xuesen's article in the newspaper further fueled the calamity by suggesting, based on photosynthesis analysis, that grain yields per are could reach an astronomical 200,000 jin. This unfounded claim exacerbated the disaster. In 1959, grain production plummeted by 50 billion jin compared to 1957, equivalent to 25 million tons. Despite this shortfall, a staggering 4.19 million tons were exported in 1959, a 2.24 million-ton increase from 1957. This surplus alone could have sustained 30 million people for half a year—from autumn 1959 to summer 1960. Yet, in 1960, national grain output dwindled to 288 billion jin, nearly one-fifth less than in 1959. Amidst widespread starvation, 2.65 million tons were still exported (1983 "China Statistical Yearbook" pp. 422, 438). Localities exaggerated their output to meet "surplus grain" quotas, pressuring party cadres at all levels to fulfill "national tasks." Consequently, grain earmarked for peasants' rations was sold to the state as "surplus grain" by local cadres eager to meet quotas, only to be shipped abroad for foreign currency. Before the 1960 wheat harvest, peasants suffered from food shortages not due to natural disasters but due to government-imposed "plus grain" quotas.

Due to the Communist Party's expropriation of peasants, they lost their sense of independence and enthusiasm for production, leading to the largest man-made catastrophe in the Chinese rural economy. I worked in rural areas in Suxian County, Anhui Province, from 1969 to 1978, during which the prevailing slogan was "We would rather have socialist grass than capitalist seedlings." Peasants were coerced into becoming commune members, forfeiting their freedom to farm according to local conditions. Directives from above mandated that only production squads could cultivate grain and cotton, while peasants faced criticism for raising chickens and sheep, as cadres sought to eliminate their "capitalist tendencies." Consequently, poverty pervaded every household, making even basic necessities like salt unaffordable. Following the establishment of People's Communes, higher authorities mandated the creation of public canteens, ceasing food distribution to members. Since the harvested grain was only handed over to the state and sent to the commune canteen, the commune members received no share. Under this system, peasants lost personal freedoms. Food wastage in public canteens reached unprecedented levels, depleting already insufficient rations within months. Peasants lost their private plots, leaving the canteen as their sole source of sustenance. However, daily rations proved inadequate for survival. The canteen system, coupled with land confiscation, became the dual tools of oppression, leaving peasants destitute.

Desperation led to extreme measures like consuming tree bark and cotton wool from quilts. Some resorted to cannibalism, with the dead becoming sustenance for the living. "People eating each other" became a chilling reality, with local cadres indifferent to starvation deaths. Bus and train travel required commune-issued letters, deterring escape attempts. Those fleeing in search of food faced detention in labor reform farms, euphemistically termed "custody and resettlement," effectively treating them as prisoners. Despite normal climatic conditions and the absence of war or plague, tens of millions succumbed to hunger due to the failures of a highly centralized political and economic system. In Suxian County, I witnessed the aftermath of the 1960 Great Famine—a landscape dotted with deserted villages and crumbling walls. Villagers cautioned against venturing near, citing the presence of plague. Declassified national archives from 1958 to 1962 reveal a staggering death toll of 37.55 million from hunger, exceeding the 15-22 million overall casualties in World War I, and 450 times the death count wrought by the Nagasaki atom bomb.

The Great Famine stands as the central and defining event of Mao Zedong's era, stemming directly from a series of ultra-leftist movements such as the "Anti-Rightist" campaign and the "Great Leap Forward." It served as the foundational catalyst for Mao's subsequent launch of the Cultural Revolution. In 1959, critical remarks made by Peng Dehuai in his "Ten Thousand Character Petition" during the Lushan Conference, and Liu Shaoqi's assertion at the "Seven Thousand People Conference" that "three-tenths of the disaster was natural and seven-tenths man-made," deeply wounded Mao. Convinced that Liu Shaoqi and his cohort would eventually hold him accountable for the Great Famine, akin to Khrushchev's denunciation of Stalin, Mao resolved to neutralize this threat. Having defeated Peng Dehuai, Mao resolved to oust Liu Shaoqi and eradicate him to forestall any future reckoning. Mao's primary objective in instigating the Cultural Revolution was to shield himself and preempt any attempts by Liu Shaoqi and his allies to indict him for the Great Famine in the future. Terms like "anti-revisionism" and "continuation of the revolution" served as cover stories for Mao's true agenda.

After four years of meticulous planning, Mao initiated the "Cultural Revolution." His initial aim was to inflict torment upon Liu Shaoqi until his demise. Following Liu Shaoqi's death, Mao sought to "continue the revolution" to establish his own "dynastic realm," showing no hesitation in dismantling the existing "party realm." Mao's methods exceeded the CCP leadership's expectations. In a swift maneuver, Mao rallied individuals long suppressed by the party to "rebel." During the early stages of the Cultural Revolution, Mao inspected the Red Guards in Beijing on eight occasions, inciting both the uninformed "Red Guards" and the aggrieved "rebels" to seize power from the "party realm" and assail his former comrades. Since the "party world" had failed Mao, Mao discarded all pretense of politeness towards the Communist Party. After Mao was forced to step aside for inspection at the Seven Thousand People Congress, he began to turn his cynicism towards the Communist Party. Since the party is no longer willing to bite the people, let the people bite the party instead. Once Mao achieved his objectives and observed the Red Guards transform into a source of societal instability, he initiated measures to address these audacious youth. Mao ordered their relocation, urging them to "head to the mountains and villages," banishing them to desolate, impoverished regions where they grappled with destitution and deprivation. Like numerous others with problematic familial backgrounds, I found myself suffering the same fate as the burial objects of the Red Guards. Ultimately, it was Lin Biao's resistance that shattered the myth of Mao Zedong. The Lin Biao incident delivered a fatal blow to Mao, compelling Mao to give in to the party he had defeated. Throughout the Cultural Revolution, the tally of lives lost proved impossible to enumerate. During interviews conducted on August 21-23, 1980, Deng

Xiaoping responded to Italian journalist Oriana Fallaci's inquiry about the death toll of the Cultural Revolution by remarking, "The actual number of casualties from the Cultural Revolution is astronomical and can never be accurately determined."

The essence of the "Cultural Revolution" lay in Mao's power struggle between the "dynastic realm" and the "party realm." Regardless of which emerged victorious, it would ultimately culminate in autocracy, with the people enduring continued oppression. Mao Zedong's triumph would have meant autocracy, just as victory for the party also signified autocracy. The "Cultural Revolution" concluded with the ascendancy of the "party realm" over the "dynastic realm." Following the downfall of the "Gang of Four," the era of Deng Xiaoping began. Many intellectuals hailed Deng Xiaoping at the time. However, it would be overly optimistic to regard Deng as the "son of the people." During the tumultuous events of the Tiananmen Square massacre on June 4, 1989, amid the thunderous presence of tanks in Tiananmen Square, Deng Xiaoping revealed his ruthless persona as an executioner. This grim reality echoed his role in purging intellectuals as Mao's deputy during the "anti-rightist movement." The party wields power like a sharp sickle and axe, while the people are mere leeks and screws. Its "core interest" lies in perpetuating the enslavement of the entire Chinese populace under the dominion of the "party realm." As long as the "party realm" endures, any notion of establishing an equitable contractual relationship between the party and the people remains forbidden.

Similar to the Soviet Union and Nazi Germany, the CCP not only perpetrated atrocities but was fundamentally a criminal syndicate. To ascend to the inner circle of power, one must bear responsibility for heinous acts and earn trust. Once ensconced within this organization, the higher you climb the career ladder, the greater your authority and the more lavish your rewards. At the pinnacle of the party's power hierarchy, one possesses everything. Communism may ostensibly be achieved within a single nation, but only for the select few who attain power. In the 1960s, officials begrudgingly acknowledged that over 37 million people perished due to famine. However, Mao Zedong's life had already entered communism in advance. The Communist Party, under the guise of public ownership, monopolizes almost all land and wealth, even including our bodies, thoughts, and love. Once they have seized all of this, there is, of course, no utopian paradise—only the paradise of power and privilege they have already attained. That is their paradise, but it can only be a hell for the common people!

The Cultural Revolution wrought complete destruction upon the ancient civilization and traditional culture that had underpinned the Chinese nation for millennia. Concurrently, the CCP rejects adherence to the norms of other civilizations and international standards, resulting in the erosion of the moral and ethical foundations of the Chinese populace. Human nature embodies both virtuous and malevolent aspects, immutable. What can be altered, however, is the system and environment. A sound political framework fosters citizens with refined character, nurturing the inherent goodness of human nature to flourish and thrive. By the same token, a flawed political system can breed malevolence among its populace. When malice finds fertile ground for proliferation, its vicious visage emerges to inflict harm upon others. A nation's political structure and governmental conduct dictate the moral fabric, social mores, and civilized conduct of its people. Following the "political mutual harm model" of the Cultural Revolution, wherein individuals forsake their dignity and integrity, forfeit their humanity, and readily resort to violence. China's contemporary culture regresses to a primal state akin to the law of the jungle, which might make right and the weak suffer at the hands of the strong. The corrosion of authority inevitably precipitates the collapse of societal morality. This "political mutual harm model" has undergone mutation and escalation, giving rise to the "economic mutual harm model" characterized by a mentality of "Every man against me, I against every man." This phenomenon pervades every facet of society, spanning from infrastructure development like construction projects to essential services such as food processing and garment manufacturing; from pharmaceuticals to the air and water. This pervasive erosion has transformed citizens into a cohort of crude barbarians who venerate power, exhibiting apathy and insensitivity, blurring the lines between right and wrong, flouting legal norms, spurning civility, lacking integrity, resorting to opportunism, and resorting to any means to achieve their ends.

Chen Duxiu once said, "We love a country that seeks happiness for its people, not a country where the people make sacrifices for the country." However, 100+ years after the inception of the Communist Party of China in 1921, especially after the establishment of the People's Republic of China, the results of the revolution completely contradicted Chen Duxiu's original intentions. During his 30-year rule, Mao Zedong launched over 50 campaigns, resulting in 80 million wrongful deaths, 30 million unjust cases, and over 300 million people persecuted. Mao Zedong treated human lives with utter disregard, creating widespread injustices. His crimes surpass the combined atrocities of all tyrants in Chinese history. The international community commonly regards Hitler and Stalin as the archetypal tyrants of the 20th century. Hitler caused the deaths of 6 million Jews, and Stalin caused the deaths of 20 million Soviets. Compared to Mao Zedong's crimes against humanity, their actions pale in comparison. Stalin surpassed Hitler, and Mao Zedong surpassed Stalin. The CCP's authoritarian rule has nullified the Chinese nation's century-long pursuit of freedom and liberation, rendering the struggles of countless outstanding Chinese individuals for freedom, democracy, and progress utterly futile.

Since the establishment of the People's Republic of China in 1949, the political landscape has veered towards authoritarianism. Despite economic growth, the populace finds itself grappling with increasing poverty. Prime Minister Li Keqiang lamented, "Over 600 million Chinese struggle with low to moderate incomes, barely making 1,000 yuan monthly." Internationally, Xi Jinping has eschewed diplomatic norms and exhibited an arrogant and confrontational stance towards the world. Drawing parallels with the crisis year of 1900, when Empress Dowager Cixi waged war against 11 Western nations simultaneously, history seems to echo. Xi views modern Western nations as hostile entities, with the United States at the forefront as the primary adversary. Sino-US relations have reached an unprecedented nadir, resulting in China's isolation within the global community and calls for reprimand. This is not due to China's weakness but its rogue behavior. Charles de Secondat, Baron de Montesquieu (January 18, 1689 ~ February 10, 1755) was a French Enlightenment thinker, sociologist, lawyer, and the founder of state theory and legal theory. Together with Voltaire and Rousseau, he is known as one of the "Three Swordsmen of the French Enlightenment." He proposed the "Ten Evils" of human society: 1. inhuman politics, 2. worship without thought, 3. science without humanities, 4. business without ethics, 5. knowledge without conscience, 6. no real history, 7. no independent spirit, 8. happiness without freedom, 9. prosperity without labor, 10. unchecked power. Examining these in the context of contemporary China, one finds a striking resonance with the nation's current deficiencies. The Ten Evils of Montesquieu's theory are all occupied by the CCP. In today's China, an unwavering reverence for authority pervades society, reminiscent of Germany in 1933. Diplomatically, China's belligerent rhetoric echoes the bellicose posturing of 1933 Germany, challenging the Western world. Will China's future mirror the errors of Germany's downfall and subsequent reconstruction? Only time will unveil the answer.

6. Summary

Contrary to Marx's prediction, the developed capitalist countries of the contemporary world—Western Europe, Northern Europe, North America, Australia, and Southeast Asia—did not experience proletarian revolutions. Instead, they mirrored Britain's "Glorious Revolution" by adopting its system of parliamentary rule. In the "Glorious Revolution," rather than resorting to violent upheaval, the King and the British populace engaged in dialogue. The King pledged to return governance to the people, and in turn, the people agreed to retain the royal family, with both sides honoring the pact for the next three centuries and on into the foreseeable future.

Today's human historical development is guided by several key principles: people-oriented, democratic constitutionalism stands as the sole legitimate source of governmental power; republicanism and the separation of powers serve as essential checks and balances on state authority, fostering a service-oriented government; a standard of justice and morality is established upon the sanctity and inviolability of private property; faier trade and free competition flourish within the framework of a market economy, enabling individuals to realize their talents to the fullest, driving technological progress, economic development, and market prosperity. In a state of abundant material resources, society possesses ample means to ensure that disadvantaged groups can lead lives of decency and dignity. Furthermore, adherence to the principles of non-violence, contractual spirit, and rational dispute resolution is paramount. The key to a nation's ascent into the ranks of advanced civilizations lies in one fundamental secret: freedom. This encompasses the freedom to develop one's potential, express opinions, and engage in competition and trade within the marketplace. Friedrich Hayek（1899～1992）dedicated his life to demonstrating that human prosperity, happiness, and dignity emanate from individual liberty, not collectivism. Utopian systems that trample on private property and disregard fundamental human nature ultimately lead to economic collapse, moral decay, and the erosion of truth. Hu Shih (Dec. 17, 1891 ~ Feb. 24, 1962), a Chinese Nationalist scholar and diplomat, once fervently declared, "To fight for one's own freedom is to fight for the freedom of the nation! To fight for one's own dignity is to fight for the country's dignity! A country founded on freedom and equality cannot be built by a crowd of slaves." Similarly, Yang Zhenning reflected on the importance of freedom through the lens of the renowned physicist, Richard Feynman, emphasizing how Feynman's groundbreaking work was only possible in a society that embraced such individual development. Yang Zhenning speculated that had Feynman been in China, he would likely have faced imprisonment or insanity due to the stifling lack of freedom.

The highest state of life comes from freedom. Within the limits of the law, people can live freely in this world, which includes freedom of thought, freedom of movement, the freedom to manage their time and money, the freedom to choose a political system, and the freedom to choose their leaders.   Indeed, freedom weighs more than democracy in significance. In a country without freedom, democracy becomes nothing more than an empty promise. A fundamental element of a democratic system is the citizens' right to vote. In China, the government leaders are elected through the National People's Congress. However, the representatives are not free to choose the leaders when they vote. Those who voice dissenting opinions are imprisoned or disappear without reason. Since the Chinese Communist Party (CCP) took power, it not only aggressively pursued "class struggle" as its guiding principle and brazenly stripped people of their property rights but, more sinisterly, maximized the deprivation of people's freedom.

Throughout Chinese history, feudalism was the political system during the pre-Qin era, which means "to establish a state by granting land." The emperor would distribute lands outside the royal domain to lords, who could establish their states and armies with significant autonomy in their territories. In 221 BC, Qin Shi Huang conquered the six states and unified all of China, establishing a centralized government. However, the centralization of power during the imperial era was limited to the realm of public authority, with government administration reaching only the county level. The imperial court's interference in civil society and the lives of the common people was very limited; it was rare for the emperor and the court to proactively trouble the populace. The saying "The mountains are high, and the emperor is far away" reflects the broad space for personal freedom that people enjoyed, allowing them to easily find idyllic places to live and lead a leisurely life. The people had the freedom to relocate and choose their livelihoods, and even the gentry and scholars had the freedom to act according to their principles rather than blindly follow the emperor. Moreover, individuals could transcend social classes: a farming family could become wealthy through hard work and frugality, and a poor scholar could realize the dream of achieving high honors through diligent study. The power of an oligarchy is limited.

However, the Communist Party of China's totalitarian system is different; it has taken centralization of power to the extreme. In its class dictatorship, there are dictators everywhere. The CCP's rule is like mercury spreading across the ground, with unprecedented strength, pervasiveness, and penetration. It intervenes in every aspect of people's lives without any gaps. The complete politicization of society extends throughout all levels of social organization, penetrating into every cell of society: every grassroots work unit, every community, neighborhood, village, and even every family. People have lost all freedoms, including the freedom of thought. The Communist Party encourages people to inform on each other, betray one another, and tear each other apart, achieving total control over society with no empty spaces. The entire country has become a vast prison, and everyone has become a modern slave.

China is a miserable nation ruled by Confucianism and Legalism. The history of China is just a history of the reincarnation of dynasties. Over the past two thousand years, there has been no glorious intellectual history, only a typical slave cultural history. For those attuned to the darker facets of Chinese society, figures like Lu Xun in the modern era and Chen Danqing in contemporary times stand out. In his novel "Medicine," Lu Xun employs Xia Yu, a character symbolizing the revolutionary martyr Qiu Jin. Confined in prison, Xia Yu engages in a futile dialogue with the jailer Ayi, asserting, "This Qing Dynasty belongs to all of us." Yet, Ayi, proficient with fist and rod, responds with a brutal beating. As Xia Yu faces the executioner, bystanders fail to muster the expected sympathy for a dying soul. Following his beheading, Xia Yu's martyrdom takes a grotesque turn as his blood is transformed into steamed buns, consumed by Hua Laoshuan's tubercular son. Meanwhile, patrons in a nearby teahouse animatedly discuss Xia Yu's beating and demise, oblivious to his noble intentions of emancipating the impoverished and ignorant masses. Lu Xun's short stories stand as exemplars of the genre for over a century, renowned for their profound insight, incisiveness, and lingering impact akin to thorns lodged in the psyche. With poignant criticism, Lu Xun exposes the ignorance and callousness of the masses while harboring a deep well of compassion for them. His narratives wield an authentic pen, depicting the grim realities of society to jolt the collective conscience from its slumber. Yet, to the benighted, sobriety proves an unwelcome revelation. Many prefer the blissful stupor of ignorance, shunning awakening. Those daring to rouse them face the grim fate of consuming the metaphorical "human blood buns." I can only imagine the profound sorrow that gripped Lu Xun as he penned these words, driven by an earnest desire to shake the populace from their stupor and ignite a flame of enlightenment.

I've never had the opportunity to meet Chen Danqing in person. Judging from his photographs, his demeanor bears a striking resemblance to that of Lu Xun: serious, resolute, as if nursing an unspoken grievance and poised to push back against injustice at any moment. Like Lu Xun, he possesses the audacity to rebuke, the courage to confront, and an unwavering refusal to shoulder unwarranted blame, embodying a lifelong commitment to challenge the status quo. In recent years, Chen Danqing has emerged as a prominent public figure, dedicating himself to rekindling enlightenment in China. I find his speeches particularly captivating, for they blend the astute social and political awareness of a classical scholar-official with the nuanced sensibilities of an artist. His discourse spans a wide spectrum, encompassing both praise and critique of current affairs. With a unique linguistic flair, his words resonate with profundity, wit, sharpness, and unvarnished candor. Occasionally, a well-placed curse word escapes his lips, seemingly a release of pent-up frustration. Yet, amidst it all, a fleeting smile occasionally graces his face, evoking the innocence and cynicism of his youth. What strikes me most about Chen Danqing is his incisive analysis of contemporary Chinese society. He astutely observes, "If you lack connections and aspire to goodness, you're destined to languish at the bottom rung of society. Even if you possess talent and insight, societal filters will likely sift you out. The more virtuous, principled, and compassionate you are, the more susceptible you become to elimination. All your strengths morph into liabilities in the ruthless arena of competition." Like Lu Xun, Chen Danqing's laughter and rebukes are etched in words. Reflecting on governmental corruption, he quips, "The greatest irony lies in a cadre of billionaires masquerading as proletariat revolutionaries, positioning themselves as the vanguard. Even more absurd is their assertion that they're the dutiful servants of destitute commoners like us! They never forget to serve us wholeheartedly. Hence, it's no wonder to take pride in being Chinese. Despite any hardships, we're at least bestowed with an abundance of 'servants' as opulent as the nation itself!"

After the CCP took the stage of history, why were they able to bring authoritarian rule and the scale of repression and murder to such an unprecedented peak? Why were they able to completely silence the voices of dissent and utterly crush human morality? First and foremost, it is because the communist regime is extraordinarily cruel and evil. The Russian revolutionary Leon Trotsky once said, "Our system claims that those who do not work shall not eat, but in reality, it means those who do not obey shall not eat. In a country where the government is the only employer, rebellion equates to starvation." Hayek also remarked, "In a country where the government is the sole employer, rebellion equals a slow death by starvation. The old principle of 'those who do not work shall not eat' has been replaced by 'those who do not obey shall not eat.'" During Mao's era, the method of dealing with dissenters was, first, to take away their means of livelihood, leaving their entire family to starve. If they still did not comply, they were thrown into prison to be slowly tortured, destroying their health and eventually their body. This approach is still employed by the CCP to this day.

On the other hand, the CCP's success in seizing and maintaining power is inseparable from the weaknesses of Chinese intellectuals themselves. Throughout Chinese history, the period of the Republic of China under Chiang Kai-shek was a time when intellectuals were most free, influential, and abundant. Among them, there were many who criticized and opposed Chiang Kai-shek. However, in the Republic, they still enjoyed status, fame, and substantial income, living comfortably. Unfortunately, having knowledge does not equate to having insight. Many intellectuals, when in privileged social positions, exhibited arrogance and left-leaning tendencies. They cheered for the Communist Party and played a significant role in overthrowing the Nationalist government. They failed to see the bloody nature of the communist regime and did not perceive Mao Zedong's deep-seated hatred for intellectuals, his narrow-mindedness, and his vindictive personality. At the critical juncture of the Chinese Civil War, they demonstrated political shortsightedness and lack of insight, recognizing only their connection to the land beneath their feet and failing to understand the greater importance of choosing a political system and leadership. When the Nationalist Army was about to lose Beijing, Chiang Kai-shek sent planes to evacuate people from the city. The ones he aimed to rescue were not military or political leaders, nor high-ranking officials, but intellectuals with academic achievements. However, most chose to stay. Only a few, such as Hu Shi, Mei Yiqi, and Fu Sinian, decided to leave. Hu Shi said, "For the Nationalist Party, freedom is a matter of more or less; for the Communist Party, freedom is a matter of existence or non-existence." Regrettably, having knowledge does not equate to having wisdom, and having academic learning does not equate to having insight. There were too few intellectuals like Hu Shi with such insight.

After the Chinese Communist Party successfully seized power, it immediately launched campaigns in the 1950s to denounce Hu Shi and criticize Hu Feng. China's intellectual elite, who had once reached the dazzling heights of prosperity with the flourishing of great scholars during the Republican era, were suddenly plunged into a state of utter disgrace and irreversible ruin. The harsh governance and tyrannical rule magnified human weaknesses to an extreme. Many intellectuals, particularly prominent figures, groveled at the feet of those in power, employing every means to flatter, betray their integrity, and seek personal gain. They resorted to slander, informing on others, kicking people when they were down, and losing all moral decency. Competing to demonstrate loyalty and preserve themselves, some sullied their own reputations, others repaid kindness with malice, turned on former allies, distorted the truth, or fabricated lies. Each one became a double-faced individual, utterly losing all dignity and intellectual integrity. It was a complete exposure and catastrophe for human nature and morality—a tragic disaster of the human heart.

After 1949, intellectuals in the humanities and social sciences in China were gradually incorporated into various units, and the class of freelancers disappeared. Intellectuals found themselves under the control of an omnipotent state, with an inescapable net. Without affiliation to a unit, there was no means of subsistence. Through ideological reform and continuous political movements, the Chinese intellectual community was left with no choice but to follow power. The modern notion of intellectuals, characterized by independent personalities and free thought, essentially vanished. Chinese intellectuals, as a whole, transitioned from losing the consciousness of independent thought to abandoning their independent personalities, willingly becoming tools of the regime.

Mao strongly supported criticizing Confucius and promoting Legalism, applying Shang Yang's harsh policies and his "five techniques for controlling the people" (weakening, impoverishing, exhausting, humiliating, and deceiving the people) to the extreme. The strategy of subjugating the populace proved highly effective in cementing authoritarian rule. Through relentless indoctrination spanning decades, the CCP succeeded in cultivating a legion of ignorant slaves. The upper echelons of society are filled with political careerists and opportunists. Renowned scholar Chen Yinke aptly summarized this phenomenon, remarking, "Chinese people exhibit ignorance at the grassroots and deception at the helm." He posited that every calamity from the Boxer Rebellion to the Red Guard Movement stemmed from a collusion between the "ignorant masses" and the "deceptive elite"—both indispensable in fomenting chaos. As Ms. Zi Zhongjun observed, even a century later, the top remains occupied by empress dowagers, while the Boxers linger at the bottom. I believe that tyrants are born from the soil of the mob. The Cultural Revolution was the result of a conspiracy between the tyrant and the mob, and both are equally indispensable. Without a transformation in the societal fabric, the recurrent emergence of tyrants remains inevitable.

The ignorance of society's underclass leads to the ubiquity and normalization of the "banality of evil." When an individual abandons free thought and an independent personality, fully immersing themselves in the collective, even if they are merely a powerless pawn or a "weed" in the grand scheme, they inexplicably feel a sense of glory and strength.

This is the allure of military uniforms, official attire, or even a small red armband. When harming the innocent in the name of revolution, such individuals become numb and indifferent, believing that committing murder as part of a group absolves them of personal responsibility. This is a twisted and perverse manifestation of human nature. Far too many people blindly obey authority, evade responsibility, pursue personal gain, and fail to recognize the evil in their actions. This "banality" of wrongdoing allows any ordinary person, in specific social and political contexts, to become an executor of atrocities.

During Mao's three-decade reign, he systematically dismantled the intellectual elite, breeding a new group of opportunists who traded integrity for expedience, all clamoring to pen sycophantic tomes. The post-1980s elites metamorphosed into shrewd egoists, adept at pandering and adeptly advancing personal interests. Since Xi Jinping ascended to power, a surge of ignorance has heralded a resurgence of fervent loyalty. Ignorant masses eagerly extol the virtues of power, belting out red anthems and performing "loyalty dances," with even monks and nuns joining the chorus. Many intellectuals have devolved into "refined egoists and consummate conformists," cozying up to power and leveraging their connections for personal gain. After Xi assumed the supreme power, numerous internationally renowned movie stars shamelessly pledged allegiance, reminiscent of the sycophantic fervor of 1966. Despite their exposure to the wider world, these "social elites" prioritize self-interest over principles. Their collusion with power, coupled with the pervasive ignorance of society's underbelly, lays fertile ground for authoritarianism to thrive.

Today's conflict between China and the world, especially the marked deterioration of U.S.-China relations since Xi Jinping assumed power, is viewed through a cultural lens as a clash between civilizations. On one side, there's the perceived universal civilization represented by advanced nations rooted in Christianity, while on the other, there's the CCP's perceived anti-humanity and anti-civilizational stance. The chasm between these two cultures leaves little room for reconciliation. Experience has shown that attempts at humane goodwill, compromise, and appeasement by civilized nations have not only failed to alter China's trajectory but have emboldened its disregard for norms and encouraged aggression against civilized societies. Hopes for self-correction and internal reform within the country have often been dashed due to entrenched historical traditions and national practices resistant to transformation.

EPILOGUE

Since the 17th Century, Western developed countries have entered a civilized stage characterized by popular sovereignty, compromise and tolerance, a spirit of contractual agreement, protection of private property, and the containment of violence within legally defined and publicly accountable institutions. Today, more and more countries around the world are proudly advancing along the broad path of democracy, freedom, and republicanism, sharing the rapid advancements in technological innovation and achieving common prosperity. Only China, still using the excuse of having different national circumstances, insists on "feeling its way across the river" while creating turmoil in the process. Who knows when this will end? The level of corruption and darkness in Chinese society today surpasses even that of medieval Europe. China today urgently needs a Renaissance.

The term "Renaissance" means "rebirth." Europe's transforma-tion from the dark Middle Ages into a developed, civilized society began with the Renaissance. Its motivation was to address the increasing corruption of medieval society and revive the democratic and republican systems of ancient Greece and Rome. The Renaissance reflected people's strong desire for fairness, justice, republicanism, and good governance. While Europe flourished culturally and artistically during the Renaissance, its scope extended beyond these realms. China's Renaissance can draw nourishment from the inherent genes of Chinese culture embedded in pre-Qin traditions. Concerning the political system, the enfeoffment system laid the groundwork for the Zhou Dynasty's rule for eight centuries. Two crucial aspects emerge: firstly, the emphasis on the governing ideology of the educated class. While the Zhou Dynasty expanded through force, the Huaxia people propagated civilization for centuries not solely through conquest, but by nurturing civil and military prowess, leveraging advanced agricultural practices, and promoting etiquette and music culture. Secondly, the implementation of local autonomy and the division of powers. The hierarchical distribution of aristocratic authority curbed royal power and the monarchy. This decentralized structure fostered multiple local power hubs that checked and balanced each other. This autonomy fostered competition among princes, facilitated talent mobility, and spurred intellectual innovation during the Spring and Autumn Period and the Warring States Period. In terms of ideological heritage, pre-Qin culture stressed etiquette, emphasized duty, prioritized familial values, and underscored a people-centric approach. The Chinese nation embodies a pluralistic yet unified community. The pre-Qin era marked a crucial period wherein this community transitioned from diversity to unity while preserving its rich pluralism. Chinese civilization during this period bequeathed invaluable resources for future generations to study and harness.

Since the founding of the Qin dynasty, China's political system has remained largely unchanged for over two thousand years. As a result, authoritarian thinking has become deeply ingrained in the Chinese psyche—a cultural imprint etched into generations. This authoritarian mindset is a double-edged curse, manifesting in two opposing yet intertwined traits: the mentality of the slave, and the mentality of the ruler. The slave mentality is marked by blind obedience and worship of power. Even in the face of starvation, rebellion is unthinkable. Loyalty to superiors is paramount; as long as personal benefits are assured, concepts like justice, truth, or morality are treated as irrelevant luxuries. From this submissive mindset, one would fervently support the downfall of Liu Shaoqi, then enthusiastically back the purge of Deng Xiaoping, and later applaud the fall of the Gang of Four. And should Xi Jinping be overthrown tomorrow, the same person would again proclaim unwavering support—without the slightest sense of contradiction. On the flip side, the ruler mentality reflects an insatiable desire to climb upward and dominate. Many dream of becoming "masters of others." Once granted even a sliver of power, they wield it ruthlessly, suppressing those below without mercy, often seeking to eliminate any potential threat entirely. To break free from the chains of this authoritarian mindset is no easy task. It will take generations—and more importantly, a radical awakening of thought. Only through such profound enlightenment can the cycle of tyranny and submission finally be dismantled.

Where does China's hope lie? It lies in a shift in concepts and the evolution of its system. Both are essential and deeply intertwined with the welfare of every Chinese individual. Institutions play a pivotal role. An authoritarian system cannot transform into a developed and civilized nation. The foundation for systemic change lies in altering the mindset of the populace. Changing concepts requires enlightenment. Why has China's autocratic structure endured for two millennia? From the Qin Emperor and the Han Dynasty to the Tang, Song, Yuan, Ming, and Qing Dynasties, "old wine in new bottles." This continuity persists because figures like Zhu Yuanzhang (an Emperor of the Ming Dynasty), Zhang Xianzhong (a leader of the turmoil of the late Ming Dynasty), Hong Xiuquan (the leader of the Taiping Rebellion), Yang Xiuqing (an organizer and commander-in-chief of the Taiping Rebellion), and Mao and Xi share common traits. The Communist Party cloaks itself in Leninism but mirrors the Taiping Rebellion. Their convictions echo the law of the jungle: "the strong prey on the weak," "might makes right," "political power emanates from the barrel of a gun," and "lagging behind leads to subjugation." Chinese and Communist Party ideologies intertwine agrarian thought, unity, familial, and hierarchical cultures. The Chinese people's acquiescence to dictators nurtures authoritarianism. China's millennia-old centralized political system stems from a cultural tradition of venerating power and acquiescing to servitude. Hence, some perceive the Communist Party as "the Chinese people in power" and the Chinese populace as "the Communist Party without power." There's truth in this observation. Chinese individuals lack the consciousness of being capitalized "humans" and struggle to grasp the concept of "human rights." They do not know what "freedom" feels like. Even if one dictator falls, successors may echo the same ethos. It's challenging for this demographic to move toward civilization through its own efforts.

Although leaders such as Deng Xiaoping, Zhao Ziyang, and Wen Jiabao put forward proposals for political reform to varying degrees, the structural reality of "deception from above and ignorance below," inherited over thousands of years, has remained fundamentally unchanged. For a long time, the authorities have strictly suppressed dissenting voices, and the news media have been confined to serving as instruments of political propaganda rather than platforms for public information. The news accessible to the public is largely filtered, edited, and reconstructed by the propaganda apparatus, with genuine information distorted or concealed. After decades of ideological indoctrination, many people have grown accustomed to treating official media as the sole credible source of truth. Within the vast ranks of grassroots Party members, a significant portion are primarily concerned with immediate personal gain and limited privileges. Their behavior is governed by short-term calculations of self-interest. Skilled in opportunism and marked by narrow-minded utilitarianism, they devote themselves to currying favor with power and extracting minor benefits, while remaining indifferent to the nation's future, social justice, public responsibility, and the common good. In 1988, the Communist Party of the Soviet Union convened its Nineteenth Party Congress, attended by more than five thousand delegates. The Congress adopted a historic resolution that formally repudiated and dismantled the Communist Party's monopoly on political power. Regrettably, political transformations of this kind—initiated from within the ruling system, as seen in the Soviet Union and Eastern Europe—are unlikely to occur in China.

If we measure from the British "Glorious Revolution" (1688), China lags behind the world by over three hundred years. If we measure from the United States' Declaration of Independence (1776), China is over two hundred years behind. It's highly improbable for the Chinese to spontaneously alter a culture shaped over millennia. Guo Songtao (April 11, 1818 ~ July 18, 1891), a Chinese diplomat and liberal statesman, believed it would take nearly three hundred years for China to overcome the ills accumulated since the Qin and Han Dynasties. In a November 1988 interview with Hong Kong's "Open" magazine, Liu Xiaobo, the 2010 Nobel Peace Prize winner, remarked, "China should emulate Hong

Kong and allow British rule for three hundred years." Their point was that China needed the influence of foreign civilizations and should adopt British and American systems. Germany and Japan serve as relevant examples. Before World War II's conclusion, all Germans supported Hitler, and all Japanese were loyal to the emperor. The likelihood of Germans and Japanese overthrowing Hitler and the Imperial Japanese Army was minimal. However, after their total defeat and subjugation, Britain and the United States compelled them to embrace constitutional systems. Only then did they renounce violence and barbarism, embrace concepts of fairness and justice, and integrate into global civilization. Taiwan stands as an exception, producing Chiang Ching-kuo, who, as the last dictator, ended the dictatorship. It took immense courage and foresight for Chiang Ching-kuo to alter Taiwan's political course. Taiwanese people must have accumulated significant virtue to receive such a divine blessing. Wen Jiabao from mainland China aspired to enact change but lacked the strength to do so. Deng Xiaoping had the power but was unwilling to pursue it.

The pre-Qin feudal system bears resemblance to the modern federal system. Given China's vast land, establishing local governments with a high degree of democracy and autonomy under a federal republican system could prove beneficial. Taiwan serves as a clear example of the advantages of local autonomy. Being situated offshore, Taiwanese people avoided a series of calamities such as the anti-rightist movement, the Great Famine, and the Cultural Revolution. Consequently, Taiwan transitioned from a dictatorship to a democratically elected service-oriented government. Only with the implementation of a true constitutional republic in China—where political systems uphold freedom of thought and speech, private property is sacrosanct, and citizens are liberated from servitude—can the Chinese people unleash their full potential. Through creativity, China can ascend to the ranks of advanced, civilized, and developed nations.

In the United States, each state functions as a "nation," enjoying significant autonomy in administrative management, judicial security, culture and education, transportation and commerce, healthcare, and welfare. Throughout U.S. history, every state voluntarily joined the Union. Governors, democratically elected by state citizens, hold no hierarchical relationship with the president. States compete freely, and citizens have the freedom to relocate. This system shares many similarities with the pre-Qin era. As Sir Winston Churchill once remarked, "The farther back you look, the further ahead you can see." By reflecting on the past, we can gain insights into what may come next. By examining the pre-Qin system, we can envision a federal system for a future China.

Treasured Documentary Footage

Wuxi, late 1940s. My grandmother, Sun Miaoying, and my mother, Liu Hairong.

Shanghai, late 1940s. My mother and her third auntie Wang Peizhen.

Wuxi, late 1940s. From left to right: my grandmother; my eldest great-aunt; and my youngest great-aunt.

Wuxi, 1955. Three years old.

1966, age 14, second year of junior high. The Cultural Revolution began.

Zhu Shuizhao, celebrated Yue opera actress and wife of Uncle Yihou.

1983. My mother with the four sons of her third aunt. Front row, left to right: Liu Chenghou and Liu Yihou. Back row, left to right: Liu Shaohou and Liu Dinghou.

1969, Yin Li at the Qianxi Production Squad of the Yelou Brigade.

1973, plowing the land with an ox in Yong'an.

Wuxi, 1970. With my grandmother.

Xuzhou, 1975. With Liu Gengnian.

1975. With colleagues from Shan's Village School.

Shanghai, 1976. With Shi Taihua.

1982, at Rui Yin's parents' home, Xiamen University.

1986, at Shanghai People's Park. From left to right:
my mother, my father, Uncle Bao Hongxian, and Uncle Bao Ting.

1983, the mourning hall of Rui Yin's grandfather, Mr. Ying Chengyi.

Xiamen University, 1984. My one-year-old daughter, Flora Bao, pictured with her grandparents—Professor Rui Hejiu and Professor Ying Jinxiang —and the translator Mr. Ge Baoquan (center).

1985, at the University of Iowa, with Rui Yin and Professor Nie Hualing.

1992, with Professor Marsha Lupi,
Dean of Hunter College's School of Education, CUNY.

2010, in San Antonio, Texas, with Professor John Olson.

May 1996, at the New York University commencement ceremony, with my dissertation advisor, Professor Dennis Sayers (Ph.D., Harvard University).

1996, Shen Jianhua, researcher at the Institute of Chinese Culture, Chinese University of Hong Kong.

1994, at Suxian No. 2 High School: from the left, Liu Yuankai, Li Yuming, Zhou Hualu, and on the right, Li Ming.

1998, Tangyue Village, She County, Anhui. With daughter Bao Fuluo.

The Bao Ancestral Hall, Tangyue Village.

2010, Nanchang, Jiangxi. With Uncle Liu Zhonghou and his wife.

2000, a reunion of classmates from Class 15, 1967 cohort, of Shanghai No. 62 Middle School.

2007, Glen Cove, Long Island. With brother Bao Chengquan.

2012, Columbia University, NY. Giving a lecture.

2017, Albany, NY. With colleagues at the New York State Education Department.

2020, 55+ retirement community at the foot of Mount Rainier.

About the Author

Chengmo Bao, *Born in 1952 in Shanghai. In 1966, he was forced to change his surname from Bao to Liu and adopted the name Liu Chengmo. Upon obtaining U.S. citizenship in 1994, he reverted to his original name, Bao Chengmo.*

From 1958 to 1964, he attended Changsha Road No. 2 Private Elementary School in Shanghai.

From 1964 to 1966, he attended Shanghai No. 62 Middle School, graduating as part of the "Old Three Cohorts" of 1967.

From January 1969 to February 1978, he worked as a sent-down youth in the Yong'an Commune of Su County, Anhui Province.

In the 1977 college entrance exam, he received special admission with a three-level reduction. From 1978 to 1982, he studied in the Foreign Languages Department at Anhui Normal University.

After graduating in 1982, he was assigned the least desirable post, working as an English teacher at "Guandian Forestry School," located in a remote valley, a position no one in his department wanted.

In 1984, he went to the U.S. for self-funded studies. From 1987 to 1990, he taught at Seward Park High School in New York City.

From 1990 to 2005, he served as an Education Evaluator in School District 24 of the New York City Department of Education.

From 2005 to 2018, he worked as a School Improvement Specialist for the New York State Education Department. He retired in 2018.

Education

1982: Bachelor of Arts in Literature, Anhui Normal University.

1984: Graduate studies in the Department of English, University of Iowa, USA.

1991: Master of Education, Hunter College, City University of New York.

1996: Ph.D. in Philosophy, specializing in Multicultural and Multilingual Studies, New York University.

2001: Post-master's degree in educational administration, Long Island University, New York.

www.ingramcontent.com/pod-product-compliance
Lightning Source LLC
Chambersburg PA
CBHW060402130626
46555CB00005B/1976